THE NORTH AMERICAN INDIAN ORPHEUS TRADITION

Also by the Author

Native Religions of North America: The Power of Visions and Fertility
The Attraction of Peyote
Shamanic Healing and Ritual Drama
Conceptions of the Soul among North American Indians
Belief and Worship in Native North America
The Religions of the American Indians

THE NORTH AMERICAN INDIAN ORPHEUS TRADITION

NATIVE AFTERLIFE MYTHS AND THEIR ORIGINS

ÅKE HULTKRANTZ

Afterworlds Press

www.afterworldspress.com

ABOUT THE AUTHOR

Åke in 1997

Åke Hultkrantz (1920-2006) was born in Kalmar, Sweden. He earned a doctorate in ethnology from University of Stockholm in 1946, followed by a second PhD in comparative religion in 1953. Between 1948 and 1990, he often conducted fieldwork and lived among Californian Native American tribes, the Arapaho, and the Shoshone who adopted him as a tribal member.

He held many distinguished academic appointments, and was a visiting lecturer at universities across Europe and the United States. He authored some four hundred papers and twenty-five books, including standard works on Native American religions. His interest in afterlife-related subjects, shamanism, and peyote spanned his entire career.

PREFACE

The following study of the North American Orpheus tradition does not constitute an exhaustive account of this tradition. In the first place, its rich content has not been subjected to an in all respects detailed analysis; the many interesting data that the material yields concerning the conceptions of the realm of the dead, of the journey thither, and of the dead I hope to be able to publish in greater detail on later occasions as separate investigations. And in the second place the stylistic form of the Orpheus tradition, its plan and pattern of action, as also the internal connection between the different versions, have been accorded only extremely summary treatment in this investigation, as Dr A. H. Gayton has earlier published an already classical study on these lines, *The Orpheus Myth in North America* (1935). Beyond a certain supplementation of the material upon which Dr Gayton bases her conclusions, and a consequent revision of certain of these conclusions, the account given here will present viewpoints of a predominantly comparative religious nature. It is above all the question of the value of the Orpheus tradition as a source for North American Indian religion that will occupy the foreground, at the same time as great importance is attached to the problems of the historical and psychological origins of the tradition.

This work does not in any way reduce the value of Dr Gayton's investigations. Her research results remain in essentials intact and in different ways support my own. As a matter of fact, her excellent article may be designated as the necessary preparatory work for my study (cf. the Introduction). The form and distribution of the Orpheus tradition must be established before the functional analysis of content is attempted.

In this work the hero and the heroine in the North American tradition have been designated with the same names as the chief personages in the Greek tale. It is of course not altogether happy to refer to the heroes of Indian legends with names from Greek mythology, but the author

5

has had no choice—generally the Indians do not know the name of their hero, and for the treatment and discussion it is necessary to have a "technical term" for him. It was therefore found most suitable to call the hero Orpheus; the name Eurydice, on the other hand, has been used in only a few passages.

Valuable help has in the course of the work been extended by individual researchers and other private persons, by museums and libraries. Professor Ernst Arbman and Professor Gerhard Lindblom have kindly offered criticism of parts of the manuscript. Professor Ralph Linton, now deceased, was good enough to place his account of the Orpheus tradition of the Comanche at my disposal, and to give me permission to publish it in extenso (see chap. I: 1). Dr A. H. Gayton, Professor Gudmund Hatt, Miss A. B. Hellbom, Dr Sven Liljeblad and Dr Ivar Paulson have afforded valuable assistance in connection with the collecting of sources. To all of these I proffer my sincere thanks.

I wish also to express my warm gratitude to Professor Sigvald Linné, who has consented to the printing of this work in the Monograph Series of the Ethnographical Museum of Sweden, to the Längman Culture Fund and to the Humanistic Foundation of Sweden, which have contributed to the costs of translation and printing, and to Mr Donald Burton, my excellent translator.

Stockholm, October 1957

Åke Hultkrantz

TLINGIT

TSIMSHIAN

HAIDA

HAISLA
CARRIER

BELLA
BELLA

BELLA
COOLA

KWAKIUTL

SECHELT

SARCEE

NOOTKA

NANAIMO

STALO THOMPSON

BLACKFOOT

MICMAC

QUINAULT

SINKAIETK

SNUQUALMI KALISPEL

ASSINIBOIN

OJIBWAY

MALECITE

TWANA

PUYALLUP

CHEHALIS

SKOPAMISH

SANPOIL

KLIKITAT YAKIMA

OTTAWA

WISHRAM

TENINO

KALAPUYA

WASCO

NEZ PERCÉ

MENOMINI
WINNEBAGO

HURON

TUTUTNI

SENECA

TOLOWA

KLAMATH

SHOSHONI

YUROK

KARUK MODOC

FOX

HUPA SHASTA

PAVIOTSO

POMO

NISENAN

MIWOK

PAWNEE

YOKUTS

WESTERN MONO

SHAWNEE

TÜBATULABAL

MOHAVE

NAVAJO TAOS

CHEROKEE

SERRANO

ZUNI

YUCHI

GABRIELINO

COMANCHE

WICHITA

KOASATI

TAWAKONI

ALABAMA

LIPAN

NAYARIT

Distribution of the Orpheus tradition in North America.

CONTENTS

INTRODUCTION

Like many other popular prose traditions in the field of primitive culture, the so-called Orpheus tradition[1] has a religious character inasmuch
as—even if it is not always an object for religious belief—it formulates
a theme which is taken from the supernatural world. As we shall find
later, the Orpheus tradition in North America is predominantly a sacral
tradition, embraced with sincere religious belief.[2] This means, inter alia,
that it is of equal value for us whether we study it as a narrative form or
as testimony to religious conceptions. It is a suitable object both for folkloristic research and for religious research.

An American ethnologist and folklorist, A. H. Gayton, has already
subjected the North American Orpheus narrative to a detailed analysis,
in which connection she has in the first place assessed the *formal* aspects
of the tradition, its character of popular literary product.[3] She has here
followed the methodological lines drawn up by folklorists with historical
interests both in and outside of North America.[4] The present work is deliberately concentrated upon an analysis of the *significance* of the Orpheus tradition, the presentation being orientated from the viewpoints
of comparative religious research. The formal analysis constitutes a necessary prime condition for such a study. In the interest for the origin,
distribution and migrations of the tradition both roads meet.

Elsewhere I have given a more detailed presentation of what in my
opinion constitute the folkloristic and the comparative religious viewpoints, what distinguishes them and what unites them.[5] A comparative
religious investigation of the Orpheus tradition is at once functionalistic
and historical. The content of the tradition is subjected to a functional
analysis, which makes possible a definition both of the psychological and

[1] Definition, see below pp. 19 sq.
[2] See chap. V: 1.
[3] Gayton 1935, 263—293.
[4] Cf. the survey in Lindgren 1949, 340 sqq.
[5] See Hultkrantz 1956.

sociological origin of the tradition and of its value for the stabilization of religious belief. At the same time the investigation becomes historical, inasmuch as the tradition is connected with other mythic motifs and its migratory routes and the milieu in which it originates are charted, as far as this is possible.

In American folkloristic circles the Orpheus tradition has hitherto been referred to simply as a *myth*. This has been in conformity with a general tendency in North America to apply the term myth to every epic narrative referring to experiences or fictive events on the supernatural plane.[6] In contrast to this one may mention the view common among orientalists that only those narratives which are at the same time ritual texts deserve to be called myths.[7] It is obvious that from the viewpoint of comparative religious research the "folkloristic" standpoint is here too undifferentiated. The student of comparative religion demands a more nuanced division of the categories of the narrative tradition, a division that in the first place takes into account the religious value of the tradition.[8] A comparative religious, functionalistic investigation of the Orpheus tradition acquires significance only after it has been possible to make a more accurate determination of its value in terms of religious belief.

With reference to the religious value and significance of the folktale material, it is now customary in comparative religious circles to classify it as myths, legends and fairy-tales (stories). The criteria for what constitutes the one or the other vary, however, from researcher to researcher, and I therefore think it desirable in this connection to define more precisely what I put into the categories of tradition referred to. The basis of classification is constituted by the form of the tradition, its content (i.e. the nature of the personages, the time and scene of the plot), and its function.

The *myth* is an epic narrative dealing with figures belonging to the supernatural sphere: cosmic beings, gods and spirits. The action of the narrative takes place in a remote prehistoric period, but in principle the once consummated course of events is still of topical interest, timeless and eternal as the course of the planets. The scene of the drama is as a rule (but

[6] See e.g. the series of North American Indian "mythologies" published as *Memoirs* of the American Folklore Society.

[7] See e.g. Hooke 1933, 3. Cf. also Hyman 1955, 462 sqq. As Weisinger has pointed out, the ritual myth is especially characteristic for the Near East—Mediterranean area (Weisinger 1956, 387 sqq.).

[8] At the same time, however, it should be observed that some folklorists, too, attach importance to a more careful consideration of the traditional material from the viewpoint of religious belief (von Sydow 1948, 186; Bascom 1954, 335 sq.). Cf. also Bayard 1953, 4; Thompson 1955, 484.

not always) another world than our own: heaven, the underworld or an unknown country. The myth gives instruction concerning the world of the gods, and therewith concerning the cosmic order; it confirms the social order and the cultural values obtaining and it is in itself sacred.[9] It is therefore self-evident that it is intended to be embraced with belief and reverence.[10]

The *legend*, again, is an epic narrative, very often a memorate[11] transformed by tradition, whose main personages appear at least partly in the supernatural sphere, though without their necessarily belonging there.[12] The action of the narrative takes place in the past, but is in general not so remote; the human figures who always appear in the legend are regarded as historical personages, and the action occurs at least in part in places with which the listeners are familiar. The function of the legend is to strengthen the solidarity in the group and the group values by maintaining the continuity between the current religious belief and conduct and the religious world of the ancestors of the group. It may have a pedagogical character, but it is at the same time considered as an actual occurrence in the past, a meeting between human beings and spirits which has really taken place, and it is therefore an object of genuine belief.

The *fairy-tale* is an epic narrative whose main personages move in a world of wonders which in an obscure way oscillates between the present and prehistoric times, the supernatural sphere of the myth and the prosaic existence of practical everyday life. The actors are either fictive figures, or else divinities or historical personages who are associated with more or

[9] It is scarcely a happy solution, it seems to me, to restrict the concept of the myth to the myth of the ritual text, the myth upon which the cult is based. Many myths have this character. But what is decisive for the myth is not its ritual function but that fact that it "expresses, enhances, and codifies belief" (Malinowski 1926, 23). Also Kluckhohn holds this view, though he admits at the same time that "myths and rituals tend to be very intimately associated and to influence each other," owing to, amongst other things, the fact that they "are adaptive from the point of view of the society in that they promote social solidarity, enhance the integration of the society by providing a formalized statement of its ultimate value-attitudes, afford a means for the transmission of much of the culture with little loss of content—thus protecting cultural continuity and stabilizing the society" (Kluckhohn 1942, 65). But the Navajo Indians, the same writer observes, have "sacred tales which, as yet at all events, are not used to justify associated rituals" (Kluckhohn, op. cit., 59). The value of the rite for the student of comparative religion has been overemphasized at the expense of the study of the myth, which itself plays an essential rôle (von Sydow 1942, 108 sq.).

[10] In this respect it is difficult to refer to the Orpheus tradition as a myth, when the actors are mythic figures like Coyote and Bluejay. The Orpheus tales in which these personages figure are as a rule not sacred, although they do sometimes establish the divorce between the living and the dead. See further below.

[11] Concerning memorates, see von Sydow 1948, 73 sq.

[12] Folklorists often speak of four different types of legend: saints' legends, local or historical legends, migratory legends and religious legends. Only the last type is of interest in our analysis.

13

less fantastic events. The function of the fairy-tale is to supply entertainment, and it need not, accordingly, be given credence. But frequently enough the fairy-tale is considered to be true, at least by some category of listeners (in Europe, for example, by children), and the motifs included in the fairy-tale may be taken from the world of religious belief, regarded, therefore, as true. The latter is often the case outside of Europe, among various primitive peoples, for whom the milieu of the fairy-tale is nearer to the world of practical reality or to the in its way equally real world of religious belief.

In this connection it is worth citing what the well-known folklorist E. S. Hartland has adduced concerning such "stories told for amusement": "They may have been told at the outset for mere amusement, or they may have originated in that twilight habit of the mind familiar to humanity which does not attempt accurately to distinguish what is meant to be believed from what is meant to do no more than pass the time. In any case, it is safe to say that they must have embodied what those who first told and what those who first heard them regarded as probabilities. Had they been the wild impossibilities to their original audience which they are to us, they would never have conciliated the favour of mankind."[13] The reader may here be reminded of the fact that the Northern Ojibway (Saulteaux) in Manitoba, for instance, consider all their tales as true.[14]

The foregoing classification of oral traditions is based upon an investigation of North American Indian folktale material, of which I cannot here, however, give an account.[15] The determining factor is, as we have seen, the relation of the narrative to the religious belief, and therewith its value as a source for this belief. As I have indicated, the truth-value of a narrative varies: the myth is true because it is sacred in itself, the legend is true because it communicates events regarded as true, and the fairy-tale, or in any case its single elements, *may* have a certain truth-value. The Orpheus tradition has in other words probably had great qualifications for being accorded credence, in whatever category it has been understood. But to which of the three categories should it be referred?

Boas and after him Bidney, Lowie and Thompson, amongst others, have pointed out that one and the same folktale may pass now as a myth, now as a fairy-tale.[16] What in one place is a sacred, true text is in another

[13] Hartland 1914, 16.
[14] Hallowell 1947, 547. See further below, chap. V: 1.
[15] I hope to have an opportunity of publishing this investigation later. See further below, chap. V: 1.
[16] Boas 1938, 609, Bidney 1950, 19, 22, 24, Lowie 1954, 125 sq., Thompson 1955, 484 sq.

place a more or less fictive story, retold for the purpose of entertainment. As an instance one may mention the so-called trickster cycle. It is well known that the North American trickster figure, in most cases also a culture hero, performs a number of obscene and irregular actions flagrantly infringing the moral code of the culture.[17] It is therefore natural that in a large number of tribes the trickster cycle should belong to the group of "false stories".[18] But it is worth remarking that the trickster as such is not regarded as an unreal figure among these peoples. The Oglala Dakota, for example, who regard Iktomi's adventures as pure fantasies without any background in reality, "funny stories,"[19] nevertheless place him in the divine genealogy as son of "the Rock," according to the shaman theology the oldest of all divinities.[20] The trickster cycle of the Tlingit Indians, which has the Raven as its main personage, consists of both true myths and untrue stories. A Chilkat Indian told Boas that "among the Tlingit the Raven legend, so far as it refers to the creation, follows a regular sequence ... In answer to my question regarding the order of the other incidents of the tale, he claimed that they were told only to offset the serious parts of the tale, in order to entertain the listeners, and that there was no particular order in which these were told."[21] Among the Winnebago Indians, again, the trickster cycle is among the sacred myths, waikā, "das-was-heilig-ist,"[22] and the Wind River Shoshoni regard the narratives about the Coyote as "true stories."[23] The tricksters of both the Winnebago and the Wind River Shoshoni have a place in the religious belief.[24]

This tendency of the folktale, to occur now as myth, now as fairy-tale, complicates our efforts to make a valid pronouncement as to the category of tradition to which the North American Orpheus tale should be referred. In the majority of tribes, certainly, it appears to have the character of the legend. But as this is not everywhere the case, it is probably wisest to speak neutrally of the Orpheus tradition. As has already been pointed out, the tradition retains its value as a basis for comparative religious analysis even if it appears in the form of the fairy-tale.

In the course of the years an enormous, and as yet still largely unex-

[17] In this connection, cf. Basccom 1953, 289, Bascom 1954, 338.
[18] Pettazzoni 1954, 11 sqq., 21 sqq.
[19] Beckwith 1930, 339.
[20] Walker 1917, 82, 90.
[21] Boas 1916, 582 note 1.
[22] Radin, Kerényi & Jung 1954, 102.
[23] Hultkrantz Ms.
[24] Radin, op.cit., 133 sqq., Hultkrantz 1955, 133 sqq.

ploited, material of North American Indian myths, legends and fairy-tales has been collected by interested laymen and researchers. The time now seems ripe to examine this material from the points of departure of comparative religious research. The myths connected with the Creator, the culture hero and a number of other higher beings have, at least in part, already been subjected to such analysis, chiefly by European students of comparative religion (Schmidt, Pettazzoni, van Deursen, Müller). From several points of view the Orpheus tradition constitutes a rewarding study-object for the comparative religious researcher. In the first place, it is typologically akin to the many Orpheus tales of classical antiquity and of Asia—it is one of the good dozen folktales which are common to North America and the Old World.[25] In the second place, the Orpheus narrative gives us a good deal of information concerning the eschatological religious conceptions of the Indians: about the realm of the dead, about the journey to the realm of the dead, and about the dead themselves. (A detailed account of these conceptions will not, however, be given here, but will be saved for later publications.) And in the third place, the Orpheus narrative is an interesting example of the way in which a myth may arise in close connection with a ritual—in this case the shamanistic ritual—, but without ever having constituted, as far as I can judge, an explanatory text to the ritual in question. In other words, the myth—or the legend, the fairy-tale—reflects the ritual, has it as prototype, but has never been fixed to the rite. We are here reminded that the origin of myths is polygenetic, and that one and the same mythic explanation can be applied only to a limited number of myths.

I. THE ORPHEUS MOTIF IN NORTH AMERICA

1. The Comanche tradition

To give the reader a general idea of the form taken by the Orpheus tradition in North America, I reproduce the version of the Comanche Indians, here published for the first time. It was communicated to me orally by the late Dr Ralph Linton, who noted it down in the course of his field-studies among the Comanche (1933).[1] Particular interest attaches to the Comanche narrative, for it is the first recorded Orpheus tradition from the more easterly Shoshonean groups. No account is given of it in Wallace and Hoebel's Comanche monograph, which is otherwise a valuable source for the religion and folklore of this tribe.[2]

The Comanche tradition runs as follows.

A young man loved his wife dearly. When she died, he therefore resolved to follow her, and got ready his horse and suitable equipment. Then he set out westwards, and rode thus for months. He journeyed over the mountains, but all he had with him was worn out there, finally even his horse, and he arrived on foot in the realm of the dead. The children there skipped around him and shouted: "Look, there is a raw one!" He soon found the lodge of his father-in-law, where his deceased wife also lived. She was now torn with conflicting feelings: she did not wish to return, for she was happy where she was, but at the same time she loved her husband dearly. At last her father settled the matter. He said to the husband: "Well, go back with her. But remember this: when you leave the camp you must go eastward. And you must not touch her before you come to the place where the buffalo is. You must give her a buffalo's

---

[1] The note I made at Dr. Linton's dictation was written on the 22.8.1950. At the same time Dr. Linton authorized me to publish the tradition, as he himself had no plans in this direction.—In dictating the note Linton did not refer to written field-notes of his own, but gave the text as he remembered it. One may adduce here what John Gillin has said concerning Linton's extraordinary photographic memory: he could quote verbatim whole pages from various more or less out of the way books, both in and outside of his own special field; and "he was able, apparently without effort, to command vast bodies of esoteric data to the envy of his less fortunate colleagues" (Gillin 1954, 277).

[2] Wallace & Hoebel 1952.

kidney to eat. When she eats this she will become flesh, and after that she can live with you as your wife. But you must never strike her. If you strike her she will come back to us."

So they set off. After a time they came to the buffalo plains. The husband slew a young buffalo and gave the kidney to his wife, who now became a living human being. They both kissed and embraced each other, and they forgot all about the life in the world of the dead. Then they went on, and soon reached the camp of the living.

This happened in the spring. When autumn came round all was still well between the two. One day they lay together in their lodge, and the man grasped the buffalo hide and wanted to draw it over himself and his wife to warm their bodies. But his hand slipped and hit his wife hard. She shrieked: "You struck me on the head, now I must return to the dead!" The unhappy husband heard his wife's voice fading and finally dying away altogether.

2. Definition

No North American Indian folktale is more attractive than the story of the Indian Orpheus, the Orpheus tradition (F 81.1 according to Thompson's motif-index).[1] The version from the Comanche communicated in the foregoing gives a good idea of the fascinating, suggestive force of the narrative. It has all the attributes, it would seem, that are required to form a well-shaped whole which may be easily transferred from tribe to tribe, from culture to culture. And one does, certainly, find it scattered over the greater part of North America. But it has been doubted that it has constituted a clearly delimited tradition that has been disseminated in the way indicated above. It has been suggested that it is as a type too general and undecided; it does not contain any definitive properties over and above the actual main motif, the bringing back of a loved deceased person, a motif that easily arises in every culture; and the dividing line between this and other stories of experiences among the dead is so extremely floating.

<hr>

[1] Thompson 1932—1936. It should be pointed out that for a religio-historical analysis of a folktale the typological classification devised by Aarne and Thompson is not always of immediate value. Where the folklorist looks for formal literary aspects the student of comparative religion looks for underlying motivistic nexuses which may imply a break with the preceding ones (cf. Hultkrantz 1956, 21 sqq.). As my presentation will therefore be not se dependent on the conventional folkloristic classification of tale-types and motifs, references to Aarne's and Thompson's indices are not given in all cases.

These objections are still raised, although Dr Gayton tried to show twenty years ago that the Orpheus tradition is cast in a relatively fixed mould about a dominating motif, and a rather regularly recurring pattern of action. My own investigations confirm Gayton's conclusions, even if her analysis of the pattern of action does not hold good in every detail. In the light of the eschatological material I have collected, moreover, it is difficult for me to endorse her pronouncement that "stories of a visit to the world of the dead without the Orpheus motivation are relatively less frequent in North America."[2] The stories of living persons who in dreams, trance or coma have journeyed to the other world and succeeded in returning to the living are as a matter of fact numerous in North America.[3]

In order to create a stable basis for our investigations in the sequel, we shall here define the main motifs and leading pattern of action of the Orpheus tradition, indicate the variations that may occur in the central theme, and draw attention to those narratives which come close to this type of tradition, though without its being possible to refer to them as Orpheus traditions.

A. H. Gayton does not give any direct definition of the Orpheus tradition, but she delimits it by referring it to the group "tales of the recovery of a beloved person from the land of the dead."[4] A more detailed, descriptive definition has been given by Thompson: "A man's wife or close relative dies. He follows her to the world of the dead, and gets permission to bring her back. But there is nearly always some condition attached to this unusual favor by the rulers of the dead. This condition may be, like the classical myth, not to look at the wife, not to touch her, not to let her out of a bag, or not to be too hasty." Thompson adds that the taboo is generally broken, so that the reunion fails.[5] A detailed list of the different elements in the Orpheus tradition has been drawn up by Gayton, and (after her) by Hatt and Voegelin.[6]

What distinguishes the Orpheus tradition from all other narratives of visits to the land of the dead is in the first place that the living person tries to bring the deceased back with him to the land of the living—otherwise it is generally the case that the living person is aiming to free himself from the grip of the ghosts—and, in the second place, that the

[2] Gayton 1935, 264.
[3] See further chap. IV: 2. What are here chiefly referred to are thus memorates which have become traditions (so-called Erinnerungssagen, according to von Sydow 1948, 74).
[4] Gayton, op.cit., 263.
[5] Thompson 1946, 351.
[6] Gayton, op.cit., 263 sq., Hatt 1949, 66 sq., Leach 1950 II, 834.

living person is a close relative or friend of the deceased, in which point he differs from the shaman, who of course visits the realm of the dead on the same errand. Even this vague delimitation of the content of the Orpheus narrative is sufficient to show that the parallel with the ecstatic shaman séance and the shaman's capturing of an escaped soul is very close. In the majority of Orpheus narratives the living person is a man, the deceased his wife, and her restoration to life fails in consequence of an infringed taboo. One may therefore define the North American Orpheus tradition as the narrative of a man who, driven by love for his deceased wife, seeks her out in the realm of the dead and tries in vain to restore her to life.

As I have already pointed out, this is the commonest, but by no means the only, version. In a number of cases it is the woman who seeks her lover, or the sons who seek their mother, and so on.[7] Similarly, the story not infrequently has a happy ending.[8] But such variants must be regarded as divergences from the central theme of the narrative. The psychological presumptions of the story are such that the main version appears the most natural. As the narrators are generally men, and the narrative is of such a kind as to engage emotively the person who is telling it—it is a "tale of family love"[9]—the motif with the man who seeks his deceased, beloved woman is a natural form for the narrator's histrionic imagination and pity. The unhappy ending underlines still more the emotional force of the story: it becomes a gripping, tragic romance. At the same time it assumes a chilling element of reality; the dream of the return of the dead cannot be realized. When the Orpheus narrative finally becomes an *aition* for the origin of death, this tragical tendency has reached its climax.[10] It is created in a milieu of listeners, a literary product, far removed from the reality which in my opinion gave life to the Orpheus tradition itself.

The careful inventory of the elements composing the Orpheus tradition given by Dr Gayton shows what in a great number of cases may be included in the tradition, but from this it is a big step to allow them to characterize the tradition. Such motifs as the westward direction of the journey, the meeting of certain types of obstacles on the way, and special attributes of the dead and their world do, certainly, frequently recur, but these have probably been woven into the narrative because they constitute parts of the general popular belief concerning the realm of the

[7] See below, chap. II: 1.
[8] See below, chap. II: 5.
[9] Fisher 1946, 234.
[10] See chap. V: 3.

dead and the journey thither. The data of the Orpheus tradition must of course in reason be in accordance with this popular belief. It would at the same time be too frivolous to assume that it was the Orpheus tale that originally introduced the eschatological conceptions—even if it sanctions them, invests them with authority and value, there are many other traditions of visits to the realm of the dead which have the same function. The Orpheus story has in my opinion adopted and fused with itself the popular local conceptions which already existed, and which in large parts of North America have not been all too divergent from one another. In a later chapter a closer analysis will be given of the connection between the conceptions of popular belief and the content of the Orpheus tradition.[11]

The argument developed here does not imply that the motifs of the realm of the dead and the journey to this realm are as such inessential for the Orpheus tradition. On the contrary, they are among its inalienable elements, but the form assumed by them varies, and must therefore be regarded as secondary.[12] The features essential for the Orpheus tradition in the accounts of the journey to the dead and the stay in the realm of the dead will be treated in the following.[13]

An index that includes all the varying—and often enough mutually conflicting—elements entering in the variants of the tradition gives no clear picture of the main line of the narrative as this is consistently represented in the majority of versions. Instead of giving such an exhaustive list I shall therefore content myself here with a short résumé of the pattern followed by the majority of the North American Orpheus narratives: A young man has lost his wife, and in his grief he resolves to follow her to the land of the dead and bring her home again. She is at first unwilling to let him accompany her on the journey, but finally yields. As a living person he finds it difficult to keep up with her, but with her help he at last reaches the realm of the dead. Here he is met with sympathy by the chief of the dead (or other higher being), and with the latter's direct help or good will Orpheus is permitted to return with his wife. The dead are active at night-time, when they devote themselves above all to dancing. The wife is seized during the dance and conducted to the land of the living, although she is reluctant and unwilling. A taboo, however, has been imposed on her husband which is valid during the journey home or for the period immediately thereafter. He unintention-

---

[11] See chap. V: 1. Cf. above, p. 14.
[12] In this connection, cf. Firth 1955, 4.
[13] See below, chap. II: 2—4.

ally breaks the taboo and loses his wife, who must once more set out for the realm of shades.

The variations on the Orpheus motif are many, and not least a number of so-called oikotypes have been developed.[14] Many of these oikotypes are so individual in character that they lead the narrative away, as it were, from its central theme. One is sometimes almost tempted to refer to the category of the Orpheus traditions narratives which, although they are strikingly reminiscent of the Orpheus story, do not quite conform with it; in one way or another they prove to be outside the Orpheus tradition as we have defined this here. Either these stories are constructed after the pattern of the Orpheus tradition (or after a similar pattern), but without containing its characteristic motifs (or its most characteristic motifs), or else they diverge in their structure from the Orpheus tradition but show one or some of its essential elements. To the former type belong a rather large number of stories concerning the journeys of legendary or historically known personages to the other world (the realm of the dead, the kingdom of heaven, etc.); to the latter may be referred, amongst others, various narratives concerning a seeking for lost relatives and friends concerning the restoration to life of deceased persons.

In some subsequent sections these narratives diverging from the Orpheus tradition will be presented in greater detail.[15] A few words, however, must in this connection first be devoted to the types of narrative most nearly bordering on the Orpheus motif, viz, in the first place the stories of visits to the realm of the dead without the motif of the return to life of the deceased (Gayton: "visits to the afterworld"), and in the second place the "revival stories" whose action does not in part take place in the realm of the dead.

As has already been mentioned, there are in North America numerous narratives concerning persons who have sojourned in the realm of the dead and succeeded in returning therefrom.[16] Especially in north-western North America, where, as Gayton rightly remarks, "tales which deal with pursuit or resuscitation of the dead are common," does one find a large number of oral traditions strikingly reminiscent of the Orpheus narrative —without being identical with this.[17] There are always one or several of the main features of the Orpheus tradition which are missing. But also outside the Northwest culture one finds such stories reminding one of

---

[14] Cf. Gayton, op.cit., 283 sq. See further below, chap. I: 4.
[15] See chap. III: 1, IV: 2, 4, V: 3.
[16] See above, p. 19, and below, chap. IV: 2.
[17] Gayton, op.cit., 280, 264. Cf. also Alexander 1916, 264.

the Orpheus tradition. As an instance I will mention the classical account reproduced by Kohl of the Ojibway hunter who during a severe illness visited the realm of the dead. After many trials on his journey thither he arrived, and was happy at meeting his parents, especially his mother.[18] But immediately thereafter he returned to the living, and one searches in vain for any desire to bring his beloved mother back to the land of the living.[19]

In a way, the Orpheus story may be designated as a "revival story". But it is here not a matter of an immediate, direct resuscitation of a dead person, a magical rebirth on the spot. No, the restoration of life takes the form of a slow process, which requires, inter alia, the journey of a living person to the world of the dead and his activity there. (This, as we shall discover later, is of importance for the psychological understanding of the origin of the tradition.) One should thus not refer to the category of the Orpheus narratives such "revival stories" as lack the important motif-complex of the journey to and the stay in the realm of the dead—however romantic the relation between the living person and the deceased who is resuscitated may otherwise be.[20] Such tales as for example the story of the youth who was reunited with his deceased beloved in her burial tipi[21] thus fall outside the frame of the Orpheus tradition, although they contain two of its most important motifs: the longing for a dear deceased and the restoration of the latter to life.[22] "Revival stories" which do not contain the first-mentioned motif are of course without any interest in this connection.[23]

Even with the firm delimitation of the Orpheus tradition undertaken here it may sometimes be difficult to decide whether a certain narrative should be referred to the Orpheus tradition or not; in some cases it may be necessary to speak of a narrative of Orpheus type. Thus the Mohave know, as Devereux expresses it, "a novelistic tale of the Orpheus type." It contains—possibly—all the particular features which together form the Orpheus tradition; but it strikes us, when considered as a whole, as only a dull replica of the Orpheus narrative.

---

[18] Concerning the hunter, Radin, who has made a commentary on the tale, finds that "dessen Denken ganz von seiner Mutter eingenommen ist" (Radin 1951, 48).

[19] Kohl 1859 I, 295 sqq. Cf. Conard 1900, 257 sq.

[20] Se also Gayton, op.cit., 265. Cf. herewith Hatt 1949, 66 note 4 ('criticism of Thompson's collection of examples).

[21] See below, pp. 170 sqq.

[22] MacCulloch obviously sees these tales as a special form of the Orpheus tradition (MacCulloch 1911, 650).

[23] They are legion. Cf. also Hultkrantz 1953, 176.

The story describes how a young woman, Young Virgin, abandons a much older husband and marries Snake-Soul, an attractive young man. Their marital happiness, however, is of short duration: two wizards, hired by the woman's former husband, kill her with their evil eye. Snake-Soul is inconsolable. One morning he goes aboard his raft and floats down the Colorado River. He sees his deceased wife walking along on the shore abreast of the raft. Finally he falls into the water, checked by the pendant branch of a tree, and drowns. But much later a girl dwelling by the river finds his decayed corpse and salvages it, and from these remains there quickly grows up a youth. The girl takes him to the winter house and tells him to lie down there and not leave the place for four days, and further, in the event of his dead wife's coming to summon him, not to touch her for four days. Snake-Soul lies down in the house as he has been bidden. He hears his wife making merry in a dance in the land of the dead, and longs to be reunited with her. Then at last he sees her visiting him, she begs him to come, but he resists her. On the third day, however, his resistance is broken. He tries to embrace her, but his arms pass right through her. She wishes to take him to the land of the dead (they are evidently both dead now). But a whirlwind separates them, and Snake-Soul is later turned into a snake (gopher snake).[24]

Devereux seems to be right when of this tale he says that "it is probably a romanticized version of some concrete event, which, through a process of elaboration, eventually became blended with the Orpheus plot."[25] But has the transformation of the tale proceeded to the point at which it has become a real Orpheus legend? As I have remarked already, we have here all the constituent motifs, although in a weakened form: the man longs for his wife; he undertakes a journey which tends to be a seeking for the deceased (although perhaps the aim of the journey is not yet quite apparent to his conscious personality); he is reunited with his beloved in a land which in its character is identical with the realm of the dead[26] (the world of psychic absence—Snake-Soul lies isolated for several days, it will be remembered, in a house, and presumably has visions there); he has been promised that she will be restored to him in life, but the breach of a taboo renders this impossible. There is no doubt but that the tale is of Orpheus type. Devereux even wants to refer to it

[24] Devereux 1948, 249 sqq.
[25] Devereux, op.cit., 240.
[26] It may be added that the Mohave, who associate their mythological figures with familiar localities in the surrounding countryside, often locate the realm of the dead to the vicinity of the Colorado River. See Bourke 1889, 172, 174; Curtis 1908 II, 53.

as an Orpheus myth.[27] And it is probably, in spite of all, most reasonable to classify it among the Orpheus narratives.

There are certain other tales which only in part manifest the features of the Orpheus tradition, but which will in the following nevertheless be referred to this. In the light of the careful delimitations undertaken in the foregoing such a disposition may appear strange. The reason for its adoption, however, is that the narratives in question seem in their fundamental structure to fall within the scope of the Orpheus tradition. They have, in other words, grown out of the same conditions as the more regular Orpheus tales, and they have developed in approximately the same direction as these. It is not impossible that some of them—e.g. the narratives on the Plateau and at Puget Sound concerning the culture hero's wooing in the realm of the dead—have been developed from more complete Orpheus tales. They may at all events be regarded as rudimentary Orpheus traditions.

3. Distribution in North America

The oldest records of the North American Orpheus tradition derive from the eastern parts of the continent. It is the Jesuit Fathers in New France who have the honour of having noted down the first versions of this tradition to become known to the Occident. However strange this may seem, they drew no parallels between the classical Greek myth, well-known to them, and its counterpart in the New World. The designation "Orpheus narrative" for the latter is, moreover, of late date. Tylor seems to have been the first to compare consciously the traditions of North America concerning visits to the beyond with the classical Orpheus myth,[1] closely followed by Bancroft,[2] while Thompson coined the term "Orpheus tale" for the North American variations on the Orpheus theme.[3]

The earliest record was made by Brébeuf (1636), and refers to the Huron. The missionary found the story very primitive. He writes: "Now this false belief they have about souls is kept up among them by means

---

[27] Devereux, op.cit., 249.
[1] Tylor 1871 II, 42 sqq.
[2] Bancroft 1875 III, 530.
[3] Thompson 1929, 337. Ehrenreich employed the term "Orpheus myths" for certain South American traditions, but was not willing to admit the North American Orpheus traditions to the same category (Ehrenreich 1905, 70). H. M. Lloyd, the editor of Morgan's study on the Iroquois (1904), discovered in Brébeuf's Orpheus legend "the story of Eurydice, and a suggestion of Peter Pumpkin Eater as well" (Morgan 1954 II, 254).

of certain stories which the fathers tell their children, which are so poorly put together that I am perfectly astounded to see how men believe them and accept them as truth." Brébeuf then recounts "two of the most stupid ones," including the Orpheus legend, which he received "from persons of intelligence and judgment among them."[4] The legend of the Huron, with its motif of the looking taboo which is infringed, is reminiscent of the corresponding Micmac legend which was noted down fifty years later by Le Clercq.[5] Brébeuf's Orpheus legend was later reproduced by Lafitau, through whom it became generally known.[6]

As among the earlier documents concerning Indian Orpheus traditions one may perhaps also reckon the totem poles on the west coast of Canada and Alaska. Many totem poles along this coast, and especially many from the Haida, appear to constitute a sort of illustration to the type of Orpheus legends current in this culture area.[7]

It is, however, chiefly the notes taken by American folklorists and ethnologists during the last hundred years that have given us a conception of the wide distribution of the Orpheus motif over the North American continent. A summary of the account of its occurrence given by Gayton will be presented here, with certain additions; for a more precise account of the content of the different narratives the reader is referred to Gayton's investigation. Only the fresh data not included in that investigation will be instanced in the following.[8]

The Orpheus tradition occurs most frequently on the west coast of North America. In the Northwest Coast culture proper (the coastal regions along the Pacific in Alaska and Canada down to the Strait of Georgia) one finds the Orpheus motif in all the bigger tribes. Gayton records it among the Tlingit, Kwakiutl and Nootka, at the same time adducing from the Bella Bella and from the Nisqually farther south a couple of narratives which, however, are in my opinion not to be regarded as typical Orpheus traditions but deal with another, though nearly related, narrative motif: the woman who returns from the realm of the dead with a skeleton baby.[9] On the other hand, Gayton dismisses as irrelevant a number of narratives in this culture area which in accordance with the definition given here may without hesitation be designated as Orpheus

[4] JR X, 147 sqq.
[5] Le Clercq 1910, 208 sqq. Concerning the value of Le Clercq's information, see Hultkrantz 1953, 74 note 11. Cf. Barbeau 1915, 28 sq.
[6] Lafitau 1724 I, 402 sqq.
[7] Barbeau 1950 I, 269 sqq., especially 288—9; Barbeau 1953, 255 sqq., especially 260—269, 301—304.
[8] See appendix, 313 sqq., for a complete account of all the sources.
[9] Gayton 1935, 281 sq. See below, pp. 172 sqq.

26

traditions. Barbeau, who, though less critically than Gayton, has dealt with the Orpheus theme in the Northwest, adduces against Gayton— and against Thompson—that these researchers "seem to have overlooked one of the most significant branches of the same theme on our continent: that of the north Pacific Coast."[10] Barbeau is referring to the tale, rather widespread along this coast, of the carrying off of the hunter's wife by killer whales. To what extent this narrative falls entirely within the scope of the Orpheus tradition is open to discussion. It has, however, seemed reasonable to me to include it; upon what grounds this has been done will be discussed in detail later.[11]

On these presumptions we may constate that the Orpheus motif has occurred among the Tlingit, Haida, Tsimshian, Haisla (Kitlobe), Bella Coola, Bella Bella (Rivers Inlet), Kwakiutl and Nootka.[12] We find the regular Orpheus tradition among the Tlingit, Haisla and Kwakiutl. Indisputably of Orpheus type is the Bella Coola narrative of the seal-hunter's wife who "lived" dead among ghosts in her husband's village; but as this story diverges in vital points from the main theme of the Orpheus tradition it can scarcely be referred to this tradition.[13]

Among the coastal tribes in the southern periphery of the Northwest, too, the Orpheus narrative has been common in one form or another. Gayton is acquainted with it from several Salish tribes, viz, the StsEélis (=Stalo, a Cowichan group), the Snuqualmi, Puyallup, Green River Salish (=Skopamish), as well as from two Chinook tribes, the Wishram and the Wasco.[14] She also includes the Nisqually, but as mentioned above, the Nisqually narrative cannot be regarded as an Orpheus tradition.[15] Gayton further adduces a number of tribes that have had tales which at least as regards certain elements are reminiscent of the Orpheus narrative, and which "may be generically related to it."[16] The majority of these stories do not belong to the Orpheus tradition, since they merely describe experiences of sick persons and persons with suspended animation in the other world. But some of the tribes referred to—the Quinault and the Twana—have indisputably possessed the Orpheus tradition in the form defined by us. Furthermore, also the version of the Orpheus tale

[10] Barbeau 1950 I, 271.
[11] See below, pp. 43 sqq.
[12] Besides the sources adduced by Gayton: see works by Barbeau, Boas, Deans, Krause, Sapir & Swadesh, and Swanton mentioned in chap. I: 4, and McIlwraith 1948 I, 508 sqq. (Kitlobe).
[13] McIlwraith, op.cit., 505 sq. See further below, p. 170.
[14] Gayton, op.cit., 278 sq., 281.
[15] See above, p. 26.
[16] Gayton, op.cit., 281.

noted by Barbeau can be instanced within the region, viz, among the Sechelt and the Nanaimo, and the Chehalis have known the Orpheus tradition in the form instanced from e.g. the Snuqualmi and Puyallup. The traditions of Orpheus type deriving from this region—the Strait of Georgia, Puget Sound, western Washington and Oregon—are very individual in character and are perhaps not all completely deserving of the designation Orpheus narratives. Nevertheless, it does appear to me most suitable to refer them all to the Orpheus tradition.[17] All in all, one finds the Orpheus motif represented among the following tribes in this coastal region: the Sechelt, Cowichan (Nanaimo, Stalo), Snuqualmi, Puyallup, Skopamish, Quinault, Twana, Chehalis, Wishram, Wasco and Kalapuya.[18]

In the Plateau area inhabited by the Salish and Shahaptin peoples, which is as we know closely allied, geographically and culturally, to the Northwest Coast, the Orpheus tradition has been widely represented. According to Gayton, one finds it among the Thompson, the southern Okanagon (=Sinkaietk), Sanpoil, Kalispel, Klikitat and Tenino.[19] In this connection it should be remarked that the Sinkaietk version presents the same problem as certain of the narratives in the foregoing group.[20] The traditions noted by Dr Gayton may be supplemented with stories from the Yakima, from a Shahaptin group that is not more precisely defined, and from the Carrier. The unknown Shahaptin group may possibly be the Nez Percé, if Spier's localization is correct.[21] The Carrier may be suitably classified with the Plateau tribes in this connection. We thus find the Orpheus motif on the Plateau among the Carrier, Thompson, Sinkaietk, Kalispel, Klikitat, Yakima, Tenino and Nez Percé.[22]

One of the foci of the Orpheus narrative in North America is thus the Northwest Coast and the Plateau; another is California, together with

[17] See the discussion in chap. I: 4.
[18] Besides the sources adduced by Gayton: see works by Boas and Hill-Tout mentioned in chap. I: 4, and Hill-Tout 1904 b, 321, 339 sqq., 1907, 214 sqq. (Stalo); Farrand 1902, 100 sqq. (Quinault); Curtis 1913 IX, 163 sq. (Twana); Adamson 1934, 21 sqq., 24 sqq., 27 sq., 29, 293 sqq., 349 sq. (Chehalis); Curtis 1911 VIII, 126 sqq. (Wishram); Frachtenberg, Gatschet & Jacobs 1945, 199 sqq., 226 sqq. (Kalapuya). See also Spier 1935, 15.
[19] Gayton, op.cit., 278, 281.
[20] See below, chap. I: 4. Gayton's account of the Sinkaietk myth after Spier's (Cline's) then unpublished manuscript does not tally with the content of the version of the myth which has since been printed (Spier 1938, 235 sq.).
[21] Spier 1935, 15. Various indications suggest that not the Nez Percé, but a more westerly Shahaptin group, should come into the question. Cf. below, p. 63 note 13.
[22] Besides the sources adduced by Gayton: Jenness 1934, 143 sqq., 1943, 537 (Carrier); Spier 1938, 235 sq., 258 (Sinkaietk); Lyman 1904, 248 sq. (Yakima); Boas 1917 a, 178 sq. (possibly the Nez Percé).

southernmost Oregon. In this area Dr Gayton has found the Orpheus motif among the Klamath, Modoc, Shasta, Karuk, Yurok, Hupa, Maidu, Miwok, Yokuts, Western Mono, Tübatulabal, Serrano and Gabrielino.[23] She also adduces what she considers to be an uncertain case: the Pomo story of a man who follows a close relative who has just died (he is represented as a son or a brother) to the realm of the dead, though without trying to take this relative with him on the return journey to the land of the living.[24] This story may, as Gayton opines, have been influenced by the ghost dance, but it should probably nevertheless be regarded as an Orpheus legend, even if a rudimentary one. It certainly falls more within the category of the Orpheus narratives than does the Takelma story of Coyote's escapades in the realm of the dead, which is included among the Orpheus traditions by Gayton.[25]

The Orpheus traditions are thus numerous within this relatively circumscribed area. As far as I have been able to ascertain, we find the genuine Orpheus tale among the Klamath, Modoc, Shasta, Karuk, Tolowa, Tututni, Yurok, Hupa, Pomo, the southern Maidu or Nisenan (Nishinam), the Miwok, Yokuts, the Western Mono, the Tübatulabal, Serrano, Gabrielino and Mohave.[26] As one departs from the North American west coast the instances become less frequent. From the highlands of the Southwest Gayton was able to note the Orpheus motif only among the Navajo and Zuni Indians.[27] She remarks that "the Orpheus tale is evidently not a favorite among the Pueblos," but mentions some narratives whose contents constitute closely allied themata.[28] Such stories are plentiful enough, as well here as on the Northwest Coast. Very close to the Orpheus motif is a

[23] Gayton, op.cit., 267 sqq., 279 sq.
[24] Gayton, op.cit., 270; see Loeb 1926, 292 sq., Barrett 1933, 379.
[25] Gayton, op.cit., 279; see Sapir 1909 a, 97 sqq. Gayton's account of the Takelma myth does not exactly reflect the content, and it therefore gives a false idea of the close connection of the myth with the Orpheus tradition.
[26] Besides the sources adduced by Gayton: Dixon 1910, 19, Voegelin 1942, 238, Voegelin 1947, 52 sq. (Shasta); Kroeber 1946, 14 sqq., Voegelin 1947, 54 sq. (Karuk); Barnett 1937, 185 (Tolowa, Tututni); Kroeber 1907 c, 193, 1907 d, 272, Gayton 1930 a, 77 (Yokuts); Voegelin 1935, 203 sqq., 1938, 6, 47 sqq. (Tübatulabal); Kroeber 1925, 625 (Gabrielino); Devereux 1948, 249 sqq. (Mohave). Commentary on the Nisenan tale (as given by Powers, Powers 1877, 339 sq.): Kroeber 1907 c, 175, 188; cf. also Bancroft 1875 III, 531 sq. Commentary on the "Miwok tale" (referred to by Hudson, Hudson 1902, 106): Kroeber 1907 c, 188, Kroeber 1925, 452. I must, however, admit that I have not been able to control the versions from the Tolowa and Tututni communicated by Barnett; he observes only that an "Orpheus myth" occurs among them.
[27] Gayton, op.cit., 271 sq.
[28] Gayton, op.cit., 272. Cf. also the psychologically interesting narrative in Stevenson 1894, 143 (Sia).

29

Tewa narrative communicated by Gayton: in San Juan (and probably also in Nambé) one is told of the man who out of longing for his wife, who had recently died, visited her in a house where she was awaiting her departure to the realm of spirits. But when he arrived at the house he was sickened by the odour of death and took to flight, pursued by his wife. The story has become a star myth.[29] Although in character it is reminiscent of the Orpheus motif, it cannot be reckoned as belonging to the Orpheus traditions.—However, a closer investigation of the literature that has been published since the appearance of Gayton's study shows that the Orpheus motif had a somewhat wider distribution in the South-west than Gayton assumed, and that it has occurred among the Navajo and the Lipan Apache, in Zuni and Taos.[30]

In the Great Basin area Gayton found the Orpheus motif represented, east of California, only among the Paviotso at Pyramid Lake in Nevada; and from her investigation it is apparent that it is missing also just east of the Rocky Mountains, on "the high western Plains."[31] These results of her investigations must now, however, be in part revised in the light of fresh material. Thus a version of the Orpheus narrative is known among the Shoshoni around Fort Hall.[32] A tale of Orpheus type from the Lemhi (whether Shoshoni or Bannock is uncertain) has been communicated to me by Dr Sven Liljeblad in Pocatello.[33] This describes the vain attempt of an antelope hunter to bring from the bowels of a mountain a supernatural woman whom he had married—the dwarf-spirit *ninïmbi's* sister—to the land of human beings. He infringes the taboo pronounced by *ninïmbi*, never to scold his wife, and she vanishes. One can scarcely refer this story to the Orpheus traditions proper.

From the Plains proper Gayton reports the occurrence of the Orpheus motif among the Wichita (with the Tawakoni), the Pawnee (three groups), the Blackfoot and Sarcee.[34] To these tribes may probably be added the Comanche, possibly also the Assiniboin.[35] One can, however,

[29] Parsons 1926, 22 sqq.; cf. also Parsons 1929, 266 note 494.
[30] Besides the sources adduced by Gayton: Haile 1942, 411 sqq., Wyman, Hill & Osanai 1942, 19 note 25, 33 note 58, Wyman & Bailey 1943, 8 (Navajo); Opler 1940, 100 sq. (Lipan Apache); Parsons 1916, 250 (Zuni); Parsons 1940, 23 sqq., 27 (Taos).
[31] Gayton, op.cit., 271, 277 sq.
[32] Steward 1943, 287.
[33] The informant's father was a Bannock, his mother a Sheepeater Shoshoni.
[34] Gayton, op.cit., 276. Gayton's material from the Sarcee (an unpublished text recorded by Sapir) may now be supplemented with Jenness 1938, 97 sq. A version from the Pawnee not mentioned by Gayton occurs in Dorsey 1904 b, 74 sqq.
[35] For the Comanche, see above pp. 17 sq.; for the Assiniboin, see Lowie 1909 b, 168 sq. (The Orpheus motif here introduced in the narrative about Lodge-Boy and Thrown-Away; see below, chap. I: 4).

still agree with Gayton where she remarks that the Orpheus narrative "certainly was not a fundamental constituent of Plains mythology."[36] It is possible to distinguish two centres for the occurrence of the motif on the Plains: a southern centre, dominated by the Caddoan peoples (the Tawakoni, Wichita, Pawnee), and a northern centre, dominated by the Blackfoot confederation (Blackfoot, Sarcee). Curiously enough, there are no signs that the Orpheus tradition occurred among the central Plains peoples. Kroeber, who has carried out ethnological investigations among the Arapaho and their linguistic kinsmen the Atsina (Gros Ventre), points out that both these tribes are without "a tradition of a visit to the land of the dead, other than in stories told as the actual experience of persons recently alive or still living."[37]

In the Middle West the Orpheus motif occurs, according to Gayton, among the Shawnee, Menomini and Winnebago, possibly also among the Fox.[38] It has, however, further been known among the Ojibway and the Ottawa.[39] Very close to the Orpheus tradition is the legend concerning the Ojibway Indian Ogauns, who in an ecstatic vision sought contact with the spirit world in order to acquire eternal life for himself and his people. He failed, however, because he happened to sneeze.[40]— There is, altogether, an abundance of traditions concerning visits to the other world in the Central Woodland area. And outside the west coastal region it has nowhere, in a limited area, been possible to record the Orpheus tradition so often as precisely here.

Nor has it been unknown farther eastward. In the Eastern Woodland area Gayton found it among the Montagnais, Malecite, Micmac, Seneca and Huron.[41] If it has not been possible to trace the Orpheus tradition among the coastal Algonquin farther south, this is doubtless due to the fact that these tribes succumbed completely to the white intruder in the course of the 17th century.

Finally, the Orpheus tradition has been noted down among the Indians

---

[36] Gayton, op.cit., 277.
[37] Kroeber 1907 a, 58.
[38] Gayton, op.cit., 274 sqq. Apart from the sources adduced by Gayton one may mention: Voegelin 1936, 5, 16 (Shawnee). The main source for the Shawnee, Gregg's *Commerce of the Prairies,* has been used by me in a later edition, Gregg 1954, 387 sq.
[39] Ojibway: Jenness 1935, 109; cf. also the survey of the literature in Conard 1900, 225 note 1. Ottawa: Schoolcraft 1851 (I), 321 sqq. (cf. herewith Hallowell 1946 a, 148: no. 38); McLean 1892, 180 sq. The Ottawa legend, however, has not the motif of the bringing back of the beloved, and Fisher does not give it in her list of Algonquin Orpheus traditions (Fisher 1946, 250).
[40] Jenness 1935, 55 sqq.
[41] Gayton, op.cit., 274 sq. The best source for the Huron legend is JR X, 149 sqq. In a deviating form we find the same legend in Spence 1914, 260 sqq.

of the Southeast, or to be more precise, among the Alabama, Koasati, Yuchi and Cherokee.[42] The Wichita and Shawnee, who are sometimes reckoned as belonging to the peoples of the Southeast, have, as we have seen, also narrated the Orpheus story.

The distribution of the Orpheus tradition in North America shows, as Gayton was able to establish, a strong concentration on the west coast, a weaker concentration on the east coast, and a more diffused occurrence in the interior of the continent.[43] Perhaps the most remarkable thing about this distribution is the absence of any instances from the whole of the Mackenzie region; of the many Athapascan tribes in Canada, only the Carrier and the Sarcee are acquainted with the Orpheus motif. This is presumably at least partly due to the fact that the Athapascan legend material has not yet been recorded to a satisfactory extent. One is here reminded of the way in which, since the publication of Gayton's work, the notes taken in the Great Basin and the adjacent regions have completely changed our knowledge of the occurrence of the Orpheus tradition there. Gayton's pronouncement that "it is practically unknown to the Shoshonean and Yuman tribes" was motivated in the middle of the thirties, but is untenable today.[44]

The probability is, however, that if the Orpheus motif occurs in northern Canada to the west of Hudson Bay at all, it is not common there. Thompson believes he has met with it among the Eskimo;[45] but the instance he adduces, after Rink, is not an Orpheus narrative but a "revival story," as Hatt has pointed out.[46]

The absence of the Orpheus motif in the Mackenzie region is in marked contrast with its intensive occurrence along the west coast, including the Plateau and the interior of California. In the Northwest area, where since presumably very remote times there has existed a religious complex of ideas with the stress on the relation between the living and the dead,[47] the frequent occurrence of the Orpheus motif is perhaps rather natural. The Plateau, too, may—possibly—be included within this circle of ideas. Also parts of California, certainly, are characterized by a sort of "death cult," the "mourning anniversary" deriving from southern California which, as

[42] Gayton, op.cit., 272 sq.
[43] Gayton, op.cit., 265 sqq.
[44] Gayton, op.cit., 265.
[45] Thompson 1929, 337; see Rink 1875, 298 (also a Danish edition, 1871).
[46] Hatt 1949, 66 note 4. Gayton finds that among the Eskimo the tradition does not exist "in any comparable form" (Gayton, op.cit., 266).
[47] Wike 1952, 98.

Kroeber has expressed the matter, apparently gives a "first impression of being one of the most typical phases of Californian culture."[48] But the fact that the Orpheus tradition has been mainly noted to the north of the centre of this ritual complex does not, at all events, favour the assumption of a direct connection therewith.

However this may be, the Orpheus motif is very popular in California —especially among the Yokuts[49]—and it has here only in a couple of quarters been conspicuous by its absence, above all in northern central California.[50] Whether the tradition has occurred in the coastal region between San Francisco and Los Angeles is now very difficult to decide.[51]

In the Southwest the Orpheus motif becomes less common—perhaps, with Benedict (and with due reservation for the generalization it in many cases implies), one may here adduce something to the effect that the Pueblos were too sober to occupy their imaginations with a "tale of passion", while the nomads (the southern Athapascans) have always been known to fear death and the death-stuff.[52] And yet, as we have seen, the Orpheus motif has not been altogether unknown among the Navajo and Apache—even if the latter have only known it as a memorate.

The Piman peoples, too, appear not to have had any great interest in the Orpheus motif. It is absent among the Piman tribes of both Arizona and northern Mexico until one comes down to Nayarit, where we find it once more (though it is not certain whether it is among the Cora, Huichol, Tepecano or Colotlán).[53] In a peculiar form with which we shall deal later, the motif occurred also among the Old Aztecs.[54]

It is evident that the Orpheus tradition has been known among the Basin Shoshoni, though to no very great extent, and about the same applies to its occurrence among the Plains Indians. This is possibly connected with the circumstance that the Shoshoni conceived death as a dreadful phenomenon which one should flee,[55] whereas the Plains Indians,

---

[48] Kroeber 1925, 859 sq. See also Kroeber 1907 b, 335.
[49] This emerges from Gayton's investigation, and was long ago pointed out by Kroeber (Kroeber 1907 c, 196).
[50] Kroeber, op.cit., 198.
[51] No Orpheus legend has been noted here by Harrington (Harrington 1942). In an earlier work Gayton believed she had found the Orpheus motif among the Salinan (Gayton 1930 a, 77); her literature refence, however, Mooney 1896, 195, is incorrect. (Probably she is referring to Mason 1912, 195, though no Orpheus legend is mentioned there.) In her Orpheus study of 1935 Dr. Gayton only mentions that "the Salinan and Costanoan peoples west of the Yokuts may have had the tale" (Gayton, op.cit., 270).
[52] Benedict 1932, 4 sqq., 10 sq.
[53] Bancroft 1875 III, 529 sq.
[54] Hatt 1951, 872, 906. See further chap. IV: 4.
[55] Cf. e.g. Benedict, op.cit., 13 sq., Stewart 1942, 319, Stewart 1941, 415.

with their realistic view of life, have not been interested in the world of the dead.[56] The Orpheus tradition has here had no natural soil in which to grow, except among the agricultural Caddoan peoples. It is, as we know, in agrarian cultures that the relation between the living and the dead becomes more intimate: the dead are here conceived in the same animistic schema of death and renewal as the vegetation, and are then frequently identified with the life-promoting vegetation spirits.[57]

Perhaps in this same circumstance we may find the explanation of the fact that the Orpheus tradition plays such an important rôle in the eastern agrarian cultures. It should, however, be remarked that the distribution here goes far to the north of the boundary for the cultivation of maize.

The inventory of instances given here permits at once of the conclusion that the Orpheus myth has had a wide distribution in native North America, and that the Orpheus tradition has been among the commonest folktales there. It is therefore not calculated to surprise us that it has been deeply anchored in the Indian view of life and that it has been so modified by cultural conditions that characteristic oikotypes have been developed.

4. Cultural integration and oikotypes

A scrutiny of the Orpheus traditions occurring in North America shows that the narratives are everywhere surprisingly alike, if one excepts the locally diverging tales on the Northwest Coast. Gayton, who has made a special investigation of the Orpheus traditions from formal literary points of view, observes that "the plot, using the term in its widest sense to include motivation, incidents, and succession of incidents, has been maintained with remarkable consistency throughout its wide distribution."[1] She adds that "the most significant attribute of the Orpheus tale is the marked similarity of all its versions."[2] We are not here called upon to show in detail all the similarities that exist between the Orpheus tales in the most widely different quarters in North America; a number of them will probably be apparent from my presentation of the main motifs of the tradition.[3] The resemblances of course strongly

---

[56] Cf. e.g. Lowie 1925 b, 199, Lowie 1954, 164.
[57] See further chap. III: 2, IV: 4.
[1] Gayton 1935, 282.
[2] Gayton, op.cit., 284.
[3] See below, pp. 56 sqq. See also Gayton's tabular list, op.cit., 263 sq.

support the assumption that it is in the main one and the same narrative that has been disseminated over the whole of North America.

It would, however, be surprising if the uniformity in the composition of the tradition did not allow of certain marked differences in different culture areas as regards the content of the tale. That this may vary was of course observed by Gayton. She writes that the Orpheus tale "is thoroughly integrated with cultural forms."[4] In the first place the cultural milieu has left traces in the 'stage properties' of the tale and in the conceptual elements, and in the second place variations of the main motif have crystallized out in connection with the culture pattern ("oikotypes" according to von Sydow).

It may seem superfluous to occupy oneself with the problem of the extent to which the content of a local Orpheus tradition constitutes the mechanical reflection of culture pattern and culture content. It has long been apparent to folkloristic and ethnological research that a myth, legend or fairy-tale must, if it is to elicit positive responses in the hearers, refer to their milieu and values, even if some single features in the narrative may be strange for the environment. The degree of this integration may, however, vary: a number of European folktales have been adopted by the Indians in a strikingly unchanged form, others have been flexibly adapted to the culture pattern.[5] For the comparative religious historian this is of interest, since the truth-value of the narrative is as a rule in direct proportion to its level of integration. One has here, in other words, one of the best criteria for an assessment of the value of a story as a document of religious belief.

The cultural integration of the Orpheus tale shows itself in part directly and in part indirectly. One finds a direct reflection of the local culture pattern in the indications of material, social, ethical and religious conditions occurring in the tale.[6] It may without hesitation be said that the agreements between the details of the Orpheus tradition and local culture elements are everywhere, as far as I have been able to judge, complete. Clothes, tools, houses or descriptions of family conditions and religious customs in the narrative have all their close counterparts in the external culture milieu.

As an instance of this one may here mention the burial customs reflected in the Orpheus tradition. It is one of the frequently recurring particular

[4] Gayton, op.cit., 282.
[5] Cf. e.g. Thompson 1919, passim.
[6] Gayton, op.cit., 283.

features in this tradition that for a period—as a rule four days and nights
—the mourning Orpheus awaits, near his wife's grave, her departure to
the realm of the dead.[7] In the Twana tale it is the one of two good com-
rades who has died. The surviving party, who mourned him deeply, sat
one day under his friend's grave—a canoe on poles—, and here he witnessed how the deceased was fetched to the realm of the dead by other
deceased persons.[8] The canoe on poles or on an elevated platform is a
common type of grave among the Twana and other Coast Salish.[9] In the
Serrano narrative we are told that the deceased wife was laid on a pyre.
"The people immediately brought brush, and piled it up. They put her
body upon it, and burned it, so that when her husband returned that night
the body was all consumed." The husband remained at the pyre, and later
witnessed how his wife was delineated in the contours of whirling dust
over the site of the funeral pyre.[10] It is the burial custom common among
the Serrano that is here described.[11] A couple of the Orpheus legends
from Zuni relate how the mourning husband comes upon his deceased
wife preparing her departure from the grave in which she has been
buried.[12] It is well known that the people in Zuni buried their dead in
the earth.[13] The version of the Orpheus tradition among the Skidi Pawnee
has it that the young girl who was the object of Orpheus' love died and
was buried in the tipi of her family, after which the parents moved from
this.[14] Burial in a tipi occurred among several nomadic Plains tribes, e.g.
the Oglala, and was presumably also common among the Pawnee when
they left their earth-lodges to go hunting buffalo or on a campaign against their enemies.[15]

In all of these cases there is an exact agreement between the burial
customs of the legend and the burial customs of the actual culture. The
case is somewhat otherwise among a number of tribes and groups in
western North America, above all on the northern Northwest Coast and
in central California. We may first consider the Carrier, the only one
among the tribes of the Mackenzie region that is included in our tribal
inventory.

The Carrier are well known for their remarkable crematory customs:

[7] See below, pp. 60 sqq.
[8] Curtis 1913 IX, 163 sq.
[9] Curtis, op.cit., 85, 158. Cf. Barnett 1939, 263 sq.
[10] Benedict 1926, 8.
[11] Kroeber 1925, 618; Drucker 1937, 36.
[12] Benedict 1935 II, 133, 157.
[13] Bunzel 1932, 482, 540.
[14] Dorsey 1904 b, 71.
[15] Cf. Bushnell 1927, 41, 80. See also below, p. 171 note 38 and p. 172 note 44.

the widow of a deceased husband was forced to embrace his corpse on the funeral pyre until she was almost choked by the smoke and singed with the flames.[16] But in the Orpheus legend it is stated that the husband of the deceased woman, who was a medicine-man, "wished to accompany her to the Spirit Land in order to discover what the place was like. So the people did not burn her body, but buried it in the ground with the living husband beside it." Then follows the story of how the two spouses journeyed together to the Spirit Land.[17] The motive for the husband's desire to go to the realm of the dead seems rather strange in this connection, and accords ill with the sequel of the narrative, which tells how the woman is restored to the world of the living. As a matter of fact, the motive has probably been woven into the narrative to provide an explanation of the divergent mode of burial. But why, then, is a burial in earth introduced inte the story? One can imagine two possible explanations: either the tale has been incorporated with the Carriers' stock of traditions without being completely integrated with their cultural premisses, or else the Carrier formerly buried their dead in the earth, but later abandoned this mode of burial. The last-mentioned alternative is probably the one which should be applied. We know that the Carrier, like other Athapascans, adopted much of the culture of the peoples surrounding them, especially in the sphere of social organization (social rank, potlatch, etc.). Probably they also adopted the custom of burning the dead from the coastal peoples—thus chiefly from the Tsimshian.[18] Concerning the adjacent Athapascans in the north, the Sekani, an older source reports that they buried their dead in the earth or the ground in former times but, after establishing themselves in their 19th century settlements west of the Rocky Mountains, they adopted the method of cremation.[19] It is probable that a similar development took place among the Carrier, even if at an earlier date (as with the Sekani, for the rest) the method of burial was perhaps not their only way of disposing of their dead, the corpses being sometimes left on the ground or in hollow trees.[20]

One is thus probably justified in asserting that the Carrier legend re- flects the burial customs of an earlier Carrier culture. The legendary tra-

---

[16] Wilkes 1845 IV, 453; Yarrow 1880, 51 sqq. (quotes Ross Cox); Morice 1889, 145, 1906, 210 sq.; Jenness 1943, 534.
[17] Jenness 1934, 143.
[18] Morice 1906, 199; BBAE 30: 2 (1910), 675.
[19] Harmon 1903, 266 (first edition, 1820); Jenness 1937, 59 (cf. also Jenness 1932, 382).
[20] Cf. Morice 1889, 146, 1906, 199 (Sekani); Morice 1911, 640 (Carrier; see also the legend in Morice 1889, 159: the entrance to the world of the dead through a hollow tree). Cf., however, Morice 1910, 230! (cremation earliest).

dition thus shows, just as do the European fairy-tales, a stubborn con-
servatism—though apparently without succumbing to the fate of becoming pure fiction, as has happened with our fairy-tales.[21]

The same applies to the other cases in which there is an apparently
marked discrepancy between the burial customs of the Orpheus legend
and those of the historical culture: this discrepancy is only apparent.
Certain traditions from the northern Northwest Coast—from the Tlingit
and Haisla, and one may here also mention a pseudo-Orpheus tale from
the Tsimshian which will be discussed later[22]—assume or mention the use
of skeleton burial, though in practice cremation was the commonest
usage in this culture area.[23] Skeleton burial is, however, known to have
occurred, especially in the case of chiefs and shamans;[24] and in earlier
times cremation appears not to have been so common.[25]

Orpheus traditions describing or referring to earth-burial are met
with among three Californian tribes, among which, however, only
cremation is reported in some ethnographic works: the Pomo, Nisenan
and Yokuts.[26] Yet from other reports it appears that these tribes also
buried their dead.[27] According to Powers, the action in the Orpheus
myth of the "Nishinam" is supposed to have occurred before the period
marking the inception of cremation.[28] However this may be, the burial
customs of the Orpheus tradition do not, among any of the tribes here
referred to, constitute an alien custom.

The close conformity of the milieu of the tradition to the culture pattern is apparent also indirectly: the religious conceptions occurring in
the Orpheus traditions are found also in the patterns of religious belief
of the tribes in question, and these in their turn reflect the cultures. I am
here thinking above all of the eschatological ideas which have taken
form in the Orpheus tales. Gayton is of the opinion that an examination

[21] That the European fairy-tale has its anchorage in an older culture milieu is of
course obvious. See von Sydow 1941.
[22] See Jenness 1932, 195 sqq.; cf. further below, p. 174.
[23] Drucker 1950, 217; Goddard 1945, 98 sqq.
[24] Swanton 1908 b, 430 (Tlingit), Garfield 1939, 241 (Tsimshian). The hero was in
both the Tsimshian and Tlingit legends the son of a chief.
[25] Drucker 1943, 107; Martin, Quimby & Collier 1947, 469.
[26] Pomo: Kroeber 1925, 253; Loeb 1926, 286; Gifford 1926, 376; Merriam 1955, 40.
Nisenan: Beals 1933, 376. Yokuts: Aginsky 1943, 440. See also the distribution maps
in Kroeber 1922, 295, Spier 1928, 294.
[27] Pomo: Gifford & Kroeber 1937, 152; Essene 1942, 36, 66. Nisenan: Kroeber 1929,
265; Voegelin 1942, 136, 229. Yokuts: Kroeber 1925, 499; Driver 1937, 99; Gayton
1948 I, 46, 107, II, 149.
[28] Powers 1877, 340; cf. op.cit., 341, and Voegelin, op.cit., 229.

of such agreements is valueless, as "in many instances it is evident that the recorder has derived his notions of native belief from the Orpheus tale itself."[29] This, however, I do not find very credible, even if nowadays—as we shall see—the Indians refer their eschatological knowledge to Orpheus' experiences.[30] Eschatological notions have been common, both in and outside of North America, without the occurrence of any Orpheus tradition.[31] And that the Orpheus tradition as such can scarcely have set its stamp upon the eschatological conceptions emerges from the fact that the content of these conceptions as a rule accurately follows the actual cultural picture. The Orpheus tradition has obviously in many cases modified already established eschatological ideas, but its eschatology has in the main been adapted to the religious conceptions actually obtaining, and these have in their turn emerged from the culture pattern.

We may for the time being postpone further discussion of the problem of the relations of the eschatological conceptions in the legendary tradition and in the living religious belief, to give instead some instances of the complete correspondence between the forms assumed by the realm of the dead in the Orpheus legend and the actual culture. Some random examples from the various culture areas should be sufficient. It should be pointed out that one does not always find more precise details concerning the other world in the Orpheus tradition—from the viewpoint of the plot these details are of course of subordinate interest.

In the Cowichan-Stalo legend we are told how day after day the mourning husband followed his wife's trail to the land of the dead. "At last he came to a settlement where there was a long-house", where the chief of the dead had his residence. When darkness fell, the dead came to the place to dance, "and they all entered the building. Now all round the sides thereof were planted swing-poles for hanging cradles upon, and as soon as the people were come in the women hung up the cradles they were carrying on these poles."[32] This picture of the realm of the dead at once calls to mind striking features of the historical Cowichan culture. Their dwellings, as usual on the Northwest Coast, of wood, were in some cases extremely long; and a single house could hold the entire population of a village.[33] Such long-houses were also used for ceremonial dances.[34] The cradles were generally suspended with ropes, so that they could be

[29] Gayton, op.cit., 282 sq.
[30] See chap. V: 2.
[31] Cf. above, p. 21.
[32] Hill-Tout 1904 b, 339 sq.
[33] Duff 1952, 47 sq.; Drucker 1955, 60.
[34] Duff, op.cit., 49.

swung to and fro.[35] The chief or village leader occupied an important position.[36]

The Orpheus of the Carrier Indians arrived at "a city, divided into two parts. On the one side all the houses and canoes were black, on the other red; and between them stood a totem-pole named tsim'yak'yak. The black houses were the homes of the dead, the red the homes of the robins, which dwell on earth during the day and depart to the underworld at evening."[37] This spirit land constitutes a remarkable parallel to the data concerning former housing conditions in the tribe given in the native, more or less credible historical tradition. Thus we are told of a now vanished village, Dizkle on the Bulkley River, that is consisted of two parts, separated from each other by a river (not by totem poles, though these are not rare among the Carrier). The one part of the village had a very large house, where resided the chief of the Thin-House clan.[38] This clan and its house were also referred to as "Robin's House," "because tradition stated that its founder had once visited the nightly home of the robins in the land of the dead".[39] The Orpheus legend has here become the origin legend of a clan.

In the Orpheus legend of the Yokuts the mourning widower arrives in the land of the dead, where the deceased are dancing the round-dance. "The chief's messenger went to the chief, Tipiknits, and told him there was a living man there. Then he got out tule mats for the man to sit on. Then he called him to eat, and the messenger's wife came to serve him."[40] The circumstances reported here are the common usages familiar to the Yokuts Indian. The round-dance referred to is the ghost dance (of which the Orpheus tradition is the origin legend).[41] Every village had one chief or more, and the chief was accorded great respect.[42] His nearest executive was the messenger, *winatum*.[43] Mats made of tule-stems sewn together were common among the Telumni Yokuts, among whom the Orpheus legend here in question was noted down.[44]

The Orpheus tradition from Taos relates how a sister of the deceased

[35] Drucker, op.cit., 70; cf. Duff, op.cit., 90, Barnett 1955, 132.
[36] Duff, op.cit., 81; Drucker, op.cit., 117. Cf., however, Barnett, op.cit., 245.
[37] Jenness 1934, 144. Morice's interpretation to the effect that the colours of the houses represented the feelings of joy and sorrow respectively is of debatable value (Morice 1910, 230).
[38] Jenness 1943, 475 sqq.
[39] Jenness, op.cit., 484 sq.
[40] Gayton 1935, 267.
[41] Gayton 1930 a, 77 sq.
[42] Gayton 1930 b, 385.
[43] Gayton, op.cit., 366, 368, 386.
[44] Kroeber 1925, 521.

woman—her name is Yellow Corn girl—on arriving at the river of death "heard some one calling out like the Governor, 'A new person is coming! People, go and put out a bridge for her'!" When the bridge had been built "the people were calling, 'Build a new estufa, so we can have a dance'. So at once they built the estufa and took Blue Corn girl [this was the name of the deceased woman] down to dance. Yellow Corn girl was peeping in through the hatch."[45] This affords a glimpse of the typical culture milieu of the Pueblo Indians, and especially of the Pueblo of Taos. This latter is ruled by a "governor," who is elected annually and invested with great power.[46] The governor generally shouts his orders himself, amongst other things the summons to collective works.[47] Taos has seven cult-rooms (kivas or estufas), which are all wholly or in part subterranean, and they are entered through a "hatch" in the roof. "The kiva ladders project from ten to fifteen feet beyond the hatch," reports the historian of Taos, Elsie Clews Parsons.[48]

The Orpheus legends in the Great Basin and on the Plains show us another milieu. The Orpheus of the Fort Hall Shoshoni found, on his arrival in the land of the dead, that "his relatives lived near one another in a row of tipis."[49] This conforms with what we know of the camping forms among the mounted Fort Hall Shoshoni.[50] Intimately associated with the life on the Plains is the camp-scene among the dead in the Orpheus legend of the Sarcee. We are told that the hero "after travelling for many days sighted on top of a hill some ragged tents, the tents of the shades. A man's shade approached him and said 'Human being, our chief invites you to his tent'. Following his guide he entered the chief's tent, to which flocked all the other shades in the camp." Here he was offered water and pemmican.[51] Thus in this account we find some of the typical ingredients in Plains culture: the tipis on the open Plains, the formal invitation to the chief, the pemmican diet.[52]

The Orpheus traditions of the Woodland Indians, too, faithfully reflect the culture conditions actually obtaining. The wanderers of the Micmac legend "were equally surprised and comforted to see on their arrival [in the land of the dead] an infinity of spirits of moose, beavers, dogs, canoes, and snowshoes, which hovered pleasingly before their eyes."

[45] Parsons 1940, 27.
[46] Parsons 1936, 71.
[47] Parsons, op.cit., 72.
[48] Parsons, op.cit., 17 sq.
[49] Steward 1943, 287.
[50] Steward 1938, 198 sq.
[51] Jenness 1938, 98.
[52] Lowie 1954, 30 sqq., 113, 25.

Shortly after this they reached "a wigwam like those which they had in their own country."[53] Elk and beavers were indisputably accounted as among the best game of the Micmac Indians.[54] Canoes of birch-bark and snowshoes facilitated the hunt.[55] The dwelling was a conical wigwam of birch-bark.[56]

The Orpheus of the Winnebago comes to a very big village with many bark houses. In the middle of the village there is a long lodge: this is the dance-lodge.[57] One is here reminded of the appearance of a typical Winnebago village in former times.[58]

From the Southeast there is an almost complete lack of any detailed accounts of the realm of the dead in the Orpheus tradition.[59] This is possibly connected with the fact that more than two hundred years have elapsed since the culture of the Southeast was intact.[60] References to the old culture conditions must have been embarrassing for the more modern narrators of the tradition, who have, moreover, perhaps not always understood them. They have at all events been meaningless in the new culture milieu.

We may now summarize our findings as follows: the instances given in the foregoing of what I have called direct and indirect mechanical reflections of the culture patterns in the oral tradition—the Orpheus tale —show unequivocally that this tale has been well integrated with the different culture milieus. It is important to bear this in mind in our assessment, later, of the value of the tradition for the religious belief. The "indirect reflections" in particular will then be of great importance.

The characteristically local variations of the Orpheus tradition, or the oikotypes of this tradition, are of evident interest from the viewpoint of literary analysis. But this differentiation of the tradition is interesting also from the viewpoint of comparative religious research, since it affects not only the forms of the tale, but also its motifs. A survey of the most

[53] Le Clercq 1910, 209.
[54] Wallis 1955, 34 sqq.
[55] Wallis, op.cit., 42 sqq., 52 sq.
[56] Wallis, op.cit., 57 sqq.
[57] Radin 1926, 35.
[58] Radin 1923, 104 sqq., 188 sq.
[59] Certain details representing the conditions obtaining in the realm of the dead are, however, given in the Shawnee versions listed by Voegelin, see Voegelin 1936, 5.
[60] Cf. what has been said concerning the more southerly Coast Algonquin above, p. 31.
[61] In connection with the following, see also Alexander 1916, 264, 302 (note 53); Gayton 1935, 283 sq. The big grouping of the Orpheus traditions of the hunting peoples and the agrarian peoples will not be treated here, as it calls for a special and deeply ramifying discussion. See below, pp. 126 sq., and chap. II: 6, III: 2—3, IV: 4.

42

important oikotypes will be given in the following,[61] and in this connection a more detailed discussion will be devoted to the completely diverging tales from the Northwest Coast.[62]

Among some of the tribes from the Northwest, viz, the Tlingit, Kitlobe, Kwakiutl, Stalo and Twana, one finds the Orpheus tradition in the conventional form: a spouse, a father, a friend follows the recently deceased person to the realm of the dead and tries to bring her or him back to life. But at the same time there occurs within this same culture area another series of narratives, which is reminiscent of the foregoing one, but has a diverging sequence of events. In his well-known work on totem poles Barbeau has drawn a clear line of distinction between the two types of narrative. The ordinary Orpheus tradition known from the Tlingit and other tribes he refers to as the "inland form," while the other type is referred to as the "sea-coast form." He writes: "Although the Tlingit version, recorded by J. R. Swanton, is from the north Pacific Coast, it belongs to the inland branch of the myth, as those who journey to the other world must go up the road, and when they return they step down... In bold contrast, the sea-coast form of the same myth takes the woeful couple to the undersea abode of the Killer-Whales, where human souls resort after death."[63] This is a clear differentiation according to eschatological motifs. Barbeau finds the "sea-coast form" among the Haida, Tsimshian, and perhaps also among the Bella Bella (Rivers Inlet).[64]

Barbeau is the first to associate the Orpheus motif with the tales of the woman who is carried off to the country of the killer-whales. But justified objections may be raised against his reasons for this combination. In the first place, is it sufficient to characterize the "sea-coast form" by referring to the fact that the journey to the other world runs downwards? And in the second place, is it always so certain that this other world is identical with the realm of the dead? Have we, in other words, to do here with an Orpheus legend in the proper sense of the term?

It would seem to be a shallow definition of the "sea-coast form" that differentiates it from the "inland form" solely on the basis of the downward direction of the journey. In the Kitlobe tradition, which obviously constitutes a variant of the "inland form," the deceased person sojourns in a world that is situated under the grave; and if we turn to the Pueblo

[62] These are, as we shall see, not, in point of fact, oikotypes of the main tradition.
[63] Barbeau 1950 I, 272.
[64] Barbeau, op.cit., 279 sq., 282 sq. (Tsimshian); 283 sqq., 286 sqq. (Haida); 289 (Rivers Inlet); Barbeau 1953, 255 sqq., 290 sqq., and 295 sq. (Haida); 269 sqq., 280 sqq., 296 sqq. (Tsimshian). Barbeau also cites Swanton 1905 b, 202 sq., 220 (Haida); Deans 1899, 71 sqq. (Haida); Boas 1912, 147 sqq. (Tsimshian).

43

Indians, we find that the realm of the dead visited by Orpheus is situated in the underworld. Otherwise it is the fact that the realm of the dead in the Orpheus tradition is more frequently on or above the earth than under the earth.[65] But the "sea-coast form" is best characterized by the sequence of events, firmly patterned in all its versions, and everywhere remarkably uniform. A white sea-otter (or other marine animal) has been caught on the sea-shore and clubbed to death by the skilfulest hunter in the village. The latter hands over the skin to his wife. While she is cleaning it on the shore she infringes a taboo, and the offended sea-spirits let the otter drift out to sea with the woman. The hunter pursues them in his canoe. They disappear into the deep just above the dwelling of a powerful sea-spirit. Here the hunter casts anchor, and climbs down the anchor-chain to the residence of the sea-spirit, i.e. of the killer-whale. He overcomes all obstacles on the way, even being helped by some animals, rushes into the palace and seizes his wife. He succeeds in making his way back to the canoe, and returns happily home with his wife. An appended, unhappy end of the spouses' relation also occurs in certain versions (among the Haida).

It may seem rather hazardous to connect this strictly rounded-off legend with the Orpheus tradition. Boas, who has made a careful, exhaustive comparative study of the "sea-coast form"—he refers to it as "The Woman Carried Away by the Killer Whales"—treats it as an independent tradition that has been combined in a secondary way with other traditions, so that among the Tsimshian and Skidegate Haida it constitutes an episode in "the Story of Gunaxnesemga'd." But the break between this episode and the other episodes is evident enough, and among the Rivers Inlet it has been combined with quite a different tradition.[66] Judging from the evidence, the "sea-coast form" is an earlier independent tale. Boas reports it from a number of tribes along the north-west coast, from the Tlingit to the Sechelt and Cowichan (Nanaimo); in all, he has noted down thirteen versions.[67] If one adds later published versions—communicated by Barbeau, Sapir and Swadesh— then it is probable that at least twenty-one versions are now known.[68]

[65] See chap. III: 3.
[66] Boas 1916, 835 sq.
[67] Boas, op.cit., 840.
[68] Besides the works adduced above, p. 43 note 64, see the following: Swanton 1909, 26 sqq., 215 sqq. (Tlingit); Swanton 1908 a, 495 sqq. (Masset Haida); Swanton 1905 a, 244 sqq., 338 sqq. (Skidegate Haida); Krause 1885, 275 sqq., Boas 1895 b, 299 sqq. (Tsimshian); Boas, op.cit., 259 sqq. (Bella Coola); Sapir & Swadesh 1939, 63 sqq. (Nootka); Boas, op.cit., 55 sqq. (Nanaimo); Hill-Tout 1904 b, 52 sqq. (Sechelt). Boas also communicates an unpublished version from the Rivers Inlet.

Now it should be pointed out that none of the versions gone through by Boas shows any evident connection between the realm of the killer-whales and the conceptions of the realm of the dead. When in his Tsimshian study Boas wants to refer the reader to tales dealing with the life after death, he recommends quite other traditions.[69] The picture of these Indians' land of the dead which he evokes diverges in all essential points from the marine realm of the above-discussed tale: "The Ghosts live in a village of their own on the other side of a river, which is crossed on a bridge. The chief lives in a house in the middle of the village, and sits in the rear of the house. The river is the Boiling-Oil River; and if a Ghost falls in, he dies a second death and becomes a cohoes salmon if old, a fisher if young. When a person dies he crosses the river and is led into the house of the chief of the Ghosts, who asks the newcomer to sit by his side."[70] This, as may be seen, is far from the scene of the supernatural world presented by the legend of the killer-whale. And it is difficult to understand how Barbeau can declare without reservation: "Among the Tsimsyans of the Northwest Coast, the home of the dead is in the Killer-Whale centre at Kwawk out to sea."[71]

A short synopsis of the conceptions of the realm of the dead held among the remaining relevant tribes of the Northwest Coast shows that this realm is in general not located at the bottom of the sea, however natural this might appear to such maritime tribes. A very common notion is that the land of the dead lies behind a river, or on islands out at sea.[72] Sometimes the land of the dead is conceived as subterranean,[73] and among the Kwakiutl and Bella Bella it is both subterranean and beyond a river,[74] while among the Bella Coola different parts of the individual go to heaven and the underworld respectively.[75] It should be remarked, however, that in these cases the underworld is not conceived as located in the depths of the sea, but somewhere under the dwellings of the living. In some

[69] Boas 1916, 544.
[70] Boas, op.cit., 455. Cf. also the Niska legend in Boas 1895 a, 582.
[71] Barbeau 1950 I, 271.
[72] Tlingit (Boas 1890, 843 sq., Krause 1885, 280 sq.); Haida (Swanton 1905 b, 34); Tsimshian (see above, note 70); Kwakiutl (Boas 1921 I, 711); Puget Sound Salish (Haeberlin & Gunther 1930, 81).
[73] Rivers Inlet (Drucker 1950, 229, 290, Olson 1954, 250); Kwakiutl (Boas 1932 b, 216, Drucker, op.cit., 291); Nootka (Swan 1870, 84 sq.; cf. Drucker, op.cit., 229, 290).
[74] Kwakiutl (Boas 1935 a, 125, 132); Bella Bella (Boas 1932 a, 142, Drucker, op.cit., 290 sq.).
[75] McIlwraith 1948 I, 495 sqq. Curiously enough, an older source speaks only of the subterranean realm of death (Boas 1898, 37 sq.), while a younger source only mentions the celestial realm of death (Drucker, op.cit., 290). Cf. the discussion in Hultkrantz 1953, 32 note 78, 477 sq.

45

quarters the realm of the dead is even thought of as on the earth, not all too far removed from the living.[76] Only the Tlingit (and, as we have seen, in a way also the Bella Coola) are acquainted with a general realm of the dead that is situated above the surface of the earth.[77] Still higher up in the sky is the realm to which go those among the Tlingit and Haida who have died a violent death.[78] A number of the Nootka have evidently imagined that the chiefs go to heaven.[79]

Generally speaking it may thus be said that the Northwest Coast Indians' land of the dead for ordinary persons was located on the earth or under the earth, often separated from the world of the living by a river or bay. This is the eschatological milieu with which the Orpheus tradition has been associated on the Plateau and at Puget Sound—thus among the Salish and Shahaptin tribes—and the Northwest Coast tribes having the "inland form" may be added to them. Whereas the Northwest Coast tribes that tell the "sea-coast form" are as little acquainted with a general realm of the dead at the bottom of the sea as other north-west tribes. This is remarkable, and would seem to indicate that the "sea-coast form" is not a real Orpheus tradition. An Orpheus tradition that does not deal with the carrying off of a person to the realm of the dead is of course no Orpheus tradition.

It must, however, be borne in mind that it is not easy to distinguish deceased persons and ghosts from other supernatural beings in the world of untrammelled religious conceptions characterizing the Indians of the Northwest. In their tales there are often obscure references to "supernatural beings", and the natives themselves may be uncertain whether natural spirits or ghosts are intended.[80] To a certain extent this confusion is probably due to the fact that after death the persons have happened upon places which belong to the animals. A curious symbiosis appears to have arisen between two originally distinct lines of thought: man's fate after death and the life of the animals before and after death. And the animals are supernatural beings that in their own realm—in their dancing house—doff their animal shapes and appear in human form.[81]

[76] Gitksan Tsimshian (Drucker, op.cit., 291); Haisla (Olson 1940, 182 note 17); Kwakiutl (Boas 1932 b, 216, Boas 1935 a, 132).
[77] Swanton 1908 b, 461.
[78] Tlingit: Boas 1890, 843 sq., Swanton op.cit., loc.cit.; Haida: Swanton 1905 b, 36.
[79] Drucker, op.cit., 290; Boas 1891, 597.
[80] Drucker 1951, 156 sq.
[81] The animals are according to the Indians of the Northwest Coast supernatural beings, and in their own realm they appear, not in animal shape, simply as spirits. See further the discussion in Swanton 1905 b, 16 sq. (Haida) and in Nieuwenhuis 1924, 126 sqq. (commentary on Swanton's presentation).

Among the fundamental principles for the religion of the Indians of the Northwest Coast are, according to Drucker, "a set of beliefs revolving about the immortality of certain economically important species of animals, combined with a series of ritual practices to ensure the return of those creatures."[82] It is, in other words, the hunting magic of the old North Eurasiatic hunting culture, with the conceptions connected therewith, that one finds among these Northwest American hunters who have adapted themselves to maritime conditions. The slain game was treated ceremonially, so that its spirit, reconciled with the hunter, could return to its home, where it was invested with a new body, which it would then once more present to the hunter in future hunts. Each animal species had its realm. Thus the land of the salmon lay far out to sea in the west; every year the salmon hurried to the country of the Indians to provide them with food. The killer-whales likewise had their country, which was at the bottom of the sea. And to this went certain categories of human beings after death.

It must thus be realized that the existence of a general realm of the dead among the Northwest Coast tribes by no means implies that all persons would end up there after death. On the contrary, there was often in one and the same tribe a belief in manifold realms of the dead: every village had its realm of the dead, or there were different such realms for physically or socially marked persons, or different places of abode were allotted to people according to the manner of their death. By way of illustration one may here mention the eschatology of the Haida on the Queen Charlotte Islands. The majority of people were conceived as going to a general realm of the dead situated beyond a bay in the direction of the mainland. Here "the towns of the Land of Souls lay in numberless inlets, like Haida towns on earth," and also other supernatural beings than the dead had towns there. The dead who were great gamblers were allowed to visit a country beyond the Land of Souls, ruled by a chief who "owns the dog-salmon." Those who had drowned went to the land of the killer-whales in the sea, those who had died a violent death went to Taxet's house up in the sky, those who had died of hunger went to the Greatest-Stingy-One's house (wherever this might be situated), those who had been killed in a fall went to a land up in the air, House-hanging-from-the-Shining-Heavens, and the shamans, finally, went to "a Shamans' Island, having houses down its sides deep into the sea."[83]

One thus finds that among the Haida the drowned go to the land of

[82] Drucker 1955, 138; cf. 140 sqq.
[83] Swanton 1905 b, 34 sqq.

the killer-whales at the bottom of the sea.[84] The same belief occurred among the Tlingit,[85] while among the Kwakiutl it is the marine hunters who after death end up in the world of the killer-whales.[86] The drowned among the Kwakiutl, on the other hand, go to a land situated beyond the ocean.[87] Not only the killer-whales, but also other marine animals took charge of human beings who had drowned. The belief among the Haisla is that "if a person is drowning all the animals race toward him. At death he becomes the actual animal which reached him first, regardless of his clan affiliation and regardless of whether the body is found."[88] This belief shows how it was possible for the association between the drowned and the whales to arise: the marine animals that had devoured the drowned were evidently also later combined with them in the conceptual world of the natives.

For the sake of completeness, however, it must be mentioned that the Northwest Coast peoples also conceived other fates after death for the drowned.[89] One of the conceptions to be found along the entire coast was that drowned persons become land-otters.[90] Drowned Nootka Indians become invisible spirits that continue their existence on the shore, shivering with cold,[91] while the drowned among the Bella Coola Indians fall into the clutches of the cannibalistic sea-god Qomoqwa.[92] The last-mentioned conception is in a way connected with the belief in the deceased as sojourning among the whales at the bottom of the sea. The land-otter idea lacks this connection with the underworld of the sea; the abode of the land-otters seems in general to be located on an island out in the ocean.

[84] See also Dawson 1880, 121 B sq., Harrison 1892, 20 sq., Hill-Tout 1899, 706, Drucker 1950, 291.
[85] Swanton 1921, 352; cf. also Swanton 1908 b, 461.
[86] Boas 1896, 579, 1910 a, 341, 1921 I, 714, 727; cf. Boas 1935 a, 132, 159.
[87] Boas & Hunt 1902, 249 sqq.
[88] Olson 1940, 200.
[89] Here, of course, I abstract from the notion, widespread over the whole of northern North America, that the dead who pass the river of death without success, i.e. who fall into the water, are transformed into fishes and toads—see, for Northwest America, Boas 1916, 326, 330, 455 (Tsimshian).
[90] See the account of sources in Boas 1916, 862 (the occurrence of the motif is instanced among the Tlingit, Haida, Tsimshian, Kwakiutl) and the following: Birket-Smith & de Laguna 1938, 236 sq., 508, 513 sq., 522 (Eyak); Swanton 1908 b, 456 and Jones 1914, 165, 234 sq. (Tlingit); Boas, op.cit., 345 sq., 758, 860, 862 (Tsimshian); Boas 1932 a, 58 and Drucker 1950, 291 (Bella Bella); Boas & Hunt, op.cit., loc.cit. (Kwakiutl); cf. also Swanton 1905 a, 225 note 19, 270 (land-otters cause mental disorders among Haida who have been close to drowning).
[91] Boas 1891, 597.
[92] McIlwraith 1948 I, 52 sq. Qomoqwa is presumably a male counterpart of the Sedna of the Eskimo (cf. Alexander 1916, 273 note 7).

It is obvious that the so-called "sea-coast form" is a narrative of Orpheus type in which the action takes place in the realm of the dead associated with the drowned. This emerges clearly from the Nootka legend referred to by Sapir and Swadesh as "The man who brought his wife back from the dead." The submarine realm is here called "the land of ghosts." The killer-whales are, certainly, not mentioned—they are here "ghosts" pure and simple—and the beings that pursue the husband when he is fleeing with his wife from the land in the sea are sharks. But the tale is otherwise in detail the same as among the coastal peoples farther north.

The tale presumably originated far to the north, among the Tlingit and Haida, and gradually spread southward. It is probably incorrect to associate it, from the viewpoint of the history of tradition, with the ordinary Orpheus legend. It is doubtless quite independent of this. On the other hand, as we shall see later, it has probably grown up from the same psychological root. And it appears to be most correct to designate it as an Orpheus legend of a particular kind—why not the "sea-coast form" of the Orpheus motif, as Barbeau formulates it.

One can thus not define the legend of the carrying off of human beings by the killer-whales found on the Northwest Coast as a variation of the current Orpheus tradition, even if it is a variation of its underlying theme. The legends that we shall group together in the following pages, on the other hand, constitute characteristically individual local forms of the ordinary tradition, "oikotypes" in the usual sense of the term.

As has been mentioned, the Orpheus tradition occurs in the conventional form among several tribes in the Northwest, from the Tlingit to the Twana.[93] To these may be added some tales from the immediately adjacent interior, from the Carrier to the Sanpoil; the Carrier presumably got their narrative and its details from the Northwest Coast and the Plateau.[94] A special category is formed by the narratives of the Thompson and the Sanpoil: only as a dead man may Orpheus enter the world of the dead. This has a certain significance for our interpretation of the Orpheus tradition, as will appear from the following account.

Over the greater part of the Plateau and at Puget Sound the Orpheus tradition has what must certainly be called a mythic form, at the same time as it constitutes an *aition* for the divorce between the living and the dead. Its central theme is that the culture hero—among the Shahaptin,

[93] See above, p. 43.
[94] Cf. Gayton 1935, 281 note 8.

the inland Salish, the Kalapuya and the Chinook Coyote, among the coastal Salish as a rule Bluejay—sets out for the realm of the dead.[95] But the
goal of his operations varies greatly, and it does not always fall strictly
within the frame of the Orpheus motif. Among the Sinkaietk and Wasco
Coyote appears in the character of suitor; his unsuccessful attempt to
bring back a wife from the land of the dead—it is described according to
the pattern of the ordinary Orpheus tradition—constitutes at the same
time the motif of the inevitability of death.[96] In their present form these
tales are not genuine Orpheus myths. But it seems most reasonable to assume that they are paraphrases of the Orpheus tradition, more especially
as they are strongly reminiscent of the more complete Orpheus narratives
among the respective neighbour tribes. They have therefore for functional
reasons been listed by me as Orpheus traditions. To a category of the same
type may be referred the here fairly numerous myths concerning the visit
paid by the culture hero to a recently deceased relative—wife, daughter or
sister—in the realm of the dead. Among the Chehalis (Upper Chehalis,
Humptulip and Satsop), for example, Bluejay longs to see his sister, who
has at his own instigation married a ghost and is now in the spirit land.
He pays a visit there, but after a time prepares to return; that he would
in this connection like to take his sister home again is nowhere indicated.
On the journey home he succumbs to the difficulties he meets with and
returns, dead, to the realm of the dead. After this men are therefore unable to visit the dead. This myth has not much in common with the Orpheus tradition to a superficial view. And yet it is undoubtedly an offshoot of it, with some key elements still retained. In one of the Chehalis
versions the mutilated Orpheus motif is strengthened: it is Bluejay's beloved daughter who dies, and he is inconsolable; he visits her in the land
of the dead, receiving her baby from her as a gift; but through the infringement of a taboo on his way home he loses the baby, and dies himself.[97]
Here, as may be seen, the Orpheus theme is more distinct. In the Kalispel
myth, this, too, describing the visit of the culture hero—in this case Coyote
—to his daughter, we are told how Coyote brings his grandchildren from
the realm of the dead in a sack; but by infringing a taboo on the way he
loses them. "Now you have lost them forever, and I am lost too," he hears

[95] The culture hero's journey to the othed world is a well-known theme in these
tracts, but no connection with the Orpheus motif is discernible. See further chap. III: 1.
[96] In connection with the following, see the list of sources in the appendix.
[97] Adamson 1934, 29. Parallels to the Chehalis myths are to be found in the Orpheus
myths among the nearby Snuqualmi, Puyallup and Skopamish (Green River Salish),
where the culture hero is (Old Man) Pheasant, Transformer, Owl or Groundsparrow.

his daughter cry.[98] Here the Orpheus tendency is quite clear. Among the Yakima and Wishram Coyote and Eagle try to bring their wives and children back from the land of the dead to the land of the living;[99] here, then, the Orpheus myth is complete.

All in all, these myths constitute an interesting special form of the Orpheus complex, not always orthodox, it is true—one feels the influences from the unsentimental trickster cycle—, but psychologically and in their motifs all these myths belong to the Orpheus pattern. That at the same time they constitute precedents for the divorce between the living and the dead does not affect their character of Orpheus myths.[100]

The myth-complex around Puget Sound and on the Plateau has offshoots far to the south. Also in a Shasta version of the Orpheus tale we find the motif of Coyote's journey to Hades (this time after a lost son), and the etiological addition—the explanation of the definitive dominion of death—is likewise included in this version.[101] Otherwise, the Californian Orpheus narratives are characterized by the fact that the chief actors, a seeking man and his deceased wife, are human beings, and the relation between them on the journey is embellished with plenty of detail. The journey to the realm of the dead is in general well described among the Californians, as also, for the rest, among the Woodland Indians in the east. Other characteristic features also occur.[102]

The more varying Orpheus tales from the Southwest reflect the widely differing habits of life in this culture area and cannot be brought together as an uniform "type." It is, however, possible to establish a certain basic pattern dominated by the Pueblo ideology, though it is rather vague: the Orpheus tradition is combined with the chthonian myth of descent and with the belief in fertility spirits. This may at all events be said concerning the Pueblo and Navajo traditions, while the narrative communicated from the Lipan Apache constitutes a special case to which we shall revert later.

[98] Curtis 1911 VII, 97.
[99] Coyote and Eagle appear together in the Orpheus myths of the Yakima and Chinook (Wishram, Wasco).
[100] See chap. V: 3.
[101] Dixon 1910, 19. In another Shasta version the two main actors are woodpeckers (Voegelin 1947, 52 sq.)—a reminiscence of Bluejay farther north? In the Modoc myth, which has been noted down, however, by Curtin, who is not always reliable, it is the Creator who is seeking his daughter (Curtin 1912, 40 sqq.), while the myth communicated from the Nishinam (Nisenan) by Powers, who is inclined to romanticize, deals with the first man and his wife (Powers 1877, 339 sq.).
[102] The so-called imitative burial (see below, pp. 62 sqq.) occurs in a characteristic form in Central California; and Gayton has been able to observe, for southern Central California, "the formation of an addendum to the tale" (see further on this subject Gayton, op.cit., 283 sq.).

The Shoshonean Orpheus traditions from Great Basin (the Mono, Paviotso, Fort Hall Shoshoni) are characterized by, inter alia, the eschatological milieu: according to the Paviotso and Shoshoni legends the "father," i.e. the Supreme Being, dwells in the camp of the dead,[103] and in the Mono legend the realm of the dead is called "Wolf's camp," i.e. the camp of the high god.[104] It is this divinity that gives the mourning Orpheus practical advice as to how he is to win his wife back.

The Paviotso legend is otherwise strongly reminiscent of the Orpheus narratives of the Plains, which often have the common feature of the Orpheus figure bringing from the realm of the dead a ceremony or a dance to the land of the living.[105] Apart from the strong local colour, the Plains versions do not otherwise show a clearly defined type, but come very close to the Orpheus legends of the Woodland. The gifts that the Orpheus of the Woodland Indians brings home from the spirit land are probably most nearly comparable with the ceremonies of the Plains Indians' Orpheus.

Among two northern Plains tribes, the Sarcee and the Assiniboin, the Orpheus legend has been contaminated with another narrative, Skeleton-Baby and Lodge-Boy respectively.[106] Unfortunately, as regards the Assiniboin, it is not at all definitely established that we have to do with a real Orpheus tradition. As mentioned already, there is a kind of Orpheus motif in the introduction to the Assiniboin variant of the tale of Lodge-Boy and Thrown Away, or Afterbirth, so popular on the Plains (T 581 according to Thompson's motif-index).[107] Here we are told of a woman who in her husband's absence was visited by a stranger. The latter cut the foetus out of her body, "then ran around every lodge-post with the woman, went to the fire-place, and thence descended underground with her." Soon the husband returned from the hunt, and he understood then what had happened. "Then he ran around every lodge-post and descended through the fire-place. After a while he went above ground, and saw lots of people camping by a lake. His wife's lodge was also there." He was informed by an old woman that those who lived here were wicked and were unwilling to part with his wife. They succeeded, certainly, in killing

[103] Gayton, op.cit., 277 sq., Steward 1943, 287.
[104] Gifford 1923, 341. Concerning Wolf as the "father" among the Mono, see Gayton 1948 II, 280. Cf. also Gayton 1930 a, 77, 78. Concerning the relation Wolf—the "father" among the Eastern Shoshoni, see Hultkrantz 1955, 134 sq.
[105] See Gayton 1935, 284. One may thus characterize certain Plains variants as origin-legends to sacred dances. Cf. below, pp. 145 sqq.
[106] Concerning the tradition about Skeleton-Baby, see closer below, pp. 172 sqq.
[107] See Reichard 1921, 272 sqq.

him, but he stood up again by magic, and was able to take his wife home.[108]

Several points indicate that the wife in this story was taken home from the realm of the dead. The mystical departure from the house to the strange country reminds one of the way in which among the Ojibway and Malecite Orpheus sets out on his journey to the realm of the dead through an extra exit in his lodge.[109] That is was a supernatural people who were visited by the Assiniboin man is immediately evident. Now in other versions of the Lodge-Boy tradition (among other tribes) it is mentioned that the woman died after the operation performed on her by the stranger, and that is was later her sons who brought her back to life from the grave through an act of resuscitation.[110] It therefore seems most reasonable to believe that also the Assiniboin narrative represents her as dead, although not in the grave, but in the land of the dead. The scanty details concerning the strange country that are communicated in the tale are not at variance with what we know concerning the conceptions of the realm of the dead held among the Assiniboin. This is generally described in our sources as a warmer and happier reflection of the milieu in which these Indians lived daily.[111] Opinion seems to have been divided as to the situation of the land of the dead, and also as to the way there. Denig's account would seem to be the most correct, that "this place does not appear to be either on the earth or in the heavens."[112]

In the Central Woodland the Orpheus tradition emerges with great wealth of detail. Especially does this apply to the journey to the realm of the dead, with its temptations and difficulties—a motif which was also with great interest narrated independently of Orpheus traditions.[113] Rather characteristic for this group of Orpheus traditions, furthermore, is the circumstance that on returning home the hero and his spouse run through fire, whereupon they return to consciousness, another motif which may occur outside the Orpheus tradition.[114] One must regard as a special form of the Orpheus tradition the Ottawa legend, reproduced by

[108] Lowie 1909 b, 168 sq.
[109] See below, pp. 71 sqq.
[110] See Thompson 1929, 104.
[111] Wied 1839 I, 446; De Smet 1905 III, 942 sq.; Denig 1930, 498 sq.; Bushnell 1927, 48 sq. (who quotes the *Diary of Martin McLeod*, Minn. Hist. Bull. 4: 7—8, 1922, 407 sq.); Lowie op.cit., 50. I abstract here from the other world of the wicked—this is obviously copied from Christian notions of Hell.
[112] Denig, op.cit., loc.cit.
[113] See especially Kohl 1859 I, 288 sqq.
[114] Cf. De Smet, op.cit., 1047 sqq.; Hallowell 1940, 32. The fire motif occurs in the Orpheus tradition in the Menomini legend and (in a modified form) in the Ojibway legend. Cf. also below, p. 152.

Schoolcraft, concerning the white stone canoe.[115] It should, however, be stressed that its central element—the voyage over the lake of the dead in a coloured stone canoe—also occurs on the Plateau; thus the Carrier legend mentions a red canoe in which the hero glides over the waters of the dead.[116] The celebrated legend "Qu'appelle?" among the Algonquin in Manitoba has by some researchers been represented as an Orpheus legend.[117] But this is an incorrect designation for a narrative describing a young man's journey to the camp of his bride-elect. That she had just died, that he hears her voice in the woods—this is not sufficient to characterize this lovely legend as an Orpheus tradition.

The Orpheus tales occurring in the Northeastern and Southeastern Woodland area may be grouped together as an uniform type. Characteristic for them is the detailed layout, especially of the particulars of the journey, the way in which the deceased is restored to life and the bringing home of heavenly gifts. In the north the passage to the land of souls is undertaken over a shaking bridge (in other tales also described as a snake), while in the south the traveller must make his way through the rising and falling curtain of the horizon—the Symplegades motif. The Alabama and Shawnee legends combine both of these motifs.[118] In the north there are only two chief actors, the one who seeks and the one who is lost; in the south the seekers are more than one.[119] The Micmac narrative in the northern group constitutes an exception here, inasmuch as the mourning father is accompanied on his journey by a number of persons.[120] Everywhere the deceased, i.e. his or her spirit, is transported home in a calabash, a bag or a hollow tube. In the realm of the dead Orpheus is furnished with gifts, moreover, from its chief or another representative; or he acquires a number of precious goods by gaming. It is here always a matter of foodstuffs of some kind, maize or "plant seeds," and of tobacco. A special form of the Orpheus tradition is constituted by the Cherokee narrative, which is obviously a sun-myth.[121]

A number of the oikotype traditions communicated here have common features, above all where they are adjacent to each other; thus the traditions of the Eastern Woodland and the Central Woodland are strik-

---

[115] See above, p. 31 note 39.
[116] Jenness 1934, 144.
[117] A. F. Hunter in JR X, 153 note 14; Barbeau 1950 I, 271, 1953, 258 sq. The narrative occurs in McLean 1892, 179.
[118] Swanton 1929, 141 sq., Voegelin 1936, 5. Cf. Gregg 1954, 387.
[119] In the Shawnee legend communicated by Gregg it is a matter of only one seeker, but Voegelin's Shawnee notes speak of four persons.
[120] Le Clercq 1910, 208 sqq.
[121] Concerning this see further chap. IV: 4.

ingly reminiscent the one of the other. But also widely separated oiko-types may show points of resemblance: the accounts of the course of the journey coincide in a remarkable way in eastern North America and in California.[122]

---

[122] The same remarkable geographical agreement has been shown by Rooth with respect to the creation myths (Rooth 1957, 498).

II. DOMINANT MOTIFS IN THE
ORPHEUS TRADITION

In the following is given a collocation of those motifs in the Orpheus tradition which either deserve attention on account of their prominence in or their significance for the tradition, or else claim our interest in view of their importance in connection with the psychological and historical reconstruction to be undertaken later. As has already been mentioned, there is here no reason to dwell upon the eschatological ideas as such, as these in general only constitute the background for the events forming the red toga of the Orpheus tradition. Only certain eschatological factors which play a direct rôle in the chain of events of the Orpheus tradition or for its interpretation will be discussed. Of the motifs treated in the sequel, there are also a few which are not specific for the Orpheus tradition, but also occur in other folktales.[1] These have a particular value, however, on account of their association with the Orpheus tale. Whether they originally arose in this tale is a question we can in this investigation go into only in part.[2]

The internal coordination between the elements of the tradition now to be discussed emerges from the short sketch of its content given earlier.[3] The elements are adduced in the main in the order in which they have been presented by Gayton.[4]

1. Main personages of the tale

In the Orpheus tradition the main interest attaches to the personal happiness and unhappiness of two people. Their relation to each other constitutes the motif of the story. One asks oneself what the external

---

[1] See Thompson 1946, 351 note 14.
[2] Cf., however, our discussion in chap. III: 1.
[3] See above, pp. 21 sq.
[4] Gayton 1935, 263 sq.

conditions for their emotional engagement have been; in what formal relation to each other have they stood?

In the majority of cases, just as in the classical Greek myth, there is an account of how a man—a husband, a lover—loses his wife or sweetheart and follows her to the realm of the dead. Gayton, who has also paid attention to the mode of the woman's decease, finds that in certain western tales—viz, some Zuni and Yokuts versions—she "is accidentally killed by her lover."[1] It may be presumed that in this way the narrator has wished to emphasize the man's deep grief and will to make good his mistake.

But other combinations of persons also occur.[2] In the Karuk legend we are told how two girls seek their dead lovers, or their common dead lover, in the realm of the dead.[3] In connection with this legend Dr. E. Wheeler-Voegelin writes that in the light of the material presented by Gayton she has been able to conclude "that of all the North American tribes which tell the Orpheus myth, only the Karok reverse the sex of the pursuers."[4] Her conclusion, however, is premature, for this reversal of the sexes is known both from the Southwest and from the Northeast. Benedict notes a marked "evenhandedness in the role of the sexes in Zuni folklore"; "the sexes of the protagonists are constantly reversed"; and, as regards the Orpheus tradition, "either men or women follow their spouses or sweethearts to the world of the dead."[5] And up in the north the Ottawa, the Ojibway on Parry Island and the Seneca tell of a woman who followed her dead lover or husband into the realm of the shades.[6] A feature common to all these versions of the Orpheus tradition in which the man follows his woman or the woman her man is the youth of the two protagonists; death puts a period to their young happiness. As romantic tragedy the Orpheus tradition has in this form doubtless gripped the listeners most strongly; and it is in this form, significantly enough, that it is most widely disseminated.

Less common are the versions in which persons otherwise related to each other appear in the main rôles. A naively moving tale of family love

---

[1] Gayton 1935, 284.
[2] Cf. Hatt 1949, 66.
[3] See the bibliography in the appendix, under "Karuk." In the version according to which the girls have common lovers they are at the same time represented as two sisters — which indicates that sororal polygyny has been practised among the Karuk, although our sources say nothing of this. Cf. especially Driver 1939, 345.
[4] Voegelin 1947, 55.
[5] Benedict 1935 I, XXI. See also op.cit., II, 299.
[6] The active rôle which in the legend is assigned to the Seneca wife agrees well with Iroquois social organization—a viewpoint which is in a way applicable also in the Zuni case.

is exemplified in the Thompson legend: two sons seek their mother for years, to find her, at last, in the realm of the dead.[7] Curiously enough, there is no corresponding tale concerning the search for a father. On the other hand, several tales describe a father's search for his children: among the Micmac, Pawnee, Kwakiutl and three Californian groups—the Modoc, Shasta and Pomo—it is the son, while among the Kalispel, Nez Percé, some coastal Salish groups at Puget Sound and among the Lipan Apache it is the daughter that a despairing father tries to fetch from the realm of the dead.[8] In the Kalispel myth, where the girl's father is Coyote, we find also as a secondary motif Coyote's vain attempt to save his daughter's children and grandchildren—obviously mankind—from the world of the dead. The motif recurs in a weakened form among the Chehalis and Upper Puyallup.

One may designate as the apotheosis of sibling-love those tales describing the appearance of a brother or sister in the rôle of Orpheus. Among the Chehalis, the Zuni Indians, the Shawnee, Huron and Koasati a brother follows his sister to the realm of the dead.[9] In a Pomo version two brothers follow each other to the same country.[10] Among the Taos Indians, finally, a girl tries to bring home her deceased sister from the realm of the dead.[11] It is worth noting that the last-mentioned tradition is at the same time a fertility myth concentrated about the figure of the maize goddess.

Among the Twana and to a certain extent among the Wichita two friends play the main rôles.[12] The bond of kinship is here replaced by the bond of friendship, which in primitive communities may be equally firm. Less emotionally engaged, it would seem, are the two men who in the Alabama legend try to bring back a woman from the world of the dead. Here, presumably, the relation of the two main persons to each other has been lost in the narrative. Probably the case was originally the same as that occurring among the nearby and closely related Koasati: the two men were brothers of the lost woman.

In some Orpheus traditions we find several figures in the rôle of the seeking hero. In the case most commonly occurring the seekers are two—

---

[7] Cf. a similar motif in the Taos myth (Parsons 1940, 23 sqq.).
[8] Cf. above, pp. 49 sqq. The Pawnee legend here referred to derives from the Skidi Pawnee (Dorsey 1904 b, 74 sqq.). Sources for the Shasta: Dixon 1910, 19; for the Pomo: Loeb 1926, 292 sq.
[9] Zuni: Cushing 1931, 18 sqq.; Shawnee: Gregg 1954, 387 sq.
[10] Barrett 1933, 379.
[11] Parsons, op.cit., 27 sq.
[12] The real goal for the friend's expedition to the beyond in the Wichita legend appears, however, to be his deceased wife.

two sons (Thompson River), two brothers (Koasati), two sisters (Karuk) or, as at Puget Sound, two friends (Wishram, Wasco, Yakima).[13] It is probable that two-brother tales and twin myths have here served as models. In these cases the party sought is always one person—a mother, a sister, a beloved husband—except in the versions from Puget Sound: here it is Coyote and Eagle that jointly seek their loved ones, wives and children. Among the Taos Indians it is a whole family, husband and children, that seek the departed wife-mother, i.e. the Corn woman. Also in the Cherokee myth—which is at the same time a sun myth—there are a number of seekers, seven in all—possibly an expression of astral speculation.[14] Among the Micmac the seekers who have joined the sorrowing father on his journey to fetch his son from the realm of the dead appear to have been still more numerous; a legend concerning the search for the culture hero in the other world may possibly have served as the pattern here.[15] In some Shawnee versions and in the Yuchi narratives the seekers are four in number: four men, who try to bring their wives back to life. The number of the seekers is undoubtedly connected with the fact that here (as in most places in eastern North America) the sacred number is four.[16] As I have tried to show earlier, it is upon this mysticism of numbers, too, that the division into four souls among the Yuchi is based.[17]

Here it may also be remarked that the person who has departed to the realm of the dead frequently symbolizes a higher value and therefore in himself constitutes a higher being, a spirit, a divinity. The discussion of the character of these figures must be postponed for the moment.[18] It must here suffice to observe that the values they represent are germinative force and fertility in the widest sense, and the therewith intimately associated idea of immortality. In one Ojibway legend which in many respects runs parallel with the Orpheus legend (though without its being possible to reckon it as an Orpheus legend), it is eternal life itself that an Indian seeks in the other world.[19]

[13] Two seekers whose character is not specified are mentioned also in a Karuk version and in the Alabama legend.
[14] Concerning astral influence in the Orpheus tradition, see below, p. 103, and chap. IV: 4. It should be remarked, however, that among the Cherokee the sacred number is seven; see BBAE 30: 1 (1907), 354.
[15] One finds this legend in Rand 1894, 232 sqq., Parsons 1925, 69 sqq.
[16] Cf. Speck 1909, 109. In a Bella Coola legend there is an account of how via a cave four men succeeded in entering the realm of the dead (McIlwraith 1948 I, 506 sqq.) Cf. also the Thompson legend, Teit 1912 a, 379: four men seek their mother in the other world.
[17] Hultkrantz 1953, 115 sq.
[18] See chap. II: 4, IV: 4, V: 3.
[19] Jenness 1935, 55 sqq.; cf. above, p. 31.

When making a synopsis of the different Indian Orpheus traditions one is soon struck with this detail: the anonymity of the two main personages. This, certainly, is not to say that they occur everywhere without name. In the myths from the southern Northwest Coast and the Plateau, as well as from the Southwest region, Orpheus and his partner are well-known figures; and by all the evidence the Orpheus narrative of the Lipan Apache constitutes a late memorate, and is thus connected with an historical personage.[20] But in the overwhelming majority of legends there is no mention of the names of the main personages. They are lost in a distant past. In this circumstance I am much inclined to see an indication that the prototypes of the main persons did long ago exist as historical personages, whose names have been lost as the narratives of the original events in which they took part have been fictionalized.[21]

2. Circumstances at the outset of the journey

In several traditions it is indicated that after the decease of his beloved, Orpheus is depressed. Among the Chehalis Coyote mourns his daughter so deeply that he is on the brink of suicide. The Sanpoil hunter who has lost his wife leaves, in his grief, both the camp and his secondary wife and goes off into the wilderness. The Pawnee Indian who had first lost his wife and then his son "did not know what to do, whether to kill himself or to wander over the country. He decided to wander over the country. He mourned four days at the grave of his son; now he was to roam over the country."[1] Examples of this kind might be multiplied. In the majority of cases we are told that it is the grave of the beloved that is visited by the mourner, who then abandons himself night after night to his anguish. The above-mentioned Pawnee Indian kept watch at the graveside for four days; without doubt what is here referred to is the ritual four-night watch, also mentioned in the Orpheus narrative of the Winnebago.[2] But the vigil might also be spontaneous. From the Tlingit legend (the "inland form") we learn that the young son of the chief was unable to sleep for two nights in his grief at the death of his wife.

[20] See below, p. 228.
[21] See further chap. IV: 1, 3.
[1] Dorsey 1904 b, 74.
[2] Radin 1926, 33.

This watch, whether spontaneous or ritual or both combined, further accentuates the mental exhaustion of the mourner. Even apart from this, the hero lapses into a psychic twilight state. The Lipan man who had lost his little girl "got sick too from thinking about his lost child all the time. I don't know what happened, whether he died or fainted, but he was unconscious. It is not known how long he was in this condition."[3] The Nisenan myth gives a dramatic description of the first man's reaction to his wife's death. "He dug a grave for her close beside his camp-fire, that he might daily and hourly weep above her silent dust. His grief knew no bounds. His life became a burden to him; all the light was gone out of his eyes. He wished to die, that he might follow his beloved Yototowi. In the greatness of his grief he fell into a trance. There was a rumbling, and the spirit of the dead woman arose out of the earth and came and stood beside him."[4] Also other Orpheus narratives describe how the mourner lapses into unconsciousness—especially at the grave—and has an hallucinatory experience in which he meets the deceased. In two of the Orpheus versions of the Zuni Indians we are told, for example, how the mourning youth sees a light at or in his wife's grave while sitting beside it after dusk.[5] The Mohave Orpheus, who has refused to eat after the death of his young wife, sees her spirit at a distance making those movements and calling out to him the phrases that were familiar to him from the happy days of their life together.[6]

From many Orpheus traditions it appears that the hero has purposely put himself in a situation in which he has fallen into a trance and received visions. In the legend of the Tachi Yokuts we are told that the husband of the deceased "went to her grave and dug a hole near it. There he stayed watching, not eating, using only tobacco. After two nights he saw that she came up, brushed the earth off herself, and started to go to the island of the dead."[7] The trance has here been prepared by a vigil and by fasting and smoking, and the intimate connection with the dead, the removal to the world of the dead, has taken place through a kind of sham or imitative burial. Both of these elements, the ritual training and the sham burial, occur in Orpheus traditions in different parts of North America; but their simultaneous occurrence, as among the Yokuts, is not described

[3] Opler 1940, 100. The editor adds that by constantly thinking of the dead the hero has developed "ghost sickness" (loc.cit., note 1).
[4] Powers 1877, 340. Unfortunately it is not possible to decide to what extent Powers has coloured the description with arts of his own.
[5] Benedict 1935 II, 133, 157.
[6] Devereux 1948, 251.
[7] Kroeber 1907 c, 216.

among many tribes. It may here be as well to consider them somewhat more closely, as they are of importance for this account.

The sham burial is, as mentioned above, a means whereby the mourning Orpheus may put himself in the same situation as the deceased, a means of getting into contact with her. It is a kind of imitative magical act, and at the same time a translation of the living individual to the supernatural world of the dead (a translation that of course also the ritual fast is intended to bring about). It is in the grave that the sorrowing Orpheus is able to behold the deceased, it is in the grave that he sees the outlines of the road leading to the land of the dead. In certain Orpheus traditions this is rather crassly expressed. When the Bluejay of the Chehalis myth lost his daughter "he went to the burial-grounds, dug a hole, and went under ground. Not long afterwards he found the trail that led to the Land of the Dead."[8] And the Haisla Indian who was mourning at his wife's grave suddenly discovered at his side a passage leading down into the earth, and crept into it.[9] In the last analysis these tales are probably based on the notion of the life of the deceased in the grave, a notion that is natural enough wherever earth burial is resorted to.[10] The sham burial is most frequently associated with the earth burial. Above all, it belongs together with the skeleton burial, the type of burial most readily associated with the idea of a sham burial.

Generally speaking, the Orpheus tradition appears to belong chiefly to those cultures in which the skeleton burial—and the ideologies connected herewith—have been practised. With cremation and the conceptions corresponding to this the Orpheus tradition has little in common. One does, it is true, find the tradition also in those cultures in which the custom of cremation has prevailed (at least in more recent times), viz, among the Tlingit, Tsimshian, Haisla, Klamath, Modoc, Shasta, Pomo, Nisenan, Yokuts, the western Mono and the Mohave. In this connection, however, it should be noted that in many of these tribes earth burial has occurred at the same time as cremation, or has even constituted the earlier burial custom.[11] But the burial custom referred to in the Orpheus narrative is even in such cases often enough, as we have seen, the skeleton bur-

---

[8] Adamson 1934, 29.
[9] McIlwraith 1948 I, 508.
[10] This conception has been as natural in regions with earth burial as the belief in wandering ghosts in the woods or on the plains in regions with burial above ground. The subterranean grave, on the other hand, is not, as older researchers believed, a prototype for the belief in the realm of the dead as such, but it does tend to instil the belief in a subterranean realm of the dead.
[11] See above, pp. 36 sqq.

ial. From the functional viewpoint the Orpheus tradition is better adapted to the practice of skeleton burial,[12] and this chiefly for the following two reasons. Firstly, the notion of the dead person's return to life is more natural if he rises up from the grave—as in the Carrier Orpheus tradition (see below). And secondly, the motif of the sham burial characteristic for the Orpheus tradition enters as a natural stage of the narrative where the latter is based upon the custom of keeping intact the bodies of the deceased.[13] For these reasons, and in the light of what has been adduced earlier concerning the integration of the Orpheus tradition with older customs relating to skeleton burial in regions in which in the course of time cremation has become the prevailing form (the Carrier, Nisenan), it appears most reasonable to conclude that the Orpheus tradition was from the outset connected with the concept of skeleton burial.

The sham burial among the Yokuts, as we have seen in the foregoing, took the form of the mourning husband's digging of his own grave beside that of his wife. In an Orpheus legend from the Telumni Yokuts we learn that "he hollowed out a little place in the ground and lay down in it". After a couple of nights in his grave he saw his wife rise from *her* grave, arrange her dress and her ornaments and shake out her hair.[14] One is doubtless justified in designating this form of sham burial as less primitive, as it seems at variance with the very idea of the sham burial: to be brought at all costs nearer to the deceased and his existence.

The form of sham burial found among the Carrier, Menomini and Zuni Indians—in one of the Zuni variants[15]—is much closer to this constitutive idea, for here it is presumed that the mourning party is buried in the same grave as the deceased. Among the Carrier and the Menomini,

---

[12] There is an interesting compromise with the custom of cremation in the ingress to the Orpheus myth among the Shasta: "A man and a woman lived together. The woman fell in the fire and burnt. But he imagined she went up with the flame into the smokehole—it looked as though only feet were sticking after her as she went out of sight. So he wanted to find her—he tracked around outside and found her track in back of the house. He followed her, also going up into the air" (Voegelin 1947, 52). Cf. also below, note 13.

[13] This notwithstanding, there have been tendencies to combine the ideas of sham burial and cremation. In the Shahaptin myth recorded by Farrand Eurydice—Coyote's daughter—is burned to death. To be able to follow her Coyote must throw himself into the fire. But "as soon as he felt the pain, he jumped out again. He was so badly blistered, however, that his daughter allowed him to go along" (Boas 1917 a, 178). The myth shows, one may say, how ill the custom of cremation accords with the idea of sham burial which was evidently in the narrator's mind. Cremation was common among some Shahaptin peoples in eastern Washington (cf. Spier 1930, 229; Martin, Quimby & Collier 1947, 458 sq.), but not among the Nez Percé (Spinden 1908, 252), to whom Spier wishes to refer this myth.

[14] Gayton 1935, 267.

[15] Benedict, op.cit., II, 157.

63

moreover, it is said that Orpheus brings his wife back to life in such a way that they both rise from the grave at the same time. In the Carrier legend we are told that the dead woman's husband, who was a medicine-man, had himself buried alive together with his wife. "Both their spirits then travelled together to the Spirit Land." From here he succeeded in bringing his wife back to life. The way back "led them to their grave; and now at their journey's end they re-entered their bodies and the medicine-man called aloud to his kinsmen. Weeping and lamentation changed to cries of gladness; quickly the earth was moved from the grave and husband and wife stepped joyfully forth into the happy circle of their friends".[16] The end of the story is thus the logical consequence of its beginning: just as the husband's burial with his wife implies that he is translated to her world and that of the dead, so does her rising fram the grave with him imply that she is removed to his world and that of the living. The sham burial here appears clearly and distinctly as a magic rite. Also in several Orpheus traditions from the Eastern Woodland the deceased woman comes to life efter a time in the grave, though without its having been necessary for the Orpheus figure at the samt time to take his place beside the corpse.[17]

As belonging to the category of sham burials must also be accounted the numerous cases in which the mourning party does not actually enter the grave, but in some other way quite evidently demonstrates his intention to try to get into contact with the deceased at the grave. This seems especially to be the case in regions in which the custom of cremation is now the prevailing one. Thus we are told that among the Pomo the mourning survivor lay for four days and four nights on the grave of his deceased brother, to follow him, after this, to the realm of the dead.[18] In one of the Orpheus tales of the Yokuts it is stated that for three days and three nights the husband of the deceased woman lay fasting beside his wife's grave; "during the fourth night he was crying for her to come back to him," whereupon she stood up from the grave and the two of them then started out on the journey to the country beyond the grave.[19] Among some peoples, e.g. the Yaudanchi Yokuts and the Taos Indians, the mourning

---

[16] Jenness 1934, 143, 145.
[17] Thus among the Ojibway, Malecite and Seneca. Among the Micmac and the Huron an awakening to life of the same type is planned, but it fails.
[18] Barrett 1933, 379. In a narrative very close in character to the Orpheus tradition and known from the Carrier and/or Tsimshian—this will be discussed in chap. III: 1 —we are told how every night the man who had lost his wife slept on her grave until there were signs of life from it (see Jenness 1932, 197, 1934, 150).
[19] Hudson 1902, 104.

relative waits for four days for the rising of the deceased from the grave and the setting out for the realm of the dead.[20]

Even where other forms of skeleton burial than the burial in the ground (in the widest sense) obtain one may possibly trace tendencies to sham burial in the Orpheus tradition.[21] It should, however, be stressed that in many cases the tales represent the course of events that should correspond to the sham burial as something completely incidental, not planned. In the Twana narrative, in which one of two very good friends is snatched away by death, there is a description of how the deceased, according to the custom obtaining among the coastal peoples in western Washington, is interred in a canoe set on 'poles. The surviving friend mourned alone in the woods, but sat down one day under the canoe. When darkness fell he felt afraid, but nevertheless decided to keep watch at his friend's coffin all night. Late that night he heard paddles dipping in the water—it was the dead who were approaching in a canoe to fetch their new comrade. The Skidi Pawnee relate in their Orpheus tale that the deceased girl was buried in her tipi, after which the people abandoned the village.[22] Her bereaved lover "walked to the tipi and found the grave, and he stayed in the tipi and made his home there. He mourned for the girl for several days and nights." Finally, he was taken by a helpful spirit to the realm of the dead.[23]—It is, as will be seen, rather uncertain whether the action here contains reminiscences of any sham burial.

The imitative interment is *one* phase in Orpheus' activities to reach the sphere of death, the world of the supernatural; an analogous or complementary phase is the method to which he has recourse to attain this goal on the psychic plane: the fast, the vigil are to pave the way to the trance, the beyond. The means employed are well-known in the religious world, and especially in North America, where fasting rites were commonly practised in connection with the acquisition of a guardian spirit.[24] We have already seen how in certain Yokuts versions of the Orpheus tale the hero has paved the way to the appearance of the supernatural visions by fasting, keeping watch and smoking.[25] Such ritual training occurred above all on the Northwest Coast.[26] The Nootka Indian whose wife was

---

[20] Kroeber 1907 c, 228; Parsons 1940, 23.
[21] Cf. also above, p. 63 note 13.
[22] Cf. above, p. 36.
[23] Dorsey 1904 b, 71 sq.
[24] See Benedict 1922, 1 sqq., 1923 b, passim; Blumensohn 1933, 451 sqq.; Frazer 1910 III, 370 sqq.
[25] See above, pp. 61, 64 sq.
[26] Of instances from other quarters we may mention here one of the Shawnee versions (Gregg 1954, 387).

snatched away to the land of the ghosts "began to bathe, training ritually so that he might see his wife."[27] Ritual bathing was on the Northwest Coast intended to make the individual "pure", so that he could get into contact with the world of the spirits.[28] In the Stalo narrative we are told that the husband of the deceased woman "went a long way off into the mountains to seek supernatural powers. He bathed regularly every day through four summers and four winters. When he had thus done he attained what he sought. He could easily see the shades of the departed, and even follow the trails they made. He sought and found the trail his wife's ghost had made on her way to the Land of the Departed."[29]

The visions which appeared after such "spiritual exercises" or after the change of consciousness spontaneously provoked by vigils and deep grief are classifiable in four groups. These are: visions of guardian spirits; visions of the dead person; visions of the journey to the land of the dead, and visions of the experiences had there. Visions of the dead person we have seen exemplified in the foregoing (and to these we shall revert later); visions of the journey to and the stay in the realm of the dead we shall discuss in greater detail below. Here, however, it will first be suitable to mention something of the preliminary visions of guardian spirits (we shall return later to the function and significance of the guardian spirits on the journey).[30]

The activities of guardian spirits in connection with the Orpheus motif occur in narratives from extensive parts of the distribution area of the Orpheus tradition. The help and counsel given by these guardian spirits to the Orpheus figure *before* the setting out for the realm of the dead frequently correspond to the assistance which in other tales—or in the same tale—is extended by the deceased party *in the course of* the journey (sometimes, however, also before the journey) and by the ruler and guardians of the realm of the dead in that region (though sometimes during the journey). In the Haida tradition—of the "sea-coast form"— we are told that the husband who intended to seek his ravished wife took with him on the journey, on the advice of a medicine-man, "two servants", a martin and a swallow: "the martin to go on before and smell, the swallow to fly about overhead and watch."[31] The Karuk relate that the two girls who had lost their lovers mourned them at the graveside every morning, "the water coming out of their eyes." But one morn-

[27] Sapir & Swadesh 1939, 63 sq.
[28] Goddard 1945, 115.
[29] Hill-Tout 1904 b, 339; Hill-Tout 1907, 214 sq.
[30] See below, pp. 82 sqq.
[31] Barbeau 1950 I, 284; cf. Barbeau 1953, 290.

ing "all at once a person sat down by them there... Behold it was A'ikren." The latter then took them to the land of the dead.[32] A'ikren is "the mythic Duck Hawk who lives on top of Sugarloaf Mountain", the guardian spirit of the village of Katimin.[33] In the Thompson legend the guardian spirit of one of two brothers reveals to him in a dream where he shall seek his deceased mother.[34] In the Wichita legend a man loses first his best friend and then his wife. On one occasion, when he is mourning at his wife's grave, he goes to sleep, and in his dream his dead friend speaks to him and promises to help him get his wife back on condition that he submits to a four-day test. The surviving friend "wished that the dream would come true. He soon woke up and there was his friend standing before him. His friend touched his eyes, and he found himself in another world, still with his friend."[35]

In several Pawnee versions, too, there is mention of a meeting with supernatural powers at the graveside of the beloved. In a Skidi Pawnee version the mourning lover in the funeral tipi "saw something like a rainbow standing over the grave. He watched, and after a while he saw a man standing there. This man spoke to the young man, and said: 'I have taken pity on you. You are poor. I am going to help you get this girl back, so that you can live with her and be happy'. When this being said this (sic), he went toward the entrance and disappeared, and the man saw nothing but a skunk going out".[36] The guardian spirit is here a skunk, that follows the young man to the realm of the dead.[37] In another Pawnee version the supernatural helper is a boy,[38] while in a third version he is a "mysterious being" that can only be heard but not seen. In an invisible form this helper accompanies his protégé on the journey to the realm of the dead; when the strength and faith of the wanderer begin to flag, he admonishes him as follows: "Keep up your courage; keep right on."[39] When in the two last-mentioned versions the supernatural ally has finished his mission he reveals himself as "the Breath" or "the Wind."[40]

It seems natural that the belief in guardian spirits so closely associated

---

[32] Harrington 1932, 33.
[33] Harrington, op.cit., 2, 31 note 67. Concerning Katimin, see Kroeber 1936, 32.
[34] Teit 1898, 85.
[35] Dorsey 1904 a, 300 sqq. It is very rare, according to Benedict, for deceased persons to appear as guardian spirits in North America (Benedict 1923 b, 47 sqq.). This does, however, occur more frequently than she believes.
[36] Dorsey 1904 b, 72.
[37] Cf. Dorsey, op.cit., 342 note 126.
[38] Dorsey 1906, 536 sq.
[39] Dorsey, op.cit., 411 sq.
[40] According to Fletcher, one of the most important Pawnee spirits is "Hoturu, the invisible Wind, the bearer or giver of breath" (Fletcher 1904, 284).

in North America with the vision complex should occur in contexts like these. In a Stalo legend, a revivalistic narrative which comes close to the Orpheus motif, the acquisition of a guardian spirit is connected with the bringing of the deceased person back to life: after four years' exercises in the mountains a widower succeeds in acquiring a supernatural helper who invests him with the ability to resuscitate the dead by stepping four times over their bones. In this way he brings his wife back to life.[41] No deliberate seeking of a guardian spirit of this kind occurs in any genuine Orpheus narrative.

From the survey given in the foregoing it should have emerged that several elements in the Orpheus tradition are represented by the narrators themselves as phenomena experienced in psychic twilight states. This gives rise to the suspicion that the Orpheus tale in its entirety may reflect phenomena that have taken place during a person's psychic absence. This suspicion is to a certain extent supported by the Ottawa legend. The young man whose beloved has died follows her to the other world, journeying, finally, in a canoe to the isle of the dead, where he discovers his sweetheart in another, exactly similar canoe. "It seemed to be the shadow of his own. She had exactly imitated his motions, and they were side by side." This peculiar event in itself reveals the dream character of the whole, and this becomes quite evident when the end of the tale is reached: the youth wakes up. "It was the fancy work of a dream, and he was still in the bitter land of snows and hunger, death and tears."[42] Even if the narrative has been influenced by Schoolcraft's literary taste, it seems clearly to testify to the origin of the action. The Blackfoot legend, too, is represented in such a way that it must presumably have originated in a dream. We are told, at all events, that on his way to the realm of the dead—the Sand Hills—Orpheus repeatedly fell asleep, and in his dreams he experienced the meeting with the helpful old women and—probably—the visit to the realm of the dead.[42a] The same kind of testimony is also given by the Shahaptin myth concerning Coyote's following of his daughter. And the course of events in the Lipan tradition is frankly represented as experiences in an unconscious state. "I don't know what happened, whether he died or fainted, but he was unconscious," declared the narrator to Dr. Opler. "It is not known how long he was in this condition. Afterwards he told about what happened."[43]

---

[41] Hill-Tout 1904 b, 338.
[42] Schoolcraft 1851 I, 322, 323.
[42a] Grinnell 1912, 127 sqq.
[43] Opler 1940, 100.

A further confirmation of the connection here indicated is to be found in the Orpheus narratives from the Modoc and the Carrier. These tell how the Orpheus figure undertakes the journey to the land of spirits "in the spirit." According to the Modoc myth Kumush follows his deceased daughter; they journey westwards, both "leaving their bodies behind. Kumush was not dead but his spirit left the body."[44] We have already mentioned that the Carrier Indian allowed himself to be buried alive together with his deceased wife. The narrative then states that "both their spirits then travelled together to the Spirit Land."[45]

Who would be in a position so deliberately to free the soul from the body? Only beings possessing or able to exploit supernatural power, one is inclined to answer. The Kumush of the Modoc myth was the creator and culture hero of these Indians.[46] And as regards the main personage in the Carrier legend, he was a medicine-man. It is doubtless no accident that the Haida hero who saved his wife from the world of the ocean beings "was endowed with supernatural powers."[47]

3. Characteristic features of the journey to the realm of the dead

The general character of the journey to the realm of the dead according to the Orpheus tradition has already been adumbrated in the foregoing. We have seen that the journey might take place "in the flesh" or "in the spirit;" and we have found that it might be accompanied with great difficulties or be performed in relatively easy conditions—sometimes, as in the Wichita narrative and in a couple of Pawnee versions, reproduced above, the traveller is transported to the realm of the dead in a trice.[1]

The description of the journey is an integral part of the Orpheus tradition and adds to its dramatic force. It does happen, however, that in some narratives it plays a very subordinate rôle, or is even wholly or for the most part omitted. The Shasta myth in which Coyote seeks his son in the realm of the dead states merely that he set out and "arrived at that

---

44 Curtin 1912, 40 sq.
45 Jenness 1934, 143. The Shawnee hero in Gregg's Orpheus narrative entered the land of the dead, towards the end of his journey, in the shape of a spirit (Gregg 1954, 388).
46 Curtin, op.cit., V; Kroeber 1925, 322.
47 Barbeau 1953, 294.
1 Cf. also the journey home, see below, p. 130.

place," the realm of the dead.[2] The most detailed accounts of the journey derive, as has already been observed, from California and the Eastern Woodland area.[3] With reference to what has been said at the beginning of this chapter we shall here only dwell upon some aspects of the journey to the beyond, viz, the setting out, the general character and main motifs of the enterprise, the significance of the guardian spirits and the relation between the Orpheus of the narrative and the fleeing figure of the deceased.

One of the aims of the ritual activities of the Orpheus figure after the decease is, as has been pointed out, to find the way to the land of the spirits. Through the sham burial he attains this aim in an effective way: he sees how the dead person rises from the grave, and he has then only to follow her on her way or to walk in the tracks she leaves behind. But there are also other ways in which the mourner can find his way to the realm of the dead. We have seen how in a couple of cases the surviving party has discovered the route to the underworld by descending into the grave (which is then understood as an extension of the realm of the dead).[4] In some cases—e.g. in the myths around Puget Sound—it is assumed that the living personage, i.e. Coyote or Bluejay or Pheasant or Ground Sparrow, the culture hero-trickster, knows the way to the beyond. In other cases, e.g. in the Ottawa legend, the hero wanders aimlessly until he reaches the realm of the dead. And in other cases again, e.g. in a Pawnee legend, the hero follows the route that is pointed out to him by his invisible guardian spirit.[5]

Sometimes, then, what is described is the simultaneous setting out of the living party and the deceased;[6] sometimes—especially where there has been no sham burial or vigil at the grave—the deceased has embarked on the journey to the spirit land long before, and the hero's starting point is not the burial place. These versions, however, are less frequent.

The departure generally takes place from the grave, where the deceased is first revealed to the watching and fasting Orpheus, who is also sometimes recumbent in a sham burial. A graphic account of the course of events is given in one of the Yokuts variants: "As the great star stood overhead he felt the ground tremble and saw the earth moving on her grave. The clods rolled back and she arose and stood brushing from

[2] Dixon 1910, 19. Another instance: Benedict 1935 II, 157 (Zuni).
[3] See above, pp. 51, 55.
[4] See above, p. 62.
[5] Dorsey 1906, 411 sq.
[6] Cf. below, p. 86.

herself every speck of dust until she was clean. He stared, but was silent (a man dies instantly when speaking to a ghost). She started away."[7]

Some variations of the version according to which the journey to the realm of the dead starts in the grave must be noted. We have earlier seen examples of the place of the earth-grave being taken by a canoe in an elevated position or a burial tipi.[8] But the point of departure may also be a funeral pyre. In the Serrano legend we are told that the husband went to the place where his deceased wife had been burned, "and stayed there motionless. Curls of dust rose and whirled about the charred spot. He watched them all day. At night they grew larger, and at last one larger than all the rest whirled round and round the burned spot, and set off down the road. The man followed it. At last when it was quite dark, he saw that it was the figure of his wife that he was following, but she would not speak to him."[9] Interestingly enough, among the Gabrielino who live in the vicinity and who are linguistically akin to the Serrano Eurydice's ghost is represented as a whirlwind which rises from the grave and starts southward, towards the realm of the dead.[10]

In some tribes one finds a remarkable deviation from the basic pattern: the way to the realm of the dead begins inside the house, or behind the house in which the deceased has lived. We have already referred briefly to the Assiniboin legend concerning the man who found his way to the realm of the dead by running round every lodge-pole and then descending into the ground via the fire-place.[11] We find certain parallels to this route to the other world among three Woodland tribes, the Malecite, Ojibway and Seneca, and a Californian tribe, the Shasta—thus one more instance of the remarkable agreements between the versions of the Orpheus tradition occurring in the extreme west and the extreme east.[12] According to the Malecite legend, the hero cut a hole in the bark of his wigwam just near the place where his beloved lay dying, in the conviction that she would go out this way. He then sat down outside the wigwam beside the hole and waited. Soon "he saw something go out through the hole which had the appearance of a puff of smoke", and immediately

[7] Hudson 1902, 104. Cf. above, pp. 61, 63. The notion that one may not speak to a ghost has been common in California, and may be glimpsed in several of the Californian Orpheus narratives.
[8] See above, p. 65.
[9] Benedict 1926, 8. There is a similar description in one of the Pomo legends: the deceased arises from the ashes (Barrett 1933, 379).
[10] Reid 1926, 40 sq. Among the Pomo one notion that obtained was that the journey of the deceased to the other world began in a whirlwind from the funeral pyre (Gifford & Kroeber 1937, 203).
[11] See above, pp. 52 sq.
[12] Cf. above, pp. 54 sq.

understood that this was his wife's spirit. "He, therefore, collected the things necessary for the journey and followed in the direction taken by the departing spirit."[13] Concerning the Ojibway woman who followed her deceased husband to the western realm of the dead, we are told that "after he had ceased to breathe she pulled out one of the front poles of the wigwam and saw the path that his soul had followed westward." She "planted the pole along the path the soul had taken,[14] its end pointing to the west, told her child that she would soon return, and at night she set out to overtake her husband."[15] The Seneca legend begins with the story of how a young man died, just before daybreak, in his wife's arms. Filled with grief, she went out to see how near it was to dawn. "Presently she heard the door, which she had just closed after her, open, and looking back again she saw her husband come out of the lodge and walk briskly past her without speaking to her. At once she followed him as rapidly as she could, but she could not overtake him."[16] In the Shasta myth, finally, the story concerns a man who lost his wife—Woodpecker—who was burned to death. "He thought he saw her ghost go up toward the sky, and went out back of the house, where he found her trail. He followed this, and reached the sky."[17]

Now it is easy enough, it is true, to explain away these agreements between the narratives cited as apparent. The events of the Iroquois tale may be regarded as an hallucinatory experience removed from the grave to the home—thus from the last resting place of the deceased to the place where he died—; the localization of the starting point of the route to the other world to the back side of the house that we find in the Shasta myth may be merely accidental; and the mysterious descent to the spirit world related in the Assiniboin legend is possibly to be referred to the sphere of the magic arts. But these explanations are not adequate. They are constructions, and do not fit even the Malecite and Ojibway cases. In point of fact, the curious events of these five narratives probably belong together, they are separate manifestations of one and the same complex of phenomena.

The central theme for this complex is that the deceased is imagined as journeying to the realm of the dead via a special exit in her dwelling, as a rule at the back. This motif does not emerge clearly in the Seneca leg-

---

[13] Mechling 1914, 88.
[14] It was thus to serve as a signpost. Cf. also Jones 1907 b, 267 (Fox).
[15] Jenness 1935, 109.
[16] Curtin & Hewitt 1918 II, 570.
[17] Dixon 1910, 21.

end, but it was presumably originally connected with it. It appears most clearly in the Shasta and Malecite variants. In the Shasta myth, it is true, there is no mention of any aperture; but this is probably tacitly understood. And in the Malecite legend an exit for the ghost is cut near the wife's corpse, i.e. at the further end of the cabin.[18]

The notion that the journey to the land of the dead begins inside the cabin and leads out through the further wall facing the door does not, as far as I have been able to find from a scrutiny of a large eschatological material, occur outside the Orpheus legend. Is it then not conceivable that the legend actualizes an older conception, according to which the deceased has departed for the realm of the dead via a special opening in the house in which he has been buried? In many places in North America—in the forests of Canada, on the Plains, in the Great Basin and in the Southwest—the dead have among the nomads been buried in the cabin they inhabited during their lifetime; but I have nowhere come across the notion that the deceased has left his dwelling through a special opening. Among some of the Central Algonquin, the Ojibway and Menomini, the deceased has been buried in a low house with a saddle roof and an opening in the short wall.[19] Skinner declares that among the Menomini this hole was intended "to permit the ghost, which is supposed to linger about the cemetery, to leave and enter."[20] It is possible that this function has sometimes been ascribed to the opening. Otherwise the rule has been that it has been used by the survivors when they have given food and tobacco to the deceased.[21] Hoffman states, also concerning the Menomini, that it was a matter of food "on which the shade of the departed may feast before it finally sets out for the land of the dead."[22] Nowhere, how-

---

[18] Among the Penobscot, and doubtless also among their neighbours the Malecite, who are linguistically related to them, the wife's place was in the rear of the lodge behind the fireplace (Speck 1940, 29).

[19] See, concerning the Ojibway: Bushnell 1920, pl. 5 a, Bushnell 1927, pl. 4, Lindquist 1926, 104 (fig.), Kinietz 1947, pl. 39; concerning the Menomini: Bushnell 1920, 35 (fig. 1), pl. 5 c; cf. also Skinner 1921, 260 (fig. 20).

[20] Skinner, op.cit., 80 sq.; see also, concerning the Ojibway, Lindquist, op.cit., 106.

[21] Ojibway: Bushnell 1920, 29; Densmore 1929, 75; Cooper 1936, 21; Kinietz, op.cit., 146, 147 sq. Menomini: Bushnell, op.cit., 34; cf. next note. Burial lodges with an aperture are also reported from the Naskapi (Speck 1935, 52) and from the Nootka, where their function was "to afford opportunity for the dead to 'peer', as it were, into the daylight" (Koppert 1930, 113). Among the Lenape an opening was made at the head of the coffin for the spirit of the deceased, "damit er nach Belieben ein- und ausgehen könne, bis er den Ort seines künftigen Aufenthalts gefunden hat" (Heckewelder 1821, 468). The same custom and the same motivation is reported from the Iroquois (Morgan 1954 I, 169 sq.).—The custom of making openings in burial lodges or coffins is obviously circumpolar. It has occurred among Karelians, Volga Finns and Ostyak (Holmberg 1927, 28 sq., 31 sq.), Gilyak (Karutz 1925, pl. I: 24, III: 19), Gold, Olchi and Orochi (Harva 1938, 310; Karutz, op.cit., pl. I: 23).

ever, is it said that the ghost has made use of the passage when he left for the spirit world.

As a matter of fact, we find the real prototype of the extra exit from the death-house in the Orpheus narratives in the custom, widely disseminated among Northwest Indians, Californians, southern Athapascans and northern Algonquin, of taking the corpse out of the cabin through a special opening.[23] The motives for this custom are the fear of the deceased and the "death-stuff." By making a temporary opening, which may afterwards easily be blocked up, one can confound the deceased: if by chance he should return, he will be unable to find the entrance to the hut. The custom takes the place of the usage obtaining in other quarters of either abandoning the dwelling (the nomads in the northern, eastern and central parts of Canada, the Plains and Basin Indians, the Athapascans in the Southwest), or else purging it with extensive and time-consuming lustration rites (settled and half-settled tribes in southwestern and southeastern North America).

Now one also finds this usage of a special exit for the corpse among the majority of the tribes having in their Orpheus tradition the motif of the departure of the deceased through an extra opening in the cabin. The exceptions are the Assiniboin, who according to Lowie carried the corpse out through the ordinary entrance,[24] and the Seneca, who appear to have done the same. Among the Shasta the deceased was taken out through an opening that was made in the roof or the wall.[25] Kohl tells us that the Ojibway did not transport the corpse through the doorway: "Vielmehr schneiden sie hinten ein Loch in das Haus und schicken da den Todten hinaus."[26] Jenness writes that the Ojibway on Parry Island "carried out the corpse, feet foremost, through a hole in the back wall."[27] The Jesuit Relations have similar observations concerning the burial customs among the Algonquin in New France, i.e. chiefly the Montagnais-Naskapi and their neighbours (among whom may be accounted the Malecite). Thus Joseph Jouvency observes: "They never bear out the corpses of the dead through the door of the lodge, but through that part toward which the sick person turned when he expired."[28] It appears probable that in all

---

[22] Hoffman 1896, 240 sq.
[23] Concerning the dissemination of this custom, see Bendann 1930, 58 sqq., Birket-Smith & de Laguna 1938, 470 sq., Frazer 1936 III, 95 sqq., Klimek 1935, 42, Skinner 1913, 64 note 1.
[24] Lowie 1909 b, 41.
[25] Dixon 1907, 465; Kroeber 1925, 300; Holt 1946, 324, 346.
[26] Kohl 1859 I, 149 note. See also Skinner 1911, 166, Lowie 1917, 455.
[27] Jenness 1935, 104. Cf. also the Menomini (Skinner 1913, 64, Skinner 1921, 79).
[28] JR I, 261; cf. also JR V, 129 (Le Jeune), JR VI, 209 (Le Jeune).

the tribes here mentioned the Orpheus narrative has spun variations upon a motif taken from the death rites. It is not certain, however, that the episode in the Assiniboin tale has this origin.[29] The Seneca legend gives a faint echo of the account of the departure of the deceased given in the Ojibway and Malecite legends—which is probably due to the fact that the Seneca were unable to exploit the death rites as prototypes in the same way as the two Algonquin tribes.

It is no accident that both in the Orpheus tales and in the death rites the passage of the deceased out of the cabin is sometimes effected through a *back* opening. Paulson has pointed out that in North America as well as in northern Eurasia the further part of the tent or house is often regarded as a sacred place.[30] And Ränk has shown how for cultic reasons North European and North Asiatic peoples have had an extra exit in the further part of the dwelling.[31] It is probably these circumpolar usages that have had repercussions on some of the Orpheus traditions. The actual utilization of an extra opening for the carrying out of the corpse has had a still wider distribution.[32]

We have thus been able to constate that the ideas concerning the departure of the deceased occurring in the Orpheus tales have been derived, in certain cases, from the death ritual. When the spirit has then loosed its moorings to this world, the burial customs no longer play any rôle for the account. The patterns are sought elsewhere—inner experiences in combination with traditional folkloristic and religious conceptions must supply the material.

Many aspects of the descriptions of the journey to the realm of spirits show that inner psychic experiences, dreams and visions have supplied the basis for the account. One may remark, for example, that in most of the Orpheus tales the deceased is depicted as a spirit whose airy, volatile consistency seems to correspond directly to the thin, metamorphic figures which may occur in dreams.[33] The fantastic changes of scene during the journey (e.g. the Symplegades motif, ascents to heaven, swift transportations) seem to have been inspired by dream experiences. And the difficult obstacles encountered by the traveller (shaking bridges, great conflagrations, dangerous monsters) often appear to reflect the world of dreams —where they have not, as in the case of the flight motifs occurring, been

[29] See chap. III: 1.
[30] Paulson 1952, 63 sqq.
[31] Ränk 1949, 194 sqq.
[32] Birket-Smith & de Laguna 1938, 471.
[33] Cf. Hultkrantz 1953, 388, 396.

taken from other popular tales.[34]   Several of the actions and motifs
are frequently iterated, as happens in dreams: the Sarcee hero passes three
camps and finds his wife in the fourth; the Malecite hero visits three wig-
wams, each a day's journey from the preceding one, and three old women
give him advice. Many of the experiences of the journey give the impression, moreover, of obscure, dream-like scenes.[35]

One cannot here make any general pronouncement as to the possibility that the motifs of the Orpheus tradition have been *directly* based
upon dream experiences. This has at all events *indirectly* been the case,
i.e. the latter have entered via other narratives or folkloristic motifs,
and may thus be said to have constituted the prototypes for a number
of motifs in the Orpheus tradition. We shall find later that some of the
dominant motifs of the journey are derivable from ecstatic visionary
experiences. Here we shall content ourselves with showing a direct dream-
origin for a relatively insignificant and regionally limited motif, the
journey with closed eyes.

The motif according to which the surviving party (sometimes also the
deceased) must close his eyes on the journey to the realm of the dead and
during his sojourn there occurs frequently in the Orpheus myths on the
western Plateau and in the coastal regions to the west of this. Behind this
motif is the conception of the world of the dead as a subreal world, which
can be experienced only in states of psychic absence.[36] "Close your eyes,
then you will find the way", says the dead girl in the Puyallup myth
to her father. "If your eyes are open you will not see." The father closed
his eyes and then clearly saw the way, but as soon as he opened them the
way vanished.[37] In a Skopamish version it is said that Orpheus (Groundsparrow) "traveled with his eyes shut, trailing his daughter."[38]   In another
Skopamish version we are told the following concerning the deceased
daughter: "She said to the father, 'Sleep and follow me.' At the lake she
said to him, 'Sleep and you shall see the people come'."[39] Here there is a
convincing allusion to the insight that the long journey to the land of the
dead can only be experienced in sleep, in dreams and states of trance.

[34] See chap. III: 1.
[35] Cf. above, p. 68 (the Ottawa legend). It must, however, be observed that some
motifs which have been presumed to have originated in dream-experiences probably
came into being in some other way, e.g. the yawning at the river of death (see below,
88 note 96).
[36] Cf. below, pp. 90, 109. In one of the myths discussed here the following commentary has been intercalated: "When the Indian doctor closes his eyes he can see into
the spirit world beyond" (Ballard 1929, 131).
[37] Ballard, op.cit., 129.
[38] Ballard, op.cit., 132.
[39] Ballard, op.cit., 130.

As we have seen earlier, in several cases the circumstances attending the start of the journey are in themselves sufficient to show that it has been undertaken as it were at a subconscious level.[40] We find a symbolic indication that the journey takes place in another sphere than the world of waking consciousness in the Thompson legend. The two young men who had for a long time vainly sought their absent mother said to each other: "Thus we have travelled for four years. We have passed through all countries, even to the edges of the earth, but have not found our mother. We have asked often, but nobody has seen her. She must be dead." But finally one of the brothers was told by his guardian spirit in a dream that the mother was in the land of the dead. "After imploring the aid of the spirits, they took their canoe and started on their voyage to the spirit land, over a great lake. After paddling several days in a dim atmosphere, it grew lighter, and they saw the shore of another country."[41] It was the realm of the dead. The way thither was thus not by the paths and geographical localities of this world; it was a mysterious route, and to travel it the assistance of the spirits—i.e. the guardian spirits—was required.

In other Orpheus narratives the journey to the land of the dead is, certainly, described as a journey on the earth, but it does at the same time take place in another world than that of daily experience. A good illustration is the Orpheus legend of the Tachi Yokuts. The deceased, a beautiful woman, set off from the grave in a south-easterly direction, then turned westwards "and crossed Tulare Lake (or its inlet)". Little by little she came to "a river which flows westward to San Luis Obispo, the river of the Tulamni." She then turned northward, and found herself now "somewhere to the west of the Tachi country". She "went on northward, across the San Joaquin river, to the north or east of it", whereupon she "went down along the river." In this way she finally arrived at the water which separates the land of the dead from that of the living.[42] Thus here the journey has been conceived as a travelling by known routes in this world—but nonetheless it has belonged to the other world. It is the husband of the deceased who has observed her movements, for he has followed her himself in a state of trance. He has sought vainly to embrace her etherial figure, his eyes have sought vainly to catch her in daylight. The journey to the realm of the dead has, despite its geographical realism, taken place in the sphere of dream consciousness.

We shall have occasion to revert to these experiences and to their signi-

[40] See above, p. 68.
[41] Teit 1898, 85.
[42] Kroeber 1907 c, 217 sq.

ficance for the form taken by the Orpheus tradition. Certain phases in the account of the journey have undeniably been inspired by dream experiences, while other elements owe their origin to migratory legends. The difficulty is to distinguish between what has emanated from the one quarter and what from the other. The next chapter will in some measure show in what degree the account of the journey has been built up with folkloristic elements.[43]

If we now leave on one side the considerations relating to the general foundations of the story of the journey, to turn instead to a phenomenological account of the narrative, we distinguish the following dominant motifs: the journey is characterized by obstacles and difficulties, which culminate towards its end; Orpheus receives assistance from different beings (his wife, guardian spirits, old men or women); the relation between Orpheus and the deceased is betokened by their belonging to two different worlds. Summarizing, one may say that the journey is as a rule represented as a difficult passage between this world and the beyond.[44] It functions as an obstruction between two mutually incompatible forms of existence, so that Orpheus' attempts to cross the boundary are exceedingly difficult, while on the other hand the fleeing figure of the deceased is led easily, almost mechanically over the dividing line between life and death.

The description of the obstacles and difficulties encountered by the traveller on his way is not a feature characterizing only the Orpheus traditions, it occurs in the majority of the narratives dealing with journeys of the living or the dead to the other world. The notion that in order to reach the realm of the dead one must cross water—a river, a lake, or a sea—is thus common over the whole of North America, especially in the northern part of the continent; in the Southwest, in the Southeast and in the Great Basin it does not recur with the same frequency as in other areas.[45] Boas gives it as his opinion that "the most common notion" of the realm of the dead among the Indians of North America "is that of the world of the ghosts lying in the distant west beyond a river which must be crossed by canoe."[46] That the realm of the dead is situated on

[43] See chap. III: 1.
[44] The Ottawa legend constitutes a remarkable exception: the traveller meets with no other difficulties than a long journey, and the landscape—which is unfortunately coloured by the romantic attitude of the American writer who reports the legend—shifts from winter to lovely summer (Schoolcraft 1851 I, 321 sq.).
[45] The diffusion investigations upon which these general observations are based cannot be communicated in this connection. I hope later to have an opportunity of presenting this material.
[46] Boas 1910 b, 618.

the yonder side of water is, moreover, a conception that we find among the most widely differing people all over the world; Acheron, Styx, Gjöll, Tuonela are names sufficiently familiar from European mythologies. There is thus no reason to believe that this conception was created by the Orpheus tradition.[47]

The same applies concerning the otherwise so peculiar Symplegades motif, which is found among the Orpheus traditions of the Southeast area (and which here to a certain extent replaces the water motif). Its rôle in the religious life of the peoples of the Southeast has been formulated by Speck as follows: "The common [mythological] element to the whole region is the eastward or westward journey of the soul and the obstacles it meets with. The most general type of obstacle is the cloud swaying at the end of the earth, where it and sky meet. This is the barrier to the spirit world, through which everyone desiring entrance to the spirit realm must pass."[48] The Symplegades motif is in the Southeast not restricted to the Orpheus traditions; it occurs also in the accounts of journeys to the other world apart from the Orpheus narratives which have been given by the Cherokee,[49] Yuchi,[50] Creek,[51] Chickasaw,[52] and it enters in the cosmological conceptions of the Chitimacha.[53] We find the same motif in a form more reminiscent of the Greek Symplegades—two rocks which strike against each other—among the Caddo.[54] The notion of the "horizon curtain" has, as Thompson has shown, a wide distribution in North America, from the Kaska in the north to the Navajo and the Louisiana tribes in the south.[55] But the examples adduced by Thompson might be multiplied.[56] Even if the notion is perhaps most common in the Southeast, it has not been of rare occurrence in other parts of North America. The distribution and the frequency with which it has been instanced support the assumption that the Orpheus tradition did not give rise to this motif, but adopted it. And the same trend is found in the instances adduced by Hatt from north-east Asia and the Philippines, where, too, the horizon curtain has not been associated with traditions of Or-

---

[47] Behind the notion of the realm of the dead beyond water, presumably, there lies, in the last analysis, the idea that—as Bertholet has formulated it—"Wasser trennt das Jenseits vom Diesseits" (Bertholet 1931, 1192).
[48] Speck 1909, 142.
[49] Mooney 1896, 971, 1900, 255 sq.
[50] Speck, op.cit., 97.
[51] Swanton 1928 b, 512 sq.
[52] Swanton 1928 c, 256.
[53] Swanton 1911, 358, 1907, 287.
[54] Dorsey 1904 a, 227.
[55] Thompson 1929, 275 sq.
[56] See above, p. 78 note 45.

pheus type.[57] As hinted above, the North American Symplegades motif occurs also in another form, which is close to the Hellenic myth. But in this form it does not play any prominent rôle in the Orpheus tradition. Among the obstacle motifs adopted by the Orpheus tradition from current eschatological notions belong also the dangerous monsters which make their appearance on the way to the realm of the dead, and which may as a rule be placated with food sacrifices and the like. Among these dangerous creatures may be noted the Dze-enk of the Tsimshian legend, a double-headed monster of the type common in the mythology of the Northwest,[58] and the terrible dog of the Algonquin, described in the Ojibway tradition as "the dog with bloody mouth that devours the souls of those who have tormented dogs."[59] Among the Seneca the dog has been replaced with two panthers. Outside the Orpheus tradition one finds the notion of the watch-dog of the realm of the dead widely distributed, from the Eskimo to the Indians of Nicaragua; and it has occurred very generally in the Eastern Woodland area.[60]

In several Orpheus tales we are told how Orpheus overcomes the many obstacles encountered on his journey by singing magical songs which subdue them. Barbeau has rightly drawn attention to the resemblances in this point between the North American hero and the Thracian musician Orpheus: each "chants incantations to overcome the monsters blocking the ghostly trail."[61] The North American instances are from the Tsimshian (possibly also the Haida), the Yakima, Chehalis and Wishram. Of the hero of the Tsimshian legend it is said that he sang a magic song which helped to cast a spell upon the giant clam guarding the entrance to the underworld.[62] The Yakima myth describing the journey of Coyote and Eagle to the realm of the dead tells how at the lake of death the former summoned the Charon of the dead with his song.[63] According to one of the Wishram variants it was Eagle who induced the dead to

[57] Hatt 1949, 78 sqq.
[58] Cf. Barbeau 1952, 119 sqq., and Locher 1932, passim (concerning the last-mentioned work, however, see Boas' criticism in RLC, 446 sqq.). This marine monster belongs presumably to the same group of water-beings as the horned water-snake among the Pueblos, Cherokee and Central Algonquin, noted particularly by Radin (Radin 1915 b, 285, 1944, 57 sqq., 62, 247).
[59] Jenness 1935, 109. This dog is mentioned in the Ojibway, Menomini and Shawnee legends (for the Shawnee, see Gayton 1935, 274).
[60] See Kretschmar 1938 II, 101 sq., 136. As Kretschmar has shown, the idea of the dogs of the realm of death has been widespread also in the Old World. Cf. also Arbman's investigation on Yama's dogs in India (Arbman 1928, 214 sqq.).
[61] Barbeau 1950, I, 272, 1953, 259.
[62] Barbeau 1950 I, 279. The Orpheus of the Haida, too, appears to have charmed the powers of the underworld with his magic song, see Barbeau 1953, 260, 266.
[63] Lyman 1904, 248; cf. also below, p. 88 note 96.

come over the water to fetch himself and Coyote: "he produced an elder-berry stalk, made a flute, put the end into the water, and whistled."[64] In one of the Chehalis myths on the Orpheus theme Bluejay is accompani-ed to the realm of the dead by the mysterious Wedge. We are told that Wedge succeeded in subduing the burning prairies they had to cross by spraying a little water and singing magic words.[65] Of another nature is the song sung by Coyote in the spirit world of the Californian Shasta: this is a dancing song, probably connected with the ghost dance.[66] It is a remarkable fact that the magic episode referred to here occurs only within a restricted area on the Northwest Coast.

The friendly counsellors met with on the way are not, any more than the numerous obstacles, characteristic only for the Orpheus tradition. The native eschatologies from the whole of North America are familiar with these figures, even if they are here not always represented in such a favourable light as in the majority of the Orpheus tales.

In the Orpheus tradition the counsellors are found chiefly in the more easterly versions, but they do also occur farther west. Among the Ala-bama, Koasati, Malecite, Pawnee, Blackfoot and Karuk there is mention of one or more friendly old women who give counsel. Among the Tsim-shian and Kwakiutl the "Mouse Woman" is not only the one who gives counsel, but she also counteracts practically the negative forces encoun-tered by the traveller. But male helpers are also mentioned, viz, among the Alabama, Koasati, Seneca, Huron, Ojibway and Winnebago. Parti-cularly interesting is the description of the hairy man of the Winnebago Indians whom Orpheus encounters several times in the course of his journey, and who appears alone the first time but as two the second time, and on the third occasion as three hairy men; on the fourth occasion, when Orpheus is in the realm of the dead, four hairy men come towards him, all in principle identical with the man he saw the first time.[67]

Thus the Winnebago narrative locates the activity of the counsellors, at last, in the realm of the dead. This reminds us of the fact that in several other Orpheus tales it is precisely the spirit world that is the place in which the helpful figures make their appearance.[68] In such contexts there

[64] Curtis 1911 VIII, 127; cf. Sapir 1909 b, 109.
[65] Adamson 1934, 296 sq.; cf. 300 sq.
[66] See below, p. 145 note 124.
[67] This motif, that a spirit multiplies itself, is found in many Indian folktales and is probably in part influenced by the visionary experiences. The Orpheus traditions of the Zuni Indians refer to the helper in the other world alternately as Owl or the Owls —the number even varies in one and the same context (Benedict 1935 II, 157).
[68] On this subject see further below, pp. 94 sq.

is as a rule no mention at the same time of any ruler of the dead—otherwise the latter is generally the good helper.[69] The circumstance that the functions of the counsellors and the ruler here become identical probably throws some light upon the real nature of the former. As "folkloristic" conceptions they may, certainly, have, at least in part, an independent origin outside the eschatological tradition.[70] But as spiritual beings within this tradition they have been intimately associated with the old motifs, known also from the Eurasiatic high cultures, of the guardians and the ruler of the realm of the dead.[71]

One arrives at the same conclusion on comparing the eschatological conceptions outside the Orpheus tradition. We find, just as in the Orpheus tales, that the traveller on his way to the spirit world meets with one or several counsellors.[72] (Where there are several of them, their number is generally determined by the sacred number of the tribe.) How close these counsellors come to the conception of the ruler of the realm of the dead emerges from several descriptions. As an example we may adduce here the description of the Thompson Indians.[73] These assume that the realm of the dead is situated in the underworld, towards the sunset. The way thither, leading over, inter alia, "a wide shallow stream" is known down to the least detail. "Three guardians are stationed along the trail of the souls," writes Teit, "one on this side of the river, the second one between the river and the land of the ghosts, and the third one at a lodge which is situated at the end of the trail of the ghosts . . . All these men are described as very old, gray-headed, wise, and venerable-looking." The third and last is a powerful man, "who is considered their chief, and who is an orator who sometimes sends messages to this world with returning souls."[74] It cannot be more clearly stressed that the "counsellors" have been understood as replicas of the ruler of the dead.

If one wishes to bring forward what most strikingly *distinguishes* the journey to the dead in the Orpheus tradition from other Indian accounts of such journeys, two essential features may be adduced. In the first place, Orpheus is often accompanied by a guardian spirit to the other world. In the second place, the difficulties which are in other accounts said to overtake the dead on their journey are according to the Orpheus tradi-

[69] See chap. II: 4—5.
[70] See further below, pp. 175 sq.
[71] As we shall find, these two functionaries are often identical (see below, pp. 95 sq.).
[72] In the Orpheus tradition the counsellors, if they are more than one, are two (Alabama, Seneca), three (Malecite) or four (Alabama, Koasati, Winnebago).
[73] Concerning its relation to the Orpheus tradition, see chap. V: 1.
[74] Teit 1900, 342. Cf. the commentary in Schmidt 1933, 126.

tion encountered only by the living—i.e. Orpheus—,while in contrast to the journey of the living that of the dead is represented as easy and free of obstacles. It is above all in this point that the Orpheus tradition diverges from other eschatological accounts. In juxtaposition to this last-mentioned viewpoint it may further be adduced that the descriptions of journeys given in the Orpheus traditions always refer to the journey of a living person to the realm of the dead, something which distinguishes them from most other accounts with a similar content.

The appearance of the guardian spirits in the Orpheus traditions has already been referred to in the foregoing, where several examples have been adduced to illustrate how even before his departure to the land of shades Orpheus has had visions of supernatural beings who were or were to become his personal guardian spirits.[75] These then accompanied him on his way. In the majority of cases nothing at all or very little is said of their actions during the actual journey; Orpheus' successes are, however, presumed to be due to their assistance. In some cases, though, the activity of the guardian spirits on the journey is gone into with more detail.

We may select as examples some Orpheus traditions from the Southwest. Thus a number of Pueblo versions tell how in the course of his expedition Orpheus is assisted by supernatural beings in the shape of animals that he has got into contact with in various ways. In a Taos tradition it is a crow, in some Zuni traditions it is a squirrel, a rat ("woodrat"), an owl or a spider. Only the latter accompanies Orpheus from the start, the others are met with in different places, the crow and the owl obviously only in the realm of the dead. All of them give immediate assistance, or at least practical advice. They may therefore be regarded as guardian spirits, i.e. in those situations in which they give assistance—unless they are to be accounted as belonging to the great category of counsellors (see above).[76] As Ruth Benedict has stressed on several

[75] See above, pp. 66 sqq., 77.

[76] They are not individually acquired guardian spirits, but function secondarily in this rôle. This is shown in their behaviour. Owl behaves in the same way as the ruler of the dead in other Orpheus traditions. Squirrel and Rat do practical services as fellow-beings who are friendly disposed, but they have no obligations towards the one they help. Crow gives advice and sends help (an eagle) at a time when Orpheus despairs of his possibilities of bringing his beloved back to life; but after this is does not show itself again. Spider has temporarily undertaken to accompany and second the Zuni girl who is seeking her lover: "Spider Woman sat in her ear and advised her and she was successful" (Benedict 1935 II, 299). It may be added that strictly speaking those functions which are generally ascribed to the guardian spirits, the counsellors on the way, the guardians or the rulers of the other world, are mixed in these figures, and it is not easy to know to what category they should really be referred.

occasions, the Pueblo peoples lack the guardian spirit complex otherwise so common in North America. Many of the elements connected herewith are present, but "it is the guardian spirit itself that is lacking as an institutionalized element of religion." The group ceremonies have taken the place of individual experience as a means of establishing contact with the deity.[77] The spirits assisting the Orpheus of the Pueblo peoples are therefore primarily tribal divinities or spirits of the collective; but they may also assist individuals as their temporary guardian spirits. This applies in an eminent degree as concerns the spider, "Spider Woman."[78]

The guardian-spirit complex has set its stamp on many Orpheus traditions, and doubtless it may be brought to light in many other Orpheus narratives where it is not discoverable to a superficial scrutiny.[78a] It should be observed that in a large number of cases the deceased assumes the legitimate functions of the guardian spirits. In the Shahaptin narrative communicated by Farrand, for example, the deceased daughter of Coyote discovers herself to her father in a dream and instructs him how he may journey to the realm of the dead. She then, though invisible to him, sets off to the other world and he follows her voice.[79] There are plenty of such Orpheus tales. It seems legitimate to me to keep open the door for an interpretation according to which the rôle of the deceased as guide, counsellor and helper is not an original feature, but a substitute for an earlier guardian-spirit activity.

It would, however, be over-hasty to believe that the rôle played by the guardian spirits in the Orpheus tradition cannot also be traced in other eschatological narratives. As I have remarked in another context, the deceased is in many quarters in North America conceived as being accompanied to the land of the dead by his guardian spirit.[80] This is perhaps not so remarkable: through some sort of law of sympathy (to speak with Frazer) the deceased and his *mana* are led to the same goal after death.[81] What is more remarkable is that in certain cases living persons

[77] Benedict 1923 b, 40; cf. op.cit., 36 sqq. See also Benedict 1946, 62 sq., and Underhill 1948, passim.
[78] Concerning Spider Woman as a guardian spirit, cf. Parsons 1939 II, 1054 note. Concerning the function of the spider in the mythology and ritual of the Pueblos, see Parsons, op.cit., I, 192 sq., II, 664 ("the mother of all").
[78a] It should be observed that in e.g. the Blackfoot legend "a bundle of medicine" plays the same rôle as the guardian spirit (Grinnell 1912, 128, 131).
[79] Boas 1917 a, 178.
[80] Hultkrantz 1953, 346.
[81] What is more common, however, is for the deceased to be accompanied by dead relatives who come to his bier (another version of the notion of the kidnapping of souls by ghosts), or for spirits sent from the other world to come to meet him (cf. e.g. the

who have visited the realm of the dead have gone there with their guardian spirits. We do not need to be in any doubt, however, as to the category of persons here in question: they are, of course, the medicine-men, the shamans, who, accompanied by their assistant spirits, have tried to fetch the souls of sick persons from the realm of the dead.

This recovery of souls has been described in a great number of ethnographic reports, but unfortunately it has not yet been made the object of a satisfactory comparative analysis. And without such a more careful investigation it is at this juncture not possible to define precisely the rôle of the guardian spirits in this connection. They are so vaguely glimpsed in the reports that one does not always know whether they accompanied the shaman on the journey to the beyond, or whether they only invested him with the power to perform the journey successfully. In his account of a shaman séance among the Thompson Indians Teit says nothing of the contributions of the guardian spirit; but it is possible to interpret him to the effect that the guardian spirit was actually together with the shaman.[82] In most of the reports of this kind from the Northwest Coast it is hinted that either the guardian spirit or the medicine-man himself journeyed to the land of souls, but not both of them at the same time.[83] Or else the shaman is conceived to visit the realm of the dead, "possessed" by his guardian spirit.[84] When a Quinault shaman was about to set out for the land of the dead he was possessed by his assistant spirit, who thereafter spoke with his voice. The spirit showed him the way, encouraged him and gave him good advice at dangerous places. The shaman was the whole time in a trance.[85] Among the Dwamish, on the other hand, the shaman and his guardian spirit were separate personalities on the journey to the realm of the dead. In the imitative séance in which a dramatic representation was given of the way in which the soul of the sick person was sought out in the other world and returned to its owner, the guardian

Seneca: Converse 1908, 51, Curtin & Hewitt 1918 I, 254). A dead Omaha child is protected on the journey to the other world by a deceased enemy warrior who has been killed by the father (Fletcher & La Flesche 1911, 594), and the Sinkyone Indian is accompanied to the realm of the dead by the assistant spirit of the shaman (Nomland 1935, 163, 168, 169).

[82] See Teit 1900, 63, and Bouteiller 1950, 129.

[83] Cf. Drucker 1950, 227; Barnett 1939, 273, 1937, 191, 1955, 215; Ray 1942, 247 sq.

[84] I will not here go into the delicate problem of whether the possession was genuine or not; presumably both possibilities have occurred (cf. Barnett 1955, 274). Boas, the foremost connoisseur of the religious life of the Northwest Coast, does not express himself unequivocally on the subject (see Lowie 1937, 152 sq.). Cf. further Stewart 1946, 323 sqq., Clements 1932, 189 sq., 224 sq.

[85] Olson 1936, 160.

spirits were symbolically present in the form of carved wooden posts.[86] The collaboration between the spirit and the shaman in this mimic drama bears a definite resemblance to the relation between the Orpheus figure and his guardian spirit on the journey to the other world.

The active collaboration of the guardian spirit in the hero's attempts to restore his beloved to life is thus one of the more striking features in the account of the journey in the Orpheus tale. Another prominent feature is, as already pointed out, the great difference between the two main personages in the narrative with respect to the difficulties encountered on the journey. While it is often only with great difficulty that Orpheus reaches the realm of the dead, his deceased spouse glides there with ease, almost automatically or mechanically. The discrepancy between their possibilities of advance emerges, of course, only in those versions of the narrative which speak of the *simultaneous* journey of the hero and the deceased to the other world. These versions are to be found chiefly in California,[87] the Southwest[88] and the Northeast,[89] but there are also isolated occurrences within other culture areas.[90] It is not, however, in all these cases assumed that there is any difference between the travelling abilities of the hero and those of the deceased: the Twana Indian succeeds in concealing himself in the canoe which takes his comrade to the land of souls; the Modoc hero follows his deceased daughter without difficulty, for he is a divinity; and the Carrier Indian, who is a medicine-man, walks abreast of his deceased wife.

Otherwise, the narratives bring out very clearly the differences between the two main personages. The deceased woman of the Mono legend "went up into 'heaven'" as soon as the corpse had been buried; her husband, who set out at the same time, had, on the other hand, to overcome various obstacles in the course of a difficult journey: "First he encountered fleas, innumerable fleas, which nearly bit him to death. Then he encountered lice, exceedingly large lice, which nearly ate him. Next he encountered ants of many sorts, but after much suffering passed through them. Subsequently he encountered mosquitoes, gnats, yellowjackets, and hornets. After these he passed through swarms of horse flies and blow

---

[86] Waterman 1930, passim; Dorsey 1902, passim; Haeberlin 1918, passim. See also Underhill 1945, 197 sqq.
[87] Among the Modoc, Shasta, Yurok, Hupa, Pomo, Nisenan, Yokuts (all the tribal divisions); Western Mono, Tübatulabal, Serrano, Gabrielino.
[88] Among the Navajo, in Zuni, and in Taos.
[89] Among the Ojibway, Malecite, Seneca and Huron.
[90] Among the Twana and Carrier.

flies. Then he came to gopher snakes, then to water snakes, then to racer snakes, then to rattlesnakes, then to king snakes. Nevertheless, he passed through all of these. In succession he then met with foxes, raccoons, dogs, coyotes, pumas, wild cats, bears, and wolves."[91] In one of the Zuni narratives we are told that in the shape of a spirit but with a visible feather in her hair the deceased wife glided easily and smoothly towards the realm of the dead, while her husband was overwhelmed with fatigue and lagged behind. "They went down to Caliente and he began to be very tired. She crossed great fields of cactus and her husband followed her. He cried for they cut his shirt and wore out his moccasins. He put on his second pair and they were worn out. He put on his third pair and they were worn out. Then he put on the fourth pair. When he got to the end of the field he looked back and there was no cactus; there was just open country. They went a little way farther and they came to a chasm and he saw the feather way down below. He cried because he could not get down."[92] And in the same way in the Malecite and Seneca traditions we are told how the surviving party tries in vain to catch up with the deceased.

Especially does Orpheus run into difficulties when he has reached the last great obstacle, the river or ocean. The departed passes over the water without further ado, but her husband is checked as he attempts to follow: he does not get over the bridge, or he does not get down into the boat. (That he is nevertheless helped over at the last moment is in this connection an irrelevant detail.) In short phrases the Yaudanchi Yokuts Orpheus legend describes how the hero and his deceased spouse "came to the bridge of the world of the dead. There the woman crossed. Her husband was unable to. On the other side were watchmen. They saw the man across the water. Then the watchmen were told to make a bridge for him. Then he crossed."[93] In another Yokuts legend within the Orpheus tradition the deceased crosses "a great roaring water" by going over "a bridge, slender and fragile like a spider's web." Her husband is left on the shore, but touched by his grief she helps him over: "She stretched a hand toward him, and he felt strong and comforted."[94] The same scene recurs in exactly the same form in the Modoc myth and—in a modified version—in the Serrano legend.

[91] Gifford 1923, 340. Concerning the various obstacles, see above, pp. 78 sqq. Obstructing monsters occur in the Northwest Coast Indians' tales of the "sea-coast form," and here and there also in other narratives, e.g. in the Ojibway legend.
[92] Benedict 1935 II, 133.
[93] Kroeber 1907 c, 228.
[94] Hudson 1902, 104; see also op.cit., 105.

The Orpheus of the Hupa Indians succeeds in crossing the water in a boat after having put the watching water-gods to sleep with a powerful medicine. The Pomo legend, about a father who follows his deceased son, tells how at the edge of the ocean the son was lowered into a black canoe, while the father was denied "on the grounds that he was still alive."[95] Later, however, he succeeded in crossing in another canoe. Also the Carrier tradition reveals a certain difference in conduct as between the Orpheus figure and his deceased partner on their arrival at the river of death: the dead woman yawns, and at once a canoe leaves the other bank and comes towards her to fetch her; her husband, on the other hand, calls out, and another canoe comes to fetch him.[96]

This theme, the difference between Orpheus' journey and the journey of the deceased beloved, runs like a red thread through many Orpheus legends. It illustrates, of course, the essential difference between the living, who is still in this world, and the deceased, who from the moment of death belongs to another world.[97] He is, as we have already pointed out, destined for that world, and is therefore drawn to it as to a magnet.[98] This clearly emerges in several ways in the texts of the Orpheus tradition. Observe, for example, the wording in the Taos myth: "So Magpietail buried his wife, and they had four nights after death to watch for her departure to the other world. After four days she had to live in the world of the dead."[99] Or compare the Yokuts legend, where a husband follows his deceased wife: "She often turned and warned him back, declaring

---

[95] Loeb 1926, 292.

[96] Jenness 1934, 144. The notion that one must summon the ferrymen of the other world by yawning is found in the Orpheus traditions of the Salish and the Shahaptin tribes (thus among the Snuqualmi, Puyallup, Skopamish, Chehalis, Sinkaietk, Kalispel and Tenino) and in the Orpheus legends of the Carrier and Kalapuya. It is possibly the same notion that one glimpses in the Sanpoil legend, if Gayton's interpretation is correct (Gayton 1935, 281). Variations on the theme are to be met with in other Orpheus narratives from the Northwest Coast and the Plateau: one must whisper (Tlingit), sigh (Kalapuya), speak under water (Klikitat), whistle (Wishram) or sing (Yakima); cf. also above, pp. 80 sq. One finds yawning as a means of communication also in the eschatological conceptions outside the Orpheus tradition, viz. among the Tlingit (Swanton 1921, 352), Bella Bella (Boas 1932 a, 142), Coast Salish (Curtis 1913 IX, 89) and Carrier (Morice 1889, 160 note 1, 1910, 230; Jenness 1934, 100, 146). The psychological root of the notion is probably not, as Morice thinks, to seek in the close connection between yawning and sleep, "the very gate of dreams," in which the spirits reveal themselves; rather is the yawning to be understood as one of the numerous expressions of the reversed character of the realm of the dead: there everything is topsy-turvy (Morice 1910, loc.cit.; Holmberg 1925, 31 sq.).

[97] Concerning the moment of death according to the Indian view, see Hultkrantz, op.cit., 459 sq.

[98] See above, p. 78. Cf. also Hultkrantz, op.cit., 379 note 22, 435.

[99] Parsons 1940, 23.

that she was bound for the Tib'-ik-nitc, the home of the dead."[100] Not only does the deceased person change outwardly, he (or she) shows his complete emancipation from the conditions of this life by changing personality, by giving up his emotional attachment to the home and the family. When in the Seneca tradition the deceased husband has just stopped breathing, his spirit sets off westward without delay, and does not pay any attention to the cries of his despairing wife to return to their child. "Do you yourself go back and take care of the child" is his only answer.[101] In the Orpheus tradition of the Telumni Yokuts it is said of the deceased, who is closely followed by her husband, that "she looked back and saw him but she ignored him."[102] In several cases, however, there is in the Californian and Southwestern traditions an element of conciliation: the deceased begs the husband to return, for he is alive and does not belong to the other world.[103]

In this connection it is very interesting to note that the deceased party flitting to the other world is sometimes caught by her living pursuer, though without his being able to retain his grip of her. The Shasta husband sought vainly to seize his deceased wife, but he could not hold her, she was "nothing but air."[104] The same difficulty in embracing his deceased wife was experienced by the Orpheus of the Tachi Yokuts. "Whenever he tried to hold her she escaped. He kept trying to seize her, however, and delayed her." Finally she said to him: "What are you going to do? I am nothing now. How can you get my body back?"[105] Thus the deceased is described again and again as a spirit: she is a breath of air, a "puff of smoke" (Malecite), or a whirlwind (Serrano, Gabrielino).[106] She is scarcely visible: she shows herself only for short moments during the journey (Seneca), or is only observable through the feather in her hair (Zuni Indians); or she is visible at night but disappears in the day (Navajo), or is then at least changed into a piece of wood (Yaudanchi Yokuts), a grasshopper (Navajo) or a jackrabbit (Taos Indians).[107] It is in complete accordance with her spirit nature that—as in one of the Zuni

[100] Hudson, op.cit., 104.
[101] Jenness 1935, 109.
[102] Gayton, op.cit., 267.
[103] Thus in the traditions from the Nisenan and Yokuts, and from Zuni and Taos.
[104] Voegelin 1947, 52. Cf. the Mohave, above, p. 24.
[105] Kroeber 1907 c, 216. Cf. also the Pomo legend (Barrett 1933, 379).
[106] Concerning the deceased in the whirlwind, cf. above, p. 71.
[107] The appearance of the deceased as a grasshopper among the Navajo (see Wyman, Hill & Osanai 1942, 19 note 25) reminds one that among the Cahuilla the soul of a sick person can assume the same form (Hooper 1920, 340). Concerning the deceased as a jackrabbit, cf. below, p. 127.

versions—she is unable to eat food but can receive sacrificial food that has been thrown into the fire.

But, as is always the case in such contexts, the "spirituality" of the deceased is not consistently represented. It is only, as in the Shasta, Yurok and Zuni traditions, that we find the surviving party catching up with the deceased on her way to the beyond.[108] The Orpheus legend of the Huron tells how at night-time the deceased sister appears "with a dish of meal cooked in water, after the fashion of the country," which she hands to her surviving brother. And the Taos myth relates how on the journey the dead woman suckled her child, that her husband had brought with him. Reluctantly, the deceased gives instructions concerning the nature of the journey and how it is to be managed,[109] indeed, she even gives practical, tangible help on the journey.[110] In some cases it is even the desire of the deceased that her surviving husband should accompany her. Thus the Modoc myth describes how the deceased guides her surviving father on the way to the realm of the dead; but he must keep his eyes closed, for, says his daughter, "if you open them you will not be able to follow me, you will have to go back and leave me alone."[111] The Euryd-ice of the Tübatulabal helps her husband to travel "on top of the water" and "in a dustspout."[112] And the Orpheus of the Serrano succeeded in entering the realm of the dead because his wife took him on her back.[113]

The road to the other world is a perilous road, and several figures of Orpheus type have lost their lives on the way.[114] In one case, in the Yurok legend, the hero succeeds in catching up with and taking home his beloved before she has reached the realm of the dead.[115] But other-wise it appears to him absolutely necessary first of all, in the land of the dead, to obtain permission from the dead or their ruler to bring his be-loved back to life. In the realm of the dead, however, the problems al-ready revealed in the course of the journey are actualized on a bigger scale: the absolute essential difference between the living and the dead.

[108] According to the Shasta traditions, Orpheus has contact with the deceased every night, but during the day she is again a long way ahead of him.

[109] Cf. the Shahaptin myth (see above, p. 84). In such cases the deceased replaces firstly the guardian spirits, secondly the counsellors (guardians etc.) who are otherwise met on the journey.

[110] Thus among the Yokuts, and among the Taos and Zuni Indians.

[111] Curtin 1912, 41. See also the discussion above, p. 76.

[112] Voegelin 1935, 205.

[113] Benedict 1926, 8.

[114] In the Yuchi and Micmac narratives one or several of the seekers succumb in the course of the journey. But it is to be observed that there still remain several persons, who continue the search and succeed in entering the realm of the dead.

[115] Kroeber 1925, 47.

4. Orpheus in the other world

Orpheus' visit to the other world is characterized chiefly by the difficulties he encounters in the carrying out of his task, to bring his beloved one back to life. To throw some light on the background to his dilemma we may here give a brief account of the realm of the dead and its inhabitants. We shall concentrate less upon this realm as such, as it appears in a number of variations and with details having no direct significance for the Orpheus theme.[1] Our main attention will instead be given to those foreground figures with whom Orpheus enters into significant contact: the guard or ruler of the dead, the dead themselves, the ravished spouse. We shall also discuss the practical measures with which Orpheus tries to keep himself free from the infection emanating from all that belongs to the dead and to their world.

The picture that from the Orpheus traditions we get of the notions obtaining about the other world is in certain essential respects very uniform, at the same time as (according to what we have already observed) local variations exist as a result of the influence of the cultural environment.[2] These variations, however, refer chiefly to what we may call the externals, i.e. material and social structure, and not to the essential ideological aspects.

The realm of the dead is as a rule described as a beautiful country situated in a remote world of another nature than this, where the inhabitants lead a relatively pleasant existence and devote themselves to, amongst other things, music and dancing.[3] Generally, this world is located in the sky, or beyond the horizon. But it does also happen that it is located on the earth (the Plains) or in the underworld (the Southwest, northern California, the Northwest Coast in the "sea-coast form"). Where the realm of the dead is the underworld, however, it is sometimes regarded as unsatisfactory and gloomy, a world worse than the scene of this life. "Life in that world is not to be desired. The spirits live on dead salmon and other unfit food. They are much given to brawls and fights. Dampness and darkness reign there." It is in these terms that the underworld Hades of the Hupa is described, a world that was visited by their Orpheus hero.[4] But how differently the land of the spirits is esteemed among the neighbour tribe, the Karuk! It is known as "that

[1] See the more detailed survey in chap. V: 1.
[2] See above, chap. I: 4.
[3] Concerning the import of the dance, see below, p. 124.
[4] Goddard 1903, 74.

place where people go underground, and where they forever dance every kind."[5] It is obvious that the notion of happiness, so dominant in other versions of the Orpheus tradition, has also set its stamp upon the underworld realm of the dead, which otherwise, in itself, has so little to do with happiness.

Thus the character of a happy land ascribed to the realm of the dead is striking. It is tempting to imagine that this valuation has been due to the whim of a raconteur, who has wished to strengthen the dramatic force of the narrative by painting the realm of the dead in bright colours, and at the same time to give a rational explanation of the attraction this abode exercised on the deceased. But a closer examination shows that this train of thought is not tenable. A realm of the dead described in terms of horror would provide a more effective dramatic frame for Orpheus' expedition to rescue his love. And as regards the attraction of the other world, it has already been pointed out that the deceased person is automatically drawn towards that world; one has not the impression that the person in question has longed to go there before becoming acquainted with it.—One possible theory, on the other hand, would be that the Orpheus tradition had the etiological function of serving as the vehicle for the tale of a happy world in the beyond for uneasily questioning human beings. This line of reasoning has more to justify it, since—as we shall see—one of the most essential functions of the tale has been, in point of fact, to spread a knowledge of the life after this.[6]

Here, however, it will be fruitful to apply quite a different perspective, which by no means excludes the foregoing viewpoint: it is obvious that in North America the Orpheus tradition has arisen among tribes who have had a bright and optimistic eschatological belief. Even if we do not yet wish to go into the relation between the Orpheus tale and the current religious belief, we may confidently assume that the basic pattern, the emotive tone, must have been identical in the conceptions of the other world found in the tradition and in the actual religious belief. In the last analysis this pattern probably reflects the national character of these tribes as this was developed under the influence of the cultural and natural environment.[7] One may, in other words, regard the happy

[5] Kroeber 1946, 16. In an ethnological report it is stated that the Karuk have had an ethically differentiated eschatology, with heaven and hell (Driver 1939, 413). One must presume that we have here to do with Christian influence from more recent times.

[6] See chap. V; 2.

[7] The investigation of national character is still at a preliminary stage, but in the future it will probably assume great importance for the interpretation of the eschatological notions of different peoples.—See further below, pp. 207 sq.

realm of the dead in the Orpheus tradition as the creation of people with a balanced and harmonious view of life.

One must not, of course, give undue emphasis to the blissful character of these realms of the dead. It is well known that the Indians considered even the happy lands of the dead to suffer from serious defects as compared with the land of the living. Jenness points out that wherever the realm of the dead was located, "the soul that reached it enjoyed happiness indeed, but only a shadowy happiness compared with the joys of earth."[8] An existence in another, vaguely imagined world can of course not have the same force of attraction as one in the world of actual waking life, even if it outbids the latter in alluring privileges. The main theme of the Orpheus tradition is in itself convincing proof that the Indians found it to be an advantage to live in the world of the living. Only for ghosts can the other world appear equally attractive, or more attractive than the world of living men. This emerges clearly in the Salish and Shahaptin traditions concerning the journey of Coyote (or another culture hero) to the realm of the dead. In the Humptulip version Bluejay was conveyed over the river of the dead in a canoe which was filled with skulls and which had a large hole; but the skulls were the children of his sister, and for the living every canoe in the land of the dead appeared to have a hole in it.[9] When Bluejay next arrived at the river of the dead he had died, and the skulls seemed to him to be beautiful children, and the old canoe with a hole appeared to him now as a handsome boat.[10] Thus a pronouncement to the effect that the realm of the dead is a happy and beautiful land has only a relative validity: the other world is happy and beautiful for the dead.

In the realm of the dead, as it is represented in the Orpheus tradition, the highest authority is generally exercised by a central figure who may be designated as its ruler or its guard—the term will depend upon his placing in the region and his influence over the dead.[11] In many cases there are at the same time a ruler over the land of the dead and a guard at its gate. But in must also be borne in mind that in some cases the dead themselves—*in corpore*—exercise the supreme control over their affairs. In the Orpheus tradition the ruler or guard of the dead fre-

---

[8] Jenness 1932, 165.

[9] Adamson 1934, 297, 302.

[10] The canoe mentioned here has its prototype in the burial canoe pierced with holes in which the corpse was placed (see Drucker 1955, 160, Barnett 1937, 183, 1939, 263; cf. the interpretation in Olson 1936, 111).

[11] Cf. above, p. 82.

quently appears, functionally, as a representative for the dead, their spokesman—his jurisdictional authority over them is not always clear. This is why it is in so many Orpheus tales so difficult to decide whether the man who assists Orpheus in the other world is its ruler or a more insignificant person. Since, however, whether he is a god, a custodian spirit or an ordinary dead person, this figure plays a key rôle in the Orpheus drama, it may be as well to consider him for a moment, though without entering upon a discussion of all the intricate historical problem-complexes connected with him.[12] The viewpoints to be advanced here relate chiefly to the account of him to be found in the Orpheus tradition; but for functional reasons reference will here and there be made also to other eschatological sources.

In certain traditions, where there is otherwise no express mention of a custodian or ruler of the other world, it is possible for the representative of the dead to appear as anonymous. There are, as has been mentioned, several Orpheus tales of this type. In a number of Salish and Shahaptin accounts, in some Californian traditions and in some Athapascan and Pueblo versions the people, i.e. the dead as a collective, constitute the authority that decides Orpheus' possibilities. The Serrano legend, for example, describes how the dead woman came to her earlier deceased parents, brothers and sisters. "They were glad to see her, but they did not like the man for he was not dead. The woman pleaded for him, however, and they let him stay."[13] Here there is no mention at all of any single authority; in the sequel we are told how the dead *in corpore* impose certain taboos on Orpheus as a condition for his wife's restoration to life. But sometimes in such narratives one glimpses a person who may be regarded as a representative for the dead, or in any case as their natural spokesman: the Orpheus of the Lipan Apache is charged by a man in the crowd to return to the living. The rôle played by these representatives for the dead is generally that of the helper—a circumstance that supports the assumption of their association and presumably identity with the divine ruler of the realm of the dead in other traditions. They occur in the most various shapes, but the commonest are undoubtedly the old woman (among e.g. the Carrier and Assiniboin) and the bird-helper among the Pueblos.[14] There is nothing to contradict the assumption that such apparently lower functionaries as the fire-tender among the Shasta

[12] I am here thinking of problems like the age of the Supreme Being as ruler of the realm of the dead, or the chronological relation between different kinds of rulers of the other world.
[13] Benedict 1926, 8.
[14] Concerning the bird helper, see above, p. 83 note 76.

94

or the fetcher of wood among the Nootka may actually have been dominant persons in the world of the dead.[15] In the Twana legend it is the
shaman Rat who, behind the backs of the dead, helps the young man to
get his comrade back; Rat's importance is very close to that of the potentate of the other world in other narratives. By way of comparison
it may be mentioned that the Tsimshian, too, know of a powerful shaman
in the realm of the dead. The latter is the ruler of the dead and assists
living shamans who have come to fetch souls.[16]

The correctness of this interpretation is favoured by the earlier mentioned circumstance that the ruler-custodian and the helper in the realm
of the dead appear to be mutually exclusive.[17] There are, however, exceptions to this rule: according to the Ojibway tradition adduced by
Jenness, Djibweabuth is the Lord of the Dead, but it is his grandmother
Nokomis, "Grandmother Earth," also identified with the moon, who
prevails upon the ruler to allow the mourning widow to get her husband
back.

One observes, however, that in the majority of cases Orpheus negoti-
ates with one of the dead, and that this person is as a rule either the ruler
or else the custodian of the other world. Everything supports the assumption that this was originally one and the same person.[18] Both in the
Orpheus tradition and in other eschatological accounts these two figures
are represented in such a way that it is easy to confuse them. Very often
the representative of the dead is equipped with such properties and functions that it is difficult to decide whether he should be referred to as
ruler or custodian.[19] And frequently enough the leader of the dead has
his abode precisely at the entrance to the realm of the dead, just like a
custodian.[20] It appears probable that precisely in his function as the custodian and ruler of the other world the Lord of the Dead has been moved
to the critical boundary zone between the worlds of life and death in

---

[15] The fetcher of wood among the Nootka has his hair clipped short, but this does
not signify, as one might be tempted to think, that he has the status of a slave. Cf.
Drucker 1951, 128 sq.

[16] Boas 1916, 329 sq.

[17] Cf. above, pp. 81 sq.

[18] This is denied, however, by Radin (Radin 1937, 284).

[19] It is thus extremely uncertain to what category the man at the gate of the other
world, in the first version of the Orpheus legend of the Alabama reproduced by Swanton, is to be referred (Swanton 1929, 141). Although he is obviously in the periphery
of the realm of the dead—or even outside this realm—and is not taking part in the
activities of the dead, his words of greeting, his friendliness and the nature of the
assistance he gives are most reminiscent of those of the divinity in the second Alabama
version (Swanton, op.cit., 143).

[20] Cf. above, p. 82 (Thompson River).

order here to occupy the place which otherwise—and presumably primarily—was taken by e.g. the automatically hindering river (see below) or the terrible dog-demon.[21] In the Orpheus legend of the Micmac the ruler of the dead is expressly described as also the custodian of the other world. "I am Papkootparout the guardian, the master, the governor, and the ruler of all souls," says the giant armed with a club who bars the way for Orpheus on the latter's entry into the land of the dead.[22] Unfortunately, it is by no means out of the question that the identification was made by Le Clercq in retelling the tale.

Nevertheless, it is here for practical reasons most advantageous not to take the two functionaries in the realm of the dead as being identical. In the first place, it is in the source-material generally possible to see whether it is a matter of a being with predominantly guardian character or a being with predominantly the character of ruler. Decisive factors in this connection are the place of domicile and the degree of the authority of the personage in question. But his attitude to Orpheus' request may also throw light upon his character: the guardian generally reacts more negatively than does the ruler. There are, of course, exceptions here— the above-mentioned Djibweabuth in the Ojibway legend is only placated through the mediation of his grandmother—; but as a rule it may be said that on account of his controlling function the guardian or custodian cannot be as obliging as the ruler of the dead. Furthermore, it must be remembered that in some cases the guardian and the ruler occur as two separate persons (Ojibway, Ottawa, Huron, Seneca). According to Schoolcraft, the Orpheus of the Ottawa found, on his arrival in the realm of the dead, "an old man with white hair, whose eyes, though deeply sunk, had a fiery brilliancy. He had a long robe of skins thrown loosely around his shoulders, and a staff in his hands." This man, who, for the rest, extended a warm welcome to the traveller from the land of the living, is afterwards described as "my messenger, who keeps the gate" by the Master of Life, who, himself invisible, makes his voice resound in the realm of the dead.[23] Here, then, is a clear distinction between the ruler of the dead and their guardian, who is represented as a functionary subordinate to the ruler.

The guardian of the other world is generally male, a circumstance that in view of the nature of his work seems quite natural; only among the

---

[21] See above, p. 80.
[22] Le Clercq 1910, 209 sq.
[23] Schoolcraft 1851 I, 321, 323.

Kwakiutl is a woman mentioned as guardian. The guardian is found at the periphery of the realm of the dead, or even outside its limits. Sometimes there is mention of two guardians (Hupa, Yaudanchi Yokuts), or of a series of guardians met successively long before the gates of the other world are reached (Seneca). It is the duty of the guardian to stop the living who try to penetrate to the land of the dead (or to destroy them if they have succeeded in getting there and afterwards try to return to life's domains again). In the exercise of his office he underlines the idea of a difference in kind between the respective domains of life and death. But although he incorporates this idea, the idea itself is maintained even where there is no mention of any guardian: generally it is a natural barrier like the river of death or water that functions as the impassable dividing line between the two incompatible worlds, that of life and that of death.[24] That the figure of the guardian here constitutes a superstructure on a mechanically regulative principle emerges with all desirable clarity if one compares certain Orpheus traditions more closely. The hero in the Sanpoil legend dies automatically when he is conveyed over the river of death. And the first man in the Nisenan myth dies when at the river of death he has spoken to his deceased wife.[25] When in the Thompson tradition the guardian appears simultaneously with the river motif, the mechanical function of disunion is transferred to him. In the narrative we are told how the guardian on the yonder side of death's water tried vainly to persuade the youth who wanted to be united with his mother to refrain from entering the realm of death—"you cannot enter alive to see her, neither can you take her away." But the youth persisted. "Then the man took his body or mortal part away from him, and he entered."[26] It is only natural that when he performs his duty in this way the guardian should come to appear as not only a hindrance, but also malevolent in the Orpheus tradition. For the Orpheus of the Hupa it is a matter of escaping the guardians of the other world, and in this he is successful when he has managed to get them to sleep by magical means.

In this connection the so-called brain-smasher or brain-preserver conception in a couple of Orpheus tales is of interest. In the Ojibway and Huron versions it is said that the guardian deprives travellers to the land of the dead of their brains. Outside of the Orpheus tradition the motif is widespread in the Central and Northeastern Woodland area.[27] Probably

[24] See above, pp. 78 sq.
[25] Concerning the taboo against speaking to the dead, cf. above, p. 71.
[26] Teit 1898, 85.
[27] Hultkrantz 1953, 215 note 42.

the original import of the motif was, as I have elsewhere explained, that the loss of the brain is tantamount to the loss of the memory-soul (ego-soul).[28] That is to say, the deceased definitively forgets this life and has no longing to return to it. The realm of the dead is, as the Sanpoil Indians opine, the land of forgetfulness.[29] And for the living the loss of memory constitutes a guarantee that they will not be visited by ghosts.

There is in general something demoniac about the brain-catching guardian, despite the fact that his actions are calculated to ensure the welfare of the living. In the eschatological conceptions of the Sauk and Fox Indians, however, the guardian is sometimes conceived as solely destructive: the deceased perishes altogether if he is unable to save himself from the "brain-smasher."[30] A typical feature is that the terrible dog who confronts the wanderer is according to the Sauk in the service of the guardian.[31] This more horrible character of the brain-catcher motif is, however, undoubtedly a secondary phenomenon which is not well integrated with the general tendency of the eschatological conceptions.[32] In the Orpheus tradition the motif occurs in its original, meaningful form. The "keeper of the storehouse of brains" in the Ojibway legend comes towards the living woman with his knife, but when he hears her errand he lets her pass. And the brain-keeper of the Huron shows Orpheus the greatest kindness and gives him good advice. In this he reminds us of the ruler of the other world, whom we will now discuss.

In the great majority of cases the supreme representative of the dead is described as a personage who has gained his special position in their community as a consequence of his experience and wisdom, or as a consequence of his power, his position as a supernatural being. If a dead person occupies a respected place in the beyond in virtue of his deeper experience and wisdom, it is understood that he acquired this during his life-time, and that even in his life-time he had therefore reached a social position that he then retains after death. The leader of the realm of the

---

[28] Hultkrantz, op.cit., 215 sq. It is not impossible that the notion has been taken from the practice of trepanning. Hrdlicka does, certainly, state that this was unknown north of Mexico (Hrdlicka 1907, 838); but Professor S. Linné has been kind enough to inform me that it did occur in prehistoric cultures in Alaska, British Columbia, New Mexico, Michigan and Ontario. See also Popham 1954, 204 sqq.

[29] Ray 1942, 233. Cf. Hultkrantz, op.cit., 215.

[30] See, concerning the Fox, Jones 1907 b, 265 sq., 1939, 68; Michelson 1925, 358, 381, 399 sq.; Joffe 1940, 274; concerning the Sauk, Skinner 1923, 35 sq. It is interesting to note that the guardian in Jones is an old woman, Cracker-of-Skulls, but in Joffe the god of death himself, Machi Manitou—according to Joffe an older conception (Joffe, op.cit., 274 note 14). Joffe's conclusion is in accordance with what has been said here earlier concerning the relation between the ruler of the other world and the guardian.

[31] Skinner, op.cit., loc.cit.

[32] Cf. Hultkrantz, op.cit., 215 note 42.

98

dead thus constitutes a replica of the leader in this life.[33] The Orpheus
tradition has several clear examples of this: the leader among the dead
appears as the head of a family (Comanche, Sarcee), a chief (Cowichan,
Pomo, Yokuts, Tübatulabal), "chief ghost" (Blackfoot) or a governor
(Taos). Where he occurs as the head of a family it is in the shape of
Orpheus' father-in-law—the father-in-law exercises the same authority
over his family and his son-in-law in the realm of the dead as he did
during his life-time. Similarly, the "chief" of the other world shows all
the significative features characterizing the chief in the land of the
living, and the "governor" in the Pueblo eschatology constitutes an
exact copy of the town governor in this world.[34]

While the "chief" of the dead constitutes in this way a projection of
the social order to the eschatological picture of the world—an extension
of the culture pattern to the existence beyond death—the leader of the
other world who is equipped with mythological features must be considered in quite a different context, the religio-cosmological. One may
even say that almost all the divinities who serve as rulers in the realm of
the dead are cosmogonic figures: the Supreme Being, the mother-goddess,
the dead twin-brother, the first man. They have all taken part in the great
drama of the inception of the world. This is why they have been placed
as masters of the land of the dead, which according to the mythological
tradition has existed ever since the creation or shortly thereafter.[35]

It is undoubtedly the Creator or the Supreme Being who in a number
of Orpheus traditions is mentioned as the Lord of the Beyond. How this
can be compatible with his rôle as a deity also for the living is a question
which we shall not go into here; I can in this connection only refer to
the in my opinion correct view held by Preuss and Müller, that the
Supreme Being incarnates the cosmic world order, which in the present
case implies that he also has charge of the realm of the dead.[36] When, as
is frequently the case in the Orpheus tradition, this is located in the sky,
where the Supreme Being generally has his residence, he can of course
easily function as a god both for the living and the dead.

It is in the Orpheus traditions from the Great Basin, the region of the

[33] See above, pp. 39 sqq.
[34] See above, pp. 40 sq.
[35] See chap. V: 3.
[36] See Müller 1956, 249 sq., and the literature adduced here. I cannot, however, at
the same time agree with Preuss' and Müller's view that the Supreme Being also com-
prehends mankind and the different objects of existence. At the most, what has been
attained in North America is a so-called emanatistic speculation (see, on this subject,
Hultkrantz, op.cit., 182 sqq.).

Great Lakes and the Southeast (with outcrops in the Plains) that the Supreme Being is mentioned as the ruler in the realm of the dead. We have already pointed out that the Shoshoni Orpheus narratives from the Great Basin are characterized by, inter alia, the fact that the high god, here called "the father" or Wolf, rules the world of the dead.[37] Also the death-god Tipiknits mentioned in a Yokuts version is referred to as "the father."[38] This designation is of course in many primitive religions a common appellation for the Supreme Being.[39] It occurs, too, among the Pawnee, who generally refer to their supreme god as Tirawa atius, the last-mentioned word signifying "father."[40] It is under this name that the divinity in the Pawnee Orpheus legends appears. And here we find a feature typical for the Tirawa cult, that an application to him must be made through the lower gods: through the mediation of the western gods the Orpheus figure prevails upon Tirawa to bring together, though the latter lays down certain conditions, the living and the dead.[41] The Winnebago assume that the supreme god, Earthmaker, has control over the realm of the dead; but, like the Tirawa of the Pawnee, he does not reside in this realm. The same seems to apply to the Ottawa Master of Life, discussed in the foregoing.[42] According to Gregg's Shawnee legend, their Orpheus comes to "the abode of his grandfather—which seems but another name for one of the good spirits."[43] But in the Shawnee versions noted down by C. F. Voegelin and E. Wheeler-Voegelin the place of this male divinity is taken by a female deity, "Our Grand-mother." Now, as the same writers have pointed out, during the last hundred years a change has taken place in the Shawnee pantheon im-plying that, under the probable influence of the Iroquois, a male Supreme Being has been ousted by a previously subordinate female goddess, the "Creator's grandmother" well-known from the whole Northeastern Woodland area (A 31 according to Thompson).[44] It is probable that the god mentioned by Gregg is the original Supreme Being. The Orpheus legend of the Koasati refers to the Supreme Being residing in the realm

[37] See above, p. 52. He is among the Mono "the creator of the present world who departed to make a home for dead people after he had completed this one for the living" (Gayton 1930 a, 78).

[38] Gayton 1930 a, 77. It is interesting to observe that like the Greek Hades, Tipiknits is the name of both the realm of the dead and its ruler (Gayton 1935, 267). Tipiknits thus personifies death.

[39] Cf. Schmidt 1930, 259.

[40] Cf. Dangel 1929, 113 sq.; Fletcher 1904, 216.

[41] Dorsey 1904 b, 76; cf. Fletcher, op.cit., 27.

[42] See above, p. 96.

[43] Gregg 1954, 388.

[44] Voegelin 1944, 370 sqq. Cf. below.

of the dead—i.e. the sky—as "Never-dying"; in the Alabama legend his name is "High-living."

One may possibly also refer to the circle of the Supreme Beings the death-god mentioned in the Nayarit legend, "the keeper of the souls."

A female ruler of the land of the dead, generally known as "The Old Woman," occurs in several Orpheus narratives from both the west coast (Karuk, Wishram) and eastern North America (Seneca, Yuchi). In some versions her character and influence are vaguely described, in others they emerge clearly; and the information we have concerning her justify the inclusion of this "old woman" in the same category with the death-goddesses of the Huron and Shawnee. What we are here confronted with is the conception, which has a wide distribution especially in the agrarian cultures, of the goddess of the earth—"Mother Earth," the mother of men and of vegetation.[45] Her association with the plant-world is well known, and just as the plants grow from her lap, to decay, after their withering, and return there, so, too, human beings are sometimes conceived to be united with her, after death, in her underworld realm. For natural reasons this belief has flourished especially in the agrarian regions, and it has also occurred in North America, though here with the modification that she is not so frequently connected with the underworld, particularly not in the Eastern Woodland area. It is only to be expected that in North America one should find her among the maize-cultivating peoples of north-western Mexico, the Southwest and the Eastern Woodland area; but strangely enough, she is also found among some tribes in northern California and western Oregon.[46] In North America, as in the Old World, the earth and death goddess has lunar mythological associations.

Let us adduce some instances of the occurrence of this deity in the Orpheus tradition. The "grandmother" of the Shawnee was presumably, at an earlier date, the earth-goddess, though this function is no longer so obvious since she has taken the place of the high god. But here and there one does get glimpses of her original nature: we find her as the creator of the maize-woman, "Corn person";[47] she offers the Orpheus men food

[45] Confused with this notion is the goddess of vegetation, in America the Corn Mother, whom we shall meet with later (see chap. IV: 4). Se further Alexander 1916, 289 sq.

[46] Viz, the Yana and Siletz (Sapir & Spier 1943, 284; Dorsey 1889 a, 60). Cf. also the above-mentioned Karuk, who may perhaps be referred to this group, and the Wishram (see below). Among the Eskimo the female ruler of the other world has another character.

[47] Voegelin 1936, 7. The narrative of "the Rescue of Corn" has definite features of the Orpheus tradition (Hatt 1951, 857; cf. below, chap. IV: 4).

in a little clay vessel, but however much they eat, it is never finished;[48] and her figure is reflected in the moon.[49] As has been mentioned, this death-goddess is also what Thompson has referred to as "the Creator's grandmother." This includes her among the mother-goddesses who among the Central Algonquin and some tribes of the Northeast are conceived as mothers or grandmothers of the creative twin-gods (see below).[50] We have met with one of these goddesses in the Nokomis of the Ojibway Indians.[51] Another member of this series is Ataentsic, the Huron ruler over the dead; Orpheus "enters the Cabin of Aataentsic, where he finds that they are indeed dancing for the sake of her health."[52] The Orpheus legend of the Seneca mentions a berry-picking old woman as the "head woman" of the ghosts, "the hostess of the country."[53] It seems probable to me that this old woman is identical with Ataentsic's counterpart among the Iroquois, Awenhai ("Fertile Earth").[54] Farther south the grandmother motif does not occur, but we do find the earth-goddess in the realm of the dead. Among the Yuchi her name is "Old Woman."[55] Curiously enough, the Orpheus legend represents her as the sun,[56] which in other contexts is described as a masculine Supreme Being.[57]

It is as a moon being, on the other hand, that the death-goddess makes her appearance among the Wishram on the west coast: when the Orpheus men—Eagle and Coyote—have seen the dead assembled for dancing in a large underground house, the goddess rises up and swallows the moon, so that is becomes dark; at dawn she vomits it up again.[58] In the Wasco myth the same trick is performed by a male or female supervisor of the dead who is said to be a big frog.[59] Among the Yakima, who live in the

---

[48] Voegelin, op.cit., 5. We find the motif in several Orpheus legends, and it is sometimes connected with the persons Orpheus meets on the way. See: Jenness 1938, 98 (Sarcee); Speck 1909, 145, Wagner 1931, 86 (Yuchi); Swanton 1929, 142 (Alabama). Cf. also below, p. 112, and p. 175.
[49] Voegelin, op.cit., 4, 6; Trowbridge 1939, 5, 40.
[50] Interestingly enough, the same motif occurs also in northern California, i.e. in the region where in the foregoing we have shown the existence of female death-divinities (Thompson 1946, 310; Voegelin in Leach 1949 I, 260).
[51] See above, p. 95.
[52] JR X, 151.
[53] Curtin & Hewitt 1918 II, 571.
[54] See the comparison between the respective cosmologies of the Iroquois and the Huron in Hewitt 1910, especially 720, 722.
[55] Speck 1909, 108.
[56] Speck, op.cit., 145. The sun occurs as ruler for the dead (at least for deceased persons belonging to certain social groups) here and there among Mexican tribes, among the Indians of the Southwest and the Eastern Woodland area, and also in some quarters on the west coast.
[57] Speck, op.cit., 102 sq., 106.
[58] Curtis 1911 VIII, 127; cf. Kunike 1926, 24.
[59] Spier & Sapir 1930, 278.

vicinity, it is Coyote who in the myth swallows the moon, so that in the resulting darkness he and Eagle may carry away some of the dead in a box.[60] It is obvious that in this region the Orpheus myth has been fitted into a lunar mythological complex in which there was probably to begin with a close association between the moon and the earth and death goddess.[61]

We find the notion that one of the so-called twin gods functions as the ruler of the land of the dead in a couple of Orpheus legends from the region of the Great Lakes and northern California. It has its background in the myth of the two twins, the good and the bad, who together created the world or gave it its institutions—a myth which constitutes a particular form of the old myth of dual creators.[62] The myth of the twin brothers belongs chiefly to the agrarian cultures, but it also occurs outside these, as we found above in our discussion of the grandmother motif often connected with this myth in North America. In North American mythology one comes across the twin myth among the Iroquois-Huron, where the two twins are each other's ethical opposites,[63] among the Central Algonquin, where the two are represented as ethically equivalent, i.e. as good beings (although the one of them, the culture hero proper, has definite trickster features),[64] among the Indians of the Southwest, where they are regarded as war-like culture heroes and slayers of monsters,[65] and, finally, among the Modoc.[66] We have earlier found an echo of the mythic twin motif in a tale tradition that has been widespread in eastern North America and has among the Assiniboin been blended with the Orpheus legend.[67] A dominant element in the twin myth of the Central

[60] Lyman 1904, 248 sq. In the Wasco myth, on the other hand, Coyote slays Frog, devours the moon and then spits it out in order to be able to see when he and Eagle capture the dead. In the Wishram myth, too, Coyote behaves in the same way, but the dead are not caught until dawn—so that here Coyote's behaviour is unmotivated.

[61] Cf. also the interpretations below, p. 123 note 24, and p. 178.

[62] We are here not called upon to give a detailed account of the lively discussion that has been carried on concerning the twin motif. Cf., however, Rendel Harris' older studies on the subject (Harris 1906).

[63] Through influences from the Iroquoian peoples twin myths occur with the same kind of dualism among the northern Algonquin (Micmac, Malecite), Delaware and Dakota. See Dixon 1909, 1 sqq., van Deursen 1931, 98, 100 sq., 184 sq., Fisher 1946, 229, Müller 1956, 90 sq., 197.

[64] The Central Algonquin here referred to are the Cree, Ojibway, Menomini, Pottawatomi, Mascoutens, Fox and Sauk. Cf. Müller, op.cit., 198 sqq.

[65] The reference here is to a number of Pueblo Indians (the Indians in Taos, Zuni and Hopi), the south-western Athapascans (Navajo, Apache) and Pima-Papago. One may probably include also the Kiowa on the South Plains.

[66] The majority of the mythologies mentioned here are described and analysed in van Deursen, op.cit. (see his table of contents). See also Alexander 1916, 295 sq., Thompson 1929, 277 sq., Fisher, op.cit., 229 sqq., 240 sq., and Wheeler-Voegelin in Leach 1950 II, 1135 sq.

[67] See above, pp. 52 sq. Cf. also Müller, op.cit., 165.

Algonquin is that the brother of the culture-forming twin, here called Wolf,[68] is drowned through the instigation of evil beings, after which he becomes the master of the other world and the dead. This is the death-god who appears in the Ojibway Orpheus legend under the name of Djibweabuth of Wolf, and who is said to be the grandson of the moon-goddess Nokomis and brother of the culture hero, Nanibush.[69] It is prob-able that the "old man" mentioned in the Menomini legend as regent in the land of the dead is identical with Wolf, who also among these Indians is the brother of the culture hero; for the Menomini do not know of any other ruler of the dead.[70] In the Orpheus myth of the Modoc Indians, too, we glimpse the brother of the culture hero, here known as Wus-Kumush, ruler of the dead.[71]

The dead twin-god was the first to descend to the land of shades, and for this reason he became its ruler. In some quarters the first man or his wife has become the regent of the dead in the same way: at the same time as through his death he has set the basic pattern for human life that must be followed by all subsequent generations of men he has become the pro-totype for the dead, i.e. the supreme representative for the dead.[72] The conception of the first man as the master in the other world is not wide-spread in North America,[73] but it occurs in the Orpheus myths of the Navajo and N'isenan. In this connection it should be borne in mind that the Orpheus myth, to be precise, describes how the first man or woman becomes the ruler in the realm of the dead; the Orpheus myth is in other words associated with the personal experiences of the first human beings. According to the Navajo myth it is the first dead woman who becomes the ruler in the realm of the dead; her husband tries in vain to bring her back to the upper world, the world of the living.[74] And the Orpheus

[68] Also among the northern Algonquin the brother of the culture hero is called Wolf. One asks oneself, for the rest, if there is any connection with the Shoshoni Creator, Wolf, whose brother Coyote has the character of trickster.

[69] Jenness 1935, 108 sq.

[70] See Hoffman 1890, 249, 1896, 73, 115; Skinner 1913, 86, 1920, 103 sqq., 1921, 45.

[71] Curtin 1912, 43, 46 sqq.

[72] Cf. Tylor 1871 II, 282.

[73] In North America the first man appears as the ruler of the dead among the Navajo and Nisenan (see the continuation above) and among the Winnebago, where it is believed that the first in the clan to die functions as chief of the clan members in the other world (Radin 1909, 312). Schmidt's opinion, that the first man among the Salish peoples is the master of the dead, seems to be without foundation (Schmidt 1933, 129). Outside North America one finds the first man as ruler of the dead among, inter alia, the Itelm (Steller 1926, 272).

[74] Haile 1942, 411 sqq., 420. The first dead woman, "woman speaker," is not formally identical with "First Woman," but she does nevertheless belong to the same generation of primaeval beings. For the rest, the Navajo conceptions of the primaeval era and the first death vary from locality to locality and are rather confused. See Matthews 1897,

myth of the Nisenan tells how the wife of the first man, the first dead person, betook herself to "the dance-house of the ghosts," followed by her inconsolable husband. But he died himself, and went to the land of the spirits, where he became "a good and great spirit."[75] This, probably, is to be interpreted to mean that he now has charge of the dead.[76]

All these cosmogonic beings who function as rulers in the other world are in the Orpheus tradition conceived as rather benevolent beings—the great exception is the goddess of the Navajo; but she is of course also identical with the woman, essentially changed by death, whom Orpheus tries to recover. In general, the narratives in the main line of the Orpheus tradition relate how the exalted ruler first asks in wonder who the living man is, or how he has come there, to sympathize resolutely with him, subsequently, and help him, if possible, to realize his goal—even if this must be done behind the backs of the dead or cause them unpleasantness. We shall soon see examples of this.[77]

Very different are the descriptions of the potentate of the dead in the independent Orpheus tradition ("the sea-coast form") among the Indians of the Northwest Coast. Here he is a malevolent monster, who has for his own pleasure stolen the hunter's wife from the world of living men. But he is not—and the point must be stressed—a ruler of the dead in the ordinary sense. His figure betrays who he is. The Tsimshian and Haida describe him as the "monster," "killerwhale," "blackfish"; the Sechelt refer to him as the "thresher." In a Tsimshian legend we are told that he is "the monster of Qwawk," chief of "the supernatural beings of Qwawk."[78] In another Tsimshian legend it is clearly stated that he is "the Killer-Whale master," surrounded by killer-whales.[79] Similarly, the Haida legend declares that the monster is "the king of the Scannahs"[80] —the latter are the killer-whales.[81] In a third Tsimshian legend, in connection with the pursuit by the submarine beings of the hunter who has recovered his wife, we are told that "All these pursuers were Blackfishes, and the slaves were their captives who had been taken by the great

77 sq., 220; Wyman, Hill & Osanai 1942, 35; Spencer 1947, 108 sq.; Reichard 1950 I, 41 sq.; O'Bryan 1956, 31.
  [75] Powers 1877, 340.
  [76] Later notes concerning the Nisenan eschatology do not mention the first man, but the vague data communicated indicate that the old belief is now decaying (Beals 1933, 380 sq.; Voegelin 1942, 148 sq.).
  [77] See below, pp. 118 sqq.
  [78] Barbeau 1953, 297.
  [79] Barbeau, op.cit., 271.
  [80] Barbeau 1950 I, 284.
  [81] Barbeau 1953, 255.

Blackfish."[82] There can be no doubt but that the ruler in animal shape, whether killer-whale or blackfish, is identical with the guardian of these marine animals.[83] As has been pointed out above, that he has become the ruler of the dead—i.e. of the drowned—is only a secondary development.[84] His indifference and even hostility to human beings thus becomes quite understandable.

In the Orpheus tradition the ruler or guardian of the dead is the figure that plays, by the side of the two main personages, the most important rôle. Yet, when he is represented as a divinity of the type Supreme Being, he is only in a slight degree the prototype for the dead he has in his care. The very fact that he must outwit or directly counteract the dead to be able to help Orpheus indicates his essential difference to them. The properties characterizing ghosts are rarely found in their guardians and rulers.

The majority of the Orpheus traditions make it quite clear that it is not this monumental figure, but the dead as a collective who in the other world offer resistance to Orpheus. The chief reason for their doing so would appear to be that they represent other interests than the living human being; the whole of their existence is so otherwise, so essentially different. The narratives give concrete instances of this. We shall give below a selection of the special features characterizing, according to the Orpheus tradition, the dead and their world. In principle, of course, these do not differ from what we find in eschatological religious material of other kinds, popular notions and memorates.[85] In the Orpheus tales there is nothing to indicate any other source for their descriptions of the dead than religious belief; and nothing in these descriptions seems to favour the assumption of any notion of the dead that should be typical only for the Orpheus tradition.[86] The regional differences in the con-

---

[82] Barbeau, op.cit., 283. In all Orpheus tales of the "sea-coast form" Orpheus is assisted by the slaves he has liberated (in the Haida version, Barbeau 1950 I, 288, these are Raven and Crow).

[83] Concerning the conception of the animal guardian (the "master" of the animals) in North America, see Hultkrantz 1953, 497 sqq.

[84] See above, pp. 46 sq.

[85] This comparative material cannot be communicated here.

[86] Possibly, however, one may here refer to the episode of the dance of the dead, which occurs in the majority of Orpheus traditions all over the continent, as a typical element in this narrative—although as an expression for the happy character of the realm of the dead such dances are very common also in other eschatological descriptions. Also in the Orpheus tales the dances testify in a way to the blissful character of the other world, except in the Huron legend, in which we are told that the dance was arranged to cure Ataentsic, who is ill. Concerning the real import of the dance, see further below, p. 124.

ception of the dead that one may find in the Orpheus tradition tally with the differences in the religious material outside this tradition.[87]

The peculiarities attaching to the dead and their world are, as we have said above, in the main only evident for the living.[88] The dead themselves are presumed not to notice anything strange in their appearance or their circumstances.[89] Rather is it the truth that the dead, as we shall soon see, regard the living as curious, inhuman beings. The world of death is topsy-turvy for the living, just as the world of the living is topsy-turvy for the dead.[90] Only the chief of the dead, and perhaps in some cases Eurydice herself, is aware that it is the world of the dead which is—in the last analysis—the only topsy-turvy world, a sham world. "This is a bad country," says the Tachi Yokuts' ruler in the realm of the dead; and he adds, turning towards the newly arrived deceased: "You must stay here. You cannot go back. You are worthless now."[91] And the regent of the dead among the Tübatulabal exclaims to Orpheus: "Your wife is bad."[92]

But it is in the first place the living who see the topsy-turvyness and wryness in the existence of the ghosts. The appearance of the dead, their form of life, their surroundings, everything, despite its resemblance to our existence, is nevertheless so strange, so opposed to all that we are accustomed to. Not least does this apply to the outer shape of the dead. They appear in the queerest shapes, especially when they are passive, when they are sleeping or resting: the ghosts of the Quinault are skeleton beings that hoot like owls;[93] the ghosts of the Chehalis, in the day-time, look like heaps of unrelated skulls and bones, that roll around and utter "ko-ko-ko";[94] when passive, the Shasta dead look like white ash[95] or like pieces of charcoal.[96] But, as is always the case with the dead, the con-

---

[87] See further chap. V: 1.
[88] See above, p. 93.
[89] There are, however, a few exceptions. According to the Sanpoil narrative, the dead person perceives both other deceased persons and himself as skeletons (Boas 1917 a, 113).
[90] Cf. Holmberg 1925.
[91] Kroeber 1907 c, 217.
[92] Voegelin 1935, 205.
[93] Farrand 1902, 101.
[94] Adamson 1934, 22, 295, 298 sq., 349. A humoristic element in the narrative depicts the trickster Bluejay kicking the skulls about. The motif is also popular in the Orpheus narratives of the Snuqualmi, Puyallup and Skopamish (Ballard 1929, 128, 129, 130, 133). See further below, p. 122.
[95] Dixon 1910, 21.
[96] Voegelin 1947, 52. Cf. the Yuchi: glowing coals are attached to the legs of the dead (Speck 1909, 146). Among the Maricopa the dead are in their fourth existence believed to become pieces of charcoal (Spier 1933, 298), and among the Yuma the deceased are transformed finally into "bits of cinder" (Forde 1931, 180). The Siberian Yakut conceive one of their souls as a piece of charcoal (Paulson Ms, after Seroshevski.)

ceptions oscillate between massiveness and incorporeality.[97] The latter is the tendency with the Karuk notion, that the dead are boneless beings —they must doff everything they have had with them, clothes and bones, before entering the realm of the dead.[98] In the Pomo legend the dead are represented as diffuse "shades."[99] In several narratives it is stated that the dead are for the most part invisible (this is the case among the Sarcee, Shahaptin, Gabrielino, Serrano, Winnebago, Micmac, Huron, Yuchi etc.); though sometimes, as in the case of Coyote among the Shahaptin, one may hear them joke and give themselves over to mirth.[100] Several Orpheus narratives describe how the dead are able to change from visibility to invisibility (see below). A contrary process is described in the Sarcee legend: Orpheus' father-in-law assembles all the shades, and through four dances they are transformed successively to human beings.[101]

Perhaps the distance of the dead from the living is still more clearly manifested in the order of their lives; the distance between the two groups is here complete, the two forms of life emerge as diametrically opposed. For in many places the dead turn day into night, and night into day. In the day-time have disappeared without trace, or they are sleeping in their lodges (when they appear in the strange shapes described above). But as soon as evening comes on they enter the dancing lodge to devote themselves to their darling occupation: singing and dancing—and now they are more reminiscent of human beings, though they are often conceived as owning a brittle, almost immaterial substance—it must not be forgotten that they are spirits. This dancing lasts the whole night; the Wishram and the Wasco suppose it to take place in complete darkness, i.e. with the lights of heaven extinguished. But when morning comes they are scattered: their shapes dissolve until they merge into nothingness, or again, they are transformed to bones and the like. Descriptions of this kind enter in the Orpheus traditions from the whole of North America.[102]

It is not, however, only when the sun rises that the dead, like the Scandinavian trolls and ghosts all over the world, vanish into air. The same thing occurs when the dead are startled or feel themselves threatened. One may, certainly, wonder how it can come about that supernatural

---

[97] See Hultkrantz, op.cit., 395 sq.
[98] Kroeber 1946, 14 sq.
[99] Loeb 1926, 292 sq.
[100] Boas, op.cit., 179.
[101] Jenness 1938, 98. Here the leader of the dead initiates Orpheus in the so-called ghost dance of the Sarcee (cf. Gayton 1935, 277).
[102] Instances from the Sarcee, Stalo, Yakima, Wishram, Wasco, Modoc, Yokuts, Serrano, Navajo, Taos Indians, Winnebago, Huron. The Kalapuya ghosts are said to dance on their heads (Frachtenberg, Gatschet & Jacobs 1945, 203).

beings are able to feel fear, especially as the fear is of Orpheus, the representative of the world of the living. For the dead have supernatural powers which the living generally lack, they are living in their own well-guarded land, and they are so many against the lonely visitor from the land of the living—indeed, several Orpheus traditions declare that the dead in their villages are far more numerous than are the living in their villages.[103] Nonetheless, the fear of Orpheus experienced by the dead is graphically and realistically described. When the Seneca woman who has lost her husband finds him again in the realm of the dead and tries to grasp him, the ghosts flee in wild panic.[104] The Stalo and Karuk traditions tell how the dead are dissolved and vanish when the living touch them. And when the Huron hero entered the dancing lodge of the dead "the souls were so startled at the sight of the man that they vanished in a moment."[105]

To explain this peculiar behaviour on the part of the dead one may refer to various circumstances, of which especially the following three deserve attention.[106]

1. In the first place, of course, the idea of the vanishing of the dead as soon as one seizes them is a direct reflex of the realization that they are unreal, fictive creations in a fictive dream-world. And several other facts, some already mentioned, point in the same direction: the experience of the nightly dance of the dead and the bleached skulls in the daylight reflects the contrast between the nocturnal vision and the reality of day; Orpheus' passive beholding of the activities of the dead and his impotence to intervene, from his isolation, in their doings[107] interpret the powerlessness of the dreamer in certain dream-experiences. Finally, one may mention the remarkable circumstance, already referred to, that the living person—in order to be able to perceive the world of the dead as similar to his own—must move through the other world with closed eyes. As soon as he opens his eyes, the leaky boat he is in begins to take water, and the children he has observed are transformed into heaps of bones.[108] Not only the dead, but the entire realm of the dead is a sham world. The

---

[103] See, e.g., Curtin, op.cit., 42 (Modoc), Dorsey 1904 a, 302, 307.
[104] Curtin & Hewitt 1918, 572.
[105] Hill-Tout 1904 b, 340, Harrington 1932, 33 sq., JR X, 151.
[106] According to one of the Shasta narratives, the dead were terrified when they smelt the odour of the fire of wild-parsnip that Coyote had made (Dixon, op.cit., 19). We have here evidently to do with a purifying fire of the kind with which the living used to protect themselves against the maleficent influence of ghosts. To this end the Shasta generally burned the root of *Helianthus cusickii* (Holt 1946, 324).
[107] See, e.g., Parsons 1940, 24 sq. (Taos).
[108] Curtis 1911 VII, 96 (Kalispel); Adamson 1934, 22 (Chehalis). See also above, p. 76.

pueblo of the deceased Taos Indians proves in daylight to be a group of rabbit burrows,[109] and the Navajo Indian who had entered the other world "beheld nothing but rags and rubbish on the walls in place of the jewels and fine robes which had adorned them when he first leaped down there."[110]

2. If we return to the point of departure for our reasoning we can constate that a second motive for the fear of the living felt by the dead is to seek in the essential difference of the living from the dead. That is to say, the horror of the dead experienced by the living has in the reverse direction been transferred to the dead. For them the living person appears as a ghost—a corpse or a spook, and for this reason he is shunned.[111] In several Orpheus traditions it is said that the dead are unpleasantly touched by the smell of the living person—he smells so disagreeable that he is avoided, rejected, or fleed.[112] In the Wichita legend, certainly, we are told that the living person has another smell, and he is therefore not noticed;[113] but this is not typical. On the contrary, Orpheus stinks, and he is "raw,"[114] he is a "ghost."[115] According to the Stalo legend, he must be washed with "strong medicine" in the other world, so that the dead shall not disappear.[116] The procedure probably corresponds to the washing of the corpse.[117] Just as in their spiritual form the dead are invisible for the living, so Orpheus is sometimes invisible to the ghosts. According to the Twana, the dead do not see him, but they perceive his smell. The Orpheus tale of the Twana also tells us that according to the belief of the ghosts it was the newly fetched deceased who "still had a taint of earthly life upon him; and they decided that it would be necessary to have a medicine-man cure this newcomer of the sickness which those on earth call life. But it was the living man they smelled."[118] The Orpheus of the Zuni Indians suffered from not being addressed, or even noticed

[109] Parsons, op.cit., 27.
[110] Haile 1942, 413.
[111] It also happens that he is commiserated with. The ghosts of the Modoc "felt sorry for him that he was not dead" (Curtin, op.cit., 42).
[112] Instances from the Stalo, Twana, Pomo, Yokuts, Gabrielino, Blackfoot, Seneca, Yuchi.
[113] Dorsey, op.cit., 307.
[114] Curtin, op.cit., 42 (Modoc); cf. chap. I: 1, above (Comanche).
[115] Gayton 1935, 271 (Navajo).
[116] Hill-Tout, op.cit., 340. The chief of the dead among the Blackfoot had to burn "sweet pine" to get rid of the smell (Grinnell 1912, 129).
[117] Duff 1952, 94; cf. Barnett 1955, 217. There is still the possibility, however, that the legend is alluding to a custom obtaining among the living and consisting of smearing persons with medicine to enable them to resist the dead. In one of the Orpheus legends of the Pawnee an episode is mentioned which obviously has this explanation (Dorsey 1904 b, 77 and 343 note 133).
[118] Curtis 1913 IX, 164.

at all, in the other world; possibly his isolation was due to the same cause as in the preceding case: that no-one in the realm of the dead could see him.[119]

It is easy to see that with the reverse order of things obtaining in the realm of the dead the living person is not desired there—he for the dead is what a dead person is for the living. Several Zuni versions of the Orpheus tradition tell us that Orpheus was informed by his deceased wife that he could not enter the other world because he was not dead. "You are living, you cannot go."[120] In both the Zuni and the Taos narratives the Orpheus heroes are forced passively to witness what goes on in the realm of death from outside.[121] And in the Shahaptin narrative concerning Coyote's journey to the other world it is said that the dead "made him sleep at some distance from the others."[122] According to one of the Yokuts versions, Orpheus was at first forbidden to enter the realm of the dead. But when he requested to be let in the guards informed the chief of the fact, and against the recommendation of the guards the chief granted his request.[123] The Blackfoot Orpheus succeeded in entering the other world with the aid of the old woman who dwelt behind a ridge in its vicinity. She brought him an escort of deceased relatives, who assured his entry into the other world.[123 a]

If, in spite of all, Orpheus manages to get into the realm of the dead, he is looked upon with disfavour by the dead. The dead Serrano woman was well received by her deceased relatives, "but they did not like the man for he was not dead."[124] In the case of the Winnebago their dead—including Orpheus' deceased wife—did their best to provoke him to a rash deed, so that his expedition might fail.[125] When the Blackfoot hero installed himself in the realm of the dead the ghosts tried to scare him away "with all kinds of fearful sights and sounds," but these had no effect on him. And the leader of the dead said: "It is a fearful thing that you have come here. It is very likely that you will never go away. There never was a person here before."[125 a] The Modoc ghosts hated

[119] Benedict 1935 II, 157.
[120] Benedict, op.cit., loc.cit., and 134, 290.
[121] Benedict, op.cit., loc.cit., and Parsons 1940, 24. Can Orpheus' isolation be a consequence of his not having been initiated in the esoteric societies of the dead? As we know, the Pueblo peoples have several secret societies, an element in their social structure which also persists after death.
[122] Boas, op.cit., 178.
[123] Kroeber 1907 c, 217.
[123 a] Grinnell, op.cit., 128.
[124] Benedict 1926, 8.
[125] Radin 1926, 35, 36.
[125 a] Grinnell, op.cit., 128 sq.

the Orpheus figure, Kumush, because he was not dead, and every bone in the heaps of bones rose up and tried to kill him.[126] We shall see later that the resistance of the dead was the chief cause of Orpheus' quick dismissal from the other world.[127]

Against this background it is not surprising that at the gate of the beyond the hero of the Ottawa had to leave his body—together with his bow and his arrows, his medicine bag and his dog. This reminds one of the way in which the Karuk, as we have pointed out above, were forced to leave their bones behind before entering the realm of the dead,[128] or of the way in which the Thompson Indian had to abandon his body, i.e. die.[129] But the Ottawa Indian was able, when he left the other world, to put on his body again. Schoolcraft has obviously coloured his account of the journey of the Ottawa Indian into the realm of death with a little fantasy of his own when he writes that "the freed traveller bounded forward as if his feet had suddenly been endowed with the power of wings."[130]

3. As a third essential cause of the ghosts' aversion to Orpheus one may mention his possession of supernatural power. No-one, of course, can contest that the dead, too, possess such power; they are spirits, they can change their shape, make people ill, paralyse them and so forth. Indeed, the whole of the world in which they live is supernatural. One night in the land of the dead is one year among the living, we are told in one of the Karuk tales.[131] As has already been mentioned, the appearance of the realm of the dead varies radically between day and night. And the objects in it have magic properties: the Twana dead possess a canoe which moves with the fleetness of the wind and without touching the water under it.[132] Reference may here also be made of the food miracles mentioned in a couple of Orpheus narratives: however much one may eat or drink in the other world, the supply of food and drink does not become less.[133] And so forth. And this notwithstanding, the dead fear the living intruder on account of his supernatural power.

[126] Curtin 1912, 43 sq.
[127] See below, pp. 118 sqq.
[128] See above, pp. 107 sq. In these measures one is tempted to see parallels to the brain-preserver's taking over of the consciousness of the deceased in Central Algonquin eschatology (see above, pp. 97 sq.).
[129] Teit 1898, 85; see above, p. 97.
[130] Schoolcraft 1851 I, 321 sq. Orpheus is here also said to walk straight through objects.
[131] Harrington 1932, 34.
[132] Curtis, op.cit., 164.
[133] See Gayton, op.cit., 268 (Yokuts), and above, pp. 101 sq.

That Orpheus has such power cannot be doubted. Where the figure is the culture hero-trickster, as among certain north-western tribes, or a divinity, as among certain southern agrarian peoples, the matter is of course obvious. And the same is the case where, as among the Carrier, he is assumed to be a shaman, or where he is accompanied by guardian spirits, which, as we have had occasion to observe, occurs in a number of cases. But the best sign of Orpheus' supernatural power resides in the fact that as one of the living he succeeds in accomplishing the difficult journey to the realm of the dead, in entering this realm and remaining there for a time, and then returns home unharmed—which is of course the theme in the majority of Orpheus traditions.[134] To this must be added —though it is of secondary importance—that in the other world Orpheus is able to do things which are beyond the capacity of the dead. This is exemplified by e.g. the tale of the deer-hunt of the Serrano Indian Orpheus in the other world. He heard the dead call out that the game was coming in his direction, but he saw nothing. "Then he looked again, and he could see two little black beetles (such as the Serrano used to eat) and he knocked them over, and these were the deer the dead people hunted. And when all the people had come up, they praised him for his hunting."[135] In the Wichita legend, too, the living person impresses the dead by his skill in hunting.[136]

After this survey of the description of the other world and its inhabitants, the guardian, the ruler and the dead themselves in the Orpheus tradition, we may pass on to a short account of Orpheus' adventures in the realm of the dead, and especially of his relation to his deceased beloved whom he wishes to take thence.

As should have emerged from the foregoing, on entering the land of the dead Orpheus meets with troubles and difficulties at the very outset. What he needs to do is to pass the final frontiers between the worlds of life and death, marked by the river of death or (and) the guardian of the other world;[137] and he likewise needs to gain the support of the ruler of that realm (or of the dead themselves),[138] and to get a permit to stay there, at least for a time.[139] If he is successful with regard to all

[134] Concerning the possibilities of a living person to sojourn in the realm of the dead, see Hultkrantz, op.cit., 456.
[135] Benedict 1928. Concerning the food in the realm of the dead, see above, and below, pp. 114 sq.
[136] Dorsey 1904 a, 303.
[137] See above, p. 97.
[138] See above, p. 105.
[139] See above, p. 111.

this, he is immediately confronted with fresh difficulties. Above all, he must in the sequel adopt particular precautionary measures. These are intended to secure his stay in the land of the dead, his contact with and recovery of his dead relative, the journey home with her to the land of the living, and the stay here with her during the first period after their arrival home. To characterize the ritual rules of conduct here in question I use the term *taboo*, defined as follows: "Taboo are all actions, circumstances, persons, objects, etc., which owing to their dangerousness fall outside the normal everyday categories of existence."[140] As regards the Orpheus tradition, it is possible to constate that the taboos referring to the stay in the realm of the dead are in general observed without other sanction than those of current social convention, whereas the other taboos are for the most part sanctioned by the dead or, still more frequently, by their ruler or guardian. In a particularly high degree does the latter apply to the taboos imposed upon Orpheus during and after his journey home.

The particular caution Orpheus must observe in the realm of the dead is connected with the fact that he must as far as possible avoid, through contact with the dead and through touching their possessions, being involved in the sphere of death and thus risking his life. We find here the same fear of infection (contagious magic) as occurs among the living in connection with a death. In one of the Skidi Pawnee Orpheus legends we are told that people did not dare either to touch or to speak to the dead when on one occasion they were actually confronted with them.[141] The Mono Orpheus was warned by the ruler of the dead, Wolf, "not to participate in any dance in the land of the departed."[142] But above all, Orpheus must refrain from tasting the food of the dead, something which is of course an actual part of the sphere of death. Naturally it is often possible to interpret Orpheus' aversion to eating the food of the ghosts as pure disgust at the nature of the fare, for the food of the dead is not always attractive. The Carrier Orpheus was offered "dried flesh of frogs and snakes and lizards."[143] Moreover, in consequence of the reversed order obtaining in the realm of the dead, what is for the dead a tasty fare may appear to the living disgusting food. We have already seen how the deer of the Serrano ghosts appear to Orpheus as black beetles (though whether these are considered appetizing or not I do not know).[144] The salmon that

[140] Hultkrantz 1954, 51.
[141] Dorsey 1904 b, 77.
[142] Gifford 1923, 341.
[143] Jenness 1934, 144.
[144] See above, p. 113.

could be caught among the ghosts of the Quinault were "a lot of knots,"[145] while among the Humptulip such salmon are described as "a lot of bark," though they tasted good even to a living being if he kept his eyes shut while he was eating.[146] And so forth. The Carrier legend, however, relates that the food in the other world sometimes appeared better than it actually was. The dead, Orpheus was warned by a little old woman, "will seem to give you huckleberries, but the huckleberries will be dead men's eyes."[147]

In the cases in which Orpheus refrains from tasting the meals of the dead or their food at all, however, the decisive reason for his behaviour is stated to be his fear of otherwise becoming entangled in the world of the dead. This caution is sometimes instilled by warnings from higher, helpfully disposed beings. The above-mentioned old woman in the Carrier legend warned Orpheus in this way, and she added: "Warn your wife also not to eat, for otherwise she will never return with you to the land above."[148] This must be regarded as indirect evidence that the wife was not completely incorporated in the sphere of death—an extremely interesting fact when one comes to investigate the origin of the Orpheus tradition. In the Tlingit legend (the "inland form"), on the other hand, it is the ravished wife who charges her husband not to accept the food offered him by the dead. "Don't eat that," she says, "if you eat that you will never get back."[149] She herself is dead, yet, as the narrative shows, is nevertheless able to return to life. Among the Twana, again, it is Orpheus who warns his deceased comrade against eating the ghost food, with the motivation that he will otherwise not be able to escape from the realm of the dead.[150] And of the Serrano Orpheus it is stated that "special food had to be always cooked for him, for he could not eat what dead people live on."[151] What is here doubtless meant is that eating the food of the dead would prevent Orpheus from returning to life.[152]

Also in his relations with the deceased person he wishes to restore to life, Orpheus must observe definite taboos. In this connection it must

[145] Farrand 1902, 101.
[146] Adamson 1934, 295.
[147] Jenness, op.cit., loc.cit.
[148] Jenness, op.cit., loc.cit. Even on the journey to the other world the Orpheus of the Carrier refrained from eating the berries growing along the path, "for he was still alive"; and he also prevented his wife from eating them (op.cit., 143). The episode is reminiscent of the so-called wild-strawberry temptation in the Orpheus traditions of the Eastern Woodland area: a living person is forever lost if he eats of the big, appetizing strawberries growing along the route to the other world. See Gayton, op.cit., 274 sq.
[149] Swanton 1909, 249.
[150] Curtis, op.cit., 164.
[151] Benedict 1926, 8.
[152] Concerning the food taboos in the afterlife, see also Thompson 1929, 338.

be borne in mind that his partner generally belongs to the other world. This is apparent in her appearance, and also in her behaviour. The Indian Eurydice, like other dead people, appears in the most various shapes, which we have already seen exemplified.[153] Sometimes she is invisible, sometimes a transparent shade, sometimes, again, she appears in the shape of an animal, and so on. And her ability to change her shape in some cases prevents, and in others facilitates her return as a living human being (see below). "She is in spirit. She is not in her body," we are told of the dead woman in one of the Pawnee Orpheus legends.[154] In one Karuk legend the dead person—in this case a man—is complaining that he cannot return to the living. "I cannot, for I have no bones; only thin elder stalks." The living persons who had come to the other world to fetch him tried to seize him from behind, but in vain; "he was like nothing, for he was boneless."[155] And in the Tachi Yokuts Orpheus narrative the chief of the dead describes Eurydice's nature in the following words to her mourning husband: "We have only your wife's soul (ilit).[156] She has left her bones with her body."[157] This notwithstanding, Orpheus receives permission from the chief to sleep with his wife. But when the night is over and he wakes up in the morning he sees that she has been transformed into an oaken log. The chief then exclaims: "You see that we cannot make your wife as she was. She is no good now."[158] It is characteristic that the Haida Orpheus was not able to recognize his drowned wife—so changed was she.[159]

In her (or his) behaviour with the surviving partner the dead person shows a strange indifference, which sometimes turns into actual hostility, more rarely into friendship and love. The wife feels rather indifferent to her husband. The conversation between the chief of the dead and the newly arrived deceased Yokuts woman leaves no room for doubt in the point. She is not interested whether her husband comes to the realm of the dead or not; and in answer to the chief's question as to whether she would like to return to life with her husband she only says: "I do not think so."[160] This listlessness only rarely gives place to stronger feelings, and

[153] See above, p. 89.
[154] Dorsey 1904 b, 72.
[155] Kroeber 1946, 15.
[156] Concerning the soul beliefs of the Yokuts, see Hultkrantz 1953, 139.
[157] Kroeber 1907 c, 217. Cf. also the Modoc myth (Curtin 1912, 43).
[158] Kroeber, op.cit., 217 sq. Cf. also above, p. 107.
[159] Barbeau 1953, 256.
[160] Kroeber, op.cit., 217. Cf. the following from the Telumni Yokuts: "She was not eager to go back with him and discouraged his efforts to obtain her" (Gayton, op.cit., 268).

then it is chiefly the hostile feelings which are uppermost. The Taos woman prevents her husband's entry into the realm of the dead;[161] the Navajo woman frightens him away;[162] and the Winnebago wife tries to thwart her husband's plans to save her by provoking him to rash acts calculated to infringe the taboos imposed upon him: "if you are going to be indifferent to me, why did you come here?" she exclaims to him.[163] Friendliness to the mourning husband is as a rule shown only in lending him a certain assistance to reach the realm of the dead—assistance that is for the most part rather inadequate and given without much interest. In the best case the wifely love is manifested in her obtaining the permission of the dead for him to stay in their land.[164]

In this indifference and emotional coldness to those she once loved the essential change that has taken place in the deceased finds its adequate expression. She now belongs to another world than that in which she formerly lived. She has shifted her allegiance to another interest group, her solicitude is now for the dead—the deceased parents, the deceased children—and not for her husband and other living members of her family. The Orpheus of the Lipan Apache was not even recognized by his deceased daughter in the other world.[165] And the deceased Ojibway Indian who was restored to life wept when he had to leave the dead.[166] In the great majority of cases, as we shall see, the dead person puts up a resistance when the journey home is mentioned. In the Comanche legend, however, the feelings of the deceased wife were divided;[167] and in the Tlingit legend the deceased woman makes a completely human impression: she weeps at having landed up among the dead, she protects her husband from the dangers of the other world, and she is eager to get away from it: "Let us go right away."[168] But this tale is a striking exception.

We now fully understand Orpheus' difficulties with the deceased loved one he wishes to bring home. She belongs to another world, she is another kind of being; and this means that her resistance to the journey home must be overcome, and also that this must be done with the greatest care, for the deceased person is both fragile and evanescent. This is

---

[161] Parsons, op.cit., 24.
[162] See Gayton, op.cit., 271, Haile 1942, 413.
[163] Radin 1926, 36.
[164] Thus among the Serrano (Benedict, op.cit., 8). See also chap. II: 3.
[165] Opler, op.cit., 100 sq.
[166] Jenness 1935, 109.
[167] See above, p. 17.
[168] Swanton, op.cit., 249.

fully testified to in the Yokuts versions. The dead wife of the Yokuts Indian "would not suffer his touch"; "his living scent was too strong."[169] This susceptibility to touch is the reason why—as mentioned above—she is transformed, after sleeping the night with her husband, into an oaken log. The episode is a variant of the more common version—represented among, inter alia, the Yaudanchi Yokuts—according to which Orpheus may not sleep with the deceased partner, as he would then lose her and find in her place a "rotten log."[170]

This leads us to Orpheus' fetching of the deceased loved one.

5. Restoration of the deceased to life

The foregoing discussion of the realm of the dead and its inhabitants should have made sufficiently clear the extreme difficulty of Orpheus' task in the other world. Before he can restore his deceased partner to the world of the living he must have the permission of the ruler in the land of the dead, he must overcome the resistance of the dead themselves, and he must secure the person of his recalcitrant partner. But even now the battle is not won: he must then return the lost relative to the world of the living, and this entails not merely a removal from one world to another, but also the restoration of the deceased person to life through a gradual essential transformation.

What is decisive for a successful performance of the task is the sympathy of the ruler of the other world, in some cases also his assistance. Without him—or, where he is not mentioned, without the guardian—Orpheus can as a rule do nothing. The obstacles are many, and chief among them are the entanglement in the sphere of death of the loved person and the resistance of the dead themselves. Eurydice is, as we have seen, so essentially different from the living that she has a hostile attitude to Orpheus and to the form of existence he represents. And as regards the dead themselves, they must be reckoned with as certain opponents of Orpheus. Just as the living do all in their power to prevent a death, so the dead muster all their resources in order not to lose one of their own number. The resistance put up by the dead is encountered at a number of points: they try to prevent Orpheus' entry into the realm of the dead, they try to take his life by inveigling him into eating their food, they

[169] Hudson 1902, 104, 105.
[170] Kroeber, op.cit., 228; Gayton, op.cit., 268.

provoke him to infringe the rules for a successful recovery of the deceased that have been laid down by their ruler.[1] Orpheus is simply powerless unless he has the ruler of the other world behind him.

How, then, does this potentate react to Orpheus' request to be allowed to take his partner home? We have already seen that in the great majority of Orpheus tales the ruler of the dead is a friendly being.[2] There are, it is true, some indications of the contrary; it is probably not an incidental manifestation of trickster humour when among the Wishram and the Wasco Orpheus kills the female ruler of the dead in order to be able to fetch his beloved without let or hindrance.[3] But there are only isolated occurrences of such examples. The prince of the other world is generally well-disposed to Orpheus—or at least he becomes so when he is informed of his errand. The ruler's change of attitude to Orpheus is movingly expressed in the Micmac legend; but unfortunately there seem to be signs of literary retouching by the hand that noted it down.[4] One of the Yokuts legends, too, testifies to this development from indifference to sympathy for Orpheus in the lord av the dead.[5] This in any case gradually arising benevolence of attitude has doubtless to do with the fact that the potentate in question is as a rule not a ghost but, as we have seen, a divinity—and sometimes a divinity ruling over both the living and the dead, e.g. the Supreme Being.[6]

In short, the supreme representative of the dead wishes Orpheus well; but is it in his power to help him as he would like? This is not so certain. Even where the prince of the dead and the Supreme Being are one and the same person, there are limits to his ability to assist the wanderer from the land of the living—limits which he has himself decreed, or which are entailed in the cosmic order.

In the first place, of course, the realm of the dead is the country without return, and its chief and guardian must see to it that none comes there who is not dead and none goes thence who is already dead.[7] The order of things that here finds expression has been formulated in the cosmogonic epoch in which the first death occurred and the separation

---

[1] See above, pp. 111 sq.
[2] See above, p. 105.
[3] See above, p. 103 note 60.
[4] Le Clercq 1910, 210.
[5] Kroeber 1907 c, 217 (Tachi Yokuts).
[6] See above, pp. 99 sqq.
[7] The eschatological conceptions are not, any more than other religious conceptions, without inconsistencies: that the dead appear in the land of the living to fetch souls (an inversion of the fetching of souls by the shaman) is as we know quite a common phenomenon (cf. Elmendorf 1952, 110 sq.).

between the living and the dead was made by the decree of the gods. It does happen, it is true, that the episodes of the Orpheus tradition are represented as taking place in this epoch, so that Orpheus' failure to restore his loved one to the living becomes an *aition* for the divorce between the living and the dead.[8] But this version of the Orpheus narrative is, as we shall find, a secondary form. In the majority of cases the ruler of the other world must conform to the law laid down in the primeval cosmic era.

This law, moreover, acts automatically, it is independent of the actions of the ruler in the realm of the dead. The deceased person will perhaps remain dead even if the last-mentioned potentate wishes otherwise. The chief of the other world in the Tachi Yokuts legend lets Orpheus realize through his own experience how impossible it is to restore his wife to life: she is transformed to wood in his arms. "You see that we cannot make your wife as she was," he says. "She is no good now. It is best that you go back. You have a good country there."[9] The god is powerless against the laws of existence; he cannot help the suppliant, though it is his genuine wish to do so.

To all this must be added the circumstance that the ruler of the dead must show some consideration for the resistance of the dead themselves. It is typical that, as we have earlier observed, he must sometimes go behind the backs of the dead in order to be able to assist Orpheus.

It is thus scarcely surprising if sometimes the ruler of the dead is obliged to refuse Orpheus' request.[10] For the traveller who has come so far this means that he must return empty-handed. But this does not always take place at once. Sometimes, in his despair, Orpheus lingers in the realm of the dead, near the deceased loved one whom he will not abandon. We have just seen how the chief of the dead Yokuts Indians charged him to return to the land of the living. But despite this the man persisted; he remained for six days in the land of the dead before returning—and the chief let him have his way.[11] This case may be adduced as an illustration of the forbearance and the friendly attitude of the ruler, but it is not typical; as a rule he requires Orpheus to leave immediately. Orpheus may not stay in the land of the dead, firstly because he is not

[8] See chap. V: 3.

[9] Kroeber, op.cit., 218. In the Karuk legends noted down by Kroeber the deceased lover is obliged to refuse the request of his sweethearts that he return to life, for he is without bones and is therefore unable to walk.

[10] As regards the other cases it may be observed that he does not oblige Orpheus more than once. If the attempt fails, it may not be repeated. There are, however, certain exceptions; see below, pp. 144 sq.

[11] Kroeber, op.cit., loc.cit.

dead, secondly because with his presence he offends the dead, just as in the land of the living the presence of ghosts offends the living.

That the realm of the dead is a country for the dead, not for the living, and that for this reason Orpheus may not remain there, emerges clearly from one of the Shasta Orpheus legends. Here Orpheus requests permission to stay with his deceased wife, but receives the reply: "No, you can't. You'll have to go back [to earth] and then you can come back again, from your home."[12] Thus it is only as a dead man that Orpheus can gain definitive entrance to the realm of the dead. In all those cases in which we are told that Orpheus gained permission to continue his life together with the deceased loved one in the other world he is deprived of his life—by passing the river of the dead (Thompson, Sanpoil), by infringing a taboo against speaking to his wife (Nisenan), or by succumbing in fire or the like (Quinault, Chehalis, Shahaptin).[13] In some cases Orpheus returns to the land of the living to die there, and then, as a ghost, to betake himself once more to the world of the dead (Tlingit, Shasta, Yokuts).

Orpheus thus has the possibility of choosing death in order to be allowed to remain with his deceased partner, at least sometimes. Sometimes even this choice is denied him, and this on account of the cosmic order, whose dominion even over the supreme gods we have observed above. Thus in Schoolcraft's Ottawa legend we learn that Orpheus "did not see the Master of Life, but he heard his voice, as if it were a soft breeze. 'Go back', said this voice, 'to the land from whence you came. Your time has not yet come'."[14] This idea, that the hour of the seeker has not yet struck, occurs also in some other Orpheus legends (among the Karuk and the Lipan Apache). It appears to have been taken from another eschatological narrative category, based upon the hallucinatory experiences of the seriously ill and persons in a swoon. In the Lipan tale Orpheus is without doubt a person who has journeyed to the realm of the dead in a deep coma and then returned to life.[15]

It is perhaps chiefly on account of the dead that Orpheus cannot remain alive for any length of time in the other world. It is, moreover, generally not the prince or the guardian of the dead who dismisses Orpheus, but the dead themselves; in some cases on the west coast it is Orpheus' dead partner who insists on his speedy departure (Snuqualmi,

[12] Voegelin 1947, 52 sq.
[13] Note that the Menomini legend, instead, represents the hero's return to life as being made through fire!
[14] Schoolcraft 1851 I, 323.
[15] See further chap. IV: 1.

Quinault, Chehalis, Karuk and Yokuts).[16] The motivations may be the current ones: Orpheus has not yet died, or his appointed life-time is not yet at an end. The deeper motive of the ghosts is, however, their infinite aversion to the living. Sometimes, to wit, on the Western Plateau and in the coastal regions to the west of this, there is very definite justification for the aversion. In the Klikitat narrative, after his arrival in the world of the dead, Coyote lingered there. The dead then said: "He should go back home. He is Coyote," and Coyote complied with their wish.[17] It is obvious that Coyote is here sent home because he is the asocial trickster—tales af the trickster from different parts of North America testify to the way in which all creatures avoid his company.[18] Not even in the realm of the dead is the trickster able to refrain from his practical jokes. The Skopamish Groundsparrow "used to walk over the dead people, trampling upon their bones."[19] When the Snuqualmi trickster, Pheasant, "opened his eyes he would step upon the dead people, but if he remembered and kept his eyes closed he would see the people and not offend by jostling them. By reason of this annoyance the people grew to dislike his presence there and wish him away." It is said that it was his deceased daughter who charged him to return.[20] Similarly, in the Quinault and Chehalis myths we are told that Bluejay was sent home by his wife and his sister respectively, as she and all the dead had tired of his tricks and his mischief. Thus many of these stories in which the trickster-culture hero plays Orpheus' rôle end in his returning alone to the world of the living.[21]

The majority of the Orpheus narratives, however, tell how Orpheus receives permission from the ruler of the dead to return with his deceased partner. Thus the Blackfoot legend, for instance, describes how the chief of the dead allows Orpheus to sojourn for four days in the realm of the dead, and then to meet his wife. But, he adds, "you must be very careful or you will never go back. You will die right here."[21a] When the lord of the dead thus yields in this way to Orpheus' prayers it is an extraordinary event—not only a flagrant violation of the rights of the dead, a piece of defiance against those who dwell in the land beyond

[16] Cf. also those cases in which the deceased partner prevents or renders more difficult Orpheus sojourn in the other world, or even chases him away. See above, pp. 116 sq.
[17] Jacobs 1929, 228.
[18] Cf. Radin, Kerényi & Jung 1954, 116 sqq.
[19] Ballard 1929, 133.
[20] Ballard, op.cit., 128.
[21] Cf. above, pp. 50 sq.
[21a] Grinnell 1912, 129.

the grave, but also a suspension of the order of things which was decreed in the primeval era. This is testified to by the four sacred beings who had assisted and guided the hero of the Winnebago. "Grandson," they say, "from now on, this will never happen again. Earthmaker did not ordain it thus. It is only because I and my friends blessed you that you have been successful. You may now go home with your wife."[22] How, then, has it been possible for this unheard-of thing to happen? It is not here a matter of any magical compelling of the god of death, as when the Greek Orpheus puts a spell on the underworld with his songs. In certain Orpheus tales, as in the above-mentioned Winnebago version, Orpheus seems to have gained the favour of the lord of death by passing tests (cf. below). The main motive for the decision of the ruler is, however, to seek in this positive attitude to a living person who at the risk of his own life follows the one he has loved into the dangerous world of the dead. If, previously, another motive existed, this has been ousted by the dominating romantic tendency of the tradition.[23]

Orpheus has sometimes not only the permission of the lord of the dead to take home his deceased loved one, but also his direct assistance. A number of Orpheus traditions tell how the ruler or the guardian of the dead advises the hero as to how the liberation is to be effected. These wise counsels are in many situations only too necessary, for, as pointed is not here a matter of any magical compelling of the god of death, as when out above, both the dead *in corpore* and the deceased person who is to be fetched offer resistance. The dead are embittered opponents of Orpheus and must be outwitted;[24] the deceased partner is in the great majority of cases recalcitrant, indeed, hostile to her liberator, and is, moreover, hard to catch and restore to her old shape as a living person. It must also be borne in mind that in most of the Orpheus tales the one who is to perform the deed has no previous knowledge of the realm of the dead and its conditions.[25]

In rare cases the dead are won over to Orpheus' side through the direct action of the ruler of the other world. The "chief ghost" of the

[22] Radin 1926, 36.
[23] Here it is of course a matter of the ordinary Orpheus tradition, not of the "sea-coast form," where the ruler of the dead is represented as a monster (see above, pp. 105 sq.).
[24] In a number of Shahaptin and Chinook tribes in the southern part of the Northwest Coast area Orpheus arranges for the world of the dead to lapse into darkness when he proceeds to action (see above, pp. 102 sq.). Also in the Orpheus legend belonging to the "sea-coast form" among e.g. the Sechelt and Haida, the procedure is the same (Hill-Tout 1904 b, 53 sq.; Swanton 1908 a, 499). The motif is also found in Siberia (see Thompson 1946, 354).
[25] This is not to say that, as we have tried to show on several occasions in the foregoing, he does not possess supernatural powers.

Blackfoot appealed to the dead in the following way: "Now pity this son-in-law of yours. He is seeking his wife. Neither the great distance nor the fearful sights that he has seen here have weakened his heart. You can see for yourselves he is tender-hearted. He not only mourns for his wife, but mourns because his little boy is now alone with no mother; so pity him and give him back his wife." This speech had the desired effect.[25 a]

Generally, following the instructions of his supernatural helper, Orpheus tries to seize his evanescent Eurydice while she is taking part in the dance of the dead. It has been hinted in the foregoing that the dances characteristic for the land of the dead described in the Orpheus tradition may be taken as evidence of the relatively happy conditions obtaining in this realm.[26] As we shall find later, in several of these tales the dances are taken by Orpheus to the land of the living and have here become ritual religious dances intended to cure the sick or to strengthen the connection with the dead in the beyond.[27] It is probable that this should be understood as an extension of the community which finds expression in the dances of the dead. Upon this train of thought is based, for example, the ideology of the ghost dance; and, as Gayton has shown for the Western Mono and Yokuts, the ghost dance is traceable to the eschatology of the Orpheus tradition.[28] One of the leaders of the ghost dance among the Mono and Yokuts, moreover, formulated what I have here tried to indicate in the following way: "The dead people are coming if we dance this dance. They dance this dance all the time where they are now."[29] The dance of the dead in the other world should be regarded as not only an entertainment, it has also a strengthening social function, it expresses community between the dead, and deepens this. And this is why many Orpheus tales tell how shortly after her arrival in the realm of the dead the newly deceased person joins the dancing there.

One might imagine that in these circumstances Orpheus has chosen an unfavourable occasion for his action; a situation like this can only be calculated to involve him in considerable difficulties. On the other hand, he has no choice. The deceased person he wants to fetch is on other occasions impossible to capture—invisible, or changed to the point of being unrecognizable, or vanished from the immediate surroundings,

[25 a] Grinnell, op.cit., 129 sq.
[26] See above, p. 91, p. 106 note 86.
[27] See below, pp. 145 sq.
[28] Gayton 1930 a, 77 sqq., 82.
[29] Gayton, op.cit., 70.

or constantly on the look-out. The dance offers the only possibility, she is here fully visible and at the same time absorbed in her rhythmical movements; she scarcely notices what is going on around her.

The dramatic capture of the deceased has not always the same general course. In some cases it is the ruler in the other world, in others Orpheus himself, who tries to seize the deceased. Sometimes Orpheus is obliged to submit to special taboos to be able to succeed in his enterprise. Sometimes, again, the deceased is forced into a container of some kind, a procedure which is now carried out by Orpheus, now by his powerful protector. The remarkable thing is that the catching of the deceased in the dance is always successful, despite all the difficulties in the way. We may here adduce two typical instances of the apprehension of the deceased, the one from the Stalo on the west coast, the other from the Seneca on the east coast; both illustrate all the eventualities here referred to.[30]

In the Stalo legend we learn that the chief of the dead promised to assist the young man who was asking to get his wife back if he would submit to the chief's instructions: he must hide himself and not let her see him, nor was he to attempt to catch her. "If you do, everybody will immediately disappear, and your wife will dissolve in your arms." When darkness fell, the dead came to dance. They sniffed the air suspiciously and said that they perceived the odour of a living person. But the chief convinced them that this must be a mistake, only the dead could come to this place. So the dancing commenced, and among the dancers the youth recognized his wife. He found it difficult to resist the desire to rush up and embrace her, but he contained himself; and at sunrise the dancers disappeared. The following evening they came again, and again they expressed to the chief their fears that some living person was present, but he calmed them with the same answer as on the previous evening. The night was passed in dancing, and in the morning the dead vanished once more. When they returned on the third evening they were no longer afraid, and they made no further enquiries about the cause of the strange smell. But while the dance was going on the youth was overcome with his longing for his wife, he sprang forward and tried to seize her—but both she and all the dead vanished immediately, "and he was left grasping nothing but the empty air." The chief blamed him for his weakness:[31] he should have waited another night. The following

---

[30] The account is given the more willingly as the motif of the apprehension of the deceased while dancing is lacking in the Comanche version adduced verbatim above, chap. I: 1.

[31] The Stalo Orpheus here shows a lack of the most Indian of all qualities, impassivity.

evening the dead arrived as usual and began to dance. And when they had danced four times round the lodge the youth rushed forth—this time at the instigation of the chief himself—and seized his wife; and now she remained in his arms, and none of the other dead disappeared.[32] The chief threw some of his medicine on the couple, and this made it possible for them to be together in the sequel.[33]

The Seneca, as we have already observed, had a female Orpheus. She, too, was assisted by the chief of the other world, an old woman, who concealed her in a corner of her lodge under a little bark and charged her to remain silent during the dance of the dead, for if they should discover her they would flee. As evening fell the dead arrived one after the other and the dancing was begun, while the old woman beat the drum and sang. The husband of the concealed woman did not, however, arrive with the others; he was lingering outside the lodge and was shy of all the strangers. But he was brought in and joined in the dancing. Suddenly the dead sniffed the air and shrieked that they perceived the odour of a living human being. But the old woman calmed their uneasiness: it was her they smelt, for, she said, "I am now getting very old again." The dancing then continued. When the deceased husband came dancing quite near the place where his wife was concealed, she attempted to catch hold of him. But "he deftly eluded her hand," and the terrified dancers fled. The old woman now called after them, telling them not to run away, for it was only she who had scratched herself. The dancing was resumed. But when the deceased husband drew near the old woman she seized him, and all the ghosts quickly evacuated the lodge. The old woman thrust the man into a bottle, which she then handed over to the wife, urging her to depart with all speed so that the dead should not catch sight of her.[34]

Despite the great distance between the peoples who relate them, these two narratives are remarkably similar. But they do diverge from each other in a couple of important points. In the Stalo legend it is Orpheus himself who captures the deceased; in the Seneca legend, on the other hand, it is the ruler of the dead. In the Stalo legend the deceased retains her natural size and appearance; in the Seneca legend the deceased husband is thrust into a small container. With reference to these differences, which also occur where there is no dance of the dead to serve as a frame for the course of events, one can distinguish two main types within the

[32] We may thus observe that the dead are paralysed, and their resistance is neutralized, as soon as the magic time-limit—four days—is passed.
[33] Hill-Tout 1904 b, 339 sq.
[34] Curtin & Hewitt 1918 II, 571 sq.

ordinary Orpheus tradition: the predominantly western type, characterized by Orpheus' own active intervention, and the predominantly eastern type, characterized by the receptacle-motif.[35] We shall in the sequel have occasion to keep these two types separate.[36] Now, however, we shall take cognizance of the special features characterizing both the types in connection with the apprehension of the deceased.

We have observed that in order to succeed in his enterprise Orpheus must use particular caution, which is impressed upon him so emphatically that the exhortations he receives may be regarded as taboo rules. The narratives make it quite evident that these rules must be regarded as an instrument for intercourse with the supernatural beings, i.e. the dead. As we have seen, the latter cannot be approached in the same way as one approaches living beings. Their reaction is extremely vehement —they fly, they vanish—and in consequence of her essential transformation through death Orpheus' loved one shows the same aversion to him as the other dead. She glides out of his arms like air (Stalo), or she flees him (Huron), or she changes shape: becomes foam (Kwakiutl), a jackrabbit (Taos) or "a downy eagle feather" (Zuni).[37] In the tales with the receptacle-motif we often find another change in the deceased when she is captured. In the Huron legend we are told that Orpheus "had to struggle against her all night, and in the contest she grew so little that he put her without difficulty into his pumpkin."[38] In the above-adduced Stalo legend the procedure lasts for no less than four days. As we have seen, it does not make any difference if Orpheus infringes the taboo regulations by trying to capture his beloved before the appointed time has passed; his action fails on that occasion, but when the four days are at an end he does nonetheless attain his goal.[38 a] The apprehension of the deceased is thus a gradual process which acts mechanically and automatically, although in the moment when the enterprise is successful it appears rather as a sudden occurrence.

In this circumstance alone we divine that as regards the apprehension of the deceased it is a matter of something far more than the actual seizing, to wit, the transference of the deceased to the sphere of the living. The

[35] As we shall find (chap. II: 6), the receptacle motif occurs also in the west in some quarters.
[36] See chap. III: 3.
[37] See Boas 1910 a, 447 (Kwakiutl), Parsons 1940, 25, 28 (Taos), Benedict 1935 II, 157 (Zuni). Concerning Taos, cf. also above, p. 89. Concerning the Zuni Indians' conception of the deceased as a feather, see also Hultkrantz 1953, 268.
[38] JR X, 153.
[38 a] The Kwakiutl legend is an exception: the hero failed because he tried to capture his son too early (Boas, op.cit., loc.cit.).

deceased is "normalized," as Gayton expresses it.[39] This process is thus already commenced at this early stage. It is most clearly evident in the so-called missile-motif, implying that certain objects are thrown at the deceased for her recovery. We have referred above to the way the chief of the Stalo ghosts threw his medicine over Orpheus and his deceased wife so that they might have intercourse with each other. A typical form of the missile motif occurs among the Pawnee. One of the Pawnee Orpheus legends tells how an old woman on the way to the realm of the dead gave Orpheus four balls of mud, with the following admonition: "When you enter into Spirit-Land the spirits will be dancing, and among them will be your wife. You must sit down and watch the dance, and whenever your wife passes, you must throw one of these mud balls at her. The fourth ball with which you hit her will remind her of her people still living, and they will remind her of you. She will then know you are there and will come to you. When she comes to you, go to the mud balls and pick them up, for by means of them you will return to your own country." The young man followed the old woman's instructions. When he had thrown the fourth ball his wife looked at him and went up to him, and after a short exchange of words she agreed to follow him home.[40] In the Alabama narratives the Orpheus men throw "pieces of corncob" at the deceased woman. The last piece hits her, she falls down, and they are able to seize her.[41]

In the one of the Alabama versions we are given to understand that the missile facilitates the capture of the woman: it paralyzes her, as it were, magically. Also the arrow which according to the Nayarit legend hits the legs of the dead during the dance has a directly paralysing effect. But the meaning, on a deeper view, is that she recovers consciousness of the world she has just left, and this breaks her out of the world of the dead. In the foregoing we have seen instances of the dead being deprived of their brains, i.e. of their recollections from their lifetimes, on entering the realm of the dead.[42] The missile functions as an at least partial restoration of this memory, as shown by the above-adduced example from the Pawnee legend. Characteristic, here, is that the missile consists of a ball of earth: it would be impossible to underline more clearly that it is the palpable world of sense that here intervenes in the spiritual sham world. The corncob in the Alabama story is pro-

---

[39] Gayton 1935, 266, 284.
[40] Dorsey 1906, 412; cf. also op.cit., 537.
[41] Swanton 1929, 141, 143. The corncob recurs as a missile in a Cherokee variant (Mooney 1900, 436).
[42] See above, pp. 97 sq.

bably a reflex of the prevailing tendency in the peoples of the Southeast to fit the Orpheus tale into the fertility schema of the agrarian religion.[43]

Dr. Gayton, who has reported instances of the missile motif among the Alabama, Yuchi, Cherokee, Wichita and Pawnee, is of the opinion that we are here confronted with an element that originated in the Southeast and the Southern Plains.[44] Its occurrence among the Paviotso is according to her best explained on the assumption that it "was introduced to the Paviotso by Wichita or other 1890 Ghost Dance delegates from the Southeast."[45] This is conceivable. But at the same time it must be emphasized that the motif occurs also in the Nayarit legend and in the Stalo legend, far off at the Pacific Ocean. It is probably not out of the question that originally, like certain other elements, e.g. the stuffing of the deceased into a receptacle, it had an east-westerly distribution in North America.[45 a]

The normalization of the deceased begins when the missile strikes him, or her. But the process takes a long time, it is going on throughout Orpheus' journey home and sometimes even lasts for some time after his arrival. But before discussing this theme we shall briefly mention something of the reactions of the dead after Orpheus has proved successful in the first act of the drama.

The seizing of Eurydice implies a clear defeat for the dead. Orpheus must therefore be prepared for their pursuit.[46] In the Winnebago Orpheus legend Orpheus was instructed, by the wise men who had assisted him in the realm of the dead, concerning his journey home. "Now go home," they said. "The ghosts will chase you for they are bad. Eight attendants will take you home." The friendly old men then gave him some ashes, telling him to throw ash behind him when the ghosts came threateningly near. The narrative continues: "On their way home they were chased by the ghosts. 'Alas! He has taken our wife away! Let us take her back!' they shouted. They came close to them. Then the man took the ashes the old men had given him and threw them behind him. Thereupon the ghosts shouted to one another, 'Run away, the ashes will ruin our clothes!' and they retreated. Then they pursued him again and he did the same thing. Finally they disappeared, and the eight attendants

---

[43] See chap. IV: 4.

[44] Gayton, op.cit., 266, 276 sq.

[45] Gayton, op.cit., 284.

[45 a] It should be observed that the missile motif also occurs in a Chinese Orpheus legend (see chap. III: 2).

[46] Cf. above, p. 123 note 24, concerning Orpheus' methods of protecting himself against and outwitting the dead.

9 — Hultkrantz

went back also."[47] In this legend the motif of the pursuit is described in some detail, but otherwise it plays a subordinate rôle in the ordinary Orpheus tradition.[48] What, on the contrary, is commonly here the case is that Orpheus and his partner find their journey home considerably less difficult than the journey to the other world had been for Orpheus. May this possibly be due to the fact that just as the deceased person is magnetically drawn to the realm of the dead, so the living person is magnetically drawn to the world of the living?[49] The Alabama and Koasati legends, for instance, describe in detail the difficulties encountered by the living on their way to the land of the dead, while the return journey is not described at all, as it takes place in a mystical way which the persons concerned are unable to understand: they lie down to sleep in the realm of the dead and wake up in or near their own houses in this world.[50] The Telumni Yokuts Orpheus hero also had a comfortable journey home, "he didn't step on the ground, he just glided along and reached home the same evening."[51]

On the other hand, the pursuit motif occupies an important place in the accounts of the journey home of the Orpheus of the "sea-coast form." Here, however, it must be remembered that in these versions the sea-creatures pursue Orpheus at the command of the submarine ruler, who has never granted permission for him to fetch his loved one.[52] In a Haida tradition there is a description of the way the seal-hunter ("Orpheus") throws magic objects behind him to check the marine powers when they begin their pursuit after he has freed his wife from their dominion.[53]

Whereas in the "sea-coast form" the chief attention is concentrated on Orpheus' attempts to escape his pursuers, it is in the ordinary Or-

[47] Radin 1926, 37. The fear of fire and ash experienced by the dead is a common folkloristic motif which was probably originally connected with the reaction of the skeleton-burying Indians to the encroaching method of cremating the corpses and their possessions.
[48] In the Klikitat Orpheus myth, it is true, Coyote believes that the rising murmurs behind him come from people who are catching up on him; but in reality it is the dead in the pack he is carrying who are coming to life again (Jacobs 1929, 299 sq.).
[49] At the same time, of course, it must not be overlooked that from the technical and dramatic points of view the narrative has gained by the detailed description of the journey not being repeated. Cf. also the points made regarding the size of the gourd, below, p. 156.
[50] Similar accounts of the difference between the journeys to and from the other world are given in Gregg's Shawnee legend and in the Yuchi legends.
[51] Gayton 1935, 268.
[52] See above, pp. 105 sq.
[53] The episode is reproduced below, pp. 182 sq.

pheus tradition directed towards his attempts to take home his liberated wife etc. without her gradual transition to life being jeopardized. In order to assure this transition between two forms of existence, Orpheus must observe certain precautionary measures, taboo regulations which are enjoined upon him before he embarks on the return home by the ruler or guardian of the dead or other helpful person, or by the dead themselves. Sometimes, as in the Winnebago, Kwakiutl and Yokuts legends, the taboo period is restricted to the sojourn in the realm of the dead; the narrative represents the hero's endeavours not to infringe the taboo regulation as if it were a question simply of a test motif.[54] The Telumni Yokuts legend, for example, describes how Tipiknits, the governor of the other world, promised Orpheus to send his wife back with him if he could lie beside her without going to sleep for a whole night. Orpheus failed on the first night, but was given another chance. When he failed again, there remained nothing for him but to return home.[55] There is no doubt but that the test motif is a distortion of an earlier taboo motif. It fulfils no reasonable function whatsoever in the legend.[56]

This, on the other hand, the taboo motif does, when it occurs meaningfully in association with the narratives of Orpheus' journey home. It is another and more effective taboo motif than the one we have met with in connection with the episode concerning the apprehension of the deceased: if the taboo regulation is infringed, Eurydice glides irrevocably back to the land of the dead. The taboos which must be observed by the hero are in point of fact intended to protect his partner during her transformation from ghost to living human being. This is a delicate, supernatural process which no living person may witness; Orpheus' look, his touch and so on may destroy the miracle. We may here mention the different taboos, their distribution and their import in relation to their general interpretation as this has been laid down here.

1. The so-called looking taboo (C 300 in Thompson's Motif-Index) is the most widespread of the numerous taboos in the North American Orpheus tradition. Thus it occurs in versions from the Tlingit, Klikitat, Modoc, Western Mono, Navajo, Zuni Indians, Fort Hall Sho-

[54] Concerning test motifs in North America, see Lowie 1908, 97 sqq.
[55] Gayton, op.cit., 268. Cf. also above, p. 120.
[56] See also below, pp. 175 sq. During the sojourn in the other world the hero must sometimes observe taboos of a peculiar kind, whose real origin may be elusive. The Navajo Orpheus was warned by Spider Man not to touch four stones that lighted the death-chamber when they were moved together. When despite this warning he brought them together in order by their light to try to find his vanished wife, the real character of the realm of the dead was revealed in all its hideousness, and he had to fly from the spot (Haile 1942, 412 sq.).

shoni, Blackfoot, Malecite and Huron. It assumes, however, different forms in different quarters. Thus we find prohibitions against looking in the realm of the dead (Modoc, Blackfoot), looking at the deceased (Navajo, Zuni Indians), looking back at the deceased as she follows behind (C 331) (Klikitat, Mono, Shoshoni, Malecite), looking at the deceased during the process of revivification after the arrival home (Tlingit, Huron). Of these prohibitions the first-mentioned has no direct connection with the taboos applying on the journey home with the deceased; it is a manifestation of the earlier adduced principle concerning the reversed order in the realm of the dead.[57] All the other "looking taboos", on the other hand, have directly to do with the restoring of the deceased to life.[57a]

These taboos are not, as we know, characteristic solely for the Orpheus tradition; they are found also in e.g. such traditions as the tales of Amor and Psyche, and of Lot's wife, and in religious conceptions and rites all over the world. But the explanations of these prohibitions can not everywhere be the same. As regards the Orpheus tradition, MacCulloch writes: "The tabu imposed on Orpheus—not to look back— is frequently found both in ritual and magic, especially in under-world rites, and may be explained by the idea that man may not gaze with impunity on what pertains to a supernatural plane, lest it harm him or force him to join the under-world ghosts."[58] This may well be applicable to the story of Lot's wife, but scarcely to the Orpheus narrative.[59] The looking taboo in the latter is rather referable to the notion that the living may not observe the supernatural process, the miracle, the mystical transformation from spirit to human being, for this process is intended to be concealed from him. Furthermore, in the Orpheus tradition the deceased is so immaterial and fragile that a "contact" with the sight of the living person has damaging effects. From another viewpoint, already adduced in the foregoing, one may say that the illusion of the presence of the deceased is retained as long as possible, and may not be broken through any close testing.[60]

The temptation to infringe this taboo is, naturally, strong. One is

[57] See above, pp. 93, 107 sq., 110 sq.
[57a] In the Blackfoot legend, moreover, another fresh motif has been added: "you must not open your eyes, or you will return here and be a ghost forever" (Grinnell 1912, 130).
[58] MacCulloch 1911, 653 sq.
[59] That is, provided one does not think of the loss Orpheus suffers—but probably this is scarcely what MacCulloch meant.
[60] Cf. above, pp. 109 sq. The unreal nature of the experience is perfectly expressed in the Bella Coola legend: Orpheus thinks he is sure of his wife's presence, but his daughter cannot see her.

scarcely surprised if Orpheus is overcome by his longing or his desire to see again the one who has been snatched from him so cruelly. A further consideration is that the deceased, who longs to return to the realm of the dead, deliberately tries to render void the journey back to life. The Creator's words to the Orpheus of the Western Mono are significant in this connection: "When your wife walks behind you, she will talk to you and try to get you to look back; but do not do it."[61]

The narratives give realistic details of what happens when the taboo is infringed. According to the Tlingit legend a man looked stealthily at Orpheus and his wife after their return home. "The moment that he did so, however, the people in the house heard a rattling of bones. That instant the woman's husband died, and the ghosts of both of them went back to Ghost Land."[62] The Navajo Indian who by lighting a fire in the realm of the dead disclosed his wife as a skeleton covered with ragged blankets rushed home terrified, pursued by her. When he got home he once again contravened the taboo, and again he saw her as a skeleton.[63] According to Bunzel's variants from the Zuni, Orpheus' sister or mother infringes the taboo, so that the deceased who has been brought home is transformed into an owl or a snake.[64]

2. Closely related to the foregoing taboo is the "opening taboo" (C 321-2), i.e. the prohibition against opening the receptacle in which the deceased is brought back. Thompson lists this taboo also as a looking taboo,[65] but as other reasons than the desire to see the deceased may also be adduced for this opening, it is probably desirable to distinguish this taboo-category from the looking taboos. We find the opening taboo in a north-westerly group of Orpheus traditions, viz, among the Chehalis, Wishram, Wasco, Kalispel, Yakima, Tenino and Shahaptin (Nez Percé?), and in an easterly group of Orpheus traditions, viz, among the Micmac, Cherokee, Yuchi, Koasati and Alabama. That is to say, this taboo occurs in the two regions in which the receptacle motif has been recorded.[66] More than any other taboo it is adapted to this motif, and it is therefore the commonest taboo associated with it.

As in the preceding case, it is of course in the first place the longing for the deceased that prompts the opening of the receptacle; this is most

[61] Gifford 1923, 341.
[62] Swanton 1909, 250.
[63] See Gayton, op.cit., 271. The pursuit motif brings this legend close to the character of an earlier adduced Tewa legend (see above, pp. 29 sq.). See also below, chap. IV: 4.
[64] Benedict 1935 II, 289, 299.
[65] Thompson 1929, 338.
[66] See further chap. II: 6.

clearly seen in the Wishram narrative. But the other narratives indicate also other motives. Thus in both the areas in which the receptacle motif occurs the opening is very frequently referred to the curiosity of the hero or of some other person (Chehalis, Wasco, Kalispel, Micmac, Yuchi). In the area of a westerly distribution we find the motivation that the bearer of the receptacle (which is here conceived as a large chest), Coyote, is fatigued with his burden and therefore puts it down and opens it (Kalispel, Yakima, Shahaptin). Only in the south-easterly versions of the narrative, on the other hand, do we find that the bearers of the receptacle open the lid for fear that the loved one inside will otherwise be suffocated (Cherokee, Koasati, Alabama). Here the opening is preceded by all sorts of attempts on the part of the deceased to persuade the bearers to infringe the taboo regulation. The Cherokee woman "pleaded so that it was very hard to listen to her"; the Alabama woman groaned and lamented, "you have brought me here and killed me"; and the Koasati woman cried, "I can not well live here. I want to stand up; I am almost killed."[67]

Through the opening of the receptacle the deceased recedes into the realm of the dead, for she is still an evanescent, etherial figure that has not yet regained its concrete shape in this life, and as a spirit she glides automatically out of the receptacle and returns to the land of spirits. Her return is described as a breeze; or one sees, hears or feels nothing, she is simply gone, as in the Alabama and Koasati tales. The Yuchi legend has it that "a great wind came out [of the gourd] and went up in the air."[68] In the Wishram myth concerning the journey to Hades of Eagle and Coyote we are told: "But no sooner was the cover lifted than it was thrown back violently, and the dead people rushed out into the air with such force that Coyote was thrown to the ground. They quickly disappeared in the west."[69] According to the Yakima myth, after the opening of the chest Coyote and his companion were "astonished and overwhelmed with grief to see the partially transformed spirits flit away like autumn leaves and disappear in the direction from which they had come."[70] The Cherokee men who brought home the dead daughter of the sun "lifted the lid a little to give her air, but as they did so there was a fluttering sound inside and something flew past them into the thicket and they heard a redbird cry, '*kwish! kwish! kwish!*' in the bushes."[71]

[67] Mooney 1900, 254; Swanton 1929, 143, 190.
[68] Speck 1909, 146. Cf. Wagner 1931, 88.
[69] Curtis 1911 VIII, 129.
[70] Lyman 1904, 249.
[71] Mooney, op.cit., loc.cit.

3. The taboo on sexual intercourse (C 117), too, is one of the fundamental taboos of the Orpheus tradition. This is a natural taboo wherever the hero may be expected to approach the deceased with erotic intentions, i.e. in those tales in which she is represented as his deceased wife or sweetheart. This is of course not to say that this taboo is the only taboo that is connected with these tales, which, as we have already seen, form the great majority of the Orpheus traditions.[72] The taboo against coitus occurs in Orpheus narratives from the Stalo, Sinkaietk, Tübatulabal, Serrano, Gabrielino, Mohave, Zuni Indians, Paviotso and Comanche. The distribution confirms what Gayton points out, that "the continence tabu is confined to western versions as opposed to a variety of other tabus in tales from the east."[73]

The fatal consequences of infringing the taboo are stressed in several Orpheus tales. Their tacit significance appears to be that in consequence of her incorporeality and evanescence the deceased is not yet fit for the physical strain of coitus. The Orpheus of the Gabrielino legend embraces his deceased wife on the third day of the journey home, only to find a rotten log in his arms.[74] The hero of the Tübatulabal, who lay with his wife illicitly, awoke in the morning to find that in place of his wife, a stalk of yucca lay beside him. He was able to tell his family at home that his wife had been changed into yucca.[75] The Serrano hero, by mistake, had coitus too early with his wife—he had wrongly interpreted the ghosts' injunction of three nights' continence, for they meant three years—; when he awoke he was alone.[76] In the Sinkaietk tale we are told that Coyote "froze stiff" when he embraced the woman he wanted to take home, and when he came to his senses she was gone.[77]

4. The sleeping taboo (C 735) may be regarded rather as a variation of the preceding taboo, and it occurs in the Orpheus tradition only among the Yokuts. It may be mentioned that according to the Telumni Yokuts Orpheus tried, during his sojourn in the realm of the dead, to observe this taboo; when he infringed it, his deceased wife was turned into a log.[78] We find the same story and with the same result of the contravention of the taboo in the Orpheus legend of the Yaudanchi Yokuts; but here the incident takes place during the journey home: on the third night with his wife the hero goes to sleep, to find himself, in the morning, together with

[72] See above, chap. II: 1.
[73] Gayton, op.cit., 284.
[74] Reid 1926, 44.
[75] Voegelin 1935, 205.
[76] Benedict 1926, 9.
[77] Spier 1938, 236.
[78] Gayton, op.cit., 268; cf. above, pp. (120), 131.

a log.[79] This Yokuts narrative has a striking similarity with the above-adduced Serrano tale, which further favours the assumption of a common origin for the sleeping taboo and the taboo on coitus. Gayton, it is true, connects the sleeping taboo in the Orpheus tradition with the rules for the acquisition of supernatural power in dreams: when one has had a vision of power one must not fall asleep again.[80] Whether one can in this way refer all sleeping taboos to the same source is, however, more than doubtful. The sleeping taboo of the Orpheus tradition cannot be explained otherwise than in the way indicated above.

5. We have already spoken of the food taboos (C 211) for the living which apply during the sojourn in the realm of the dead, and which are sometimes extended to apply also for the person just deceased, i.e. Orpheus' partner.[81] These taboo regulations must be observed if Orpheus (or in some cases his deceased wife) are not to remain in the grip of the sphere of death. Among the Zuni Indians, again, we meet with another food taboo, which is connected with the home-coming of the deceased, and whose aim is evidently to prevent her being too brutally introduced into the world of the living. For four days after their return to the village of the living Orpheus' wife had to abstain from food (meat); on the fifth day she and her husband feasted, for now she was out of all danger.[82]

6. Several of the afore-mentioned taboos may be grouped under the heading contact taboos (C 500); especially does the continence taboo belong to this category, since the sexual act must of course be regarded as a very definite form of contact. Several of the taboos mentioned in the following must also be regarded as contact taboos. But in addition to this we find in an Orpheus narrative of the Skidi Pawnee a taboo against contact as such, without any specification. A god said to the Pawnee man who wanted his deceased son back: "You are to be allowed to be near your son and to speak with him, but not to touch him." When the father took hold of his son, the latter vanished.[83] He was evidently too spiritual, too physically weak, to bear touch.

7. Various prohibitions against physical ill-treatment of the deceased may of course be connnected with the notion that during the journey home from the realm of the dead the deceased is physically brittle and fragile—the process of transformation from spirit to human being is still going on. As we have seen, the Comanche Indian lost his wife for the

[79] Kroeber 1907 c, 228.
[80] Gayton 1930 a, 78.
[81] See above, pp. 114 sq.
[82] Benedict 1935 II, 158.
[83] Dorsey 1904 b, 76, 77.

second time when—by mistake—he happened to strike her, thus contravening a prohibition imposed upon him by his deceased father-in-law.[84] "Do not whip your wife, nor strike her with a knife, nor hit her with fire" the Blackfoot Orpheus was admonished by his father-in-law in the realm of the dead. Shortly after her arrival home, however, he threatened her with a firebrand in wrath at her disobedience, and "all at once she vanished, and was never seen again."[84a] In a Shasta tale, Orpheus, who is carrying the deceased (obviously an echo of the receptacle motif farther north), drops her on the ground, whereupon she returns to the other world. Here there is no mention of any taboo prohibition, but it seems to be tacitly understood. A remarkable feature in this tale, for the rest, is that the hero twice succeeds in taking his wife from the realm of the dead (to fail the third time).[85]

Also in another Shasta variant there is mention of the taboo against physical ill-treatment, but it is here not alone (see below).

8. Various prohibitions against psychic abuse of the deceased are obviously intended to protect her feeble mental energies; for the transition from death to life implies also a gradual restoration of the mind, often expressed with a reference to the restoring of the free-soul and the ego-soul.[86] These souls (or one of them—they are both of vital importance for the existence of the individual) fly away if their owner is treated inconsiderately; through his speech, especially hard words and spiteful utterances, through anger, and even through entertaining evil thoughts or showing contempt Orpheus may jeopardize the life of the person he is trying to restore to life.[87] The taboos here in question, with the exception of the speech taboo, occur rarely and have an irregular distribution.

The prohibition against conversing with the dead person (C 400) occurs only among the Western Mono. It reminds one of the fear of talking to a ghost which is found in large parts of North America—it was by talking to a ghost that the Nisenan Orpheus lost his life.[88] But in the case here in

---

[84] See above, p. 18.

[84a] Grinnell, op.cit., 30 sq.

[85] Dixon 1910, 21. See further below, pp. 144 sq.

[86] See chap. II: 6.

[87] In the story of Ogauns, which is closely akin to the Orpheus tradition, it is a sneeze which causes the failure of the expedition (see above, p. 31). The significance of the sneeze in causing soul loss, stressed by Clements (see Clements 1932, 231), is not, moreover, observed at all in the genuine Orpheus tradition.

[88] Powers 1877, 340. Among the Tachi and Telumni Yokuts a prohibition against mentioning to anyone what has happened to him until six days have elapsed is contravened by Orpheus or his parents (C 423.3). The infringement of the prohibition leads to Orpheus' death (Kroeber, op.cit., 218; Gayton 1935, 268). The prohibition against telling what one knows about the world of the dead is common in North America (cf. chap. IV: 1).

question it is not the hero's life that is in danger, but that of his partner. Among the Western Mono the hero lost his wife again by infringing the taboo against conversing with her for the ten days immediately after the home-coming.[89]

The prohibition against saying "stop" if the deceased children he was bringing home should laugh was, according to the myth, imposed upon the Orpheus of the Upper Puyallup, the transformer (Xode). He disobeyed the prohibition, and "the children became nothing."[90]

The prohibition against crying out in the presence of the deceased who has just come home occurs in the Zuni variant noted down by Parsons and in the Nayarit narrative. According to the former, Orpheus was permitted to return with his wife "on condition that none would cry out on her return." But an old woman caught sight of her and let out a yell. "Straightway the *revenante* was changed into an owl and flew away."[91] The Orpheus of the Nayarit version was warned "not to speak a loud word"; when in his joy he raised his voice at a feast after the home-coming "a ghastly corpse had taken the place of the wife."[92]

The prohibition against speaking angrily to the deceased is mentioned in the Shasta tale of Coyote's bringing back of his deceased son. Here it is the deceased himself who states the condition: "For ten years you must not beat me, must not scold me." The prohibition was contravened after five years.[93] In a Pawnee variant the woman who has been brought home charges her husband to remember her and to be kind to her. But on one occasion, when he is visiting his second wife, he gets angry and speaks in contemptuous terms of his first wife. When he returns to her he finds her bones on the bed.[94] One may here also adduce the Winnebago Orpheus who in the other world was provoked by his wife so that in anger and through rash acts he might frustrate his own intention.[95]

We have seen above, in the Pawnee legend, an instance of the prohibition against thinking ill of the deceased. Another example is furnished by the Yuchi legend noted down by Wagner. Here we are told that Orpheus may never think of the fact that his wife has once been dead (C 441).[96] Such a thought is naturally in itself offensive; to be called a

[89] Gifford, op.cit., 341.
[90] Ballard 1929, 131.
[91] Parsons 1916, 250.
[92] Bancroft 1875 III, 530.
[93] Dixon, op.cit., 19.
[94] Dorsey 1906, 537.
[95] See above, p. 117.
[96] Wagner 1931, 88 sq.

"ghost" is among many Indian tribes extremely derogatory. But in addition to this, the thought that someone has been dead may have a magic effect. In the same way as the thought of the dead attracts them (hence the prohibition against speaking of them, so common in North America), the thought of a person's belonging to the sphere of death binds the person to this sphere.

Finally, we have the prohibition against the husband of the deceased being unfaithful in the sequel of the marriage, a prohibition that was in force according to the descriptions of the Orpheus drama in the Wichita versions and a Pawnee variant.[97] In the Pawnee legend it is the reclaimed woman herself who formulates the prohibition, which is very reminiscent of the other Pawnee legend (concerning the man who spoke ill of his wife) reviewed above.

One asks oneself if all the North American Orpheus traditions are connected with taboo motifs. This is not the case, as should, moreover, have emerged from the survey of the distribution given here. But it is impossible to say precisely which Orpheus tales have lacked this motif, as there is reason to assume that in a number of cases it has been forgotten by the narrator or that it dropped out of the story one or a couple of generations previously.[98] One can, however, say that the taboo motifs have a fairly regular distribution among the different culture areas, with the exception of the Northwest, for they are entirely lacking in the so-called "sea-coast form" of the Orpheus tradition.

According to certain tales Orpheus must submit to two or more taboo regulations, not counting the taboos already obtaining in the realm of the dead. Double taboos are mentioned in the Orpheus tales of the Western Mono, the Zuni Indians, the Blackfoot, the Comanche and the Yuchi; the commonest, in these cases, are the looking taboo and the taboo on coitus. In the Shasta myth concerning Coyote's journey to the other world several taboos are enjoined upon Coyote in a confusing way. It does not suffice that the son he is after charges him not to strike him or scold him; in addition to this the dead give him the following instructions: "You must not drink water in the usual way. You must not take off your pack when you sleep. You must not lie on your back."[99] One can, certainly, suspect elements of the numerous jokes of the trickster cycle in this plurality of taboos; but they are, undeniably, related to the circumstance that Coyote is taking his son home on his back.

[97] Dorsey 1904 a, 305, 310; 1906, 413.
[98] Cf. Gayton's discussion on the completeness of the tradition (Gayton, op.cit., 284).
[99] Dixon, op.cit., 19.

The interesting question of the gradual return of life in the deceased calls for a closer investigation, to which we shall revert presently.[100] In the meantime we may ask ourselves to what extent Orpheus is successful in the carrying out of his task; does a happy or an unhappy issue of the enterprise belong to the structure of the narrative? We have already seen that in several cases Orpheus is turned away from the realm of the dead, or dies on his arrival there; and to these cases must be added those adduced in the foregoing, in which his expedition is jeopardized in consequence of infringement of taboo-regulations. On the other hand, we have in several cases observed a happy issue, even if we abstract from the temporary gains (e.g. the survival of the loved one who has been brought home for a limited number of years).

Through her studies of the Orpheus theme Gayton came to the conclusion that a failure is one of the regular elements in the tradition, while a happy end constitutes the exception.[101] Thompson shares this view. He observes that of about forty versions, only three mention the successful bringing home of the deceased.[102] It is, certainly, true that Orpheus tales with a negative issue are predominant. But the material of Orpheus traditions scrutinized here—about 120 versions, see appendix—show that the percentage of successful expeditions is higher than has hitherto been assumed. Even if we abstract from the tales of the "sea-coast form", almost all of which describe the hero's success in fetching his loved one (see below), sixteen versions have a happy ending—i.e. almost one sixth of the total stock of tales in the ordinary tradition. Thus even if the tales with unsuccessful expeditions still form the majority, it is difficult in these versions to see, as unreservedly as Thompson, "the regular American Indian pattern."

The sixteen versions with a happy issue adduced above come from the Stalo, Twana, Modoc, Yurok, Zuni and Taos Indians, Sarcee, Assiniboin, Skidi Pawnee, Winnebago, Ojibway, Menomini, Shawnee, Malecite, Seneca and Yuchi.[103] In this connection it should be borne in mind that the Zuni Indians, the Skidi Pawnee and the Yuchi know other versions, in which the expedition it not successful. To the sixteen versions with a positive issue may possibly be added a seventeenth, viz, the Hupa legend. In this it is said that the man brought his deceased wife to life

---

[100] See chap. II: 6.
[101] Gayton, op.cit., 264.
[102] Thompson 1946, 351.
[103] Grinnell mentions an Orpheus narrative with a happy ending—but there is no reference to his source (Grinnell 1909, 200 sq.).

again, "but she was no longer able to enjoy the world of light."[104] Does this imply that the woman died? Or did she, as appears most probable, continue her life among the living? If the latter was the case, then the above quotation should probably be interpreted to mean that in consequence of her attachment to the sphere of death the woman was unable to resume her normal active existence among the living.[105] To the narratives with a successful home-bringing of the deceased one may, finally, refer practically all tales belonging to the "sea-coast form" of the Orpheus motif. The only exceptions are a couple of Haida versions which describe how the Eurydice restored to life was shut up in a box by her husband when he was going hunting; but she had nevertheless disappeared when he returned. In the one version, communicated by Swanton, we are told that she had escaped through a hole in the bottom of the box.[106] In the other version, communicated by Barbeau, it is said that she had been kidnapped by mountain spirits; Orpheus, who had earlier saved her from the sea-monsters, once more tried to free her, but opinion is divided as to his success in this attempt.[107]

In several cases the Orpheus tales tell of the temporary return of the deceased, which implies that the taboo infringement does not occur during the actual journey, but after the home-coming. The time which elapses before the forbidden action takes place may vary greatly. Among the Western Mono it is a matter of scarcely ten days; among the Pawnee it is obviously a matter of a longer period; the Yuchi husband (in Wagner's version) has time to see his wife give birth to several children; and the Carrier medicine-man lives together with his wife "for many summers".[108] It does not seem correct to include these special cases among the successful home-bringings. One may, however, possibly make an exception for the Carrier legend, for here the wife does not return to the dead on account of her husband's infringement of a taboo, but because, wearied by her belonging half to the world of the dead, he allows her to die a second time.[109]

Nor can one refer to the cases of successful expeditions those tales in which Orpheus brings back from the land of the spirits a substitute for the deceased. These tales are in themselves of particular interest, whether they take (in their kind) a happy turn or not, and it may therefore be

[104] Goddard 1903, 74.
[105] See further chap. II: 6.
[106] Swanton 1905 b, 203.
[107] Barbeau 1953, 295 sq.; cf. op.cit., 4.
[108] Cf. below, pp. 150 sq.
[109] Jenness 1934, 145.

worth while to consider them for a moment. To a certain extent they are reminiscent of an earlier adduced Ojibway legend—Ogauns' search for eternal life[110]—and of the narratives of the gifts that the ruler of the other world gives Orpheus to take home with him.[111] According to the pattern of action, Orpheus follows the deceased to the realm of the dead, and in this connection his longing for her seems to be the chief motive for his action (although this is not expressly stated). But he does not take her home, and if he does happen to do so her restoration to life is at all events not his main purpose. The Karuk girls who sought out their lovers in the realm of the dead remained with them there for a year, and then returned home without them, but equipped with medicine of immortality; the Pomo father who betook himself to the other world to seek his son brought home a dance; and in the Chehalis tale Bluejay returned home with a basket "full of something." But this something came out in the form of flying insects when, against the instructions he had received, he opened the basket on his way home. "Some of the insects would have become fir-cones and things like that, the rest would have become berries. All these things, Bluejay lost to us."[112] To this type of Orpheus narrative belong above all those versions which describe how Orpheus takes the dead home with him in his pack or box, though without always succeeding in his intention. These versions occur among the Wishram, Wasco, Kalispel, Klikitat, Yakima, Shahaptin (Nez Percé?) and Modoc. The Modoc myth, for example, relates how Kumush brought home from the realm of the dead a basket with the bones of his daughter and other dead people. The last-mentioned he threw out in different directions, in order that different peoples should arise from them.[113] We shall later have occasion to revert to Orpheus traditions of this type.[114]

The tales adduced here, in which the fetching of the deceased plays a subordinate rôle or no rôle at all, are most closely comparable with the Orpheus narratives which tell how Orpheus returns home alone, obviously without having desired to bring his dead partner back with him.[115] Also these tales belong to the western tradition represented by the previous ones, and occur among the Quinault, Snuqualmi, Puyallup and Skopamish.

[110] See above, p. 31.
[111] See below, pp. 145 sqq.
[112] Adamson 1934, 22.
[113] Curtin 1912, 44 sq.
[114] See chap. V: 3.
[115] This indifference on Orpheus' part may be due to his negative reaction to a being who has been drawn into the sphere of death—cf. the Tewa and Navajo myths, where from horror and disgust the hero flees from the proximity of the deceased.

142

There are thus several Orpheus traditions which cannot be listed with the narratives in which the hero succeeds in fetching the loved one, though they do not directly show a negative issue of Orpheus' visit to the other world. Just as little, however, can they be adduced as examples of Orpheus tales in which the expedition is a failure. They are and remain irrelevant for the problem here under debate.

One may ask oneself then, what factors have brought about the differentiation of the great majority of Orpheus traditions in narratives with positive and negative issue as regards the fetching of the deceased. Is there in this connection any regularity which may afford a hint as to the cause of the distribution? It is in my opinion here possible to distinguish certain patterns which may throw a little light on the problem.

In the first place one may observe that practically all versions of the independent "sea-coast form" describe the hero's success in fetching his loved one. Now this narrative cycle is, as we have already observed, formally distinct from the ordinary Orpheus tradition, although it is based upon the same fundamental motif as this. A feature in the pattern of the "sea-coast form" is, inter alia, the absence of taboo-motifs proper, something which should, of course, facilitate the hero's task.

In the second place one notes that all the versions of the ordinary Orpheus tradition which at the same time function as origin narratives of the divorce between the living and the dead, or of death as such, take an unhappy turn. It is possible, however, that the negative issue of the tale has constituted the link with the myth of the origin of death.[116]

In the third place it is obvious that the traditions in which there is no mention of taboo prohibitions will tend to a successful expedition, while the traditions containing taboo prescriptions will have a contrary tendency. In this circumstance, in my opinion, one has probably to seek the deeper causes of the differentiation. One may even constate that practically all the Orpheus traditions without taboo prohibitions have a positive issue,[117] while extremely few Orpheus versions with taboo prohibitions do end in this way. Especially fatal is the "opening taboo", which is always disobeyed (except in the Yuchi versions, where, however, one or several of the Orpheus figures acting at the same time fail). Both the "looking taboo" and the "taboo of sexual abstinence" occur, on the other hand, without being contravened (Modoc, Western Mono,

---

[116] See further chap. V: 3.

[117] The above-discussed Carrier, Hupa and Haida legends, although they do in some measure have a happy issue, constitute exceptions.

Malecite; Stalo, Zuni Indians, Comanche); they evidently constitute weaker temptations. One observes, however, that the happy issue is relatively rare in the Orpheus narratives with taboo motifs; and in those in which double taboos occur, as among the Western Mono and Comanche, one of the prohibitions, at all events, leads to infringement. Of the tales with the taboo motif, only the Stalo, Modoc, Zuni, Winnebago, Malecite and Yuchi versions tell of a happy issue, in which connection it must be borne in mind that in the Modoc and Winnebago narratives the taboo refers to the sojourn in the realm of the dead, and the Yuchi versions have a happy ending with the modification mentioned above. Only one of the many Zuni legends has a happy issue, although the hero and his deceased wife must each submit to a different taboo prohibition.[118]

On the basis of the distribution of successful and failed expeditions here adduced it is possible to arrive at certain conclusions concerning the historical main line of the Orpheus tradition in North America. It is, I think, fruitless to speculate on the question as to whether a happy or an unhappy ending characterized the Orpheus tradition as such from the outset. The majority of the North American tales noted down in historical times take a negative turn, which has undeniably been an advantage for a dramatic telling of the tales.[119] But what is more important in this connection is that all of these narratives contain the taboo motif, while tales both with and without this motif have a happy ending. It thus seems probable that the Orpheus tradition was from the outset built up about a theme which provided both possibilities as regards the ending, the issue being made to depend upon the observance of the taboo prescriptions, i.e. upon the right treatment of the deceased person.

We have already remarked that the infringement of the taboo prohibitions regulating the return of the deceased to life cannot be made good.[120] What has happened has an irreversible character, it cannot be changed—a common observation in connection with magic trains of thought. There are, however, certain exceptions to this rule. Chief among these is the Shasta narrative reported by Dixon about the man who fetched his wife, Woodpecker, from the realm of the dead. "Before he got back, he dropped his burden, and the ghost ran back to the other world. He followed her again, and the next time got within a very short distance of his door, when he dropped her, and again she ran back. For the third

[118] Benedict 1935 II, 157 sq.
[119] See above, p. 20.
[120] See above, p. 131.

time he returned to the land of the dead, but was told that he might not try again."[121] Thus here Orpheus makes three renewed attempts, two of which are evidently quite legitimate.

We also find that it is within the range of the possibilities obtaining for Orpheus' deed to be repeated by others, but then it must have had a positive issue, and its character of an unique occurrence must not be expressly stressed, as it was in the Winnebago Orpheus legend.[122] Like his predecessor, the second Orpheus had strictly to observe the limits for his freedom of action which constitute the conditions for a happy conclusion of his task. According to the Stalo legend, some time after Orpheus' achievement another man lost his wife. He trained for four years to acquire supernatural power, and then set off. Everything was repeated. He returned home with his wife, and with horses and other gifts. But on the last night of the taboo period he had intercourse with his wife, and the next morning he found himself lying alone "with no sign of wife, or horses, or other possessions to be anywhere seen."[123]

Even if the Orpheus of many tribes experiences a bitter defeat after all his efforts, this need not necessarily mean that he will return home quite empty-handed. In those versions of the Orpheus tradition, too, which tell of a successful fetching home of the deceased, there is often mention of treasures brought back from the land of the dead, given by representatives of the other world (the ruler, the dead themselves). These gifts may be of the most various kinds; but one may observe that in the main the distribution follows regional lines: a northern field, from California and over the Plains to Lake Michigan, where the gifts consist of (ritual) dances, and a southern field, comprising the Indians of the Southwest and of the Eastern Woodland area, among whom the gifts consist of agricultural products.

The gift of the dance is not very common in the Californian Orpheus traditions; it is mentioned only among the Pomo and Yokuts. It is nòt quite clear what kind of dance is here referred to, but Gayton presumes that it has in both cases been the well-known ghost dance.[124] As we know, it was the aim of the ghost dance to resuscitate the dead, to enable the reunion of the living with them and to bring about the rebirth of the old

---

[121] Dixon, op.cit., 21.
[122] See above, pp. 122 sq.
[123] Hill-Tout 1904 b, 341.
[124] Gayton 1930 a, 77 sq. (Yokuts), 1935, 270 (Pomo). The round-dance in which Coyote, the Shasta myth Orpheus, took part and to which he sang in the realm of the dead was probably, too, a ghost dance (Dixon, op.cit., 19).

tribal life—without coexistence with the whites. It seems quite natural that precisely the Orpheus tale should have become the "institution myth" for the ghost-dance movement. One may observe, moreover, that one of the central aims of this cult is also incorporated in one of the Karuk Orpheus legends, where we are told that the two girls—the heroines of the tale—brought home with them as a gift from the dead a medicine of immortality.[125] We shall have occasion to revert to this supernatural gift in another connection, when we shall also analyse other motifs in the Orpheus tradition closely related with this.[126]

The dance as a gift of the dead to Orpheus is also found among the Paviotso, with whom it obviously had the character of a procedure through which the dead woman is normalized.[127] On the Plains we find it among the Sarcee as a special kind of "ghost dance," with whose help the sick can be cured.[128] Also the "ghost dance" brought home by the Winnebago Orpheus has a similar motive, viz, to restore the soul of a sick person.[129] We may here once more observe how naturally the Orpheus legend lends itself as an "institution myth": it illustrates very well the medical drama. According to the Sarcee legend, the ghosts even become "almost completely human" when they dance this dance, which is afterwards donated to Orpheus. We may here remember what has been said in the foregoing concerning the communion of the living and dead in the ghost dance.[130] According to two Pawnee versions of the Orpheus tradition the dance brought home by the hero is the Elk dance, whose aim is evidently to enable communication between the living and the spirits of the dead.[131] It is possible that the "sacred dance" given to the Shawnee Orpheus in the realm of the dead had the same import.[132]

The gifts brought home by the hero in the Orpheus traditions of the East and the Southwest are of another character. The Taos rain spirits give him "different kinds of fruits, huckleberries, chokeberries, green corn."[133] The Alabama and Koasati legends are peculiar inasmuch as the Orpheus men are *refused* permission to take home with them the seeds

---

[125] Harrington 1932, 34.
[126] See chap. V: 3.
[127] Gayton 1935, 277 sq.
[128] Jenness 1938, 98.
[129] Radin 1926, 36 sq. See also Radin, op.cit., 33 note 1. Neither the Sarcee nor the Winnebago "ghost dances" must be confused with the well-known messianic movement with the same name.
[130] See above, p. 124.
[131] Dorsey 1906, 413, 537.
[132] Greggs 1954, 388.
[133] Parsons 1940, 26.

of the water-melon. As Gayton has shown, there is in this an indication that the whole narrative, if the Orpheus motif is subtracted, is intended to explain "the origin of seeds" among these peoples.[134] Through a game played for stakes in the land of the dead the Micmac Orpheus wins maize and tobacco.[135] The Micmac tale is remarkably reminiscent of an isolated Chehalis narrative in the Orpheus tradition which tells how when playing with the ghosts for stakes Bluejay won their berries and fruits; if he had not won, human beings would now be without them.[136] In this as in other respects the Plateau versions reveal a peculiar stamp which makes them more akin to eastern legends than with tales in their vicinity.

Gayton has drawn attention to the fact that all the Orpheus versions of the Plains area "are couched in characteristic terms of Plains culture"; to this observation may be referred, inter alia, the circumstance that they explain the origin of a ritual. Thus the Blackfoot narrative is used as origin legend for a ceremonial pipe.[137] This is correct; but the perspective should be widened. In the northern versions, as we have found, it is for the most part a matter of the bringing home of a dance, a dance that brings the dead and the living into close relation with each other. This dance is found over a large, connected area of which the Plains area is only a part. In view of the fact that this dance motif everywhere appears in regions in which a hunting culture has prevailed, whereas the motif concerning the sending home of berries and maize is on the whole (but not so regularly) met with in the agrarian cultures, it would be natural to conceive the dance motif as belonging to an older stratum of the Orpheus tradition. This assumption is rendered still more likely by the circumstance that the earlier mentioned motif of the dance in the realm of the dead[138] is universally found over the whole area of distribution of the Orpheus tradition with the exception of the Northwest (where the majority of the Orpheus tales belong to the diverging "sea-coast form"); and the ritual dance, which Orpheus takes home with him in the northern narratives, is a natural continuation of the dance among the dead.

[134] Gayton, op.cit., 273 note 2.
[135] Le Clercq 1910, 210 sq.
[136] Adamson 1934, 29. The Chehalis narrative in its turn is reminiscent of the Kalispel tale: Coyote wins when playing for stakes in the other world, thereby jeopardizing the return to life of the dead (Curtis 1911 VII, 96).
[137] Gayton, op.cit., 276 sq. Cf. above, p. 52. The pipe was "the Worm Pipe" (Grinnell 1912, 131).
[138] See above, p. 124.

6. Revivification rites

It now only remains for us to discuss the process or the processes whereby the deceased is brought back to life, i.e. is once more incorporated with the sphere of the living. It has already emerged from the foregoing that the realization of this change requires Orpheus' cooperation, and he as well as the relatives at home are subjected to severe tests, as the deceased runs the risk of being lost again both during the journey back to the living and immediately after the home-coming. The numerous taboo prescriptions we have just reviewed are of course intended to constitute a protection for the restoration of the deceased to life. And it is essential that these be observed. Firstly it is a matter of seeing to it that the deceased does not return to the world of the dead, the milieu to which for natural reasons she feels drawn. And secondly it is a matter of ensuring that in consequence of her weak health, i.e. her situation on the borderline between life and death, she is not injured through contact with or hard words from the living. One may speak of a gradual revivification of the deceased. This begins with the missile, continues more or less perceptibly during the return to the land of the living, and is concluded some time after the home-coming.

The revivification process constitutes the central element in the accounts of the journey home, which does not otherwise attract much attention on the part of the narrators.[1] The process does not everywhere, however, follow the same basic pattern, and three different themata are distinguishable: the slow, continuous transition from death to life; the resurrection via the grave; and the fetching of the deceased in a receptacle with (in the East) corresponding revivification rites.

The slow, continuous process, the progressive incorporation of the deceased in the sphere of the living, has been referred to by Gayton under the heading "normalizing of deceased," and she instances this from the Tlingit, Stalo, Tenino, Shasta, Gabrielino, Paviotso and Pawnee.[2] One might add further instances, but these would not invalidate her conclusion that we have here to do with "a feature having a western distribution."[3] The successive restoration is described both in connection with the receptacle motif and in narratives without this; here, to begin with, we shall only touch upon its occurrence in tales of the last-mentioned type. The action takes place in some cases during the actual journey

[1] See above, p. 130.
[2] Gayton 1935, 266.
[3] Gayton, op.cit., 284.

home, in some cases during the period after the home-coming; only in certain versions is the process of restoration clearly fixed to both periods.

Some narratives describe how even during the journey home the deceased slowly recovers her character of a living being. The Gabrielino legend tells how on the first day the wife newly recovered by the husband appears as a phantom, on the second day becomes fully visible and on the third day is a normal human being again—except in this respect, that she cannot stand sexual contact. We have already reproduced the account of how the Stalo hero's wife began ta regain a part of her former, living self when the chief of the dead threw a missile at her.[4] The improvement of her state progressed during the journey home, as they respected the taboo prescriptions. "By the time they reached the village, a similar period to that which he had spent in looking for his wife had elapsed, and she was now grown strong again, and accustomed to the contact of living people, so there was no longer any need to keep apart, and thereafter he lived with her as before her death."[5] The Comanche woman "became flesh" when on the way home she ate a buffalo kidney—the allusion here is probably to the life-producing force that the buffalo possessed according to the belief of the Plains Indians (cf. e.g. the buffalo cult in the sun-dance). In one of the Skidi Pawnee versions Orpheus dropped some lice on the dead girl, with the result that "the girl scratched, and the flesh came on her again, and the blood began to circulate through her veins." Her saviour was now able to observe: "You are now like myself, and your feelings are such as mine", whereupon "the girl found that is was so."[6] In another Pawnee version the hero, just before the home-coming, makes "his wife sleep each night in [a] bed of cactus, which by morning has caused her nerves to assume normal condition."[7] The last-adduced examples from the Plains area come close, undeniably, to the missile motif.

In several cases, however, the Eurydice restored to life and to the world of living men is not always entirely removed from the sphere of the dead; she retains, at least for a time, her "death-being." The Haida woman who had been freed by her husband "came back to life like a soul revived among the people of the Queen Charlotte Islands."[8] The Haisla narrative tells in a drastic way how the dead woman brought back by her husband lives in the home, invisible and inaudible; her daughter concludes that

---

[4] See above, p. 126.
[5] Hill-Tout 1904 b, 341.
[6] Dorsey 1904 b, 73.
[7] Dorsey 1906, 537.
[8] Barbeau 1953, 296.

it is her mother who moves things about when these move as if by their own volition. Of the same type is the account in the Tlingit legend of the woman restored to her home. She was visible only to her husband; her father-in-law and his family saw merely a deep shadow following the husband. "When she ate they saw only her arms and the spoon moving up and down but not the shadow of her hands. It looked strange to the people." During the day she was very quiet, but at night "the people could hear her voice very plainly." When her father-in-law joked with her "they could hear the shadow laugh, and recognized that it was the dead woman's voice." This went on until one day she declared that she would resume her living shape that she had had formerly. Unfortunately a relative of hers disobeyed a taboo prohibition, so that both she and her husband died for good.[9]

It is not only the reaction of the living to the deceased that is deserving of attention, but also the reaction of the deceased to the living. As in the realm of the dead, she finds the living repulsive and peculiar. In the Pawnee legend mentioned above the wife remained for several days after her home-coming sequestered from people, as she could not stand their odour.

As is testified in the Tlingit legend, after her return the deceased had to spend a long time growing into the milieu of the living; revivification is a slow procedure. It reminds one, incidentally, of the way in which in the Shahaptin narrative Coyote, by having intercourse with the dead, became more and more accustomed to them, and could see them more and more plainly—thus an adaptation in the contrary direction. The time which elapses before the deceased is completely incorporated in the world of the living varies considerably. In the Western Mono legend it is a matter of ten days, in the Shasta myth of Coyote's fetching of his son it is a matter of ten years. Sometimes it is quite impossible for the restored person to become normal again. What we are told in the Carrier legend is significant in this connection: "But in this her second life all the seasons seemed reversed to the medicine-man's wife. Summer was as winter to her, cold and foodless, so that she constantly asked for a big fire to warm her frame. On her feet and hands she wore thick moccasins and mittens, and instead of eating the ripe berries she chewed the bark of the jack-pine. Then when winter came she put on her thinnest clothing and went forth barefoot to gather berries and salmon.[10] So for many sum-

[9] Swanton 1909, 250.
[10] Is it a coincidence that the woman with this topsy-turvy behaviour is so strikingly reminiscent of the Dakota divinity Haokah or Heyoka? (See Eastman 1849, 158, 206, 209 sqq.; Dorsey 1894, 468).

mers the medicine-man had to waste the warm days and toil to gather her firewood." Finally he tired of this, and when she died for the second time he let her travel to the land of the dead alone.[11] We have met with a similar prolongation of the sphere of death among the Hupa.[12]

Some of the above-mentioned tales (from the Carrier, Western Mono and Skidi Pawnee) also give instances of a ressurection via the grave. As has been mentioned in the foregoing, this form of removal from the world of the dead to that of the living is a direct counterpart of the deliberately undertaken sham burial; it should consequently be understood as a magic rite, a revivification rite.[13] Such rites occur chiefly in connection with the eastern versions, according to which the soul is fetched in a receptacle and the body is restored from the grave (see below). They have, however, a wider distribution than the receptacle motif and should therefore be regarded as an older or at all events originally more independent element. The idea behind the revivification rite is based upon sympathetic magic.[14] In the first place the bones of the deceased are conceived as possessing an inherent capacity to restore the body in its entirety —a notion which is based on old hunting magic and which also finds expression, moreover, in the Orpheus myths of the Klamath and Modoc, where the god-culture hero makes the bones of the dead populate the earth.[15] And secondly, among the Carrier and Menomini the deceased reawakens to life when she rises from the grave together with her living husband—a clear expression for homeopathic magic. As in these two tribes the rite appears more meaningful than among the other tribes that refer to it, it seems most natural to assume that the Orpheus narratives of these two tribes have preserved it in its original form.

We shall here adduce four examples of the awakening from the grave, taken from four different culture areas; to the easterly forms of this revivification rite, which I regard as historically secondary, we shall revert presently. In the Carrier legend the way to the land of the living led the medicine-man and his deceased but recovered wife to their grave —the grave in which she had been buried as a dead person and he as a living one.[16] And now, "at their journey's end they re-entered their bodies

[11] Jenness 1934, 145.
[12] See above, pp. 140 sq.
[13] See above, pp. 63 sq.
[14] I follow here the classification of the forms of magic given by Frazer (Frazer 1949, 11 sq.).
[15] Cf. Hultkrantz 1953, 176 note 167. Cf. also above, p. 68.
[16] Cf. above, p. 64.

and the medicine-man called aloud to his kinsmen. Weeping and lamentation changed to cries of gladness; quickly the earth was moved from the grave and husband and wife stepped joyfully forth into the happy circle of their friends."[17] In the Western Mono legend Orpheus' wife separated from her husband to go to her grave. According to the prescriptions of the ruler of the dead, Wolf, the husband sent his mother to the grave to fetch her on his return home. In the earlier adduced legend from the Skidi Pawnee we are told that the deceased girl was able, when her circulation had started, to leave her burial tipi. When, later, she and her young adorer returned to the place and dug in the ground they found her body gone.[18] Finally, we have the Menomini legend, which constitutes a link between these narratives and the eastern Orpheus versions. Equipped with the tube in which the soul of his deceased wife is kept, Orpheus approaches the grave in which he had been buried with his wife.[19] At the grave the burial fire is burning,[20] and the man rushes straight into this. A mourner at the grave then hears faint voices from within, the grave is opened and Orpheus and his wife step forth.

The Menomini tale brings us straight to the most complicated but also most interesting of the revivification rites of the Orpheus tradition, viz, the fetching of the soul in a receptacle and its reunion with the dead body. It is evident that this ceremony found in the eastern tales is traceable to two basic elements, viz, the resurrection of the dead body via the grave, a process which we have just illustrated, and the bringing back of the soul (or rather, of the dead person) in a receptacle, a motif which occurs, apart from the eastern areas, also on the Plateau and at Puget Sound, as well as in the Southwest.[21] Let us first consider the last-mentioned motif.

The receptacle motif is differently developed in each of the areas of distribution referred to here. In the more westerly versions in which it occurs it is intimately associated with the figure of the culture hero-trickster, and the receptacle is described as a wooden box, a bag, a basket or

[17] Jenness, op.cit., loc.cit.
[18] Cf., however, above, p. 65, where I have recorded certain doubts of the occurrence here of a planned sham burial.
[19] See above, pp. 63 sq.
[20] It was common custom among the Central Algonquin for a fire to be kept alight at the grave for four days after the burial, so that the route to the realm of the dead should be lighted up. See e.g. Jenness 1932, 165, Schoolcraft 1853 III, 60, 1860 V, 64, 1860 VI, 664 sq.
[21] Cf. also Gayton 1935, 284. The instance from the Southwest was published after the appearance of Gayton's study.

a sack. The narratives here in question constitute an oikotype, which we have defined earlier.[22] In connection with the receptacle motif this oikotype is represented among the Snuqualmi, Skopamish, Chehalis, Wishram, Wasco, Kalispel, Klikitat, Yakima, Tenino, Shahaptin, Klamath and Modoc.[23] One may possibly also include among these tales the Shasta traditions communicated by Dixon, in which Orpheus takes the deceased on his back. Although there is here no mention of any receptacle, such essential motifs for the "receptacle versions" as the pack on the back and its increasing weight on the journey home do occur (see below). Curiously enough, the Haida living far in the north have in their Orpheus legend of the "sea-coast form" a fully developed receptacle motif. We are told that after successfully recovering his wife from the dwelling of the sea-monsters, the Haida hunter, out of fear of his neighbours' greed, shut her up in a box, where she had to sit while he was out hunting. "Nobody could touch her, and for greater security he fastened the cover of the box and bored two holes in the sides for her to see the light." But one day she had nevertheless disappeared.[24] A variant mentions that she was kept in the innermost of a series of five Chinese boxes, but they had a hole in the bottom, and through this she disappeared.[25] One is tempted to assume that the receptacle motif here is related to the receptacles referred to in the more southerly tales.

How, then, is the receptacle motif described on the Plateau and at Puget Sound? Let us take, as a prototype, the bringing back of the dead according to the Wishram Orpheus myth noted down by Curtis. Coyote and Eagle, who had arrived in the realm of the dead to fetch their wives and children, made a big wooden box, as big as they were able to carry, and in this they put grass and leaves. They then placed it outside the dancing lodge of the dead, and when at dawn the dead left the lodge they went right into the box, on which Eagle quickly closed the lid. The prisoners sounded like a swarm of flies. Coyote and Eagle then set off homewards, and Eagle carried the chest. When they were resting on the third night on the way home, Coyote heard the faint voices of people who seemed to be approaching. On the fourth night Coyote heard the voices again, and found that they came from the box. He applied his ear and smiled when he recognized his wife's voice. When the last day of the journey arrived Coyote insisted on carrying the chest. Somehow,

[22] See above, pp. 49 sqq.
[23] It must be due to an oversight that Gayton marks on her map the occurrence of the motif among the Puyallup and forgets the Kalispel (see Gayton, op.cit., 266).
[24] Barbeau, op.cit., 295.
[25] Swanton 1905 a, 340, 1905 b, 203.

he found himself lagging a little bit behind Eagle on the way, and from behind a hill he opened the chest to let his wife out. The dead then rushed back to the other world with such force that Coyote was felled to the ground.[26]

We find this pattern of action recurring in principle all over the Plateau and coastal region where the receptacle motif is represented. There are, however, a few striking deviations. In the Snuqualmi narrative and one of the Skopamish versions the culture hero takes the "pack" with him already on the way to the realm of the dead, and according to the Skopamish version the beings shut up in a basket—Groundsparrow's grandchildren—fly out of this; "the little ones slipped away, one by one," for "they did not wish to go to the land of the dead."[27] This is undoubtedly a distortion of the original motif. The same may be said of the observation in the Chehalis myth that it was berries and plants that Bluejay brought back to the world of the living in his bag.[28]

In the more regular traditions of this type the box or bag forms a roomy receptacle which the culture hero uses to bring back his loved ones to life. It may, as we find in several of the tales, even be roomy enough to contain also other dead persons, perhaps all the dead. This, however, is doubtless a secondary motif.[29] The box (bag, etc.) serves chiefly as a suitable instrument for bringing a spirit from the supernatural world to the natural world: the spirit is of course etherial and without contours, as we have already seen,[30] and it is, moreover, extremely recalcitrant on account of its solidarity with the other world. We have found in the foregoing that the deceased is drawn towards the realm of the dead as if by a magnet,[31] that she strives with all her might to reach the other world and desires to stay there.[32] It can scarcely be a coincidence that it is precisely in the Orpheus tales with the receptacle motif that the attraction back to the realm of the dead experienced by the deceased emerges so clearly in connection with the episode of the journey home.[33] When the receptacle is opened—however little—the dead in it are mechanically restored to the other world. In the Plateau and west-coast narratives it is said that they glide out, or flow away, or fly away with the

[26] Curtis 1911 VIII, 127 sqq.
[27] Ballard 1929, 132.
[28] See above, p. 142.
[29] See below, chap. V: 3.
[30] See above, pp. 116, 127.
[31] See above, p. 88.
[32] See above, pp. 117, 123 sqq.
[33] Compare the Orpheus narratives among the Wishram, Wasco, Menomini, Micmac, Seneca, Alabama and Koasati.

speed of lightning. The box is evidently a necessary accessory for a happy issue of the expedition; without it, the etherial volatile stuff of which the deceased is composed cannot be brought back to life. When the enterprise nevertheless comes to grief, this is because the taboo prohibition against opening the container intimately connected with the receptacle motif is disobeyed.[34] As we have already observed, this taboo is always infringed, as it implies too great a temptation.[35]

Despite the ultimately unsuccessful issue, one has time to observe how the process of revivification is already started in the receptacle. The above-adduced Wishram myth tells how at first the dead sounded like buzzing flies, but afterwards acquired increasingly human voices. The Klikitat Orpheus, Coyote, hears voices in the distance behind him; they become stronger and stronger, and he thinks he is being pursued—though it is in reality the dead in the pack he is carrying who are beginning to come to life. In the Shahaptin, Yakima and Shasta tales the revivification becomes apparent through the increasing weight of the beings in the pack. Thus we are told concerning the deceased Shasta woman who was brought back by her husband that "At first she weighed nothing, but grew heavier as they approached the earth and his house."[36] And to quote the wording of the narrative in the Yakima myth concerning the journey to Hades of Coyote and Eagle: "As the two adventurers went upon their long journey toward the earth with the precious box, the spirits, which at first were entirely imponderable, began to be transformed into men and to have weight. Soon they began to cry out on account of their crowded and uncomfortable position. Then they became so heavy that Speelyi [i.e. Coyote] could no longer carry them."[37] The narrative of the Shahaptin myth conforms closely in this point with the Yakima myth.

To proceed now to the Southwest, where the receptacle motif occurs only in a Taos version. The narration is here as follows. When Magpietail had succeeded in the other world in catching hold of his recently deceased wife, Yellow Corn woman, she was turned into a jackrabbit. As the powers had informed him, an eagle now came flying to his aid. "The eagle sat on the jack rabbit and tore the jack rabbit to pieces, into bone and hair and meat. Then he picked up all the pieces he could see on the ground and made a ball of it and tied it up in a corn husk bundle, and gave it to Magpie-tail." The latter took the ball to the rain-spirits, who

---

[34] Cf. above, pp. 133 sq.
[35] See above, pp. 143 sq.
[36] Dixon 1910, 21.
[37] Lyman 1904, 249.

placed it under a white blanket and sang a magic song. "By and by it began to move while they were singing. Then it began to move more and more and then it came to life. Then the guard uncovered her and she sat up, very tired. Raising her hair from her forehead, she said, '*Huwi!* I slept a little while'."[38] We see here how the deceased is brought back enclosed in a corncob—a circumstance which, like her name, gives definite associations; of which more anon.[39] At the same time we witness a revivification ceremony, remarkable on two counts: that it takes place in the supernatural world and that, in contradistinction to the case in other tales with the receptacle motif, the deceased is identical with the dead body.[40]

Through its connection with agrarian conceptions, for the rest, this episode in the Taos myth reminds one of the receptacle motif in the Eastern Woodland area. Here the receptacle sometimes occurs in the form of a gourd or a pumpkin. The receptacles we find mentioned, to be precise, are a box (Ojibway, Cherokee), a tube (Menomini), a hollow pipe (Shawnee), a bag (Micmac), a nut (Malecite), a pumpkin (Huron), a calabash (Seneca, Yuchi, Alabama), or a jar (Alabama, Koasati). From the above list of tribes it is apparent that the receptacle motif in the Orpheus tradition has been much more widely distributed in the east than in the western parts of the continent.[41] It would, however, be over-hasty to imagine that in the respect in question all these eastern versions of the Orpheus tradition belong to one and the same basic type. This is not the case. One can clearly distinguish two different patterns in connection with the receptacle motif, the one represented in the Southeast, the other represented among the Central Algonquin and in the Northeast.

The Southeast tradition occurs among the Cherokee, Yuchi, Alabama and Koasati; Gregg's Shawnee version marks the transition to the northern tradition. A typical feature in the Southeast tradition is that big as she is the deceased is put into the container, which thus consists of a very roomy object, a chest, a large jar, or a huge calabash (among the Yuchi "four large gourds" for the four women). On account of the size of the vessel it is not carried home, both it and Orpheus himself are transported magically to the world of the living.[42] The exception is constituted by the chest of the Cherokee, which is carried by seven men. The deceased is

---

[38] Parsons 1940, 25 sq.

[39] See below, chap. IV: 4.

[40] In a variant which will be adduced later, however (see below, p. 161), the soul is brought back to the grave, whence the resurrection takes place. But this variant lacks the receptacle motif.

[41] Gayton reports the motif also from the Montagnais (Gayton, op.cit., 266, 274). She does not, however, mention any source, and I have not been able to find this.

[42] Cf., however, also above, p. 130.

definitively lost when the taboo prohibition against opening the container is contravened. This pattern of action tallies in a remarkable way with that in the Plateau and Puget Sound narratives.

The northern tradition, represented by the Ojibway, Menomini, Micmac, Malecite, Huron, Seneca and (to some extent) the Shawnee, is characterized by a strict dogmatic defining of the constituent parts of the deceased, the spirit and the body. It is always the more "immaterial" ghost that is fetched in the container; as we shall see presently, one may in this connection speak of "the soul", the free-soul. Three circumstances especially reveal the incorporeal existence of the deceased who is being brought away: she is perceived as a miniature being; she is sometimes carried home in two receptacles containing her spiritual parts; she is confronted after the home-coming with her own body.

We have earlier adduced an instance from the Huron of the way in which, when she was seized, the deceased became so small that there was no difficulty in introducing her into the receptacle.[43] In the Seneca legend, too, the presumption is that the deceased enters the receptacle in a diminutive form; and the Central Algonquin Orpheus tales (Ojibway, Menomini) follow the same pattern. The Shawnee "grandfather" told Orpheus concerning his sister's restoration to life that "he must seize and ensconce her in the hollow of a reed with which he was furnished, and cover the orifice with the end of his finger."[44] In the Micmac legend the deceased "became in an instant the size of a nut by the command of Papkootparout, who took it [i.e. 'the soul'] in his hands, wrapped it very closely in a little bag, and gave it to our Indian."[45] The last of the supernatural old women whom the Malecite hero met on his way to the realm of the dead gave him a little nut and the following advice concerning the apprehension of his wife: "When she dances past you, open the nut, and you will thus bring her back to life. And as she goes past you, close it."[46] Here, it is true, we are not told what happens to the deceased. But we need scarcely doubt that the deceased as a spirit—in miniature form—has been enclosed in the nut. When in the sequel of the story it is said that the nut "was full of oil," this is a confusion (presumably by the narrator) with the motif with two containers.

The narrative of the taking home of two receptacles by Orpheus occurs among the Ojibway, Huron and Seneca, and in the two first-men-

---

[43] See above, p. 127.
[44] Gregg 1954, 388.
[45] Le Clercq 1910, 211.
[46] Mechling 1914, 89.

tioned tribes the form is practically the same. According to the Ojibway legend concerning the woman who brought back her deceased husband from the land of the dead, she first reached, on her journey to this land, "the storehouse of brains," whose guardian promised to give her her husband's brain if the ruler of the dead gave her his soul. The ruler "placed the man's soul in a little box and sent the woman home," after which the brain-custodian "gave her the brains and sent her on her way." Equipped with two boxes, containing the soul and the brains—here also referred to as "the shade"—she returned to the land of the living.[47] The Huron legend is told in similar terms. From the brain-custodian Orpheus receives two pumpkins, first one in which to shut up the deceased herself, then one in which her brains are kept. In an earlier work I have shown that the contents of the two containers in the Ojibway and Huron legends correspond exactly to the soul-dualism obtaining in these tribes.[48] Both the so-called free-soul, i.e. the human being himself in his extra-corporeal form of existence, and the so-called ego-soul, i.e. the potency of the conscious mind, are needed for the human being to be able to come to life again. The ego-soul is, as has been observed earlier, represented in the Orpheus tradition by the brain.[49]

The receptacle motif in the Seneca legend has a somewhat different form. The young woman who was looking for her husband in the land of shades was given the following counsel by its guardian: "You must take with you this gourd, which is closed with a tendon, for in this receptacle you will have to bring back the soul of your husband, carefully shut up. You must take also this small gourd bottle, which contains the fat or oil of man; you must take it with you for you will need it." The female ruler or "head woman" of the dead then stuffed the dead husband into the empty gourd, whereupon the young wife returned to the guardian, who gave her further instructions concerning the anointing of the dead man's corpse with the oil.[50] There can be no doubt but that the "fat or oil of man" in the Seneca legend is used as a symbol for the man's vital essence, life-fluid. In order to be able to come back to life the deceased must be furnished both with his personal identity (the free-soul) and his vital essence.

But if the integration of the psychic "parts" of the deceased has been dealt with in such detail, it may be presumed that the restoration of the

---

[47] Jenness 1935, 109.
[48] Hultkrantz, op.cit., 78 (Ojibway), 87 (Huron).
[49] See above, pp. 97 sq.
[50] Curtin & Hewitt 1918 II, 571 sq.

body will also be entailed in the context. As a rule, too, the Orpheus traditions here in question conclude with a regular revivification rite, whose aims are to unite the spiritual substances with the body and to restore the latter to life. Thus we have here a recurrence of the motif "resurrection from the grave" discussed earlier.

The revivification follows different lines. It has already been mentioned that according to the Menomini legend the deceased returned to life down in the grave to which her husband had taken her soul.[51] She had then to go through a rite of purification, which she vainly tried to avert; one divines here a last protest from a being who is with one foot still in the sphere of the dead.[51a] In the other legends the revivification takes place above ground: the corpse is brought up out of the grave and united under ritual forms with the "spiritual" parts of the deceased. In some narratives we are told that the corpse is laid out in a special lodge. The Micmac Orpheus was ordered by the ruler of the dead to return home with the bag in which his son's spirit was kept and to "lay out, immediately after his arrival, the body of his son in a wigwam made for the purpose."[52] Nothing is here said concerning the actual rite of resurrection, except that the wigwam must have no aperture through which "the soul" might fly out—a prohibition which was afterwards contravened because of a woman's curiosity.[53] The female Orpheus hero of the Ojibway returned to the earth from the realm of the dead "after an absence of one night only." "There she built a sweathouse, placed inside it her husband's body with the two boxes containing his soul and his brains (shadow), poured water over the hot stones and waited outside. Within a few minutes her husband rose up alive and well."[54] Evidently the revivification took place in a mystical way in a closed room inaccessible for all living persons—a procedure one also seems to glimpse in the above-reviewed Micmac narrative. In the Huron narrative, on the other hand, Orpheus is supposed to be present at the transformation. "When thou

[51] See above, p. 152.

[51a] The rite of purification occurs also in the Blackfoot legend, according to which the two spouses took a sweat-bath (see below, note 54) "and burned sweet grass and purified their clothing and the Worm Pipe" (Grinnell 1912, 131).

[52] Le Clercq, op.cit., loc.cit.

[53] Le Clercq, op.cit., 213.

[54] Jenness, op.cit., loc.cit. Similarly in the Blackfoot legend. Orpheus was instructed by his deceased father-in-law to get his relatives to build a sweat-house and then to use this: "wash your body thoroughly, leaving no part of it, however small, uncleansed; for if you do you will be nothing [will die]. There is something about us ghosts difficult to remove. It is only by a thorough sweat that you can remove it" (Grinnell, op.cit., 130). The resurrection from the dead in a sweat-house is a theme which has also been known among the Dakota (Wissler 1907, 201). Kretschmar's attempt to find the same motif among the Indians of California is misdirected (Kretschmar 1938 II, 257 sq.).

reachest home," said the brain-keeper to him, "go to the cemetery, take the body of thy sister, bear it to thy Cabin, and make a feast. When all thy guests are assembled, carry it on thy shoulders, and take a walk through the Cabin holding the two pumpkins in thy hands; thou wilt no sooner have resumed thy place than thy sister will come to life again, provided thou givest orders that all keep their eyes lowered, and that no one shall look at what thou art doing, else everything will go wrong."[55] Thus according to this description the living may be present, but they may not, any more than in the preceding cases, get any glimpse of the mystical change which takes place. The Huron Orpheus followed the instructions and "already felt motion in the half-decayed corpse" when the taboo prohibition was contravened by an inquisitive person. "At that moment the soul escaped, and there remained to him only the corpse in his arms, which he was constrained to bear to the tomb whence he had taken it."[56]

In the Seneca and Malecite narratives there is no mention of the ceremonial cabin, and the deceased is brought to life by being smeared with oil, i.e. life-stuff (see above). The guardian in the Seneca legend gave the female Orpheus the following advice: "When you arrive at your home stop up with fine clay the nostrils, the ears, and every other opening or outlet of your husband's body, and then rub the oil of man over his body. When you have finished this task, carefully uncork into his mouth the gourd bottle containing his life, in such manner that his life can not escape, but will reenter his body and so reanimate it again."[57] The revivification procedure could not be described more clearly! The corresponding episode in the Malecite narrative is an echo of the Seneca tale. The wise old woman near the realm of the dead told Orpheus on his return home to "dig up his wife and to grease all her joints with the oil, which would just suffice for the purpose. She also gave him a wooden comb to comb her hair." He then returned home. "With his own hands the Indian made a wooden shovel, and, having dug his wife up, he began to oil her bones. There was no flesh on her, for she had been buried for a great while. When he had exhausted his oil supply, the woman looked as natural as she had before her death. Her first words were a request for a drink."[58]

---

[55] JR X, 153.
[56] JR X, loc.cit.
[57] Curtin & Hewitt, op.cit., 572 sq.
[58] Mechling, op.cit., 90. The prescription concerning the combing of the wife's hair on her return reminds one of certain North American traditions telling how a supernatural person combs his (or her) hair or is combed. One is here reminded of the Eskimo Sedna (see e.g. Boas 1888, 583 sqq., and compare the exposition in Ehnmark 1939, 150 sqq.), of the Iroquois To-do-dä-ho (Morgan 1954 I, 63 sq.), and especially

In both narratives the oil is the vital essence, but apart from this it appears to have a magic capacity to restore the body to its former condition. The association of the receptacle motif and the revivification of the corpse is typical for the Central Algonquin and Northeastern Orpheus traditions here discussed. On the other hand, the restoration of the soul in a diminutive form and its reunion with the corpse in the grave occur in another place. In one of the Taos versions it is said that Yellow Corn girl brought back her deceased sister, Blue Corn girl, to her grave in the shape of a rabbit. According to the instructions of a rain-spirit *(łachina)* she placed the rabbit on top of the grave under a white dance-kilt. It then began to rain and thunder, and the lightning ripped up the kilt, and the sister stepped forth alive.[59]

of the woman who in certain origin myths of the Southwest is represented as the first person to die, likewise as the female ruler of the dead, who sits combing her hair: thus among the Navajo (Reichard 1950 I, 41) and Hopi (Parsons 1939 I, 242). According to the corresponding myth among the Zuni Indians, she *washes* her hair, and Parsons draws attention to the parallel with the washing of the hair of the dead (Parsons, op.cit., 220). In the same way, the combing of the hair is probably to be regarded as a purification procedure (quite obviously so in the Sedna narrative) and apparently corresponds to the tending of the body of a deceased person before the burial. Its purpose in the Malecite legend would then be analogous, i.e. to purify the deceased from the death-stuff on her reentrance into life.

[59] Parsons 1940, 28.

III. HISTORICAL ANALYSIS

With the analysis of the dominant motifs and elements of the North American Orpheus tradition (in its two forms) here undertaken it has in several points been possible to show, or at all events to indicate, that there are evident agreements between geographically widely distinct special forms of the tradition, between the North American and the Greek traditions, and between the Orpheus tradition as such and other folktales. From these points of agreement we can divine the possibility of far-reaching historical connections. Before venturing to embark on the definitive interpretation of the Orpheus tale, the determination of its origin and import, we must try to elucidate some important historical problems, the position and age of the North American Orpheus tradition.

1. Connections with other folktales

The Orpheus tradition has, as has already been pointed out, over the whole of North America a notably firm development around a remarkable, central motif.[1] It is in this connection a matter of subordinate importance that there exist oikotypes, and this with a great breadth of variation. Even the so-called "sea-coast form" of the Orpheus tradition, which is in point of fact an independent narrative from the formal viewpoint, is motivistically a part of the Orpheus tradition, and has doubtless sprung from the same root as the ordinary form of the latter.[2] This uniformity in respect of motif and general plan does not mean that the Orpheus tradition may not have been influenced by other tales and motifs. It will now be our endeavour to ascertain to what extent this influence has essentially contributed to the building up of the Orpheus tradition.

---

[1] See above, pp. 18 sq., 35.
[2] See above, p. 49. See further chap. III: 3.

To begin with, however, the scope of my presentation must be more closely defined. In the first place, for reasons that should have emerged from the foregoing, I do not in this connection distinguish between the ordinary Orpheus tradition and its "sea-coast form". These can, as compared with other traditions, in general be classified together, a twin pair in which each party represents the Orpheus motif in a genuine form. Their reciprocal relation will be discussed in a subsequent section.[3] In the second place, no related tales in the Old World will be included here for discussion unless they are also represented in the New World—it is, it must be remembered, the structure of the North American Orpheus tradition that we wish to investigate. If a North American tale which may possibly have influenced the Orpheus tradition has an European background—as many of the "Indian" folktales have[4]—this will be pointed out in so far as this influence may be of importance for an assessment of the age and original import of the Orpheus tradition. In the third place, the following short survey makes no claim to completeness. A disentanglement of the numerous threads connecting the tradition with other narratives and motifs would require a large volume of its own. We shall here only embark upon a brief discussion of those tales and motifs that may conceivably have exercised a more obvious influence upon the composition of the Orpheus tradition.[5]

An investigation of this kind must, at least theoretically, give individual treatment to motif and narrative. Every folklorist knows that narratives often lend motifs to each other, that one and the same motif may be current in a number of tales. Many migratory motifs have undoubtedly been introduced in the Orpheus narrative; some are easily identifiable, others are more difficult to recognize.[6] It is, of course, also conceivable that certain motifs may have originated within the Orpheus tradition and been assimilated thence to other folktales. These motifs do not particularly interest us here, but we shall nevertheless touch upon them in some cases.

Undoubtedly the Orpheus tradition has been enriched with many motifs which have been introduced into the narrative as less important elements in the pattern, and which have been incorporated in it as natural links in the chain of events. These are in general of subordinate interest

[3] See below, chap. III: 3.
[4] See Thompson 1919, and W. E. Roberts in JAFL 70 (1957), 52.
[5] In the following account I shall not include all the themata from the oral tradition outside the Orpheus tradition which might be discussed in connection with the latter (see e.g. the narrative of the bear-wife, below, p. 213).
[6] See above, pp. 56, 76.

for us; they cannot in any essential way affect our fundamental interpretation of the tradition. Such motifs may be suitably referred to as "marginal motifs", and with these I contrast the more important "central motifs." These, too, have probably become connected with the tradition on account of their natural place in it. But they constitute a striking element, and one must reckon with the possibility of their misdirecting the "main motif" of the narrative and thus obscuring our possibilities of reconstructing the origination of the Orpheus tradition.[7] Thus the "sea-coast form" derives its special character from the fact that the main motif—the freeing of the wife from the realm of the dead—has been pushed into the background by another central motif, her spiriting away by a supernatural being.[8]

The motifs with religious significance, however, are generally found ready-made in the popular belief; they have as a rule no revolutionary effect upon a firmly established, living popular narrative tradition. There seems to be a greater risk of the entire tradition being caught up in the perspectives of other narratives, if in their trend and complex of motifs these narratives come close to the tradition in question. The extremely pertinent problem we must pose is therefore this: has the Orpheus tradition, as regards its main form, its fundamental structure, been influenced by other narratives? It will be in the first place this question that we shall try to answer in the following.—The distinction between narrative and motif is, however, rather academic. In North America, as in other parts of the world, it is frequently the case that a narrative is built up around a single motif, which may sometimes constitute at the same time a subordinate detail in other narratives. Sometimes it may seem, at least at first glance, as if the Orpheus narrative in its entirety reflected now a motif (or rather complex of motifs), now another narrative. As the boundaries may be so floating, I have presented side by side a folktale like Lodge-Boy and a motif like the magic flight.

Certain narratives and narrative-motifs are saved for later chapters: the stories of visits to the realm of the dead by ordinary persons,[9] the fertility and sun myths,[10] and the etiological narratives.[11]

---

[7] My classification of the motifs is made on qualitative lines and has nothing to do with Rooth's "quantitative" delimitations of detail motif, principal or main motif, motif-complex and act (Rooth 1951, 32). The latter classification is, for the rest, excellent for its purpose, historico-quantitative analysis.

[8] See below, p. 213.

[9] See chap. IV: 2.

[10] See chap. IV: 4.

[11] See chap. V: 3.

The narratives (and motifs),[12] which show the closest resemblances with the Orpheus tradition are firstly revivalistic tales of different kinds, and secondly tales of visits in another world and of the fetching of beings, persons and things from this world.[13] The first-mentioned series of tales generally have the form of the legend, the tales in the last-mentioned series, on the other hand, may often be described as myths. Finally, as an extra group, we have the tales of pursuits by supernatural beings.

"Revival stories" have been common among North American Indians, especially on the Northwest Coast. Several of these tales describe how a man succeeds, either alone or with the help of shamans, in restoring his deceased wife to life, to lose her again, sometimes, on account of infringement of a taboo. As an example one may first mention the Lillooet tale of "the Ghost-Mother."

A man lost his wife through death. But he soon discovered that her ghost came every night and suckled their little child, and he resolved to catch her and restore her to life. At great cost he hired skilful shamans from various tribes, and they prepared to collaborate in the catching of the ghost. Furnished with different kinds of medicine, they concealed themselves in the house to wait for her. When darkness fell the deceased wife came, "from below, as that was the only way she could get in." The shamans immediately lit a fire, took away the child, and threw medicine at the ghost. Now she was captured, and was sprinkled with medicine the whole night, "and by morning she was so changed that she had partly left the ghost state, and had begun to resemble a living woman." The shamans worked on her for several months, and she got better and better, until finally she was able to work and to sleep with her husband. The shamans now left, but at the same time they "warned the man to take very great care of his wife, and to give her tasks by degrees, as it would take a very long time yet for her to become just as she had been before her death. If she were excited or startled in any way, she would at once change back to the spirit state." Unfortunately, these instructions were not followed, and the wife "reverted to the spirit state, and was a ghost as before."[14] Much in this tale, apart from the actual main motif, reminds one of the Orpheus tradition: the missile, the gradual normalization, the taboo.

In this narrative the widower makes use of shamans to get his wife back; in another tale from the same region he is himself the miracle-

[12] Concerning the classification of motifs and narrative types, cf. above, p. 18 note 1.
[13] See above, pp. 22 sqq.
[14] Teit 1912 b, 329 sqq. The same story is found among the Thompson River (Boas 1917 a, 44 sq.).

working magician. In a Stalo narrative we are told how a man lost his beloved wife. He buried her in a tree and betook himself to the mountains to seek a supernatural helper. After four years a spirit revealed itself to him in a vision, and said: "I will give you power to restore the dead to life. If you see a bone lying on the ground and you step over it four times the body to which the bone belongs will straightway be restored to life." The man made a successful trial of his new skill on a deer bone and a bird's bone and was delighted with his power. He then went to the tree in which he had buried his wife, brought down the corpse, and restored his wife to life. He let her be by herself for a while, apart from the people, so that she might recover her strength undisturbed. The tale finishes with a reference to another man whose wife had died, and who after training in solitude tried to restore her to life in the same way; but he failed.[15] A variant from the Lillooet mentions that after the revivification the man washed his wife to remove the smell of death.[16]

The successive normalization of the deceased appears still more clearly in a Thompson legend, which is very close to the preceding type of narrative. It concerns a young man, Otter, "who had spent much time in training," i.e. vision-quest, and the way he restored his deceased betrothed to life and thus became a famous medicine-man. Every night for four days he dug up his beloved and endeavoured to bring her back to life until dawn, when he buried her again. During the day he mourned her, without speaking to anyone, and without eating anything. But on the fourth night "he brought her so far back to life, that she was able to sit up and speak to him." He then carried her to her father's house and there lay down by her side, "spreading her robe over both." In the morning, to everybody's joy, he got up, and with him also the young girl.[17] In a variant we are told of the events in the house in connection with the awakening of the couple: "When the people saw a couple sleeping in the place where the corpse had lain, they lifted up the foot of the blanket and saw the feet of two persons. One pair of feet were quite healthy-looking; the other pair were yellow, and looked like those of a corpse ... When the couple sat up, the face of the woman was like that of a corpse. This appearance wore off in a few days."[18] Here the change from death to life is clearly described.

In a Quinault narrative it is Bluejay who restores to life a girl whom he has himself slain by magic. As the tale runs, he visited the burial

[15] Hill-Tout 1904 b, 338 sq.
[16] Hill-Tout 1905, 197 sq., Teit, op.cit., 332 sq.
[17] Teit 1898, 68 sq.
[18] Boas, op.cit., 45 (Teit).

platform, "took off the blankets and mats in which the body was wrapped and pulled it out, and it only smelled a little. He carried her to his canoe and started up the river. Whenever he came to a rapid, he stopped and sang his *tamanous* [=spirit] song and washed the body and then went on up-stream. By the time he had done this the third time, the body hardly smelled at all. At the fourth rapid the girl began to get warm." At the fifth rapid the girl sat up. She became quite healthy, but when her father refused her hand in marriage to Bluejay, she died again, and this is the reason why to-day medicine-men are not able to restore a deceased person to life.[19]

The revival stories are especially common on the Northwest Coast.[20] But they also occur elsewhere, though more sparsely. It may in this connection be of interest to mention a Pueblo narrative from the Southwest, the Isleta legend of the girl who was restored to life through help from her brother and a medicine-man summoned by him. The latter's diagnosis at the girl's burial was remarkable: the girl has died—but she is not dead! (Obviously he meant that the girl had, certainly, died, but had not been entirely incorporated in the sphere of death.) When she had arisen from the grave she was taken home. "The medicine man made a ceremony for her. She used to work at night and sleep by day."[21] Both the ceremony after the return of the deceased and her topsy-turvy behaviour for a time thereafter have their counterparts in the Orpheus tradition, where they are explained by the woman's gradual return from ghost to human being.

To summarize, one may observe that precisely this successive transition from one existence to another and the actions and precautionary measures necessitated thereby are the links connecting with the Orpheus tradition all the revival episodes referred to here. Probably this tradition has not been directly influenced by these stories, but both they and the Orpheus tradition have grown from a common presumption: the gradual recovery of health and strength by the half-and-half dead person.

There is, however, a folktale closely connected with the motif of the "successive revival of a deceased person," which according to Stith Thompson should be regarded as identical with the Orpheus tradition: the story of the woman who comes to life in a wooden doll.[22] Among the

[19] Farrand 1902, 105 sq.
[20] Gayton 1935, 280.
[21] Parsons 1932, 438. This tale is well known in several other pueblos: Hopi, Zuni and Laguna (Benedict 1935 II, 292).
[22] Thompson 1929, 337.

Iroquois this legend runs as follows. A man's wife has died, and he has buried her in his cabin. Out of his longing for her presence he makes a wooden doll of her size and dresses this in her clothes. One day, on his return from the hunt, he finds his food already prepared, but he discovers no-one who can have done this.[23] But the next time he returns from the hunt he sees his deceased wife busy in the cabin, and the doll has disappeared. The wife charges him not to touch her until they have together seen all their deceased relatives. They set off for the main camp of the tribe, but on the way there the man infringes the taboo, and the woman is once more changed into a wooden doll.[24] The whole of this narrative bears an evident resemblance to the Orpheus tradition, which has, moreover, been recorded in a rather regular form among an Iroquois group, viz, the Seneca.

Thompson, who has noted down this Iroquois legend, has found an analogous tale among the Tlingit; and interestingly enough, H. B. Alexander, too, has characterized the Tlingit version as an Orpheus legend ("the legend is made a part of the incident of the carved wife.")[25] In the Tlingit narrative we are told that a young chief on the Queen Charlotte Islands was deeply mourning his young, deceased wife. At his request a skilful wood-carver made a life-like statue of her and dressed it, and the chief thought that it was his wife who had come back to life. When he was one day sitting sorrowfully beside the image he noticed that it moved. "At first he thought that the movement was only his imagination, yet he examined it every day, for he thought that at some time it would come to life." With each succeeding day the image became more like a human being, and on one occasion "the image gave forth a sound from its chest like that of crackling wood." But it never became quite human. "The woman moved around very little and never got to talk, but her husband dreamed what she wanted to tell him."[26] In a variant from the Tsimshian the inconsolable widower is said to have made the statue half automatic; "he made it turn when he opened the door, and he pretended that the image could speak."[27]

In certain respects this narrative is reminiscent of the Orpheus tradition —the longing for the return of the deceased, finding expression in hallucinations, and the succcessive transformation of the statue into an at

[23] Here one clearly discerns the motif of "the mysterious housekeeper," Thompson N 831.1.
[24] Smith 1883, 103 sq.
[25] Alexander 1916, 264.
[26] Swanton 1909, 181 sq.
[27] Boas 1916, 152.

168

least animated being are common motifs. But otherwise we have here to do with an independent story, the North American counterpart of the Pygmalion legend told by Ovid. Apart from the tribes mentioned above the narrative occurs also among the Bella Coola, Kwakiutl (three versions), Nootka and Cowichan,[28] and in a somewhat altered form it has spread to the Stalo, Shuswap, Lillooet and Thompson River.[29] As may be seen, the narrative is concentrated to the west coast, and the Iroquois instance is quite isolated. But in two respects the Iroquois version is firmly connected with the western versions. Its statement that the statue is replaced by a living being has its counterpart in one of the Kwakiutl variants and in the Cowichan version; and the prime fact upon which the story is based, the wife's death, the Iroquois narrative shares with the Tlingit and Tsimshian legends. In all the other legends this, from our point of view significant, motif is missing; the hero here makes himself a wife from a wooden doll, and he has not previously lost his real wife. A closer study of the different variants—of which, however, no account can be given here—leaves one with the impression that the Iroquois version, like the Tlingit and Tsimshian versions, has preserved the legend in its more original form. There is a tremendous gap between the western and the eastern instances. In a certain sense, however, it can be bridged over if one conceives the narrative to have arisen in direct connection with the use of "spirit dolls" in the cult of the dead—the deceased person *in effigie*—or of any life-like representations of the deceased.[30] Such images have been used over large parts of North America.[31] It appears probable, however, that like other ghost stories of this kind the narrative originated in the first place in the Northwest area.

The North American "Pygmalion story" is thus not, as Thompson thinks, a fragmentary Orpheus tradition. It is based upon the same fundamental motif as the Orpheus tradition—the inconsolable longing for a wife lost through death—but it is in other respects a diverging creation and has, as far as may be judged, in no way affected the Orpheus

[28] Boas, op.cit., 744 sqq.
[29] Boas, op.cit., 609.
[30] See especially Emmons 1914, 59 sqq., and James 1927, 349 sqq.
[31] Concerning the general distribution, see Davis 1919, 8; Kroeber 1925, 609; Spier 1928, 297, 299; Klimek 1935, 42. As regards the distribution on the Northwest Coast and in the Plateau area, see Emmons, op.cit., and Swanton 1908 b, 430 (Tlingit), Boas 1889 a, 323 (Nanaimo), Teit 1900, 329 sq. (Thompson), Teit 1906, 273 (Lillooet), etc. The North American instances are undoubtedly connected with the northern Asiatic ones; see e.g. Harva 1938, 332, 334 sqq., 341 sqq.—The images were often clad in the clothes of the deceased.

tradition. Whether it, as Gudmund Hatt opines, shows influence from the Orpheus tradition is a more difficult question.[32]

If we now return to the genuine revival stories, we find among these a group of tales describing how the deceased lives her existence as a dead person, a ghost, in her own village or camp, and how the nearest living relative tries to restore her to life. Here, then, it is not, as in the Orpheus tradition, a matter of a journey to and from the realm of the dead. But the resemblance to the Orpheus tradition is nonetheless striking.

The Bella Coola in British Columbia tell the story of a seal-hunter who on arriving home from one of his hunting expeditions finds his wife dead in the home. That is to say, she appears here as a ghost, a "living corpse," and collapses into a heap of bones when she is touched. The entire population of the village have taken to the woods. The hunter resolves to try and win his wife back when—on the fourth day after her death—the dead come to welcome her into their circle. The dead arrive, the wife stands up and dances round the lighted fire. As she is dancing round for the fourth time the husband and the three sons rush up and seize her. But in the same moment the ghosts disappear, and the hunter is left standing with a skeleton in his arms. He does not subsequently make any attempts to restore his wife to life.[33] In this story we find many points of agreement with the Orpheus tradition, and the question is whether this has not here served as a model. But one cannot be certain of this; as we have pointed out above, there are innumerable ghost stories on the Northwest Coast. Nevertheless, it is out of the question that this isolated narrative should have left traces in the real Orpheus tradition.

Also reminiscent of the Orpheus tradition is another revival story of the same type, to wit, the tale so popular on the Plains of the deceased woman who comes to life in her burial tipi and then lives there together with her living lover.[34] The tale is known under different names. Among the Teton Dakota it is the man who is the deceased, and the recorder of the tale, J. O. Dorsey, therefore calls it "The Ghost Husband." In the other versions, on the other hand, it is the woman who has died, and Grinnell refers to the narrative, accordingly, as "The Ghost Wife." The tale is known above all on the more northerly Plains.[35] It is in many

[32] Hatt 1949, 97.
[33] McIlwraith 1948 I, 505 sq.
[34] Cf. Gayton, op.cit., 265, 277; Alexander, op.cit., 276, 280.
[35] Instances from the Sarcee (Jenness 1938, 97 sq.); Teton Dakota (Dorsey 1889 b, 148; Dorsey 1894, 490; McLaughlin 1916, 145; Deloria 1932, 224 sqq.); Winnebago (Radin 1926, 27 sqq.); Pawnee (Dorsey 1906, 126 sqq., Grinnell 1893, 129 sqq., 191 sqq., Weltfish 1937, 79 sqq.).

respects a typical product of the Plains culture: the Plains peoples some-times bury their dead in tipis,[36] they have a strong notion that the dead live in their graves (platforms, cabins, cairns); and their mourners often go to the burial places to converse with their dear deceased. It may thus be said that the narrative of the dead woman in the tipi and her living lover has had the most favourable psychological background for its emergence among the Plains Indians. To all appearances, however, it belongs to a wider narrative complex. Both among the Sarcee and among the Pawnee we find the motif of a child being born in the marriage, and of its dying when a given taboo is infringed.[37] But this motif is also known on the Plateau and among the Northwest Coast tribes in the closely related narrative "Skeleton-Baby," which we shall discuss presently.

If one now compares the tale of "The Ghost Wife" among the Pita-hauirat Pawnee with the normal form of the Orpheus tradition, which is of course also represented among the Pawnee (among the Skidi and Kitkehahki Pawnee), one finds several remarkable points of agreement. In the tale of the ghost wife we are told how a young man, who has lost his beloved through death while he was in a strange district, overwhelm-ed with grief visits her grave. This is situated on a hill near the village, which his tribe has just left on a hunting expedition. When, finally, he leaves the grave and goes down to the village he finds his beloved in one of the cabins in a half living state—as an active ghost resembling a human being.[38] He gets her permission to visit her in the night-time, but he may not touch her. The dead, who hold a dance in the cabin every night, promise him that he may keep the girl if, when the living return, he is able to seize and hold her fast. But, they add, he may not, in the sequel, hurt her. At first everything turns out well: the young man succeeds in holding fast his beloved, and she is therewith incorporated with the world of the living. They then live happily together until one day, in a fit of anger, he strikes her. She then disappears in the whirlwind, and the man dies of grief.[39]

Alexander characterizes this narrative as a "Pawnee tale on the Or-

---

[36] See above, p. 36.
[37] Jenness, op.cit., 98 (Sarcee), Dorsey 1906, 133 sq. (Pawnee).
[38] Neither among the Pawnee nor among the Winnebago was burial in the cabins of the permanent village common; this seems to be the explanation of the fact that in the narrative the scene changes rapidly from the earth-grave to the cabin (cf. Radin, op.cit., 31). The living ghost is in the Winnebago tradition consequently perceived simultaneously in two places.
[39] Dorsey 1906, 126 sqq.

pheus and Eurydice theme."[40] This is certainly to go too far. But it is quite possible that in view of its general resemblance to the Orpheus tradition the tale has borrowed motifs belonging to the latter. It is in any case evident that in essential points the Pawnee tale had the same form as the Orpheus tradition while at the same time it cannot be identified with this, as it lacks the latter's central motif of the journey to and stay in the realm of the dead.[41]

Several versions of the Orpheus tradition occur, however, among the Pawnee, and one of these versions includes, inter alia, the following elements, which are also found in the above-mentioned tale: 1. The hero sets off to find his deceased loved one (the first contact with her supernatural world taking place in "a tipi over her grave"). 2. Her existence beyond death passes away in a cabin (tipi), where she very slowly recovers her normal humanity. In this narrative, certainly, one motif is missing which does occur in the above-mentioned tale and which is found in other Orpheus versions among the Pawnee, viz, the taboo and its infringement.[42] On the other hand, the Orpheus version we are discussing has a couple of other motifs which justify its reference to the Orpheus tradition, to wit, the journey to and the stay in the realm of the dead.[43] In other words, a variant of the story of "The Ghost Wife" has been adopted by the Orpheus tradition.

Also the northernmost of all Plains Indians, the Sarcee, have these two narratives combined, though in another way. The hero, who has married a dead girl in a tent beside her burial place,[44] lives together with her until one day he loses her by infringing a taboo. He then visits her in the realm of the dead and succeeds in restoring her to the land of the living.[45] As among the Pawnee, the points of resemblance between the two legends have here obviously led to their fusing in one tale of predominantly Orpheus type.

The narrative of "Skeleton-Baby," as has already been pointed out, belongs to the same motif-complex as "Ghost-wife", and has, as we have indicated, been contaminated with the latter. It is then not unnatural

[40] Alexander, op.cit., 118. Also Barbeau is of this opinion (Barbeau 1950 I, 272).
[41] Cf. above, p. 23.
[42] Cf. Dorsey 1904 b, 77; Dorsey 1906, 411 sqq., 537.
[43] Dorsey, op.cit., 71 sqq.
[44] According to the narrative, tree-burial was practised here. Only prominent warriors and chiefs were accorded the honour of tent-burial on heights among the Sarcee (Jenness 1938, 39, Wilson 1889, 248). The same custom obtains among the neighbouring and allied Blackfoot (Wissler 1906, 176, Wissler 1911, 31, Jenness 1932, 320).
[45] Jenness 1938, 97 sq. Cf. also Gayton, op.cit., 277 (quoting from Sapir's unpublished collection of texts from the Sarcee).

to suspect that it may also have been combined with the Orpheus tradition. Like the latter, it, too, has a distribution whose climax falls within the Northwest Coast area and the Plateau region.[46] In its commonest form this tale runs as in the following version from the Klikitat.

A young chief died, and was deeply mourned by his sweetheart. One night in a dream she was summoned to the land of spirits, where her beloved was longing for her. Her father then rowed her out to the island of the dead—a burial place in the Columbia River—where at night the dead gave themselves up to singing and dancing. Here the girl met her lover and spent the night with him. But when day dawned he and all the other dead were transformed into skeletons. Overcome with horror she paddled home again; but her father, who was terrified at what might now take place, took her immediately back to the island. Here she lived for a time together with her lover, and soon had a beautiful child by him, "being half spirit and half human." The proud father sent for his mother, who was still alive, but at the same time he gave her to understand that she might under no circumstances look at the child until ten days had elapsed. The old woman was too curious, however; she lifted the cloth covering the baby, whereupon the latter died. The grieved and angry ghosts now decreed that as from that day there should be no contact between the living and the dead.[47]

This story, varied with but few changes among several peoples in the Northwest area, shows great similarities, both in its general frame and in several of its motifs, with the Orpheus tradition. As already mentioned, Gayton has listed two of its versions (among the Nisqually and Bella Bella) among the Orpheus narratives.[48] The nearest to the Orpheus narrative is in this case the Bella Bella story, according to which the mourning girl is taken to the land of the dead—here a submarine island— by the ghost of her lover. But it is a characteristic feature that she never goes after her lover to fetch him back; on the contrary, it is she who is summoned to the realm of the dead by the deceased. The concluding episode with the child does, certainly, introduce a new connection with the world of the living, but it aims only at a brief reunion and does not imply a restitution of the dead to life. Gayton acknowledges, moreover, that we have here really to do with an independent narrative, a variant

[46] Instances from the Bella Bella (Boas 1932 a, 142 sq., Olson 1955, 340); Kwakiutl (Boas 1921 I, 710 sqq., 1935 b, 110; cf. Boas 1935 a, 132); Nisqually (Curtis 1913 IX, 129 sqq.); Klikitat (Lyman 1904, 249 sqq., 1909, 28 sqq.); Klamath (Ms. by Spier, *Klamath Tales*, according to Gayton, op.cit., 282 note 1). Cf. also above, note 37.

[47] Lyman, op.cit., loc.cit.

[48] Gayton, op.cit., 281 sq.; cf. above, p. 26.

of the tale of the unnatural marriage.[49] But in this case it is over-hasty to classify it with the Orpheus tradition. Nor, as far as I have been able to find, has any Orpheus narrative been influenced by it.

Finally, mention may here be made also of a story of revival character which closely resembles the preceding tale: the tradition of the fetus which comes to life in its mother's grave, and which is caught and "normalized" by shamans.[50] This story has a certain similarity to the Orpheus tradition (the husband sleeps on his wife's grave; the process of normalization); but no direct connection between them can be shown unless one is prepared to assert that the notion of the normalization of the deceased in the Orpheus tradition has been introduced in the revival story. In view of the restricted distribution of the latter, the transference of the notion in the reverse direction is probably out of the question.[51]

The narratives so far adduced may for the most part be regarded as variations on the theme of revival in this world.[52] We shall now pass on to another series of tales, and these, too, come close to the Orpheus motif: stories of journeys to another world. This "other world"—by which, naturally, we understand the supernatural world—may either be the realm of the gods and the spirits, or else it is identical with the land of the dead. In North America these two worlds are often distinguished, but they may also be identical, as we have indicated in the foregoing.[53] In this connection, however, we shall for the sake of clarity keep them distinct.

There are several narrative traditions dealing with the journeys of mortals to the world of the gods. A frequently occurring North American narrative of this type is the legend or myth of Star Husband investigated by Thompson.[54] It has, however, no demonstrable connection with the Orpheus tradition. On the other hand, one finds good parallels to the

[49] Gayton, op.cit., 282. Marriage between living and dead persons is mentioned also in other tales from the Northwest Coast; cf. Swanton 1909, 247 sq. (Tlingit), 1908 a, 625 (Haida).

[50] Jenness noted down this tale, but represents it now as a Tsimshian legend (Jenness 1932, 195 sqq.), now as a Carrier legend! (Jenness 1934, 150).

[51] In the pattern here in question the tale is regionally limited; but one of its elements, the boy who makes expeditions from his abode near his mother's corpse, is a well-known motif in some versions of the Plains narrative "Old Woman's Grandson." See e.g. Beckwith 1938, 121 sq., Lowie 1942, 3 (Hidatsa); Lowie 1935, 137 sq. (Crow); Lowie 1956, 136 (Kiowa). Concerning the further distribution, see Beckwith, op.cit., 117 note 56. The tale is closely allied to the origin myth of the Iroquois.

[52] It need scarcely be pointed out that the tales of "Ghost-wife" and "Skeleton-Baby" constitute borderline cases.

[53] See above, pp. 99 sqq.

[54] Thompson 1953 b; cf. also Reichard 1921, 269 sqq.

Orpheus tradition in the tales in which a woman seeks a supernatural husband (Amor and Psyche, Aarne 425 A) and in which a man seeks a supernatural wife (The Swan Maiden, Aarne 400).[55] Both of these narratives are represented in North America.[56] But it is above all in a combination of the two narratives from the Cree and Ojibway, Mudjikiwis, that the parallel with the Orpheus tradition becomes evident.[57]

Here we are told how the supernatural wife of a young man is shot by his brother, Mudjikiwis. She disappears, but leaves bloody traces after her, and these are followed by her young husband. On his journey he passes three old women, the one older than the other, and all of them provided with miniature vessels containing a ration of meat which never gets less, however much of it is eaten. The old women give him magical objects, and with the help of these he climbs up into the upper world. Here, in competition, he succeeds in regaining his wife. She is brought back to the earth, accompanied by her sisters, who marry his brothers —Mudjikiwis, too, gets a wife.[58]

As may be seen, this tale has not only the actual narrative frame, but also several motifs in common with the Orpheus tradition. Thus one recognizes such central motifs as the following of the deceased (in so far as one may speak of the supernatural wife as being "deceased"), the four old women on the way with their wonderful objects (e.g. the magic food) and their helpfulness, and the testing in the other world. Now these motifs, as Thompson has emphasized, are migratory elements, occurring not only in these traditions.[59] One might thus assert, theoretically, that they have been added to the Mudjikiwis narrative on account of its general agreement with the Orpheus tradition. The only thing is, that precisely this constellation of motifs is so typical for Aa 400, not least in the Old World.[60] One can thus apparently not rule out the possibility that such motifs as the helpful old women and the testing, of subordinate importance for the central Orpheus theme, have been adopted from Aa

[55] These folktales are, as Thompson has remarked, very much alike (Thompson 1946, 99). They are discussed in Swahn 1955 and Holmström 1919.
[56] Amor and Psyche among the Zuni Indians (as a Spanish fairy-tale), Swan Maiden (as the "Goose Woman" etc.) among the Eskimo and several Indian tribes. See Holmström, op.cit., 69 sqq.
[57] The title figure of the tale has nothing to do with Hiawatha's father, who according to Longfellow bore the same name.
[58] Instances from the Cree (Skinner 1916, 353 sqq.) and Ojibway (Jones & Michelson 1919, 133 sqq.).
[59] Thompson 1946, 350 sq. The motif "inexhaustible food," for example, is extremely common in Californian Indian folklore; see Du Bois & Demetracopoulou 1931, 401 note 134. Cf. also Thompson 1929, 335 sq. note 210.
[60] See Aarne-Thompson 1928, 62 sq. (IV, V f, VI e), and Holmström, op.cit., 15 sqq. (motifs E¹, F).

400.[61] And if this is the case, we are led to further conclusions: the motif of "the helpful women" must in North America, both in and outside of the Orpheus tradition, have been connected with an older Indian notion of a guardian or adviser on the way to the realm of the dead, an hypostasis of the highest functionary in that realm.[62] In this way this advisory being would have been multiplied and furnished with new attributes. As regards the Orpheus tradition, its fusion with Aa 400 was probably effected chiefly in eastern North America, whose Orpheus narratives clearly include the motif here under discussion.[63] Especially the Winnebago tale, which is obviously very close to Aa 400, should be mentioned in this connection.

A further central motif may have been adopted by the Orpheus tradition from the Mudjikiwis legend or herewith related tales (of the types 400 or 425), viz, the motif of "the supernatural wife."[64] (This motif *may*, however, be a reflex of the supernatural character acquired by Eurydice as a ghost.) I am not here referring to those Orpheus traditions in which the deceased is a relation of the culture hero or of the first man, or the daughter of the sun goddess or of the goddess of vegetation, I am thinking of a couple of narratives in the "sea-coast form" in which the man is represented as an ordinary hunter and his woman as a supernatural being. In the Tsimshian version we learn that "a hunter married a very beautiful woman who was a *narhnorh* (supernatural). She was white, and her hair was very bright. Her husband always was successful in the hunt, and he remained away from the village for long periods. He sought only sea-otters, and he used to come back with his canoe loaded with sea-otters. It was partly because his wife gave him great powers in the hunt." When his wife was unfaithful to him his luck in the hunt deserted him.[65] The Haida say, concerning the seal-hunter's wife, that "she was a super-woman, to be reborn among the Haida."[66]

In spite of agreements of this kind with regard to motif, it is not likely that different narratives of journeys to the other world—even if in consequence of their general plan they are in other respects to a certain

[61] The testing has then presumably replaced an older taboo-motif—see above, pp. 130 sq.
[62] See above, pp. 81 sq., 93 sqq.
[63] See above, pp. 81, 102 note 48.
[64] Cf. also the story of *ninïmbi's* wife, above, p. 30.
[65] Barbeau 1953, 296 sq. The white colour, which in North America (and elsewhere) so often characterizes the deity, may possibly be connected with the experiences of the bright sky of daytime and the light-sensation of visions.
[66] Barbeau, op.cit., 296. The spouse, on the other hand, is a human being in the ordinary sense, and evidently for this reason called "Real-Person" (Barbeau, op.cit., 289).

176

extent of Orpheus type—had as concerns their composition genetic or diffusionistic connections with the Orpheus tradition. Individual motifs may have assimilated to the latter, but the narratives themselves need not necessarily have taken impressions from each other. They move in different worlds, even if they spin in the same theme. Nor does Thompson wish to connect them; he distinguishes the Orpheus narrative as a variant on the motif "visits to the lower world," a perhaps somewhat misleading distinction.[67] Gayton, too, observes that "tales of a wife stolen and pursued to some exotic place such as the sky-world are unrelated to the Orpheus story."[68] Nor does this pronouncement, in its import otherwise quite valid, meet the requirements of complete accuracy. It is probably safest to define the matter thus: that the events of the Orpheus tradition take place at least in part in a supernatural milieu, and this is the realm of the dead, wherever the latter may be situated. Precisely through the fixation to the realm of the dead does the independence of the Orpheus tradition emerge.

In connection with the tales concerning the acquisition and loss of a supernatural wife referred to above we shall here also discuss a category of narratives which come close to these tales, and which may possibly have influenced the Orpheus tradition: the narratives of the stealing of light and fire and of other necessities which are of benefit to man.

"One of the important functions of many of the American Indian Culture Heroes," writes Thompson, "is the stealing of light, or fire, or water, or game supply from some monster who keeps them from men."[69] The tales concerning the theft of light (A 1411), of fire (A 1415), of water (A 1111) and of the animals (A 1421) show the culture hero in his double rôle of trickster and benefactor of man. This cycle of myths is especially well developed on the Plateau and along the southern Northwest Coast, where the mythology is in a high degree stamped with the figure of the culture hero-trickster. We have seen earlier that in this area he also occurs with Orpheus functions.[70] His appearance in the rôle of Orpheus here is perhaps not accidental: Orpheus' actions are in many respects reminiscent of the beneficent work performed by the culture hero in the myths adduced. A further connecting link between the Orpheus tradition and these myths is the receptacle in which is kept

[67] Thompson 1946, 351.
[68] Gayton, op.cit., 265.
[69] Thompson, op.cit., 315. Cf. also Rooth 1957, 505 (map).
[70] See above, pp. 50 sq.

12 — Hultkrantz

the valuable capture which the hero tries to bring to the land of men. As will be remembered, in the more north-westerly forms of the Orpheus tradition the deceased is sometimes taken back in a wooden box, bag or sack.[71] In the culture myths adduced the stolen goods are transported by the culture hero in the same way. In a Squamish version of the myth concerning the bringing of fish to men[72]—a variant of the story of "the Release of the Wild Animals"—we are told that the fish were let out of a box.[73] In the Karuk myth concerning the stealing of fire there is mention of "the casket of fire";[74] and Thompson reports that "at least two California tribes tell that the fire was carried from the monster [that owned it] in a reed or flute," which constitutes, as he points out, a remarkable parallel to Greek mythology.[75] According to a Makah myth the culture hero Kwati brought the daylight to the world of men in a box.[76] This reminds one of how in the Orpheus myths among the Yakima, Wasco and Wishram Coyote swallows the moon—which is also a symbol of light—before setting off with the box containing the dead.[77] If one wishes to press the parallels still further, one can find analogies between the story of the way in which the culture hero scatters the fish-scales he has caught over lakes and rivers so that they shall become fish, and the Orpheus narrative of how in the same way he scatters the bones of the dead so that they shall become men on earth.[78]

So much, at all events, one can constate, that on the Plateau and in the adjacent regions the Orpheus tradition has been transformed and adapted to the local mythic pattern, more particularly the pattern of the "theft" myths. But this process has not gone very deep, it has not brought to the Orpheus tradition anything essentially new. It may, certainly, seem as if the receptacle motif has been introduced from the "theft" myths, but in view of the distribution of this motif I find this improbable.[79] One asks oneself then if at least the box motif—the box as a variation of the receptacle—does not derive from the north-westerly cycle of myths. But this, too, is not altogether a matter of course. One may probably presume

[71] See above, pp. 152 sqq. The motif of the dead kept in boxes occurs here also outside of the Orpheus tradition: cf. the Tlingit tale of "The Mucus Child" (Swanton 1909, 196).
[72] Concerning the mythic fetching of fish, especially of salmon, see Boas 1918, 301; Gunther 1928, 162; Reichard 1947, 105 sqq.
[73] Gunther, op.cit., 163.
[74] Powers 1877, 39.
[75] Thompson, op.cit., 316.
[76] Densmore 1939, 207 sq.
[77] See above, pp. 102 sq.
[78] Curtin 1912, 44 sq. (Modoc).
[79] See above, pp. 152 sqq., below, pp. 215 sq.

that in the north-western traditions the receptacle has been transformed in accordance with the box motif occurring in that area in other tales, but the influence of these tales has scarcely extended farther than this. It may of course be tempting to assume that the myth of the daylight that is brought home in a box has given a remote echo in the Cherokee myth of the bringing home of the Sun's daughter from the land of ghosts in a chest. The only thing is that in this Orpheus myth the daughter of the Sun does not represent the light itself, and that the interpretation in the light of fertility mythology is more natural.[80]

The journey to another world may thus, in North American mythology, refer to the bright spaces of the gods and the spirits. But among a number of peoples, above all agrarian peoples, gods and spirits are chthonic beings dwelling in a subterranean world of shades, and the latter is in most cases identical with the realm of the dead. To betake oneself to the underworld is to betake oneself to the dead.

A tradition common in the whole of agrarian North America tells how once in the mythic primaeval era the first human beings ascended from the underworld, where their line had first come to life.[81] To this notion of man's origin corresponds, among the same peoples, the notion of his fate after death: man returns to the place whence he came, thus to the underworld. Gayton opines that "since ghosts return whence people came, it may as well be that the direction in which the dead go influenced beliefs concerning the location of the place of emergence as vice versa."[82] But one can scarcely reason in this way. For the agrarian peoples man's life constitutes a counterpart to that of the plants; like the latter it grows up out of the earth, lives on the earth and returns to the earth.[83] It is a life-cycle in the world of belief, whose firmness and closed character were realized already by such Americanists as Fewkes and Stevenson.[84] And researchers like Haeberlin and Dieterich have since stressed that the primaeval myth of man's emergence from the underworld and the notions of his abode after death are parts of one and the same general pattern of ideas.[85]

[80] See chap. IV: 4. The resemblance to the Pandora myth, which Mooney has chosen to stress (Mooney 1900, 436), is only superficial. Concerning the Pandora motif, see chap. V: 3.
[81] Concerning the distribution of this tradition, see Loeb 1931, 538; Krickeberg 1935, 344; Parsons 1939 I, 17 note; Flannery 1939, 158; Rooth 1957, 502. As regards the distribution outside of America, see Hatt 1949, 110.
[82] Gayton, op.cit., 272.
[83] See also above, p. 101.
[84] Fewkes 1901, 86; Stevenson 1898, 24 sqq. Cf. Hale 1890, 183.
[85] Haeberlin 1916, 27 sq.; Dieterich 1913, 14 sq., 32; cf. also van der Leeuw 1956, 87.

In North America this myth has been especially common in the South-west.[86] It occurs here both among the settled Pueblo peoples and the village tribes, and among the nomadizing Athapascans. Judging from the evidence, the latter got the myth from the Pueblos; thus the origin myth of the Navajo is most nearly identical with those of the Zuni and Hopi Indians.[87] What from our point of view is interesting is the fact that among the Navajo the origin myth at the same time occurs in an elaboration which leaves room for the Orpheus theme. In other words, the Orpheus tale has been introduced in the origin myth, and it has in this way been as it were systematized with other mythology among the Navajo.[88] Wyman and Bailey formulate the case as follows: "This occurrence of the Navaho's Orpheus Myth as part of their organized mythology rather than as a separate tale is of considerable interest and might be taken as evidence of their penchant for systematization."[89] One must reckon with the possibility that a more or less regular, ordinary Orpheus narrative has here been absorbed by the dominant, Pueblo-influenced mythology and been combined with the origin myth on account of its many points of contact with the latter.

The subterranean realm of the dead of which we are informed in the origin myths of these agrarian cultures is also glimpsed in the tale of Lodge-Boy and Thrown-Away.[90] We have shown in the foregoing that among the Assiniboin this tale has been furnished with the Orpheus motif.[91] The fusion between the two tales has presumably taken place here in the same way as in the Navajo myth. Reminiscent of the Assiniboin narrative is a Thompson legend reproduced in two variants by Teit. According to this legend a man—or two sisters—lost his (their) brother in a mysterious way. It was found that he had made his way to the underworld through a hole under the fireplace in the lodge.[92] The one variant describes how the brother still living among men jumped down to the underworld and was united with the other brother; in the other variant we are told that out of pity for his sisters the brother who had disap-

---

[86] See Haeberlin, op.cit., loc.cit., and Wallis 1936, 2 note 1; Goddard 1931, 124, 184.

[87] See Parsons, op.cit., II, 1042; Spencer 1947, 116 sq.; cf. also Haeberlin, op.cit., 27 note 5.

[88] See above, p. 51.

[89] Wyman & Bailey 1943, 8.

[90] Concerning its distribution, see Reichard 1921, 272 sqq., Swanton 1929, 270, Thompson 1929, 318, Beckwith 1938, 31 note 8.

[91] See above, pp. 52 sq.

[92] It is here a matter of a so-called pithouse, with sunken floor. The usual entrance and exit was the smoke aperture in the roof, connected with the floor by a ladder. See Teit 1900, 193, figs. 135, 136.

peared came up into the lodge again.[93] Teit does not, it is true, state whether the underworld here is the world of the dead—but he does make comparisons with the latter,[94] and the description of the underworld does undeniably remind one of the Thompson Indians' realm of the dead.[95] Alexander, too, finds that the tale is reminiscent of "the myriad tales of the bereaved one, god or mortal, seeking the ghost of his beloved in gloomy Hades."[96] It is, however, difficult to make out any direct connection with the Assiniboin narrative, even if the motifs are similar.

From the Plateau and adjacent parts of the Northwest Coast there are a number of traditions concerning visits to the realm of the dead by Coyote or some other culture hero. Many of these tales are obviously without any connection with the Orpheus tradition; they are simply examples of the culture hero-trickster's adventures in different worlds, a narrative cycle which we have found to be characteristic for these tracts.[97] But when it is said that the culture hero betakes himself to the realm of the dead to visit a close relative, or that from this realm he wants to bring home a woman to whom he has there been paying his attentions, or relatives that he has lost, then these traditions more or less coincide with the Orpheus tradition. And, as I have earlier asserted, one can with a certain justification also list such tales as the myth of the culture hero's courting journey to the realm of the dead as a kind of Orpheus narrative, irregular offshoots of the Orpheus tradition.[98] It should, however, be remarked that one cannot rule out a mutual attraction between these Orpheus myths and the above-mentioned "theft" myths characteristic for the culture region. Among the Salish around the Gulf of Georgia, for example, it is narrated that Mink once visited the land of ghosts and on this occasion stole fire from them.[99] Here it is very conceivable that the Orpheus tradition has influenced the myth of the stealing of fire when the incident is located to the realm of the dead. One can perhaps glimpse a contrary influence in certain motifs in the Orpheus traditions in this region, as pointed out above.[100]

<hr/>

[93] Teit 1898, 78 sq., 1912 a, 373.
[94] Teit 1898, 116 note 254.
[95] Cf. the description of the underworld in Teit 1912 a, 373, with the description of the afterworld in Teit 1900, 343.
[96] Alexander 1916, 137.
[97] See above, pp. 177 sq. We are familiar with such tales of the culture hero's journey to the realm of the dead from e.g. the Quinault (Farrand 1902, 109 sqq.), Klallam (Gunther 1925, 146 sq.) and Takelma (Sapir 1909 a, 97 sqq.; cf. above, p. 29 note 25!)
[98] See above, pp. 49 sq.
[99] Boas 1916, 662 sq.
[100] See above, pp. 177 sqq.

A motif-complex which is not, certainly, very common but which does nevertheless occur in the Orpheus tradition, especially in its "sea-coast form", is the pursuit of Orpheus and his partner by the dead, when they are hurrying back to the land of the living from the realm of death.[101] In the regular Orpheus tradition the flight from the dead is described as a natural consequence of the fact that Orpheus has encroached upon the interests of the ghosts, and one looks in vain for influence from other tales. The case is otherwise with the "sea-coast form," whose pursuit episode shows close agreement with one of the commonest motif-complexes of international folktales, viz, "the magic flight," also referred to as "the obstacle flight" (D 672).[102] Briefly, this flight implies that in order to check his pursuer—as a rule a malicious supernatural being—the fugitive throws magic objects behind him, generally a comb, a stone or the like, in all three or (in the New World) four objects, and from these there arise mountains, forests or seas. This motif-complex occurs all over the world.[103] Boas has drawn the conclusion that it did not arise independently in America, and that it was introduced there partly in pre-Columbian time via Siberia, and partly in post-Columbian time through the Spaniards.[104] Its pre-Columbian origin is considered by Boas to be indisputable, on account, inter alia, of "the very intimate connection between this story and the religious concepts of the people."[105] In North America "the magic flight" is a rather common motif which has been combined with several tales.[106]

It has also evidently been incorporated with certain versions of the "sea-coast form" of the Orpheus tradition. Thus in a Haida tradition belonging to this form the actual narrative is introduced with an episode which is obviously "the magic flight" in a typical version.[107] In another Haida tradition, this, too, a "sea-coast form," the obstacle-flight motif is inserted in the middle of the tale. The flight of the seal-hunter and his wife from the dwelling of the sea-monsters is described as follows: "And [the people] ran after him. And when they had almost overtaken him, he threw down some of the hair-combings. He got far away, while the land became covered with bushes. And they came out from the bushy place.—And again they almost overtook him. Then he laid down the

---

[101] See above, pp. 129 sq. Cf. also the Tewa tale, above, pp. 29 sq.
[102] The motif (or motif-complex) also enters as an element in a folktale (Aa 313, 314) with the same name; see Aarne-Thompson, op.cit., 51, and Aarne 1930.
[103] Thompson 1946, 60. Aarne's notion, that it arose in India, is probably over-hasty.
[104] Boas 1915, 314 sq., 318, 321; cf. also Thompson, op.cit., 349.
[105] Boas 1940, 518.
[106] See Swanton 1929, 270 sq.; Thompson 1929, 334 note 205.
[107] Swanton 1905 b, 202 sq.

182

comb. When Nanasimgit [i.e. the seal-hunter] ran from this place, and came under the canoe, he began to shake the string that hung down from it. And he was pulled up. And the comb became a mountain."[108] In one variant the magic objects are "a handful of cotton," which is transformed into falling trees, "a dried seal stomach," containing hair-oil, which forms a great lake, a comb, which becomes a wall of trees, and a "stinking stuff," which when poured in water keeps the pursuers at a distance.[109] One need be in no doubt but that the flight episode is here a migratory motif taken from without.

At the same time it is interesting to observe that Aarne refers this motif to an original narrative of flight from the dead.[110] Hatt shares this view and points out that in the sense of flight from the realm of the dead "the magic flight" has been narrated among the peoples in north-east Asia.[111] In this case it cannot be altogether without significance that the motif-complex has occurred in the same frame in adjacent areas of North America. This is not to say that it originated in this corner of the world. But in this as in so many other respects we perceive evidence of important historical links between north-east Asia and north-west America.[112]

The foregoing survey of narratives and motifs in North America coming close to the Orpheus tradition has, despite its sketchy nature, afforded convincing evidence that in all essentials the Orpheus tradition is a narrative of individual stamp cast in one mould, which has not received any decisive influence from other tales. It has adopted individual motifs from other tales, it has adapted its form to tales with similar themata, and it has become mixed, locally, with other tales; but this is all. In so far as it shows similarities with alien tales, these similarities may be traced back to common conditions, which have in their turn implied a common association to the same notions and usages.

2. Connections with the Orpheus traditions of the Old World

It is tempting to assume that a tradition so individual and free from contact with other tales as the North American Orpheus tradition is actually a remote echo of the classical Greek Orpheus legend, a distant end-

108 Swanton 1908 a, 499 sq.
109 Barbeau 1953, 292 sqq.
110 Aarne, op.cit., 154 sq.
111 Hatt, op.cit., 94. Cf. below, p. 193.
112 Cf. also chap. III: 2.

product in a long chain of diffusion, whose other terminal point and first origin is the Greek tale. In support of this assumption one may adduce the numerous points of resemblance existing between the Greek and the North American traditions—resemblances which are so striking also as to details that one is astonished when one makes the comparison. And the suspicion arises that the Indians once listened to the tale as told by European colonizers, were fascinated by its deeply human, dramatic content and then elaborated it in their own way.

But all researchers who have formed an opinion as to the possibility that the Orpheus tradition was introduced into North America in post-Columbian time by the whites have dismissed the notion as improbable. Gayton emphasizes that Brébeuf's and Le Clercq's notes from the 17th century "show that the tale was extant at a time prior to any but the slightest European intrusion." Further, she mentions the internal evidence afforded by the tales themselves. The two narratives which might constitute the models for the North American tradition, the Greek tale of Orpheus and Eurydice and the later, Italian tale in Dante's Divine Comedy, are, opines Gayton, in essential respects so diverging: "In both sources there is an abundance of character, incident, and detail beside the mere journey to the world of shades which never appears in any version of the North American tales."[1] And it must be acknowledged that even if the likenesses are striking, there are nevertheless not so few differences; and this signifies much, where it is a matter of a direct transference of the tradition. Not a little narrative material belonging to the Greek legend which would have delighted Indian listeners is missing in the North American tales: the auspices of marriage, Eurydice's violent death, the description of the different conditions imposed upon the dead, and so forth.

An equally sceptical attitude to the loan hypothesis is taken up by Dr. Wheeler-Voegelin. After a scrutiny of the North American texts she finds that they do not contain any references to European culture elements, and are therefore probably "of native origin."[2] The conclusion is perhaps rather hasty; the tale may of course nevertheless have come from some place in the Old World. But her observation is correct and important for the problem here under discussion. Also the Danish researcher Gudmund Hatt rejects the hypothesis of the direct transference

---

[1] Gayton 1935, 283. As exceptions the author mentions the Shawnee tales, whose penal scenes are probably to be ascribed to influence from the prophet-cults affected by Christian ethics. I completely share Dr. Gayton's view on this point.

[2] Voegelin in Leach 1950 II, 834.

from the Europeans; "European influence is here out of the question," he writes.[3]

The present writer shares this view. The reasons already adduced should be sufficient to show the untenability of the theory of an European influence.[4] One may also question whether the few European pioneers in North America during the 17th century who possessed a classical education really wasted their time in telling the Greek legend to the aborigines of the country! Certainly not the missionaries, who were fully occupied with inculcating Christian ideas and Christian legends in their Indian protégés. The French *coureurs de bois*, who so often married native women, would scarcely be familiar with the Greek tale.

If we thus reject the hypothesis of a direct European influence, there remains, however, the possibility that the classical tradition gradually reached North America by devious routes over the Asiatic continent and the Pacific. Or that both the Greek and the North American traditions derive from the same first source, situated somewhere on the Eurasiatic mainland—or, to refer to Heyerdahl's theory of transpacific migrations, somewhere on the American mainland. In other words, can one over Asia assume an historical connection between the Orpheus traditions of Greece and North America?

To be in a position to answer this important question we must first take a quick survey of the Orpheus traditions of the Old World, and arrive, particularly, at some opinion concerning the problem as to whether there is any historical connection between these reciprocally. If this is the case, and if the distribution of these tales extends as far as the frontiers of the North American continent, or at least as far as places whence a transference to America may be regarded as possible, then a connection seems conceivable. And if the similarities between the North American and the Eurasiatic forms of the tradition are essential, complex and not motivated by the logic of the Orpheus theme itself, then one must assume an historical connection. Otherwise, we must be content to hold the door open for the possibility of such a connection.

[3] Hatt 1949, 65.
[4] I naturally dissociate myself entirely from the fantastic modern theories of a Celtic and Nordic influence upon the Indian cultures in pre-Columbian time that have been advanced by A. H. Mallery, just as I must reject Dr. R. Malaise's idea of an immigration from Atlantis. These theories belong to the same airy sphere as their more or less similarly worded predecessors from former periods, e.g. the thesis of the Americanist Brinton concerning an Indian immigration from Europe over a now vanished Atlantic bridge (see, for the rest, Vignaud 1922 for a survey). Such a reliable researcher as Haekel does not, however, exclude the possibility of influences over the Atlantic Ocean (Haekel 1956, 89).

Let us then first consider the myths, legends and fairy-tales from the Old World which in accordance with our earlier definition may be regarded as Orpheus traditions.[5] It should be pointed out to begin with that we cannot here give a more detailed presentation, but must restrict ourselves to a short survey. Nor do we claim to give a full account of all instances: the traditions lying outside the main routes between Greece and the Pacific will here be ignored, as they have no relevance for our problem.[6]

The classical Orpheus legend—or possibly the Orpheus myth—is naturally the Greek tale of Orpheus and Eurydice, immortalized by Virgil and Ovid.[7] Its content is all too well known for it to be necessary to reproduce it here in detail. According to the commonest version, Eurydice died in consequence of a snake-bite, whereupon she was incorporated with the underworld realm of shades. Her husband, the Thracian singer, wandered about inconsolable and listless until he finally descended to Hades, and here, with his lyre, prevailed upon the dead and their ruler to listen to his lament and his request. He was promised by the ruler of the underworld that he might restore his wife to life on condition that on the journey home he did not turn round and look at her. But on his way back to the world of the living he broke his promise, with the result that Eurydice slipped back into the realm of shades. The narrative occurs in several variants. In his *Symposion* Plato represents Orpheus as returning home empty-handed; another narrator replaces the looking taboo with a speaking taboo; and Ovid's version contains as an addition the story of Orpheus' renewed but unsuccessful attempt to descend to the underworld.[8]

There have been many scientific interpreters of the Greek Orpheus tale. One of the latest to penetrate the subject is W. K. C. Guthrie, whose work *Orpheus and Greek Religion* has now been published in a second edition (1952). Guthrie's theories carry great weight in some respects, but the chief fault of his presentation is that he has not chosen to see the Greek myth in a wider, comparative perspective. Like Harrison, he believes that Orpheus did actually exist.[9] "Probabilities are," he writes, "that he was a Greek, that he was a bard and musician, that he was officially a servant of Apollo."[10] Guthrie doubts that Orpheus was a

[5] See above, p. 20.
[6] Concerning the European traditions, see Bar 1946, 66 sqq.
[7] See Nilsson 1935, 189; Gruppe 1897—1909, 1058 sqq., especially 1163 sq.
[8] Guthrie 1952, 31.
[9] Guthrie, op.cit., 4, 26, 41, 47.
[10] Guthrie, op.cit., 56.

186

shaman, as some have considered,[11] nor will he acknowledge that his association with Eurydice is essential for the myth, which he judges entirely according to Orphic viewpoints: the important thing was that Orpheus knew of man's fate and how one could improve it for the other world. "That was the important thing. The reason which once took him there was secondary."[12] It is quite in line with this interpretation that Guthrie understands the looking taboo as "an addition by no means universally adopted until Alexandrian times, if not invented by the Alexandrians."[13] Finally, he finds every reference to the fairy-tale *(Märchen)* incorrect, since the journey to Hades in the Orpheus myth "is an instance not of *Märchen* but of sincerely held belief."[14] The point of this is directed against the well-known classicist Rose, who considers the Greek myth as a variant of "a very old tale, known apparently from Thrace to North America, of the man who went to the other world to fetch his wife and (usually) lost her after all his efforts because he broke some tabu."[15]

Guthrie's Orpheus theory has been briefly reviewed here because it is one of the latest and most well known critical contributions to research on the Greek Orpheus, and as it shows indirectly how much one loses by ignoring wider, comparative viewpoints. It is not for me to judge concerning the earlier composition of the Greek myth or concerning its exact interpretation. But it seems to me justified to assert that Rose has introduced into the Orpheus debate a more fruitful line of research; the parallels with other, extra-Greek traditions are much too obvious for it to be possible to solve the problem only with the help of the Greek material. The circumstance that the tradition may possibly be found to be a migratory legend need not vitiate its value for religious belief— this is shown by the North American Orpheus tradition.

There are several other Greek narratives of a hero's or heroine's descent to the realm of the dead to fetch some beloved deceased person (Bacchus or Dionysos—Semele, Heracles—Alcestis, Persephone—Alcestis, Theseus —Persephone, Aphrodite—Adonis, possibly also Demeter—Jason); and it is conceivable that the Orpheus myth has been influenced by them.[16]

[11] Guthrie, op.cit., 68, note 24.
[12] Guthrie, op.cit., 29; cf. op.cit., 153.
[13] Guthrie, op.cit., 31. According to, inter alia, Kern's and Heurgon's views, the myth originally had a happy ending, which was changed, however, into an unhappy end under the influence of the fairy-tale motif of punished curiosity (Heurgon 1932, 6 sqq.; cf. Nilsson 1941, 645).
[14] Guthrie, op.cit., 52.
[15] Rose 1945, 255. Note that tale and *Märchen* are not synonymous concepts! Rose's treatment of the Orpheus theme comes in his chapter on "Legends," not in the chapter "Märchen."
[16] See Bar, op.cit., 30 sq.

A whole stream of such traditions seems to have existed in the Mediterranean world and the Near East, that is, if we include among them the numerous myths of the abduction and return of the god (or goddess) of vegetation. It is doubtful, however, whether these myths should be classed together with the Greek Orpheus myth. It was, certainly, Maass' great thesis that Eurydice was none other than the goddess of the underworld.[17] But doubts of this were already voiced by Dieterich, and Guthrie has shown that Orpheus' and Eurydice's connections with the powers of the underworld are not any expression for their inherent nature.[18] If Orpheus taught the Greeks in the art of agriculture, this does not mean to say that he was a god of vegetation, but only that he was a culture hero, or rather, a civilizer—for the orthodox Orpheans.[19]

A comparison between the Greek Orpheus myth and the Babylonian fertility myths reveals considerable differences.[20] Also Tammuz and Ishtar descend to the underworld, to the realm of the dead; Tammuz (Dumuzi) betakes himself "to the womb of the earth, to the earth of the dead,"[21] and Ishtar descends to the female ruler of the realm of the dead, Ereshkigal. But the essential thing here is not the actual journey to the realm of the dead, but the circumstance that this journey and its consequences correspond to the cycle of the seasons, the dying of the vegetation in hot July and its return with the spring sun. Numerous details in the myths allude to the course of events in Nature. And at the same time rites were performed to ensure this course of events; the myths concerning Tammuz and Ishtar were, in other words, cult-myths. Finally, it is remarkable that in the Sumerian account of Ishtar's (Inanna's) journey to the underworld there is no allusion to the death and descent to the underworld of her male partner.[22] The fertility myth retains its meaning and importance without him.

[17] Maass 1895. See also Harrison 1923, 603.
[18] Guthrie, op.cit., 41, 43, 54. Cf. Rose, op.cit., loc.cit.
[19] Cf. Guthrie, op.cit., 40. There have been frequent discussions of the question as to whether the Orpheus of the Orpheus legend was identical with the religious reformer Orpheus, a problem which is not yet solved. If, as is possible, the Orpheus legend has been part of a migratory tradition, the probability is that no identity originally existed. In the course of the historical legend formation the two figures may have been gradually attracted to each other because they had an essential feature in common: the magic song, the incantation, characterizing also the founder of Orphism (see Nilsson 1935, 181; Rönnow 1943, 35, 39).
[20] Concerning the Sumerian-Accadian myths on the fertility goddess's journey to the world of the dead, see Zimmern 1909, 701 sqq. and Contenau 1941, 240 sqq.
[21] Cf. Dhorme 1949, 117.
[22] Hooke 1935, 75. In connection with the tale of Aphrodite's journey to Hades to fetch Adonis, Contenau writes: "Ce récit montre les progrès de la légende au cours du

It does not fall within the frame of our task to give here a more detailed account of the relation between the Greek and the Babylonian myths. But the general conclusions we can draw in the light of the comparative survey given here show good agreement with MacCulloch's pronouncements as early as the beginning of this century. Tales of Orpheus character but without elements of ideas relating to vegetation did undoubtedly, he considered, exist both in Babylonia and Greece. And "they would easily become part of, and give precise form to, the myths of vegetation-divinities who were thought to die and come to life again. But it is certain that the latter belief did not originate the tales themselves."[23] This interpretation is supported by the evidence afforded by the comparative material, not least from North America. It seems most reasonable to assume that the Orpheus traditions arose in a pre-agrarian, shamanistic hunting society, while the fertility myths originated independently of them in a more ritualistic agrarian society, and that gradually a mutual attraction between the two cycles of myths arose.[24] This mutual influence is presumably to be read out of the Greek Orpheus tradition and the Babylonian fertility myth; one may assume that the points of contact were constituted by two motifs, the love between husband and wife (in the fertility myth united through an *hieros gamos*), and the disappearance of one of the spouses. It is the business of the specialists in the fields of classical and oriental religions to investigate more closely the fusion between the myth-cycles. Here I shall only indicate some conceivable possibilities. The Babylonian myth may have been influenced by some Orpheus tale when it represents Ishtar as descending to the underworld to fetch Tammuz—a purpose which is not obvious in the older Sumerian version—and when it relates that Ereshkigal is subjugated by flute-playing. (It is not so likely that the combination of the underworld and the world of the dead was made under the influence of the Orpheus tradition.) The Greek Orpheus tale may for its part have been affected by the fertility mythology when the realm of the dead is represented as the underworld, and when Orpheus' wife is given the name Eurydice, "wide-ruling"—a name that is instanced only at a very late date (1st century B. C.); an older name for her is Agriope, "wild-eyed" or "wild-voiced."[25]

temps; tandis que le mythe babylonien permet seulement, grâce à une allusion, de supposer qu'Ishtar va délivrer Tammuz, la légende grecque est formelle et indique qu'à ce moment la nouvelle tradition est bien établie" (Contenau, op.cit., 237).
[23] MacCulloch 1911, 648.
[24] See the conclusions in chap. IV: 3, 4.
[25] See Guthrie, op.cit., 30.

The Greek Orpheus myth has undoubtedly exercised a direct influence on later occidental oral and literary traditions. Thompson's summary of this is worth reproducing: "The myth of Orpheus and his descent to the world of the dead to bring back his wife lived on into the Middle Ages, both in the literary romance and the popular ballad. There has been a transfer of the action from the world of the dead to the land of the fairies and, although the name of Orpheus has been retained, some of the details have dropped out, such as the marvelous harping and the prohibition against looking at the wife on the way out and the conse-quent failure of the mission."[26] We are not called upon to occupy our-selves with these more or less transformed versions of the Orpheus myth, but shall now instead proceed to the more eastern Orpheus traditions, which might perhaps be able to supply the link between the Greek and the North American texts.

Tales of living persons who visited the realm of the dead occur ab-undantly in Asiatic religion and folklore, and MacCulloch has made a collocation of the narratives describing a "descent [to Hades] to rescue a dead relative."[27] It is clear, however, that the tales based on this theme which may be adduced from the high cultures on the Asiatic main-land are only in slight measure connected with the sequence of events occurring in the Greek and North American tales. In Indian literature one notes a myth concerning Krishna's journey to the world of the dead which is found in a Purana text, *Harivaṃsa*, appended to *Mahābhāratā*. Here we are told how Krishna descended to the kingdom of the death-god Yama to fetch a deceased son of his teacher Sāndīpani. Krishna defeated Yama in a duel and succeeded in this way in regaining the de-ceased for this life.[28] A celebrated episode in *Mahābhāratā* describes how the beautiful Savitri, married to the exiled prince Satyavant, was deprived of her husband by Yama, the god of death. She followed him, however, and did not return until he had restored her father-in-law's kingdom and the life of her husband.[28a] A Tibetan Buddhistic legend tells of a young man who made his way to Hell to take the place that his mother occupied there after her death in consequence of her sins. This is refused

[26] Thompson 1946, 265. See further Labitte 1842, 704 sqq., Becker 1899, Diels 1922, and Bar, op.cit., 102 sqq.
[27] MacCulloch, op.cit., 650 sq.
[28] See Scherman 1892, 63 note 1 (from *Harivaṃsa* V, 4913 sqq.). Barbeau adduces another tale on the Orpheus theme from India, according to which a wife seeks her deceased husband (Barbeau 1950 I, 270). I have unfortunately been unable to find the source, which is not mentioned by Barbeau either.
[28a] See Keith 1927, 160 sq.(from *Mahābhāratā* III, 16616 sqq.).

190

him, but at Buddha's instigation both the young man and his mother and father are transported to Heaven, though the mother has first to go through several reincarnations.[29] A similar story is known from China: shortly after his death the Buddhist Lo Pah visited Hell in order to liberate his captive mother, and he actually succeeded in removing her thence.[30]

There are really not many threads connecting these legends with the Greek and North American narratives. A couple of apparently genuine Orpheus tales have, however, been preserved in Chinese folklore and are reproduced in Eberhard's collection of Chinese folktales. The one, no. 144, tells of a man who betook himself to the land of the dead to search for his wife. With the help of the information he was given by the waiter in an inn he succeeded in reaching the underworld, where he saw his wife fetching water at a source. He tried to communicate with her, but she did not notice him until he had thrown a coin into her bucket. She charged him to go, as she was now a spirit, but he refused. After sojourning together in the realm of the dead for a time the two fled thence. On the way home the woman went into a house and disappeared. But at the same moment the wife of the owner of the house gave birth to a daughter, and when she had grown up the man recognized his wife and (re)married her.[30a] The other tale (no. 145 II) describes a father's attempt to bring his deceased son back from the underworld; the son does not recognize him, and the attempt is a failure.[30b]

Is it possible that these two tales are relics of an older Asiatic Orpheus tradition, which in most quarters has in the course of time been exposed to Hindu or Buddhistic elaboration?

Even if it is difficult to show that this is the case, the theory does acquire a certain probability (but not more) when one finds regular Orpheus tales in the border regions of the Asiatic continent, in Siberia, Japan and the Pacific. In other words, marginal regions would, on this theory, preserve the remains of one and the same Orpheus tradition that had once had a distribution also in the central parts of the continent, but had here undergone essential changes in connection with the growth of the high cultures.[31]

---

[29] Scherman, op.cit., 80 sqq.
[30] MacCulloch, op.cit., 651; quotes *Asiatic Journal,* XXXI (1840), 211.
[30a] Eberhard 1937 a, 161 sqq., 1937 b, 198 sq.
[30b] Eberhard 1937 b, 199 sq.
[31] Concerning the validity of the "marginal theory," see e.g. Cooper 1941 and Wallis 1945.

Let us first examine the "marginal testimonies" here referred to.

A tale from the Katshin Tartars tells of a young woman, Kubaiko, who made her way to the underworld domain of Irlek-Khan, the prince of the realm of the dead, in order to find her brother's head, which had been taken there by a nine-headed monster. She passed through nightmare halls and finally reached the prince himself. The latter promised to restore her brother's head if she could extricate a seven-horned wether that had sunk into the earth right up to the horns. She tried and was successful, and brought the head up to the surface of the earth again, and she then resuscitated her brother by sprinkling him with the water of life.[32]

In a well-known Manchu poem (Nishan saman) is told, according to Shirokogorov, the following story, which must to a certain extent be considered analogous with the preceding one. A young man who lived during the period of the Ming dynasty (1368—1644) was killed in an accident while hunting. "The female shaman, named Nishan, took on herself the task of bringing back the soul of the young man, and she shamanized accordingly. Her shamanizing-visit to the lower world, meeting with the various spirits, including her own husband and other people, her finding of the young man's soul and restoring it were recorded."[33] Unfortunately, this poem has never been translated from the Manchu language. From Shirokogorov's summary it does not emerge clearly whether the young man and the female shaman had any tenderer feelings in common. One is inclined to believe that this was the case, since precisely this piece of shamanizing was made the subject of a poem. But as long as no information on the point is forthcoming the case cannot definitely be referred to the class of Orpheus traditions.

A curious Orpheus tale has been noted by Chamberlain among the Aino. A man was searching everywhere for his wife, who had disappeared. An oak-god helped him, and gave him a golden horse with which he could ascend to the sky. Here he caused a great to do, and the demon of hell stared up and forgot his duties as guard. The man took advantage of this, stole into hell and freed his wife from the box in which she was shut up. The two spouses were happily reunited.[33a] The tale does not, it is true, make the impression of a first or original version, but is included here for the sake of completeness.

---

[32] Castrén 1853 III, 147 sqq.
[33] Shirokogorov 1935, 308. We shall later have occasion in another context to revert to this tale. See chap. IV: 3.
[33a] Chamberlain 1888, 21 sq.

The Japanese Orpheus myth is at the same time a part of the Japanese epic of the Creation. It is introduced with the tale of how two divinities, Izanagi (Male-who-invites) and Izanami (Female-who-invites), are by the celestial deities sent down to earth along the "Floating Bridge of Heaven."[34] Izanagi created an island and married Izanami, who later gave birth to all kinds of living and dead entities, gods, mountains, forests and winds. But when she had given birth to the gods of fire she succumbed, and descended to the realm of the dead, Yomotsu-kuni ("the Land of Gloom"). Death had herewith been brought into the world. Izanagi followed after her. But she could not return, for she had already tasted the food in the other world. She wished first, however, to confer with the underworld divinities, and Izanagi was charged not to look at her. But, impatient to behold her again, he lit a torch (made of his comb) and then saw his wife's horrible, decaying corpse. He fled, terrified. But his wife, whom he had shamed, indignantly despatched the ghosts and "the ugly females" after him. In order to check his pursuers, Izanagi then threw at them fruits which grew on his comb, and which they stopped to consume. Finally, Izanami herself took up the pursuit, whereupon he emerged from the opening between this world and the other world and blocked it with a big boulder. Izanami had to return to the abyss, where she became the goddess of the realm of the dead.[35]

The Japanese narrative of the Creation is indisputably related with Polynesian primaeval myths.[36] Izanagi and Izanami are without doubt the heavenly father and the earth goddess, at the same time as they represent the first man and woman.[37] The Japanese myth herewith belongs to a mythic complex—the world-parents—which has occurred chiefly in the high cultures of the Old and the New Worlds.[38] One may thus presume that the connection of the Orpheus theme with this myth is, as in the Euphrates-Tigris area, a secondary phenomenon, at the same time as it is possible that the association of the tales is a heritage from the period when the central agrarian cultures were developed (wherever this process may have taken place). It is, however, also a possibility that the connection arose in Japan, although the comparative material from Oceania (cf. below) does not favour this hypothesis. It is remarkable, finally, that "the magic flight"—with the inevitable comb-motif—should here, as

[34] Probably the rainbow—see Anesaki 1928, 378 note 5.
[35] Chamberlain 1883, 34 sqq.
[36] Florenz 1925, 279.
[37] Florenz, op.cit., 279 sq.
[38] Baumann 1955, 265, and map 4, op.cit., 353.
[39] Cf. above, pp. 182 sq.

among the Haida Indians, have been woven into the Orpheus tradition.[39]

In Indonesia Thompson has found no fewer than thirty-seven instances of tales of the type Aa 400 (Quest for Lost Wife) migrating here from Asia.[40] None of these versions, however, is identical with the Orpheus tradition,[41] and it is doubtful whether the latter has ever existed here.[42] Yet fertility myths which are close to the Orpheus tradition are known from the area. A Buginese tale from southern Celebes tells how on account of man's neglect of her the rice goddess left the earth and ascended to heaven. The people were threatened with famine, but a kindly disposed divinity prevailed upon the goddess to return, and the catastrophe was averted.[43] To the same group of traditions and ideas belongs also a narrative from the Riung tribe on central Flores, relating how the first mother visits her children, who had been cut to pieces and turned into forage plants.[44]

Only when we get as far as Melanesia, however, do we meet with real Orpheus tales. The Kai on north-eastern New Guinea have, as Hatt remarks, a "wild and sinister" Orpheus tradition. Here it is a man who seeks out his deceased wife in the realm of the dead. His father-in-law, evidently the chief of the dead, protects him from the cannibalistic tendencies of the other dead persons and brings his daughter to life again by fitting together her bones (taken from her grave) and wrapping her skin about them. The husband and wife come up again to the light of day. When, shortly afterwards, the man dies, the wife puts her bones in the grave again and accompanies him to the underworld.[45]

Other Orpheus legends are known from the Banks Islands and the New Hebrides.[46] We shall reproduce here a couple of versions from the last-mentioned group of islands. Codrington reports that the natives here tell of a wizard who betook himself in the spirit to Panoi, the world of the dead. He took with him on this occasion a man who desired to bring back his wife, who had died. In vain did the man implore his wife to return. She had eaten the food of the dead and could not follow him, but she gave him instead an arm-ring as a remembrance. He then seized her hand and tried to drag her away with him—but the arm came off

[40] Thompson, op.cit., 289.
[41] Thompson has used de Vries' studies of Indonesian folktales as a basis for his calculation. I have, however, not been able to find the Orpheus tradition in de Vries' work (de Vries 1925—28).
[42] Cf. Dixon 1916, 78.
[43] Bezemer 1904, 376 sq.; see also Hatt 1951, 885.
[44] Hatt, op.cit., 888.
[45] Keysser 1911, 213 sq.
[46] See especially Codrington 1891, 277 sq. (Banks Islands), 286 sq. (New Hebrides).

194

and her body fell to pieces.[47] On north-eastern Malekula there is told a story of two women who, beside themselves with love for a dead man, followed him to the realm of the dead. They were, however, forced to return.[48]

The most remarkable development of the Orpheus tradition is that found in Polynesia. Here it appears in forms which are reminiscent of both the Japanese Orpheus myth and the North American Orpheus tales. The resemblance to the North American tales is the more interesting because Polynesian mythology otherwise shows connections westwards, with the archaic high cultures.[49] We shall therefore give a somewhat more detailed account of the Polynesian Orpheus traditions. The Orpheus tales in the area occur in New Zealand, on the Samoan Islands, Mangaia (Cook Islands), the Society Islands, the Marquesas and Hawaii.[50]

A Maori narrative from New Zealand is here given in an abridged form: Mataora married a beautiful woman, Nuvarahu, who belonged to the people of the underworld. When he struck her on one occasion she got angry and fled back to the underworld. Her husband mourned her and resolved to seek her out. He descended to the underworld (learning here the art of tatooing[51]). He begged his wife to return with him; she was at first hesitant, but finally yielded. On their way back they were advised by a bird to postpone their ascent to the earth till the summer, for, said the bird, the upper world was full of evil. They acted on this advice. When, the following summer, they came up from the underworld the guardian closed the door behind them, so that no more living beings should ever be able to visit the underworld. Now, it is only the dead who get there.[52] Another Maori narrative alludes more clearly than the preceding one to cosmic circumstances: Tane,[53] the Creator, married his own daughter, and she then killed herself out of shame and descended to the underworld, where she became the goddess of night and of death. The grief-stricken husband betook himself to the realm of the dead and tried to prevail upon her to return to the light of day again; but he had to return empty-handed.[54] The dichotomy between the re-

---

[47] Codrington, op.cit., 286 sq. The notion that one is committed to the realm of the dead if one eats its food is widespread in Indonesia and Melanesia, but is not found in Polynesia, except in New Zealand. See Dixon, op.cit., 321 note 77.
[48] Layard 1934, 126 sq.
[49] Baumann, op.cit., 239.
[50] See the succinct account in Handy 1927, 80 sqq., Dixon, op.cit., 72 sqq.
[51] The myth serves at the same time to explain the origin of tatooing.
[52] White 1887 II, 4 sqq.
[53] Concerning Tane, see e.g. Handy, op.cit., 98 sqq., Nevermann 1947, 57.
[54] White 1886 I, 131 sqq., 145 sqq.

presentatives of the upper and lower worlds is here as clear as in the Japanese myth, and one must probably assume a basic connection. In a third Maori myth the Orpheus theme has possibly been combined with a fertility myth. I am here thinking of the myth of the goddess Pani, the mother of the sweet potato. When the god Maui and his brothers discovered how she gave birth, out of her own substance, to the food that they ate, she was overwhelmed with shame and betook herself to the underworld; Maui visited her here.[55]

The Maori tale coming closest to the North American Orpheus legend is a fourth narrative, dealing with the love between two high-born persons, the virgin Pare and the chief Hutu. When the latter scorned Pare's offer of marriage she shut herself up in her house and hanged herself. Her relatives were seized with wrath, took Hutu captive and informed him that he must die. He then said: "It is good, but do not bury Pare's corpse. Allow me to depart. I will be absent three on four days, and then I will be here again." They believed him and allowed him to go, and he hurried down to the abode of the dead to fetch Pare back to life. He sought out the goddess of the night and of the dead (cf. above), gave her presents and received in return information about the way to Pare. The goddess also prepared food for him and warned him against eating the food of the dead.[56] At last Hutu found the deceased, but she was by no means disposed to return to life. When Hutu had taken part for a while in the games of the dead he hit upon a strategem whereby he might bring his enterprise to a successful conclusion. He amused the dead by getting them to sit on the top of a tall pole which with a rope fastened to the ground had been bent down like a bow; when the rope was loosed the dead were flung up into the air. Pare, too, wished to participate in the game, and sat down by Hutu's side on the pole. Hutu then had the rope pulled tauter than usual, and when it was loosed both he and Pare were flung up to the upper world. He then bore Pare (i.e. her spirit) to the place where her corpse lay; the spirit entered the body and Pare stood up alive. At her request Hutu now married her.[57]—In this tale we recognize several motifs which are typical for the North American Orpheus legend: the negotiations with the ruler of the dead, Orpheus' participation in the games of the dead, the unwillingness of the deceased to return, the revivification.

Similar, though less detailed Orpheus stories have been told on Samoa

[55] Hatt, op.cit., 891 sq. Concerning Maui, see Handy, op.cit., 118.
[56] Cf. above, p. 195 note 47.
[57] White 1887 II, 164 sqq.; Clark 1896, 1 sqq. (cf. also op.cit., 126).

and Mangaia. The Mangaia version is interesting inasmuch as here Orpheus betakes himself to the underworld (Avaiki) with the help of his guardian god.[58] His wife has been taken there against her will by the people of the underworld, and is liberated by her husband.[59] On the Society Islands the Orpheus theme has been combined with a myth—or fairy-tale?—concerning the love of the Sun for the flowers.[60]

Of particular interest are the Orpheus narratives on the more easterly islands, the Marquesas and Hawaii, inasmuch as they mention the receptacle-motif. The Hawaiian narrative (which is introduced with an episode of the type "magical flight of arrows," a motif also known in North America, on the Plains and elsewhere[61]) relates that the beautiful Kawelu dies of grief and despair when her young husband, Hiku, leaves her to visit his mother. Hiku returns and weeps over her corpse. Finally he resolves to recover her spirit from the realm of the dead. With the help of his friends he makes a long rope, smears his body with a rancid oil that makes him smell like a corpse, and procures a hollow coconut. He then lets himself be lowered through the opening to the underworld, and neither the dead nor their prince are able to tell from the smell that he is a living being. The dead delight in swinging in the rope he has taken down with him, as does also Kawelu (cf. the Maori tale of Pare). But then Hiku gives his friends up above the signal to hoist up the rope. Kawelu now tries to flee, and turns herself into a butterfly; but Hiku catches the latter in the coconut and is hoisted up. As soon as he reaches the surface of the ground he hastens to Kawelu's corpse, makes a hole in the big toe of the left foot and forces the spirit into the body; with the help of massage he gets it to slip in further and further. "Gradually, as the heart was reached, the blood began once more to flow through the body, the chest began gently to heave with the breath of life, and soon the spirit gazed out through the eyes."[62]

In the Marquesas narrative noted down by Handy we are told how the hero Kena descended to the realm of the dead to fetch his beloved, who had committed suicide on his account. He put her spirit in a basket and was then despatched to the upper world by the powers of the underworld, who could not abide his smell.[63]

---

[58] Concerning the guardian gods, see Nevermann, op.cit., 48 sqq. (guardian gods for the families).
[59] Gill 1876, 221.
[60] See Handy, op.cit., 81 sq.
[61] See Thompson 1929, 315.
[62] Thrum 1907, 43 sqq.
[63] Handy, op.cit., 81 sq.

Both the receptacle-motif and the well-described resuscitation act in the Hawaii narrative have their counterparts in the North American Orpheus tradition.

After this survey of the material—i.e. the relevant material found by me—we are once more confronted with the question we posed at the beginning of this little investigation: are the tales recounted here connected with one another by historical links, or are they "independent inventions," whose only connection is the common nature of the tales?

It is here, as in so many other similar cases, difficult to arrive at a conclusion. The difficulty resides partly in the paucity of the sources. There are of course more tales of Orpheus type on the Asiatic mainland than those of which it has been possible to give an account here; but they are buried in a terribly voluminous literature, which it is difficult for the non-specialist to exploit to advantage. On the basis of the material reviewed here it is almost presumptuous to give any opinion at all concerning possible connections between the traditions. Certain striking resemblances do undeniably exist between geographically widely separated narratives—e.g. between the Greek myth and some Polynesian tales. But it is difficult to say whether these resemblances are of such a kind as to make a diffusion appear probable, or whether they are merely the result of the dramatic dynamic inherent in a natural human conceptual motif (the Orpheus theme). The remarkable thing is that a long-distance testing of the similarities between the Greek narrative and the North American narratives is more fruitful than the scrutiny of the parallels in the Old World!

It must here be remembered, however, firstly that a stream of myths, beliefs and ideas are held in common in the enormous area from the Mediterranean to the Pacific that has been dominated by the high cultures, and secondly that there seem to be definite historical connections between the Orpheus myths in widely separated regions in the outskirts of the high cultures, viz, in Japan and in New Zealand.[64] Even if no direct connections are demonstrable between the East Asiatic-Oceanic Orpheus narratives and their counterparts in the Near East—Mediterranean area, we cannot without rashness exclude the possibility of a continuous chain of traditions comprehending the whole of Eurasia.

An hypothetical reconstruction of the historical connections would then have the following appearance. The Orpheus tradition originally

[64] See Dixon, op.cit., 321 note 60; Hatt 1949, 69. Cf. above, pp. 193, 195.

belonged to the hunting culture, to which it was well adapted on account of its shamanistic content.[65] It still occurs among pure hunting peoples (cf. the Siberian and North American instances); but in the central agrarian regions of Eurasia it has been fused with the fertility mythology, whereby Orpheus has been identified with the ruler of heaven (or the god of fertility), Eurydice has been identified with the earth goddess, who, as we know, is in the fertility religions often at the same time the female ruler of the dead. In this distorted form the Orpheus tradition has reached both the Maori and the Japanese. In view of the fact that the Orpheus myths of these two peoples are so similar, one may venture to assume that their "primaeval myth" belonged to a period when the close connections between Polynesians and Japanese which many researchers have assumed were a reality. In the marginal regions outside the immediate sphere of influence of the high cultures, in Siberia, Melanesia and Polynesia, the older Orpheus tradition has been able to remain fairly unchanged. Perhaps the Orpheus tradition once existed in an unbroken chain from the tundras in the north to the islands in the south, a chain that was broken when the invading high culture separated paleo-Asiatic and paleo-Melanesian cultures.[66]

But this, as I have remarked, is a theory which is, certainly, plausible, but which is without reliable foundation. What is, however, certain is that there has been a connection between the Orpheus tales in the peripheral areas in the Far East and the Pacific, and against this background one asks oneself whether it might not also be possible to show a connection between these and the North American tales. The prerequisites for a connection appear to be good: the Asiatic-Oceanic Orpheus tradition exists in places as near to North America as eastern Siberia, Japan and Hawaii; and on the last-mentioned island especially, as we have found, the Orpheus narrative bears a remarkable resemblance to certain North American versions. But is this resemblance accidental, or can it be adduced as a proof of dissemination of the tradition? It seems impossible to imagine that the resemblance is merely a caprice of chance.

Before making any declaration of opinion on the question of a possible connection between the Orpheus traditions on either side of the Pacific, we shall give a brief account of the views in the question that have been advanced by different researchers.

Unfortunately, Gayton has not given her opinion, unless one may

[65] Concerning this see further chap. IV: 3.
[66] See Chang 1956, 380.

interpret her silence to mean that she dismisses the whole problem as all too speculative. The majority of other writers who have occupied themselves with the problem find the notion of a connection improbable. Concerning the North American, especially the north-west American Orpheus tradition, Alexander writes: "It is not necessary to invoke the theory of borrowings for such a tale as this; the elemental fact of human grief and yearning for the departed will explain it. Doubtless a similar universality in human nature and a similar likeness in human experiences will account for the multitude of other conceptions which make the mythic universe of the men of the Old World and the men of the New fundamentally and essentially one."[67] Dixon has not made any direct communication of his view in the matter. He must, however, have been confronted with it, since he has met with Orpheus tales in both of his investigation areas, Polynesia and California. It is therefore of value to note that as regards the culture elements in general he only finds superficial resemblances. "The resemblances, so far as they exist, are analogies and not homologies, and as soon as one studies details, the differences are found to be both significant and fundamental."[68] Thompson writes of the Orpheus tradition: "The general outlines of this story with its journey to the otherworld to bring back the dear departed is of such universal interest that we might well expect to find parallels where there is little likelihood of actual contact." It is, certainly, surprising that the taboo on the return journey from the dead is mentioned both in North America and in Greece. "All evidence, however, would indicate that, in spite of the resemblances, the so-called American Indian 'Orpheus myth' is an independent growth."[69] Speaking of Orpheus and Eurydice and some other "European" stories, the same researcher states that "there is little doubt that the American Indian myths of this group have developed independently. Each has a well-defined distribution quite different from those borrowed from the Europeans."[70] One glimpses the last-mentioned argument also in Eliade; he observes that the Orpheus tradition in North America is not found among the Eskimo, "ce qui nous paraît exclure l'hypothèse d'une influence sibéro-asiatique."[71] Hatt, who more than anyone else has tested the possibility of a transpacific migration of the Orpheus tradition, is equally negative. The Orpheus motif, he says, "springs from human feelings of a general kind, and it may have origin-

[67] Alexander 1916, 264. The same views recur in Alexander 1953.
[68] Dixon 1933, 344; cf., however, op.cit., 352 sq.
[69] Thompson 1946, 265 sq.
[70] Thompson, op.cit., 345.
[71] Eliade 1951, 281 note 2.

ated many times within different cultures."[72] The thesis is somewhat encumbered by the remarkable agreement between the receptacle-motifs of the Oceanic and American tales. "Considering, however, the general human character of the Orpheus motif, there is hardly reason for assuming that this motif has come to North America from Oceania. The idea of going to the world of the dead in order to bring a beloved person back must be rather obvious for any people who has the notion of a world of the dead."[73]

Only Barbeau diverges from this dominating basic view by applying purely diffusionistic viewpoints. The American Orpheus tradition, he opines, is a remote offshoot of the same tale as the Greek narrative, and was introduced into North America by the ancestors of Indian tribes now living. "The world-wide diffusion from an unknown source of a tale so typically classical as Orpheus and Eurydice must have required milleniums. It was part and parcel, like many others, of racial migrations out of Asia into Europe and Africa, or into America with the colonists;[74] or again, the other way, from Asia into North America via Bering Sea."[75]

There is, undeniably, much to support the negative attitude to the contact hypothesis taken up by the majority of the researchers here mentioned. Above all, one must agree that the Orpheus tale is a natural, human theme, whose formation in many places ought easily to be possible—at least in places where fear of contact with the dead does not stifle the longing for them.[76] In North America, it would seem, two different traditions have arisen on the Orpheus motif, the "inland" and the "sea-coast forms." More difficult to digest is the viewpoint that the likenesses found between the North American and the Asiatic-Oceanic narratives are superficial and accidental. It is, however, worth while remembering that in her study of the traditions of the sun's capture in a snare Luomala arrives at the conclusion that the North American and the Polynesian narratives have nothing to do with each other, they represent two separate, independent areas of tradition.[77] The third argument of the opponents of diffusion, the interrupted distribution, seems less well founded if one considers the possibility of transpacific connections that is the subject of such lively debate at present. On the other

---

[72] Hatt 1949, 65; cf. op.cit., 27, 106.
[73] Hatt, op.cit., 69.
[74] Barbeau is referring to Catholic and other tales concerning visits to the realm of the dead, e.g. French-Canadian folktales such as the story of Jean de l'Ours.
[75] Barbeau 1951 I, 270; see also Barbeau 1953, 5 note 1, 257 sq.
[76] See below, pp. 223 sq.
[77] Luomala 1940.

hand, there is a wide gap between the North American and the Siberian Orpheus legends (we cannot here reckon with the uncertain Manchu case). The Japanese Orpheus myth is too peculiar for it to be possible to attach any importance to it in this connection.

This notwithstanding, there is a good deal that favours the possibility of a diffusion; and when brought together the different arguments that can be adduced do acquire a certain force, even if they cannot give us the assurance of complete certainty:

1. It is known that northernmost America and northernmost Eurasia have quite a lot of culture elements in common, not least in the fields of religious belief and oral narrative tradition. In this connection we have firstly to do with circumpolar culture elements spread from Scandinavia over the tundras of Siberia to the boreal regions of North America and the ice-fields of Greenland; important diffusion elements within this zone in the field of spiritual culture have been collocated by Lowie.[78] And secondly we have to do with ideas and customs that have been common to fisher peoples on either side of the northernmost part of the Pacific Ocean, the paleo-Asiatics about Amur and to the north of Lake Okhotska, and the Northwest Indians in British Columbia and Alaska.[79] What is particularly interesting from our point of view is the fact that a number of folktales and narrative motifs have been common to North America and northern Asia; how many, it is impossible to say, but presumably at least a dozen.[80] Dr. Francis Utley has kindly informed me that as far as he knows for certain fourteen well-known North American tales are to be found in the Old World, not counting the numerous folktales which in post-Columbian time have been introduced by Europeans and Negroes to North America and here assimilated by the Indians with their own traditions.[81] Among these fourteen, Utley also includes the Orpheus narrative. It should not surprise us if its appearance on two adjacent continents is due to diffusion, since the majority of the other tales —e.g. tales of Earth-diver and *vagina dentata*—have quite obviously migrated from the Old to the New World.

2. The distribution is very remarkable. As MacCulloch has already observed, most of the Orpheus tales are concentrated to the countries around the Pacific Ocean.[82] One wonders whether any other factor than

---

[78] Lowie 1925 a; Lowie 1934 b. Cf. also Wassén 1954.

[79] Bogoras 1902, 579 sqq.; Boas 1909; Boas 1933, 355 sqq. See also above, p. 183, below, p. 210.

[80] Cf. Hatt 1949, 102 sqq.

[81] Concerning these, see Thompson 1919. The European narratives probably run to about one hundred.

[82] MacCulloch, op.cit., 650.

the diffusion can be behind this distribution of instances. A further consideration is that the modes of occurrence of the Orpheus tradition on the two American continents can only be explained as a result of diffusion.

As regards South America, I do not know of a single Orpheus tale from this continent. Ehrenreich does, certainly, adduce from the Yurakaré "die merkwürdigste Mythe, die das Verhältnis von Sonne und Mond im Sinne des Orpheusmotivs behandelt."[83] The story tells of a man who while out hunting was torn to pieces by a jaguar. His wife, the daughter of the Sun, found all the pieces and fitted them together—except a piece from the face, which was missing. The man was ashamed, and begged his wife not to look at him on the journey home. When in spite of this she turned round and looked at him, he disappeared.[84] This may well be a Sun and Moon myth, as Ehrenreich opines (although this is not certain either), but it is not an Orpheus tale simply because the motifs "woman seeks husband" and "looking taboo" occur.[85] The essential condition, that the deceased should be in the realm of the dead and here be visited by his wife, is missing. There do exist in South America, on the other hand, tales of living persons who are fetched by the dead to accompany them to the realm of death. Among the Chane in Bolivia there is a narrative of a woman who was sought out by her deceased husband; first he slept with her, and then he took her—with her permission—to the world of the dead.[86] But such tales are not Orpheus narratives, even though they are based upon a similar theme. It is remarkable that South America is without not only the Orpheus tale, but also a myth reminiscent of this tale and known from both the Old World and North America, viz., the myth of the departure of the vegetation goddess.[87]

In contrast to the total absence of the Orpheus tradition in South America is its lively occurrence in North America. As Barbeau has pointed out, one finds a more frequent occurrence of the Orpheus motif in this part of the world than elsewhere.[88] This circumstance seems able to point to diffusion as the active factor. In addition to this, as Gayton has point-

[83] Concerning the Orpheus tradition as astral-mythological speculation, see below, pp. 220 sq.
[84] Ehrenreich 1905, 37 (quotes J. R. Barboza, *Poranduba Amazonense*, Rio de Janeiro 1890, 252 sqq., and A. d'Orbigny, *Voyage dans l'Amérique méridionale*, Vol. III, Paris 1844, 210).
[85] The tale is somewhat reminiscent of the Egyptian Osiris myth.
[86] Nordenskiöld 1912, 255 sqq.; Koch-Grünberg 1920, 297 sq.
[87] Hatt 1951, 879. On the other hand, the receptacle-motif occurs in a similar tale, Aarne 400 (see Métraux 1946, 48).
[88] Barbeau 1953, 258.

ed out, the Orpheus tradition in North America has kept "a constant form amidst a variety of cultural influences."[89] "One would expect," she writes, "that the simplicity of the essential idea, the desire to bring back a beloved person from the world of death, would have made it singularly amenable to frequent reinvention. But such is not the case."[90] Hatt has drawn the full conclusions from this: "The considerable and continuous geographical distribution must be the result of spreading. Although the motif is of a general human character, it is probably not invented more than once in North America; but when it first was there, it spread very quickly, keeping its form in the main."[91] For my own part I find it probable that the quick dissemination—so characteristic for firmly constructed popular folktales, whether legends or fairy-tales[92]— is also connected with the religious creative activity typical for the Indians of North America, "democratized shamanism."

The distribution in America thus seems definitely to support diffusion. It is then not unnatural to imagine that also the American and the Asiatic-Oceanic Orpheus tales—which latter are of course parts of one and the same tradition—are outgrowths of one and the same historical narrative. In other words, not only the motif, but the actual formal basic tradition would in this case be common to the peoples on either side of the Pacific Ocean and Bering's Strait. Although our earlier observation, that in consequence of its elementary nature and its psychological assumptions the Orpheus tradition can easily arise both here and there, militates against such a supposition, it is confirmed by the observations most students of folktales have been able to make concerning the importance of diffusion for fairy-tales and legends.[93] It is well known that certain culture elements are better suited to diffusion than others.[94] To these elements belongs without doubt the folktale; and however simple and uncomplicated it may appear, it should always be possible to expect that it has migrated from one place to another.[95] C. W. von Sydow has shown that diffusion may also take place by "jumping," so that it passes over big geographical areas without leaving a trace. The reason for this is that the bearers of tradition are few and must meet, if there

[89] Gayton, op.cit., 286. Cf. above, pp. 18 sq., 34, 183.
[90] Gayton, op.cit., loc.cit.
[91] Hatt 1949, 67.
[92] As Ström has pointed out, the serious myths—the trickster myths thus excepted— are never spread in this way (Ström 1956, 51).
[93] See e.g. Lessa's assessment of the Oedipus tradition (Lessa 1956, 70 sq.).
[94] See e.g. Linton 1936, 338.
[95] This is why diffusionistic studies have meant so much in folklore research (cf. the Finnish historico-geographic method).

is to be a possibility of the tradition spreading.[96] As Hatt has emphasized, this theory is of great interest for our assessment of the spread of culture between America and Asia.[97] As regards the Orpheus tradition, our knowledge of "the sporadic distribution" may with advantage be supplemented with what we know concerning actual cases of culture-loss (e.g. in Polynesia). In this way the break between the Northwest American and the Siberian Orpheus narratives would find a natural explanation.

That there have been communications over the Pacific Ocean between America and the Old World is now fairly established, even if both the routes and the nature of the communications are debated problems.[98] At all events, a transference of the Orpheus tradition across the ocean no longer appears as an impossibility.

3. Also in favour of the diffusion theory is the fact that in several details not characteristic for the main motif the North American tales are reminiscent of the Orpheus tales of the Old World, especially the peripheral tales outside the high cultures proper.[99] Here I would especially stress the resemblances between the North American and the Oceanic narratives (the prohibition against eating the food of the dead; supernatural guide or divine ruler gives assistance; games with the dead; the deceased resists her liberator; she is brought back in a diminutive capsule; ritual revivification). Certain of the resemblances are presumably not due to direct contact, such as the receptacle-motif, as I shall try to show later.[100] Also the Greek narrative of Orpheus and Eurydice has detail-motifs which are found in the North American tales (Orpheus wanders listlessly about after Eurydice's death, overcomes the powers of the dead with his magic song; Hades is won over for his cause; the taboo-motif; unsuccessful renewed attempt to get back the deceased).[101] The Greek

[96] von Sydow 1948, 11 sqq., 203 sqq.
[97] Hatt, op.cit., 103 sq.
[98] Regarding a possible transference of culture elements from Oceania to North America, se e.g. BBAE 30: 1 (1907), 539; Friederici 1929, 451, and passim; Olson 1930, 21; Nordenskiöld 1933, 265; Klimek 1935, 67; Quimby 1948, 252 sq. See also below, p. 211 note 24. Regarding the cultural contact between Oceania (south-eastern Asia) and nuclear America, see below, pp. 216 sq.
[99] See the reconstruction above, pp. 198 sq.
[100] See chap. IV: 3.
[101] A presumably accidental parallel to the death of the Greek Eurydice exists in the Cherokee myth. As we know, in the Greek tale Eurydice dies after being bitten in the heel by a snake. This motif recurs in a northern version of the tradition: Kalevala relates that Lemminkäinen was killed by a snake (song 14, verses 407—412; song 15, verses 575—584). In the Cherokee myth we are told that the daughter of the Sun died in consequence of a snake-bite (Mooney 1900, 253). In the Orpheus legend of the Telumni Yokuts it is Orpheus himself who is bitten to death by a rattle-snake (Gayton 1935, 268). In one of the Zuni legends the young man who dies is changed into a snake (Benedict 1935 II, 299), and according to the Mohave legend it is the young Orpheus, with the name Snake-Soul, who on his death becomes a snake (see above, p. 24).

tale hereby comes closer to the North American tradition than the tales on the Asiatic mainland, which, as I have supposed, have been subjected to a powerful influence from the dominating circle of religious ideas in the great high cultures.

The arguments here adduced for a diffusion are strong, but nevertheless not sufficiently convincing. In these circumstances it appears to me most reasonable to hold the door open for the diffusion theory, but to base nothing on it. That is to say, the conclusions we are able to draw concerning the sociological and psychological origin of the North American Orpheus tradition must allow for the possibility of its being necessary to judge the tradition in a larger historical context. It can here only be a matter of a migration from west to east, from Asia or Oceania to North America. Two circumstances here are decisive. Firstly, in the New World the Orpheus tradition is concentrated to North America, where its stable form shows that it probably had a single source; as I shall soon show, I include in the connection also the otherwise peculiar and formally independent "sea-coast form". And secondly, in the Old World the Orpheus motif has such a wide distribution—from Europe to Oceania and Japan—that the origin of the tradition in America appears inconceivable. On similar grounds Boas has found that the folktales common to America and the Old World have spread from west to east, and not vice versa.[102] We have already seen that Barbeau considers an origin in the Old World probable for the American Orpheus tradition.[103] And we may add that if there is a connection between the Orpheus tales of the Old and New Worlds—which is uncertain but not inconceivable—the direction of the movement has been from Asia or Oceania to America.

3. History of the Orpheus tradition in North America

Obviously, any attempt to reconstruct the history of the Orpheus tradition in North America can only have hypothetical validity. In the first place we do not know whether the tradition was introduced from without or not, at the same time as we are forced to reckon with such an introduction as a possibility; in the second place we are without any reliable points of reference for a relative chronology, even if on some

[102] Boas 1915, 319.
[103] See above, p. 201.

points a feeble light does fall on certain stages in the development. Still, one can assert that while in many respects the reconstruction of the historical course must appear extremely uncertain, the assessment of the original milieu of the tradition—or rather the type of milieu—stands on firmer ground. And this is of importance for our psychological reconstruction in the sequel.

What points of reference have we then for our reconstruction of the original milieu and the historical development? Four methods of approach have been utilized: those of internal evidence, distribution, archaeological combination and ethno-historical documentation.

"The method of internal evidence" was formulated by Radin, who, however, unfortunately gave it restricted possibilities through his exaggerated demands on the researcher who is to employ it.[1] Briefly, it implies that through an intensive investigation of a certain ethnographic document—e.g. the Orpheus narrative in a certain tribe—one shall be able to arrive at important conclusions concerning its history, age etc. within the tribe. It should follow naturally that such intensive investigations might also be valuable for comparative studies, something that Radin neglected to point out, which is doubtless connected with his negative attitude to the comparative, quantitative methods in ethnological research.

"The method of distribution" need not be commented upon here; the foregoing section has afforded examples of what it is a matter of. By "the method of archaeological combination" I mean, in this connection, that an element, a conception in the Orpheus tradition is brought into connection with prehistorical artefacts or usages which may be dated, or whose origin may be determined, by archaeological methods. "The method of ethno-historical documentation," finally, consists in finding points of reference between facts and conditions mentioned in the Orpheus tradition and communications given in historical documents from past centuries.

By working with these methods—which frequently reinforce one another—one can arrive at certain points of reference for the historical reconstruction of the Orpheus tradition.

To begin with, we can get an approximate idea of the original milieu and the age of the tradition. We have earlier been able to establish the fact that the Orpheus tradition has chiefly belonged to a milieu in which

---

[1] See Radin 1933, 184 sqq.

there has been a belief in happy realms of the dead in heaven or at the horizon.[2] One finds this milieu, with a few exceptions, best developed among the gathering and hunting peoples of North America. Among the majority of the Algonquin, Salish and Californians especially, the realms of the dead are described as happy places in heaven (among the Salish also in the underworld or at the horizon). On the whole, it may be said that in the hunting and gathering cultures those individuals who have been good members of the community, have died a natural, quiet death and been buried with the traditional ritual forms, have been conceived as going to a paradise, which has as a rule been located in the sky. There should be no doubt but that it is this paradise that has served as a model for the realm of the dead in the North American Orpheus tradition. In other words, the eschatology of the primitive hunters and gatherers has set its stamp on the Orpheus tradition.

One may perhaps then ask oneself whether the eschatology of the Orpheus narrative has transformed the eschatological notions of the peoples among whom it has been disseminated. This, however, need not necessarily be the case. One should instead proceed on the assumption that the narrative in itself would tend to spread especially to tribes with a bright and happy eschatological view.[3] This does not mean to say that the narrative has not also been adopted by peoples with a pessimistic view of the life after this,[4] and that in individual cases it has not modified their eschatology.[5] More on this subject in a later connection.[6]

That the North American Orpheus tradition has been maintained by representatives for the hunting culture emerges, moreover, from the circumstance that it is connected with shamanistic ideology, of which more anon.[7] Shamanism is functionally a religio-magical technique belonging to the individualistic hunting society; it fades away among the agricultural tribes, as Underhill has shown for the Southwest area of North America.[8] Genuine shamanism is closely connected with the notion of illness through the absence of the soul from the body, "soul loss." As I shall show later, this diagnosis of illness is of importance for the psycho-

---

[2] See above, pp. 91 sqq.
[3] See above, pp. 92 sq.
[4] A number of Northwest Coast and Plateau peoples (the Kwakiutl, Nootka, Kalispel, Chinook, Hupa), a number of tribes on the north-western Plains (the Sarcee, Blackfoot, Atsina) and some peoples in the Southwest (chiefly the Navajo).
[5] See above, pp. 91 sq.
[6] See chap. V: 1—2.
[7] See chap. IV: 3.
[8] Underhill 1948, 51, 1954, 645,

logical interpretation of the Orpheus tradition.[9] It is, then, of interest to note that the conception of soul loss is probably extremely ancient in North America.[10]

The Orpheus tradition alludes further to a couple of burial customs that seem to testify to its origin in an ancient hunting milieu. We have been able to constate that skeleton burial is the type of burial characteristic for and best adapted to the Orpheus tradition.[11] It is, however, also the oldest type of burial from the historical viewpoint. The custom of removing the corpse through a special opening in the cabin, of which we have also found traces in the Orpheus tradition, belongs to a primitive hunting milieu.[12] Birket-Smith wishes to refer this usage to what he himself has postulated as the oldest circumpolar culture, the ice-hunting culture.[13]

There are also other circumstances testifying to the high age of the tradition in North America, chiefly its wide distribution and cultural integration.[14] In the foregoing it has been shown how some of the Orpheus tales even allude to cultural conditions from prehistoric times.[15] Speaking of the Orpheus legends of the Yokuts, Hudson observes "the fact that a number of archaic words are found, identical in every version and which could not be translated by the Indians."[16] Similarly, Harrington reports that the death of the two Karuk youths occurred "long ago in human times," and to express this the Karuk Indians used an archaic phrase.[17]

It is, however, rather hazardous to try to ascertain *how* old the tradition is. It was certainly not maintained by the first immigrants or by the generations immediately succeeding them, since it is not found in South America. But it was presumably disseminated in North America before the agrarian cultures developed here, i.e. in pre-Christian times.[18] For us, however, it is sufficient to be able to observe that the Orpheus tradition was probably spread from tribes with hunting culture. This is not to say that these tribes created the tradition. But they did, at all events, disseminate it.

[9] See chap. IV: 3.
[10] Hultkrantz 1953, 449 sqq.
[11] See above, pp. 62 sq.
[12] See above, p. 74.
[13] Birket-Smith & de Laguna 1938, 517.
[14] Gayton 1935, 285.
[15] See above, pp. 36 sqq.
[16] Hudson 1902, 106.
[17] Harrington 1932, 31 note 63. Interestingly enough, through comparisons between the Orpheus tales of the Karuk and the Shasta, Voegelin finds that the Shasta are late-comers to the Klamath River, as also Dixon—on other grounds—has assumed (Voegelin 1947, 55; cf. Dixon 1905, 611 sq.).
[18] See Hultkrantz 1957, 311, 312.

Since by all the evidence the Orpheus tradition belonging to the Old World is likewise a product of a hunting milieu, one may very well imagine that through communications between hunting peoples on either side of Bering Strait the narrative found its way into the New World. In this connection it is of subordinate importance that the Orpheus tradition cannot definitely be said to be represented among the northeastern Siberian peoples, or among the Eskimo. As Hatt, Birket-Smith and Hallowell have shown, North America and northern Asia have several culture elements, indeed, cultural complexes, in common which are absent precisely in the coastal zones facing each other.[19]

The Canadian researcher Barbeau has tried to define the way in which the transference of the Orpheus tradition to the Northwest Coast—which he thus regards as the port of irruption—took place. He proceeds on the assumption that "the myths have travelled into prehistoric America with the ancestors of the present-day people who still conserve them."[20] He finds that "the myth of Orpheus migrated two ways across Bering Sea into North America. With the Siberians on the move eastwards, it passed from the tundras of Asia into those of Alaska at Bering Strait, where the old and the new continents stand nose to nose, as it were, on both sides of a strait fifty miles wide and frozen most of the year. With the sea folk of the Chinese and Japanese coasts it sailed north and eastwards, past the Kurile and Aleutian Islands, until it reached Kodiak Island on the Alaskan Coast, where it split two ways, northward into the Eskimo fringe of the Arctic ice cap; and southward with the North Pacific tribes."[21] This is of course a bold historical reconstruction, an hypothetic route traced on the basis of an hypothetic transmission, and it confuses the reader that the exposition is carried out in such categoric terms. But Barbeau is convinced of the correctness of his theory, for it gives him a natural explanation of the fact that in North America the Orpheus tradition exists in two completely distinct versions, which we have here referred to as the "inland form" and the "sea-coast form." The former, according to Barbeau, is identical with the Siberian narrative, the latter is the narrative introduced by the Chinese and Japanese (or their primitive predecessors on the coasts of northern Asia).[22] On account of this connection to the splitting of the Orpheus motif in North America

---

[19] See Hatt 1949, 27 sq.
[20] Barbeau 1953, 5 note 1.
[21] Barbeau 1950 I, 270.
[22] Barbeau, op.cit., 271. Barbeau has presumably taken the notion of the distribution of the Orpheus tradition to the Eskimo from Thompson (see above, p. 32).

Barbeau's theory assumes a very particular interest for us, and there is therefore reason for us to consider it more closely.

It may be constated at the outset that by fixing the possible "irruption area" for the tradition to the north part of the Pacific Ocean Barbeau has imposed on the transmission hypothesis a rather arbitrary limitation. The points of resemblance existing between the Oceanic and the North American Orpheus traditions are, as I have pointed out, so remarkable that the possibility of a connection between the traditions cannot be excluded, even if such a connection cannot be demonstrated.[23] It is in this context of less importance that one does not find any Orpheus narrative among the Luiseño, the Indians who otherwise in their store of oral tradition show the most analogies with Polynesian folklore.[24] One must of course reckon with the possibility that the Polynesian influence, if this did exist, is spread here and there along the west coast; and the Orpheus narrative may very well have been taken ashore farther north —or farther south.

There is, in et per se, nothing to object to the route of communication between North America and Asia via Japan and China proposed by Barbeau. Especially the Japanese influence in North America is well documented, both in older and more recent times.[25] What may be more debatable is whether Chinese culture elements reached North America directly over the sea; the old Chinese tradition of the expedition to the country of Fu-sang seems not to allude to America, as was for so long believed.[26] However this may be, the Chinese Orpheus legends are not very reminiscent of the North American ones, and as regards the Japanese Orpheus myth, this offers such slight resemblance to the North American Orpheus narratives—not least those belonging to the "sea-coast form"— that it may well be left out of account. The Aino tale is also very unique, and can scarcely have been exported to North America. Whether prehistoric people along the coasts of Japan and China brought Orpheus tales to Northwest America is a question that cannot possibly be unravelled in this connection. It contains far too many dubious factors.

It is quite obvious that Barbeau's theory takes us onto uncertain ground. We know absolutely nothing as to which Indian hunting tribe it was that

---

[23] See above, p. 205.

[24] Concerning Polynesian influence on the Luiseño mythology, see Kroeber 1925, .677. Cf. also Baumann 1955, 329 note 38; Hultkrantz 1953, 201 sq.

[25] Ehrenreich 1905, 92 (quotes Ch. Brooks); Holmes 1919, 26 sqq.; Quimby 1948, 247 sqq.

[26] Mortier 1930, 22 sqq. Concerning possible connections between China and America, see also Erkes 1925—26.

was first aquainted with the Orpheus tradition, and we are equally ignor-
ant as to whether the originator of this first Orpheus legend in North
America had emigrated from the Old World. Barbeau's account of the
immigration routes for the tradition is a pure construction, which can in
no wise be supported with the present source material.

As regards the differentiation between the "inland form" and the "sea-
coast form," there are good reasons for the assumption that this took place
on North American ground. The "sea-coast form" can scarcely have
been imported from without to North America, even if two of its more
remarkable motifs—the magical flight and the carrying off of a woman
in connection with the extinguishing of the light or the fire in the place
where she is kept—also occur in Siberia (which in any case does not suit
Barbeau's theory of the routes of immigration!).[27] We have seen how
closely connected with local conceptions along the north-west coast the
"sea-coast form" is; one might describe it as the oikotype in the Orpheus
tradition that has absorbed the most local culture elements and been most
boldly adapted to the existing culture pattern. On the other hand, it must
be considered as so remote from the ordinary Orpheus tradition that it
is preferable to see it as formally independent of this.[28] The likeliest
explanation of its peculiar position is that the Orpheus motif which gave
rise to the ordinary tradition, the "inland form," provoked, on the
north-west coast, a new Orpheus tradition having a strong anchorage
in the culture milieu and being influenced by other Indian tales.

Such a course of development would appear to have had the best possible chances. Gayton, who has asserted that the Orpheus motif has seldom
been an object for "reinvention" in North America, nevertheless considers
the possibility of this in Northwest America, where one finds "the greatest
reworking of the revival theme"—something which we have previously
been able to constate[29]—and where one also finds a number of tales
"related to, yet not identical with, the Orpheus pattern under consideration." These tales are, she opines, "the direct result of the cultural atmosphere."[30] One can entirely agree with Gayton's views, if one abstracts
from the fact that she has not regarded the "sea-coast form" as a genuine
Orpheus motif—she appears not to have had it in mind at all. The constant recrudescence of "the revival theme" must probably also have had

[27] Regarding the magic flight, see above, pp. 129 sq., 181 sqq.; concerning the extinguishing of the light, see above, pp. 102 sq., 123 note 24, 178.
[28] See above, p. 49.
[29] See above, pp. 32, 165.
[30] Gayton, op.cit., 286.

consequences for the Orpheus tradition. As far as I can see, it appears likely that the intensive interest on the Northwest Coast for the world of the dead led to the creation of a new form for the expression of the motif upon which the more ordinary Orpheus tradition is based. The narrative has here been connected with the notion of the fate of drowned persons after death, presumably because the Orpheus motif was not so compatible with the cremation accorded to most of the dead among the northernmost tribes, especially the Tlingit and the Tsimshian.[31] (As I have pointed out earlier, this form of the Orpheus tradition probably arose farthest north.)[32] Later, the tale was reworked with other, but related motifs; two of these have been mentioned in the foregoing. In consequence of its association with the world of the animals the narrative has probably been contaminated with a popular animal tale, the tale of the bear-wife.[33] It will be remembered that in one of the Haida versions of the "sea-coast form" the hunter's wife is carried off, after her liberation from the sea-demons, to a mountain.[34] It is not difficult to see here a variation on the main motif, brought about through the contact with other, similar motifs. Finally, one can observe that in consequence of its general character the "sea-coast form" has in part lost its eschatological anchorages and instead been changed into a tradition of a woman's being carried off to the supernatural powers—it does at all events appear in this light to a modern interpretation.

The "sea-coast form" must thus be understood as a younger, regionally limited narrative on the Orpheus motif in the older, widespread, ordinary tradition. From its original home in the north—perhaps among the Tlingit—it has spread southwards along the coast. Data from the Haida show that they have adopted it from the Tsimshian.[35] On its migration south, the "sea-coast form" finally reached Puget Sound; farther than this it has not gone.[36]

But at the same time there has existed within the same cultural area, and also among the Tlingit, the ordinary, and presumably much older, "inland form". This was originally the property of the hunting peoples, among whom it must have spread very rapidly—this is indicated by its uniform composition over the whole of North America.[37] If the recon-

[31] See e.g. Drucker 1950, 217.
[32] See above, p. 49.
[33] Thompson 1946, 354.
[34] Barbeau 1953, 295 sq.
[35] Barbeau, op.cit., 5 note 1, 255.
[36] See above, p. 44.
[37] Cf. above, pp. 203 sq.

struction sketched in the foregoing is correct, then the original Orpheus tradition in North America should be found best preserved (and most purely represented) among the modern hunting tribes—we can undoubtedly, in consequence of the cultural retardation among these technically less advanced tribes, count on many ancient conceptions and folktales being conserved. The tribes coming chiefly into the question are the Californians, especially the Central Californians[38] (who have of course been exposed to only little influence from alien culture areas), the Basin groups, a number of Plains tribes (the north-western tribes and the Comanche), and those tribes on the northern Plateau that are without the mythological motifs characteristic for the western Plateau groups. Among these tribes, moreover, we find the Orpheus tradition in a form which seems convincingly elementary: the main personages are human, not mythological, beings; they bring back from the realm of the dead a ritual dance which—among the living—has a revivalistic, magic character; Eurydice is brought slowly back to life, and without any receptacle being used. Everything supports the assumption that these central motifs belong to the oldest layer of the Orpheus tradition, and that together they formed the corner stones of the original narrative.

We must assume that the Orpheus tradition reached the Eastern Woodland Indians at a time when the latter were only hunters and collectors: the remarkable points of agreement between the Californian and the eastern Orpheus traditions (with regard to the richly embroidered journey to the world of the dead and the importance attached to the dance of the dead) must go back to a time when the Indians of California and the Eastern Woodland area had a similar basic culture.[39] Perhaps the circumstance that the Orpheus tradition is more numerously represented in the west than in the east supports the assumption that with the advancing agrarian culture it had lost something of its popularity (compare below).

Among the Athapascan Indians of Canada we find no Orpheus narratives, except among the marginal tribes of the Carrier and Sarcee, that have been affected by adjacent peoples with other tongues. Can one possibly connect this vacuum with the presumed late immigration of the Athapascans to North America?[40] In this case we should get a *terminus*

[38] In this case the Maidu, Miwok and Yokuts.
[39] It is possible that in the east this basic culture was maintained by the Algonquin (cf. above, p. 208). A. F. Hunter presumes that the Huron adopted the Orpheus legend from the Algonquin, but his assumption rests upon uncertain grounds (Hunter in JR X, 324 note 14).
[40] See e.g. Jenness 1941, 385 sqq.

ante quem for the Orpheus tradition in North America. But unfortunately the rarity of the tale among the Athapascans can also be interpreted as an expression of the fear of the dead and of the death-stuff felt by these tribes.[41]

The receptacle-motif, which has its centre of gravity in the east, appears to belong to the Orpheus tradition in a later phase. The tales with this motif have in several respects diverged from the main line which is manifested by the (hypothetically) older narratives: on the Plateau and at Puget Sound the Orpheus tradition has been contaminated with the myths centering round the culture hero-trickster, in the Southwest and in the east the same tradition has been coloured and transformed by agrarian-mythological trains of thought. We need not presume any original connection between the receptacle and the agrarian culture; as we shall see, the original and natural function of the receptacle is that of soul-container.[42] In the Northeast the receptacle-motif has been combined with a much older motif, the resuscitation from the grave (which probably belonged to the early form of the tradition in North America).[43] This combination has led to the analysis in these tales of the connection between soul and body, indeed, soul-dualism has here been fixed.[44] In the Southwest the receptacle-motif has been entirely interpreted into the prevailing conceptual schema of fertility mythology, as the deceased is brought back in a corn-cob and is evidently, moreover, in a couple of cases identical with the maize-goddess. In the Northwest (among the Salish and Shahaptin) and in the Southeast the receptacle-motif shows remarkable points of agreement: the deceased is thrust in her natural size into a huge receptacle, a chest, a sack, a jar, and she escapes when the opening taboo—characteristic for both areas—is infringed. It is, however, uncertain whether this signifies that there have existed direct historical connections between the Orpheus tales of these widely separated regions. The opening taboo is naturally connected with a receptacle of the format mentioned here,[45] and as regards this receptacle it may for various reasons have replaced a presumably more primitive notion of a smaller receptacle. Thus in the Northwest the receptacle-motif may have been modified through the influence of certain motifs in the trickster mythology[46]—the reader is here specially reminded of the notion that all

[41] See below, pp. 223, 224.
[42] See below, pp. 250 sqq.
[43] See above, pp. 151 sq.
[44] See above, pp. 157 sqq.
[45] See above, pp. 133 sq.
[46] See above, pp. 178 sq.

the dead are brought back in the same chest—and in the Southeast the size of the receptacle may be due to influences from the burial customs—the jar in the Alabama tale, for instance, reminds one of the skeleton burial in giant urns occurring among the Creek in earlier times.[47]

The receptacle-motif has been discussed in such detail here because it illustrates, better than any other motif in the Orpheus tradition, the historical and regional differentiation.

The transition from hunting culture to agrarian culture has been decisive for the later development of the Orpheus tradition in North America. The latter culture was accompanied with religious, mythological and ritual conceptions which counteracted the Orpheus tradition—they were at variance with its psychological basic idea, of which more anon—and transformed it in accordance with a new conceptual pattern with an agrarian ritualistic character.[48] The new conceptions which were disseminated (possibly even a couple of thousand years before the beginning of the Christian era) were of southern origin; in the last analysis several of them probably came from the high cultures in Central and South America ("nuclear America").

Hatt presumes that these agrarian religious conceptions had originated in the Old World. On the basis of his investigations of the Corn Mother motif he writes that "pre-Columbian America's agricultural folklore seems to have more in common with Indonesia—and Melanesia—than with any other part of the world."[49] He considers that one must presume a direct connection between the Indonesian-Oceanic instances and the American instances. The routes of communication cannot have been via Bering Strait—for how could agrarian conceptions have been mediated by the subarctic fisher and hunting peoples in these northern tracts? "If agricultural myths and rites have found their way from Asia to America, they must have been brought by agriculturists across the Pacific Ocean," concludes Hatt.[50] The consequences of this reasoning for the problem here under discussion would be that the southern form of the Orpheus tradition leavened with agrarian-mythological trains of thought would include traditional elements which had in the last analysis been added to it from the Old World.

[47] Bushnell 1920, 112 sq.
[48] See, for further details, chap. IV: 4.
[49] Hatt 1951, 853.
[50] Hatt, op.cit., 905. Baumann shares this view (Baumann 1955, 371; cf., however, op.cit., 241).

216

We are not here called upon to enter in greater detail into the extremely difficult and debated problem concerning the connection between cultures of the Old World and American agrarian culture with its offshoot, American high culture. That contacts between the high cultures of the Old and the New Worlds have been effected over the Pacific Ocean is now the opinion of many researchers, and it can scarcely be contested that several culture elements have reached America in this way.[51] It should, however, at the same time be pointed out that essential and fundamental resemblances need not necessarily be referred to transpacific communications, but may be explained as manifestations of a convergent development from similar premisses.[52] As regards the agrarian culture-complex itself, the archaeologically proven high age of maize-cultivation in America does not particularly favour the contact hypothesis.[53]

What we can definitely constate is that the conceptions, myths and rites from nuclear America closely connected with agriculture have been disseminated to the south and north and thereby overlayered the ideology of the hunting culture. Through a process whose details we shall discuss in the next chapter, also the Orpheus tradition has been incorporated in the new mythology, and its content in part or totally revised.[54] Between the Orpheus tradition and the fertility mythology there has arisen in America a connection of the same kind as we have earlier divined in the mythological world of the Near East.[55]

The North American Orpheus tales that have been transformed through the agrarian-ideological influences are to be found chiefly in the Eastern Woodland area and in the Southwest, thus among the corn-cultivators—but they do also occur elsewhere. As we have frequently pointed out, the Orpheus tales in the Plateau area and at Puget Sound have been integrated with the mythic pattern, characteristic for this area, that has been developed about the person of the culture hero-trickster.

---

[51] It is above all Heine-Geldern who has brought some clarity into this question (see e.g. Heine-Geldern 1951, 1954, 1955). His research results have been accepted by, inter alia, Fürer-Haimendorf ("It is difficult to see how the parallels and analogies discovered by Heine-Geldern could be explained in a way excluding historical connections," Fürer-Haimendorf 1955, 153) and Haekel ("Die zahlreichen charakteristischen Übereinstimmungen zwischen altweltlichen und amerikanischen Hochkulturen lassen eine andere Interpretation einfach nicht zu," Haekel 1956, 89), while a good American archaeologist like Willey takes up an attitude of reserve, though without rejecting the possibility of a connnection (Willey 1955, 585 sq.).
[52] This is e.g. Kroeber's opinion (Kroeber 1948, 783 sqq.).
[53] Cf., however, Dittmer 1954, 194 sqq.
[54] See below, chap. IV: 4.
[55] See above, p. 189.

But curiously enough, we also find in these tales elements of the religious ideology of the agrarian peoples, despite the fact that these tracts lie far to the north and west of the historically known horizon of the agricultural peoples.[56] We need here only to remind the reader of the earlier mentioned earth and death goddess who reigns over the realm of the dead, and who is closely connected with the moon,[57] or of the remarkable rôle played by berries and fruits in a Chehalis myth.[58] It is in any case conceivable that the religious conceptions in the area have been affected by the agrarian peoples farther south. Late archaeological finds seem to testify that about the year 1300 A.D. offshoots of the corn-cultivating population in the Southwest were living around the course of the Columbia River ("middle Columbia").[59]

The original Orpheus tradition is still easily recognizable under the husk of agrarian mythology, and even in a culture area like the Southwest, where the Orpheus narrative has been worked upon most strongly, the basic theme is clearly recognizable; indeed, several of the more characteristic detail motifs of the narrative recur among the hunting peoples farther off. One can, for example, adduce the remarkable resemblances that exist between the Taos myth and the Orpheus legend of the Yokuts Indians: in both we find that a special bridge is built on the arrival of Orpheus or the deceased in the realm of the dead, and in both the deceased begs her husband to return to the world of the living.[60] The same historical special form of the Orpheus tradition appears to form the basis of both tales.

The southernmost occurrence of the North American Orpheus tradition is in Nayarit in Mexico. Obviously, it reached this place before the fertility mythology spread. A tale understood entirely in the frame of this mythology is the myth of Piltzintecutli and Xochiquetzal among the Aztec. This myth was possibly to begin with an Orpheus tale.[61]

As we have previously pointed out, the Orpheus tradition has not reached South America.[62] Nor does the so-called flight-motif in the fertility mythology[63] occur here, except farthest north—a circumstance that rather tempts to the assumption that the two traditions might be identical. Such a conclusion would, however, be all too facile; it is his-

[56] See the map, Wissler 1950, 20.
[57] See above, pp. 102 sq.
[58] See above, p. 147.
[59] Smith 1956, 291.
[60] See above, p. 89.
[61] See below, pp. 266 sq.
[62] See above, p. 203.
[63] Concerning this see further chap. IV: 4.

torical accidents of various kinds that have cut them both off from the southern continent. As regards the Orpheus tradition, two causes of its absence in South America may be adduced:

1. South American religion—especially among the primitive peoples to the east and north—is characterized by, inter alia, the cult of the dead.[64] As the dead intervene in the existence of the living as acting, divine beings, the divorce between the living and the dead is less perceptible. The strongest impulse of the Orpheus motif has herewith been eliminated.[65]

2. The Orpheus tradition disseminated from North America has been unable to reach South America because before this could take place the fertility ideology spread rapidly and formed an effective barrier. As has already been hinted, the Orpheus narrative has no natural soil in agrarian regions.

Perhaps both these circumstances in combination have constituted an obstacle to the advance of the Orpheus tradition in South America.

---

[64] See Métraux 1949, 569 sq.
[65] One cannot, on the other hand, adduce the absence of soul loss as a diagnosis of illness; soul loss occurred rather often (Métraux, op.cit., 595; Ackerknecht 1949, 623, 625; Steward 1949, 690 sq., 707, 713).

IV. ORIGIN OF THE ORPHEUS TRADITION

The detailed discussion of the content, distribution and historical connections of the Orpheus tradition given in the foregoing now enables us to approach our main problem: what motives or experiences have given rise to this remarkable tale? It may seem that its occurrence in the Old World and possible historical continuity Asia-America constitute serious obstacles to an interpretation based mainly upon the American material. To this, however, it may be objected that if, as in the following I try to show, the Orpheus tradition has been inspired by religious experiences and these basic experiences have been constantly renewed within the frame of the religious life, then one need not feel any trepidation concerning the justification for the method here applied.

1. Actual basis of the tradition

The Orpheus tradition, both the European-Asiatic and the North American, has long enticed laymen and scholars to attempt interpretations. These have varied from speculative assumptions to the effect that it is the medium of an esoteric philosophic message to more romantic suppositions to the effect that it expresses the power of love and man's impotence in the face of death. Common to all these interpretations has been the proceeding from arbitrary premises and failure to use the psychological key given by the narrative itself.

While research has often identified the Greek tale as a nature myth connected with the alternations of the twenty-four hours, the year or the planets,[1] its North American counterpart has as a rule been asso-

---

[1] The tale is said to describe the vanishing of the rosy dawn at sunrise (Max Müller), the ascent and descent of the underworld goddess (Maass), the journey of the Moon after the Sun (Ehrenreich) and so forth. Edv. Lehmann understood the narrative as an Undine story.

ciated with the eternal theme of man, love and death. The North American Orpheus tradition has therewith—in fact—become the object for a more sober interpretation than the Greek tradition. A circumstance that has probably contributed to this is that through its in general simpler plan it does not invite to speculations of a riskier kind, as does the Greek narrative with its parallels within the frame of other narratives, e.g. the fertility myths. (We must remember that only a few of the North American tales have a definite fertility character.) Even such a champion of lunar mythological interpretations as Ehrenreich finds that the action of the North American Orpheus tale belongs to another plane than that of nature mythology.[2] If he had been acquainted with certain of the Plateau narratives reviewed in the foregoing, which obviously testify to pronounced lunar mythological associations, he would presumably have changed his mind.

It does, certainly, lie within the frame of theoretical possibility to conceive the North American tale as an astral myth, describing e.g. the waning and waxing of the moon, but it is gratifying that researchers have entertained a more practical view of the aim and import of the tale. We have in the foregoing adduced several investigators who have laid particular stress upon the general human trend of the Orpheus tradition.[3] It has been found that its theme expresses human feelings on encountering the death of a dear relative. Fisher characterizes the Algonquin Orpheus tradition as "a tale of devotion," to wit, a person's extraordinary devotion to his family, in the first place his wife.[4] In Barbeau's opinion the Orpheus narrative is a symbol for "everlasting faith."[5] MacCulloch, Alexander and Hatt have emphasized the intimate connection of the Orpheus motif with the deep feeling for the dear deceased and the longing for communion with them, a longing which according to MacCulloch overcomes the fear of them.[6] But when Hatt considers this positive attitude towards the dead as something characteristic of the North American Indians, and in this connection refers to the ghost-dance religion, he is seriously overshooting the mark.[7] The love of deceased relatives has, doubtless, existed in many quarters all over the world, and, as we shall soon see, it could, among the Indians of North America, easily be changed into its contrary. As regards the ghost dance, this is a revivalistic

[2] Ehrenreich 1905, 70.
[3] See above, pp. 199 sqq.
[4] Fisher 1946, 234.
[5] Barbeau 1953, 258.
[6] MacCulloch 1911, 648. Cf. Alexander 1953, 205.
[7] Hatt 1949, 67.

phenomenon, which has its counterparts in other cultures in analogous circumstances.[8]

MacCulloch has at the same time formulated a more dynamic viewpoint when he characterizes the Orpheus tradition—its "savage" forms as well as its representatives on "higher levels"—as a "most pathetic" story, "showing man's instinctive belief that love is stronger than death."[9] Lyman expresses himself in almost the same words, describing the Orpheus myth of the Yakima as "showing the instinctive desire of people on earth to bring back the spirits of the dead."[10] And Gayton observes that "the wish-fulfillment factor ... has made the Orpheus tale particularly acceptable."[11]

Radin has advanced a further viewpoint, which in the light of our exposition in the sequel is not without justification: the Orpheus narrative (among the Winnebago) shows how through mind-control a man is able to "scale the heavens and transcend death."[12]

All the authors mentioned here have caught essential aspects of the real import of the Orpheus drama, for the narrative refers primarily to events which have taken place on the human, not the mythic, plane. From the historical sketch given in the previous chapter it should have emerged clearly that in its presumably original form the narrative had the character of the legend and not of the myth.[13] Every attempt to get on the track of the original intention and import of the tale must proceed from this fact.

To get a firm grip of the tale as it appears in its here postulated oldest form, still documented among the hunting tribes of North America, we must above all take into consideration the milieu, the situation in which the tale is recounted, in this case especially the interplay between the narrator and the listeners. Malinowski, especially, as we know, has stressed the importance of such analyses when one wishes to establish the function and meaning of a narrative; but it is worth while pointing out that in North America Radin had advanced similar viewpoints much earlier.[14] Like Radin, we must proceed on the assumption that in order to succeed the narrator must as far as possible meet the needs of his

[8] Cf. Linton 1943.
[9] MacCulloch, op.cit., 650.
[10] Lyman 1904, 247 sq.
[11] Gayton 1935, 286.
[12] Radin 1948, 55.
[13] See above, p. 214.
[14] Radin 1915 a, 47.

listeners. To judge from its wide distribution and at the same time stable form, the Orpheus narrative must in a high degree have corresponded to the audiences' needs and expectations. This has also been realized by Dr. Gayton, for she writes that "the source of its [the Orpheus tradition's] stability must be sought in the relation of its subject matter as expressed through its literary form to the psychological and emotional demands of its possessors."[15]

The Orpheus theme has found resonance among the Indians, and this may of course seem self-evident. But it is not at all self-evident. Many primitive peoples show such fear of death and everything connected therewith that they carefully avoid listening to stories of events on the other side of the grave; and it is not surprising that this attitude should also be found in some North American Indian tribes.[16] Furthermore, the fear of the dead is in many places so pronounced that the survivors try to erase the memory of even very dear relatives. In North America the Athapascans, especially, have felt great fear of the deceased; among the Navajo this dread was so immoderate that they were never able to accept the ghost dance.[17] And it is striking that the Athapascans should to such a large extent be without the Orpheus legend. The Navajo have, as we have seen, combined the Orpheus tradition with the origin myth; but its horrible, nightmare character testifies to the fact that it was not a popular tale.

To illustrate further the way in which the devotion to a living close relative may turn into its direct opposite, loathing and fear, after the latter's death, I will here adduce a couple of examples from North America. When among the Kwakiutl a child has died, "the mother kicks her dead child four times. And when she first kicks him, she says, 'Don't turn your head back to me'. Then she turns around, and again she kicks him. And as she kicks him, she says, 'Don't come back again'. Then she turns around again. She kicks him; and she says as she kicks him, 'Just go straight ahead'. And then she kicks him again; and says, 'Only protect me and your father from sickness'. Thus she says, and she leaves him."[18] According to Lumholtz, a freshly bereaved widow among the Tarahu-

[15] Gayton, op.cit., 285.
[16] Thus among the Montagnais (JR IX, 117); Lenape (Hulbert & Schwarze 1910, 129, Loskiel 1789, 49); Hopi Indians (Kennard 1937, 492 sq.); Chiricahua Apache (Opler 1941, 26, 472); Yuma (Dorsey 1903, 200).
[17] Hill 1944, 525. The Navajo dread of ghosts is well documented: see Curtis 1907 I, 80; Reichard 1928, 293; Coolidge 1930, 151 sqq., 160 sqq.; Goddard 1931, 173; Benedict 1932, 9, 11; Morgan 1936, 25 sq.; Wyman, Hill & Osanai 1942, 42 sqq., and passim; Kluckhohn & Leighton 1947, 126; Ladd 1957, 233.
[18] Boas 1921 I, 708 sq.

mare adjures her deceased husband not to turn back. And the mother says to the dead child: "Now go away, and do not come back, now that you have died. Do not come back in the nights and suck at my breast. Go away with you!" Similarly, the father says to his deceased child: "Do not come back and ask me to hold your hand or do anything for you. I know you no longer. Do not come and wander about here, but keep away."[19] One can scarcely imagine a reaction more at variance with the spirit and significance of the Orpheus tale than this.

To be able fully to understand the background to the popularity of the Orpheus tradition in some quarters and unpopularity in other quarters, we must bear in mind that among primitive peoples the attitude to the dead is in general ambivalent: they are loved in the light of their importance in their life-time, but feared on account of the change that has overtaken them through death.[20] This double attitude to the dead probably characterizes the emotional life of primitive peoples more than is the case among ourselves. At the same time it happens that in consequence of the peculiar character of the culture an emotional adjustment is brought about, implying that the positive or negative affective attitude becomes predominant: the Athapascans' pure fear of the dead or the warm feelings of most Pueblo peoples for their deceased are typical examples of this.[21] We may rest assured that it is in cultures with an ambivalent or benevolent attitude to the dead that the Orpheus tradition has obtained a firm footing.[22] The reader should once more be reminded that the Orpheus tradition probably belonged originally among tribes with a bright and harmonious view of life.[23]

If we now revert to the relation between the narrator and his listeners, we may constate that the Orpheus narrative must in two respects have fascinated the hearers: it is based upon a relationship of love or friendship between two persons, and it describes how love bursts the boundaries set by implacable death—indeed, it tells how even the prince of the dead is softened by this love.[24] In most versions of the Orpheus tradition the love relation between man and woman is of fundamental importance.[25] Inasmuch as the love story has been provided with a bitter-sweet ending which has invested it with the character of romantic tragedy, it has

---

[19] Lumholtz 1904 I, 272.
[20] See also Ljungberg 1946, 23, Malinowski 1954, 48.
[21] Cf. Benedict 1932 and 1946.
[22] Exception: the Navajo legend; cf. above, p. 142, note 115.
[23] See above, pp. 92 sq.
[24] See above, p. 123.
[25] See above, p. 57.

presumably got a firm emotional anchorage in many tribes and individuals.[26] The notion that the bonds of love between two persons cannot be dissolved by death has certainly taken shape in many other tales; we may here mention the already discussed Qu'Appelle-legend (which has become so well known that it has given its name to one of the rivers in Saskatchewan) as well as a Kwakiutl song in which the deceased lover laments over his separation from his beloved and cries out for her in the other world.[27] But the Orpheus tradition acquires a greater value than the Qu'Appelle-legend, because it not only expresses man's longing for his dear ones that have departed, but compensates for the loss with wish-fulfilling dreams, where the reunion—even if temporary—has been realized. By way of illustration one may adduce Schoolcraft's Ottawa legend, where the journey to the other world is represented as a fantastic creation of dreams.[28] Such wishful dreams have possibly acquired further consequences: a psychologist like Pratt finds that the hope of reunion with one's dear ones "is certainly one of the very largest factors in the desire for immortality."[29]

It would, however, be overhasty simply to interpret the Orpheus tradition as an entertainment product, intended to fascinate a circle of listeners. The circumstance that in many quarters the tale appears as the best description of the realm of the dead should in itself be sufficient to give us food for thought. And it will be remembered that the Orpheus legend of the Carrier, for example, functioned as origin tradition of an important rite which had the practical aim of curing sick persons. It is in any case obvious that in certain quarters the narration has had a deeper aim than the giving of entertainment for the moment. We shall not here dwell on the etiological element in the tradition;[30] but even at this stage it is worth pointing out that it is no accident that in a large number of cases the tradition appears as a seriously intended explanatory legend. It has an authorizing function and must thus be based upon a foundation in a reality accepted as genuine. It is a legend, not a fairytale.

Let us, in order to come to closer grips with the problem, once more revert to the milieu in which it is related. The listener, we must assume,

[26] See above, p. 20.
[27] Boas 1921 II, 1306 sq.
[28] See above, p. 68.
[29] Pratt 1945, 235. Boas, too, has underlined the rôle played by "the desire to see the dead alive again" in the formation of the tradition (Boas 1915, 348).
[30] See further chap. V: 3.

enters into the atmosphere of the tale, identifies himself with Orpheus and shares his pains. But in what circumstances is it that Orpheus actually carries out his task? The tale describes, as we have seen, how he is overwhelmed with grief at his bereavement and wanders, perhaps, without a goal until at last, exhausted and starving, he sinks down in a state between life and death, during which he experiences the journey to the other world and the meeting with the dead or the deceased loved one. We may therefore conclude that the listeners are gripped, because they themselves are familiar with this situation, they can imagine it, or they have experienced it. It is, I think, precisely this empirical background that has assured the popularity of the Orpheus tradition: if it had been presented in a less realistic form it would scarcely have gained ground, despite the dramatic love-motif.

In the chapter on the dominating motifs of the Orpheus tradition several of these were presented in such a way as to make their origin in psychic experiences quite evident. It was my desire, amongst other things, to bring into relief the perfection with which the Orpheus narrative reproduces the psychic process leading up to experiences of the supernatural: the despair of the mourner, sometimes manifesting itself in sleeplessness, voluntary isolation and autistic flight from reality, all prepare his receptivity for suggestive impressions and pave the way for hallucinations and illusions. In order to provide further foundation for this viewpoint I will give some examples of the states here in question, taken from Indian life in different places in North America. These are a few examples from a very rich material, and their sole purpose is to show how realistic the actual foundation of the Orpheus tradition is.

From many quarters we have testimony to the way in which after the death of a dear relative a person completely loses control of himself and commits rash deeds. From the Iroquois Fenton has described several cases of suicide on such occasions, and he does not dismiss the possibility that the suicide has believed he would follow the deceased to the other world—an interpretation which finds support especially in an example reported by Lahontan.[31] In the majority of cases the grief experienced doubtless does not have such consequences, but it may take a direction that does in a high degree remind one of the events of the Orpheus narrative. From the Bella Coola the following is reported: "Some years ago a young man died without apparent reason. His sorrowing father kept wondering: 'Why has my son died? Can he have committed some crime

---

[31] Fenton 1941, 106, 115, 126. Wisse reports suicide for love of the deceased from the Ojibway, Saulteaux, Ottawa and Pottawatomi (Wisse 1933, 166 sq.).

or made some mistake?' Despondent and grief-stricken, for a whole year the man did not wash, ate little, and slept on the floor. At last he wandered away, alone, into the mountains. Night overtook him and he lay down to sleep without food. His son came to him in a dream, telling him not to lament, that he was in a better place than this world..."[32] A medicine-man, presumably a Klallam Indian, once told Eells of a dream that he had had. "A child of his died and he felt very sorry about it, crying much of the time. One night he went to sleep and dreamed that some one came to him, similar to the picture of an angel which I had shown him, and took him off to the other world... they went up until they came to a house, at which his leader knocked. They were admitted, but there was no one in the house save an old man, who told them that the child was farther on... After a time they reached a hill where were some children and persons singing, and his leader told him that his child was among them, but that he must not go over the hill and see the child." The Indian thus got no farther, he had to return, but he did so with the assurance that his deceased child was happy in the other world.[33]

The last narration has, as we have found, tendencies to develop in the same direction as the Orpheus tradition. As well the nature and motivation of the experience as its content follow the patterns which according to our interpretation apply for the Orpheus tradition. Conformities of this kind not only give one an idea of the psychic processes that have constituted the models for the Orpheus tradition, they seem also through their uniformity and their fixed order to reveal that the story is not a free invention, but really goes back to actual events, the subjective experiences of particular individuals. If the Orpheus tradition reflects experiences below the threshold of consciousness, as we have here opined, and as also Devereux presumed,[34] and if in their structure and content these experiences follow a pattern referring directly to the extraordinary experiences of particular individuals, then nothing is more natural than the assumption that we have here to do with events which once occurred in a certain context, and which have passed into tradition, even if a tradition that has in the course of time been transformed through many elaborations.

We have earlier adduced further arguments in support of this hypothesis: in the great majority of Orpheus tales the two main personages

---

[32] McIlwraith 1948 I, 37.
[33] Eells 1889, 678 sq.
[34] Devereux 1948, 234. Cf. also the psychoanalytic interpretation, op.cit., 240.

are anonymous, they are not known by name.[35] In this point the Orpheus legend differs from both mythic tales and tales understood as fictive, where the actors are named—animals' names are often used. This might indicate that the main personages of the Orpheus narrative did once exist, although their names have been forgotten. Characteristically enough, Dr. Gayton points out that in southern California the Orpheus narrative "invariably . . . is told as an historic event, i.e., a tale, although myths are a favorite literary form."[36] There are, of course, in exceptional cases also legends with named heroes, such as the Orpheus tradition of the Mohave, where the male chief character is called Snake-Soul. This legend does, certainly, belong to the so-called "Coyote tales," but it is nevertheless considered possible by the orthodox believers that it dates back to an historic event in the past.[37]

Furthermore, we may adduce with certainty one Orpheus narrative which, despite its anchorage in the historical Orpheus tradition,[38] is nonetheless in its present form based upon the experiences of a particular historical person: the Orpheus legend of the Lipan Apache. This deals with "a certain Mexican" who had been captured as a child and brought up as a Lipan. He married an Indian and had a little girl with her. But the girl fell ill and died, although many medicine-men tried to cure her. "The parents were lonesome and cried. At length this man got sick too from thinking about his lost child all the time. I don't know what happened, whether he died or fainted, but he was unconscious. It is not known how long he was in this condition. Afterwards he told about what happened." He had wandered to the land of the dead. There his little daughter was playing, but to his despair she did not recognize him. "The little girl had not even said a word. He became angry because his little girl had paid no attention to him." And when one of the dead instructed him to return because his time was not yet come he betook himself home again. "He finally got back to the place where his body was. Then the life went into his body and he was conscious again." The narrator continues: "This man died not so long ago. He died in Oklahoma. 'Came in a Wagon' was his name."[39]

Now one may wonder whether this story is really a genuine Orpheus legend, as the fetching motif is missing. Here, however, as earlier when

[35] See above, p. 60.
[36] Gayton 1935, 269.
[37] Devereux, op.cit., 236.
[38] As Opler has pointed out, in the eschatological section the tale follows a conventional pattern (Opler 1940, 100 note 2); I should like to define this as the Orpheus tradition.
[39] Opler, op.cit., 100 sq.

judging the Mohave, Thompson and Sanpoil versions, I attach decisive importance to the actual narration of the living person's following of the deceased to the realm of the dead: the aim is the reunion with the newly deceased, the actual fetching is a means for the realization of this reunion. In other words, the bringing back of the deceased to life may be discerned as the chief aim behind the expedition of the Apache to the beyond, although this is not clearly stated in the narrative. Now it does happen, as we have seen earlier, that Orpheus fails even before the fetching, or while this is being done, or after it has been accomplished. In the Lipan case Orpheus fails at an early stage: the girl does not recognize him, the dead send him home again. And we may add that he would never have been able to succeed in carrying out his intention, as he was without the special equipment with which Orpheus is generally provided—a circumstance that we shall revert to in greater detail presently.

It thus appears that the Orpheus tradition is a romanticized version of an historical event which has been connected with a person's experiences in psychic twilight states. Certain of the data given here seem to indicate that these states may have been provoked by deep sorrow at the death of a close relative. But the question is, whether this explanation is sufficient. In order to get a better idea of the nature and conditions of the supernatural experience, we shall now briefly consider the experiences that have provided material for the stories of journeys to the world of the dead.

2. Journeys to the world of the dead

If one considers the general composition of the Orpheus tradition one is struck by the amount of space allowed to the actual journey to the other world. As has been pointed out earlier, the details of the journey are especially well brought out in the Orpheus narratives of California and the Eastern Woodland area. The journey is in Thompson's opinion the central motif of the tradition[1]—i.e. according to the nomenclature employed here, its main, basic motif. Even if we are unable to agree with this evaluation of the content of the Orpheus tradition with the quantitative yardstick, the fact remains that in many essentials the tradition appears as the narrative of a journey, and this circumstance should be borne in mind in the reconstruction of its origin.

[1] Thompson 1946, 351.

Partly, of course, the detail with which the account of the journey is given may be explained in the light of its purely narrative value; a series of well-chosen, exciting actions will naturally enhance the dramatic force of the tale (something which may have contributed to the infiltration of elements from various migratory legends into the description of the journey). But at the same time one cannot rule out the possibility that subjective experiences of an extraordinary kind may have afforded material for the popular theme—indeed, in the last analysis such experiences may perhaps have formed its idea.

Only a comparison between the Orpheus tradition and other descriptions of the journey to the world of the dead can give us points of reference for an assessment of the empirical basis of the tradition. Now Dr. Gayton does, certainly, assert that it is only very rarely that such descriptions occur outside the Orpheus tradition. Tales of the bringing home of a loved person from the realm of the dead "are common in North American mythology," she declares, whereas "stories of a visit to the world of the dead without the Orpheus motivation are relatively less frequent in North America." These tales are, for the rest, she opines, "unquestionably related to the more popular Orpheus form."[2] Dr. Gayton is, however, mistaken in this view. It is incontestable that the majority of Orpheus traditions constitute important contributions to our knowledge of the Indian notions of the journey to the world of the dead. But there also exist numerous other descriptions of this journey; and if these are essentially reminiscent of the accounts of the journey in the Orpheus tradition this is not necessarily due to any historical connection with the latter, but rather to the fact that they have emerged from the same types of experience as has the Orpheus tradition. In many cases they reflect these basic experiences more directly than the latter, and in this way they are able to throw an indirect light upon the empirical background of the Orpheus tradition.

In these circumstances it is desirable that we should devote a critical examination to these independent descriptions of a journey and note the characteristic expressions for their experiential background, in order subsequently—if possible—to combine them with corresponding elements in the Orpheus tradition.

The descriptions of the journey to the land of the dead instanced outside of the Orpheus tradition are in point of fact rather numerous. We

² Gayton 1935, 263, 264.

have, it is true, seen how many peoples have no desire to remember or to listen to tales dealing with the conditions among the dead.[3] But at the same time there are other tribes with an abundance of narratives concerning individuals who have journeyed to the other world and succeeded in returning therefrom. By way of example one may mention the Wind River Shoshoni: among these Indians I have noted down three traditions of a journey to the realm of the dead through a tunnel under a mountain, as well as a number of tales of journeys by named persons to the other world in the course of ordinary dream experiences, fever dreams, delirious alcoholic states, ecstatic trance and states of suspended animation.[4] Without doubt, a similar wealth of eschatological descriptions have existed in many other quarters, and not least on the Northwest Coast. That not more have been noted than is actually the case is probably to no small extent due to lack of interest on the part of field-researchers.

In her study of the notions of the other world obtaining among the Algonquin Miss Conard tries to classify the tales referring to alleged visits to the realm of the dead by various more or less historical individuals. The classification may be used with advantage also outside the Algonquin region.[5] Miss Conard writes: "Ces histoires peuvent se diviser en trois catégories: 1° celles où l'âme est représentée visitant l'autre monde durant un rêve ou une extase; 2° celles où l'être humain se rend au pays des morts en chair et en os; 3° celles où il s'agit d'un mort qui revient parmi les vivants."[6] As the writer herself points out, "entre les histoires de la première et de la troisième classes, il y a d'étroites relations."[7] We have here to do with traditions which still reveal their connection with the structure of the experience from which they have emerged. It is a good deal more difficult to find out the real basis for Miss Conard's intermediate category; one must assume that in the course of time the traces of the basic experience have been effaced. As a further category one may adduce the tales concerning the journeys to the land of the dead by gods and culture heroes—such tales have been mentioned in the foregoing.[8]

Nearest to the Orpheus tradition are the narratives dealing with journeys to the realm of the dead by ordinary persons "in the flesh" and accounts of journeys provably based upon human experiences in states

---

[3] See above, pp. 223 sq.
[4] Hultkrantz Ms.
[5] Cf. also the classification in van Gennep 1910, 102 sq.
[6] Conard 1900, 221 sq.
[7] Conard, op.cit., 222.
[8] See above, p. 181.

of psychic absence. The first-mentioned narrative category is of no particular interest for us in this connection; as the tales in question present
clear parallels to certain Orpheus legends, however, a selection of them
will be given here. The Tlingit owe their knowledge of conditions in
the other world partly to a man who once strayed thither and succeeded
in getting away.[9] The Bella Coola tell of four men who when visiting
a cave found themselves in the realm of the dead: the cave "turned over
on itself and projected them into the land of ghosts." They succeeded
subsequently in returning home. "This was the first time that anyone
had penetrated to the land of ghosts," and the travellers' accounts of this
land were received with great interest.[10] There is in the same tribe a
similar story of four girls who landed up by mistake in the celestial realm
of the dead.[11] From the Carrier Jenness reports the following: "Two
persons, and only two, the Indians relate, have ever reached the City
of the Dead and returned to life again to describe their experiences. One
was a youth, the hero of many strange adventures; the other a medicine
man who, like Orpheus, followed his dead wife to bring her back to
earth."[12] Of the young man we are told that he—like the Bella Coola men
—reached the realm of the dead by passing through a cave or the hollow
trunk of a tree.[13] According to the Wind River Shoshoni, in a former
time several men reached the other world through a tunnel, as mentioned
above.[14] When the realm of the dead was spoken of the Montagnais used
to refer to the experiences attributed to two men of their nation when
on one occasion a long time ago they paid a visit to this place.[15]

These tales are reminiscent of several Orpheus traditions which in
their present form leave us uncertain as to their origin. More remarkable,
however, are the points of agreement between a large number of Orpheus
legends and the narratives—chiefly memorates—based upon experiences
during exceptional psychic states. These tales of journeys to the land
of the dead are, as we shall now find, of decisive importance for our
assessment of the basis in reality of the Orpheus tradition. By comparing
them with the Orpheus narratives one can get an approximate idea of
which states of psychic absence the latter reflect.

[9] Krause 1885, 280.
[10] McIlwraith 1948 I, 506 sqq.
[11] McIlwraith, op.cit., II, 495 sqq. Cf. also the tale of the man who journeyed to the
land of the dead in a canoe (Boas 1898, 38).
[12] Jenness 1943, 537.
[13] Jenness 1934, 99 sqq., Morice 1889, 159 sq., Hill-Tout 1907, 178 sq.
[14] See above, p. 231.
[15] JR VI, 181, JR VIII, 271.

Let us then try to ascertain in how high a degree and in what way the memorates here referred to bear witness, in their actual action-pattern or their general composition, to the nature of the experiential process behind them. That is to say, through which characteristic features can one distinguish between the experiences which have taken place in sleep, comatose states of different kinds (fainting fits, deep unconsciousness, temporary cessation of respiration, "suspended animation") and shamanistic trance? If it is possible to define these features in the tales referred to, and they are then found to exist in the Orpheus tradition, it should be possible to connect the latter with a specific type of experience.

It is rather rare for a person in normal sleep to have a dream experience of a journey to the other world. Dream-journeys are not uncommon, but their goal is for the most part within the frame of the natural world.[16] Hallowell, for instance, testifies that among the Saulteaux he did not hear "any personal accounts of the journey of the soul of a perfectly healthy man to the land of the dead while he was asleep."[17] Only under certain circumstances—often in connection with illness or painful states of a mental or physical kind—does the soul glide into the way to the land of the dead. Thus of the Thompson Indians it has been said that: "When a person dreams, his soul leaves the body, and walks around the earth. The soul of a person who has the nightmare is nearing the beginning of the trail leading to the world of the souls."[18]

In unhappy circumstances the soul may go astray on its dream excursion and land up in the realm of the dead. The result is then seldom slow in manifesting itself. The Cocopa Indians who reach the abode of the dead in dreams are exhorted by the dead not to return, but to stay there to escape the hunger and difficulties of this world. But the consequence of such a dream is that the dreamer falls ill.[19] Feverish Ojibway and Creek Indians may while in the state of delirium journey to the other world.[20] In fortunate cases the dreamers are turned away in time by the dead who confront them or hasten towards them. Father Boscana tells of a feverish Juaneño woman who arrived in the land of the dead in a dream. She was sent back to life, however, on orders from the ruler of the afterworld; "the woman could not live with them [=the dead] yet."[21]

[16] Cf. Hultkrantz 1953, 270 sqq. See e.g. Bushnell 1909, 29.
[17] Hallowell 1940, 32.
[18] Teit 1900, 372.
[19] Gifford 1933, 307. Cf. Hultkrantz, op.cit., 274.
[20] Kohl 1859 II, 75 (Ojibway), Swanton 1928 b, 665 sq. (Creek).
[21] Harrington 1934, 52 sq.

When in a dream experience a sick Saulteaux Indian approached the village of the dead "he could hear the voices of people shouting and laughing. But someone met him on the road and ordered him back. 'You're not wanted yet,' he was told."[22] One who does not want to risk illness or even death can as a rule not venture on a visit to the realm of the dead —unless he is a medicine-man. The Wailaki shamans, for example, frequently visited the land of the dead in their dreams; they were careful not to eat anything there, and were then able to return safely.[23]

It is probably in general the case, as Hallowell found among his Saulteaux, that healthy persons may very well approach the realm of the dead, but they can scarcely visit it.[24] Feverish persons, on the other hand, may betake themselves thither, with the risk of being unable to return, while shamans, by taking care, may freely betake themselves thither and home again. From this it is obvious that if the Orpheus tradition is based upon a normal dream experience during sleep, only a shaman's experiences can come into the question. It appears quite improbable that the source of the tradition should be visions of fever; Orpheus' rôle is not that of the sick person, rather that of the physician.

A similar objection may be raised against every attempt to build up the Orpheus tradition on the visionary experiences of sick persons in comatose states. One may otherwise with advantage compare Orpheus' state after his vigil, fasting and exhaustion on account of his grief at the decease of his spouse with those sick persons who in an unconscious state visit the realm of the dead through their extra-corporeal soul. How close is not the introductory section of the Orpheus tales to the following narrative of events communicated by a Saulteaux Indian: "I saw a man who died and lay dead for two days. He told me what had happened to him. He never felt any pain. He thought he was going to sleep. Then, 'all of a sudden,' he said, 'I found myself walking on a good road'."[25] The road here referred to is of course the road to the other world. Although unconsciousness and the therewith connected low vital activity is considered much more serious than fever, it is not believed necessarily to entail the soul's straying all the way to the realm of the dead—it may check itself before it gets there.[26] As a rule, however, the free-soul does

[22] Hallowell, op.cit., 31.
[23] Loeb 1932, 95.
[24] Hallowell, op.cit., 29.
[25] Hallowell, op.cit., 30.
[26] Cf. Swanton 1928 b, 461 (Tlingit); Jenness 1943, 536 (Carrier), 537 (Babine); Beaglehole 1935, 16 (Hopi); Steward 1933, 307 (Owens Valley Paiute).

in this case actually land up in the other world. Among the Omaha, for example, we are told that "a person who during illness, or from some other cause, falls into a swoon is supposed to pass into the world of spirits."[27] Sometimes the person who had reached the realm of the dead and who had sojourned there for a time was nevertheless able to return —this might be due to the fact that the person in question was fetched by a shaman, or it might be due to his having been maltreated in the spirit world or turned away by the dead.[28] But it was generally regarded as something extremely serious for someone in a coma to arrive in the realm of the dead: the longer the free-soul sojourned there, the greater was the risk that also the life-soul would leave the body, and the person would herewith be dead.[29]

In many cases the sick person is in a state of such profound lethargy that he appears to be lifeless. This is why many Indian tribes have not made any verbal distinction between complete unconsciousness and death.[30] One hears of people who have "died" and returned to life. Lowie's informants among the Crow concluded tales of such events with phrases like "he was eager to go back to the dead again and died once more soon after," "after this experience he did not die again until relatively recently."[31] Of a Tlingit Indian we are told that he "died and came to life again four times, after which the war spear was taken from him and he died for good."[32] Owing to the fact that the weakened respiratory and cardiac activity was not always realized by the bystanders, a sick person has in many cases been buried before he has actually died. In fortunate cases he has later, with or without the help of others, been freed from his grave. He has herewith risen from the dead. But also the return of consciousness to the unconscious person is interpreted as such a rising from the dead.[33]

In the Orpheus tradition Orpheus is represented as living, never as dead (we make an exception here for the Lipan tradition), and certainly never as a person whose condition borders upon death—as already mentioned, Orpheus is described not as a passive weakling but as an active hero. If he finally dies, his mission has therewith proved a failure. Thus

[27] La Flesche 1889, 4.
[28] See e.g. Haeberlin & Gunther 1930, 81 (Puget Sound), Olson 1936, 159, 161 (Quinault), St. Clair & Frachtenberg 1909, 37 sqq. (Coos), Hooper 1920, 342 sq. (Cahuilla), Jenness, op.cit., 549 (Carrier), McClintock 1923, 115 (Blackfoot).
[29] Hultkrantz, op.cit., 459, 460 sq.
[30] Hultkrantz, op.cit., 458.
[31] Lowie 1922, 383, 384.
[32] Swanton, op.cit., 463.
[33] Conard, op.cit., 222, 233.

the Orpheus tradition may in no circumstances be based upon the experiences a sick person has had in the state of deep coma. From this it also follows that the description of Orpheus' experiences as motivated by grief, exhaustion and so forth cannot be prototypical but must constitute an elaboration of the original narrative—even if an elaboration that is based upon direct psychic experiences of the kind indicated.

The figure of Eurydice, on the other hand, appears in a clearer light if her state in the tradition is defined as deep coma, tantamount to or understood as "death." We may add that she has in all probability been in a state of "suspended animation", though it is less certain whether in the older form of the tradition she was also represented as buried— the burial episode undoubtedly has its origin, as we shall soon find, in a ritual practice reminiscent of the burial form, which was probably made the object of a later, modifying elaboration. If the original Eurydice was only deeply unconscious or in a state of suspended animation, her resuscitation to life should not have been an imposssible enterprise.

As regards Orpheus himself, there then remains the possibility that he was sunk in a shamanistic trance—that he was, accordingly, a medicine-man, a shaman.[34] For the shaman, the miracle-worker of the hunting society, its physician and mediator between men and the supernatural powers, the trance constitutes an adequate means of bringing about contact with these powers:[35] during the trance his soul, liberated from the body, undertakes extensive journeys in the supernatural world in order to get the advice of the spirits, to acquire knowledge of hidden matters, to explore the future or restore the escaped or ravished souls of sick persons. The trance can not be compared with ordinary comatose states. In its genuine form it is a psychogenic, hysteroid mode of reaction forming itself according to the dictates of the mind. It may also be described as a mentally anormal state of introversion which may be provoked suggestively or with suggestively acting artificial means (drugs, narcotics etc.), and which is an expression for the conscious or unconscious desires of the visionary. The trance states may be of varying quality and intensity, from light trance to deep trance with amnesia—which is practically tantamount to complete unconsciousness—but the different types may

[34] For the sake of simplicity I do not here distinguish between the medicine-man and the shaman. The difference between them is extremely subtle. Both are spirit-inspired physicians and miracle-workers. The term shaman, however, ought preferably to be reserved for the ecstatic magician.

[35] Arbman 1955, 57 sqq.

gradually merge into each other. Thus the trance may be so deep that it may be compared to a state of death. But it is only rarely represented as equivalent to real death.[36] For in a primitive community everyone knows that the shaman sunk in trance is on a journey; however deathlike he may appear as he lies in his heavy absence, his return is nevertheless expected.

To pay a visit to the realm of the dead of one's own accord is a great feat, as Hallowell stresses in his splendid analysis of the Saulteaux' relation to the dead: to visit the land of shades "is very dangerous, if one wishes to return to the land of the living; so only persons with extraordinary spiritual powers could achieve the journey."[37] In other words, only the shaman, with his guardian spirits, can perform the feat, and the trance is the appropriate means for this. Innumerable are the reports from North America telling how on his own initiative the shaman has undertaken long journeys in the supernatural world, which is closed for ordinary mortal eyes. When the object of these journeys has been to catch up the escaping soul of a sick person, their ultimate goal has generally been the realm of the dead.[38] Such journeys might be undertaken on several occasions by one and the same person. Thus we are told of a Shuswap prophetess that she "could fall into a trance and go to the land of souls whenever she desired."[39]

The Indians generally refer a large part of their knowledge of the other world to the shamans and their experiences. And in many respects the shamanistic experiences have set their stamp on the current narratives of the journey to the other world. The obstacles met with on the way to the realm of the dead are intended less for the soul wandering away from its earthly existence than for the shaman who is trying to restore the soul to the body. Many shamanistic experiences—both in dreams and in the state of trance—reflect the difficulties encountered on the journey. One is scarcely guilty of any exaggeration if one ventures to assume that the notions held concerning the journey to the land of the dead are for the most part referable to the experiences had in the shaman trance.[40] "Die Ekstase . . . ist ja nichts anderes als eine Antecipation der

[36] Hultkrantz, op.cit., 280 sq.
[37] Hallowell, op.cit., 29.
[38] Cf. Hultkrantz, op.cit., 281 note 266.
[39] Teit 1909, 605.
[40] This is also Eliade's opinion (cf. chap. IV: 3). At the same time I willingly admit that both experiences during coma and dream experiences may have contributed to the origin of the notions concerning the journey to the other world (cf. Andrae 1926, 304 sqq.).

Himmelsreise der Seele nach dem Tode des Menschen."[41] The frequently recurring Indian pronouncements to the effect that the shamans knew the realm of the dead best—or that only they knew that realm[42]—are probably to be interpreted to mean that the shamans had, in the last analysis, given the eschatological belief its exact form.

If the trance is very deep—and this is undoubtedly the case when the shaman's soul sets off on distant expeditions—, the awakening to life is a difficult process, and the same applies in the case of the sick person who returns to consciousness from a state of coma in which his soul had been sojourning in another world. One may here speak of a "threshold obstacle" at the frontier between the two worlds, those of death and life. This obstacle may sometimes appear as a hazy mass without outline,[43] sometimes it is the individual's own body; and in the latter case the soul lands, as it were, upon the body and glides into it.[44] It is very common for a burning fire to constitute the obstacle. Here follows the account by a Tlingit shaman of the way in which he awoke to life and consciousness through fire: "Far away I saw a great fire, and close behind it a sword swinging around ... The fire was still at a distance. At last I reached it, and then I thought, 'What shall I do? My mother does not hear me. I hate the life of the spirits. I will die a violent death, and go to Tahī't'.[45] I put my head into the fire, right where the sword was swinging round. Then all of a sudden I felt cold. I heard my dog barking and my mother crying. I stretched my limbs ..."[46] A celebrated Ojibway legend tells of a chief who was wounded in a battle with enemies and lost consciousness. His soul wandered about for a time, but after a while returned to the battlefield where the body lay. When he approached the place "he remarked a fire in the centre of the path which he was following. Wishing to avoid it, he quitted the track; but the fire, at the same instant, changed position, and placed itself before him. In vain he tried to go from right to left, the same mysterious fire ever preceded him, as if to bar his entrance to the field of battle." Finally, "with an intense effort, he darted

---

[41] Bousset 1901, 136. Cf. Nyberg 1937, 203 sqq.: the Persian chinvat bridge is the way for both the deceased and the ecstatic, but has its roots in the experience of ecstasy.

[42] Cf. Boas 1898, 37 (Bella Coola), Smith 1940, 98 (Puyallup-Nisqually), Teit 1900, 342 (Thompson), 1930, 196 (Coeur d'Alêne), Park 1938, 41 (Paviotso), Steward 1943, 287 (Shoshoni), Gifford 1936, 318 (North-eastern Yavapai).

[43] Knight 1913, 94 sq. (Ojibway).

[44] Jenness 1943, 536 (Carrier). Concerning the phenomenon of bilocation, cf. Hultkrantz, op.cit., 443.

[45] This is the realm of the dead for those who have died a violent death; see e.g. Swanton, op.cit., 461.

[46] Boas 1890, 844.

through the mysterious flame" and awoke from his long absence.[47] In both of these cases one may almost speak of a resurrection through fire.[48] In all probability the fire motif is a paraphrase of the physical sensations accompanying the awakening to life.

If one now compares the above-mentioned phenomena, typical for the trance, with the account given in the Orpheus tales of Orpheus' experiences, the points of agreement become obvious. Orpheus has on his own initiative, and sometimes through training (fasting, guardian-spirit quest etc.), put himself into a such a state, mentally and physically, that the contact with the other world has become possible. The lethargy has got so deep that his extra-corporeal soul has been able to stray into the domains of the realm of the dead. But he has nevertheless been accounted as among the living; for this reason the reactions of the dead have been so vehement. For him, as for the shaman, the way to the other world has been full of obstacles and difficult, while the deceased he has been pursuing has progressed without any great trouble. Both have experienced the same hardships connected with the re-entrance into the world of the living. The fire motif plays a central rôle in the Menomini legend, where it has been connected with the fire burning at the grave.[49]

In addition to all this, there is the circumstance that Orpheus has not only been able to visit and leave the world of the dead, he has also had the power to bring his beloved home from this world. If we now put together the conclusions we have come to regarding the psycho-physical situation of the two main personages, it should plainly emerge that Orpheus was a shaman who in the state of deep trance carried out the wonderful restoration of an unconscious person, perhaps one in a state of suspended animation—perchance his own wife or some close relative—from the world of shades. If in many Orpheus traditions he is represented as a faithful husband who in a coma caused by his grief experiences the meeting with his spouse and the other world, this is to be understood as a later reinterpretation of the tradition inspired by the love-relationship between the husband and wife and by the wife's own condition, and nourished by the experiences of later generations.

[47] De Smet 1905 III, 1047 sqq. Cf. also Kohl 1859 I, 295 sqq., Conard, op.cit., 257 sq., Jones & Michelson 1919, 3 sqq. See also a similar Miami narrative in Trowbridge 1938, 52 sq.

[48] Edsman asserts that this conception is not found in North America (Edsman 1949, 151 sqq.), and he considers it to be Indo-European (op.cit., 159). It is, of course, debatable whether the above-adduced tales may be listed as genuine instances. On the other hand, the Ojibway narrative of "The Poor Grandson" constitutes a definite example of the idea, even if European influence is not out of the question (Radin 1914, 45 sq.).

[49] See above, p. 152 note 20.

That Orpheus was from the outset a shaman is indirectly asserted in the pronouncements to Dr. C. F. Voegelin by his Shawnee informants. The former writes: "A distinction is sometimes made between those who flit, as it were, to the Creator's home in a prophetic trance,[50] and those who make the long journey going by the well established path which the visitors in the Orpheus tale took. The latter way is extraordinarily difficult and could not be made by an ordinary mortal without the aid of a powerful guardian spirit. Sweat house doctors or other individuals who have received on their vision quest an unequivocal guardian spirit are particularly well equipped for making the difficult journey."[51] The one who travels Orpheus' road must, in other words, possess the spiritual equipment of a shaman.

3. Recovery of the soul by the shaman

In a general way we have now been able to establish it as probable that the Orpheus tale was from the outset inspired by shamanistic experiences. This is in itself not so very remarkable, as the institution of shamanism has, altogether, signified so much for the development of different religious phenomena.[1] One may here remind the reader of the rôle played by shamanistic thought in the development of the belief in the soul,[2] the belief in the high god,[3] the cosmology.[4] But in the present case we are confronted with a specific, genuine manifestation of shamanistic activity. I shall in the following try to demonstrate that the dramatic events of the Orpheus tradition reflect, at bottom, a shaman séance whose aim it has been to restore to life a sick, unconscious person regarded as "dead." In other words, the Orpheus tradition may in its core be regarded as the text to a shamanistic act—if we here exclude the meaning "ritual text."

The notion that shamanization has provided the pattern for the Orpheus tales is not new. Even to Ehrenreich it was clear that in its North American form with the receptacle-motif the Orpheus tradition derives

[50] What are here referred to are isolated ecstatic visions of nativistic-revivalistic import, revelations from "Our Grandmother".
[51] Voegelin 1936, 16.
[1] Cf. also above, pp. 237 sq.
[2] Hultkrantz 1953, 40 sq., 126, 146 sq., 182 sqq., etc.; Paulson 1956, 156.
[3] Radin 1954, 25 sq.; cf. Pettazzoni 1954, 31 sqq.
[4] See e.g. Walker 1917, 78 sqq.

240

from the shaman ritual, while in his opinion it has in Europe and in South America been an astral myth. "Solche in Nordamerika (Huronen und Cherokis) häufigen Versionen, denen das für die Orpheus- und Eurydikesage wesentliche Moment des Folgens und Umwendens fehlt, dürften auf die schamanistischen Praktiken des Seelenfanges zurück-zuführen sein. Das Verbot des neugierigen Hinsehens im Moment der Ausführung eines Tricks gehört zu den wichtigsten Suggestivmitteln der Nekromanten."[5] The reasoning is scarcely very happy, but Ehrenreich's trend must be designated as correct. Eliade has since advanced a similar standpoint. He finds that the Greek Orpheus tale "présente plusieurs éléments qui se laissent comparer à l'idéologie et à la technique chamani-ques"; but the arguments he brings forward are only partly convincing.[6] Also in the North American Orpheus tradition Eliade recognizes influen-ces of shamanistic ideology.[7] "Ce qui est 'chamanique' dans tous ces mythes, c'est la descente aux Enfers pour ramener l'âme de la femme aimée." He adds, however: "Il serait exagéré de considérer de tels mythes comme des créations exclusives des expériences chamaniques; mais ce qui est sûr, c'est qu'ils utilisent et interprètent de telles expériences."[8] This cautious attitude is understandable; but in the light of the facts already adduced and of those which will be adduced in the sequel, a bolder re-construction appears fully justified: in the whole of its structure the Orpheus tradition testifies to its shamanistic origin.

The present writer advanced these results in a lecture in Stockholm in 1949, thus two years before the publication of Eliade's work. I was at that time uninfluenced by Ehrenreich's views, with which I was then unacquainted. The circumstance that independently[9] of each other three researchers have arrived at approximately the same result is a warrant of the correctness of the view advanced here. Neither Ehrenreich nor Eliade, however, have put forward a material of binding proof for the thesis. It is my opinion that the material adduced in the following is suf-ficient to confirm it.

A closer investigation of the different phases of the Orpheus tradition shows, in fact, that they fully correspond to the phases in the act refer-red to as soul-recovery by the shaman. The significant traditional ele-ments have in the foregoing been analysed precisely with reference to

[5] Ehrenreich 1905, 70.
[6] Eliade 1951, 351 sq.
[7] Eliade, op.cit., 281 sqq. Eliade finds similarly shamanistically inspired Orpheus motifs in Siberia (op.cit., 196 note 1, 219) and Polynesia (op.cit., 331 sq.).
[8] Eliade, op.cit., 283.
[9] Possibly, however, Eliade has been influenced by Ehrenreich.

the problem posed here, and they will here be collated with comparable data from the shamanizing procedure. A number of general points of agreement have already been discussed and are not here taken up for renewed treatment.[10]

1. The shamanistic practice reflected by the Orpheus tradition presupposes the diagnosis "soul loss" in cases of illness. This commonly means that the illness has been caused by the ravishing of the person's soul, and the perpetrators of the crime are as a rule the dead, who have transported the soul to the realm of the dead. The destination is natural, for illness is a state which eventually leads to death, i.e. the transference of the soul to the land of the dead. The soul here in question is generally the free-soul, but also some one of the body-souls may come into the question.[11] Significative for the diagnosis soul loss is the loss of consciousness.[12] This agrees well with the assumption that the Eurydice figure is in a state of deep lethargy which is confused with death.

Now it may be objected that soul loss as a cause of illness is not found in large parts of North America in which the Orpheus tradition does occur, especially among the Indians in Mexico and the southern United States, and on the Plains.[13] It should, however, be pointed out here, firstly that instances of soul loss do actually occur, even if to a very limited extent, and secondly that in older times the ideas of soul loss did in all probability exist here more generally, but have in the course of time been superseded by other diagnoses of illness. In the Southwest, for example, one can observe how the individualistic methods of curing which obtain in the hunting society (shamans curing soul loss) have been superseded by the collectivistic method of curing of the agrarian society (a doctors' society curing intrusion or soul loss caused by witchcraft).[14] The Orpheus narrative thus once had the possibility of being associated with the religio-medical ideology of the Southwest, and it has subsequently persisted in the area, although in the course of time it has among the Pueblos been influenced by agrarian ideological conceptions.[15]

Among certain tribes the soul-loss diagnosis remains unchanged, but the curing procedure itself has been altered under the influence of newer

[10] See chap. IV: 2.
[11] Hultkrantz, op.cit., 452.
[12] Hultkrantz, op.cit., 451.
[13] Hultkrantz, op.cit., 450.
[14] Cf. Underhill 1948, 37 sq. Concerning soul loss and its cure among the Pueblo Indians, see Bunzel 1932, 481 sq., Parsons 1939 I, 62 sq., 425.
[15] See chap. IV: 4.

ideological currents. This implies that the method of curing has become less closely adapted to the nature of the diagnosis. In the Southeast, for example, despite the dominating intrusion theory, the diagnosis of soul loss has been retained for certain illnesses.[16] But it is characteristic that in such cases the illness has not been cured with the recovery of the soul but through the patient swallowing or being smeared with curative herbs.[17]

The changes in the view of a disease's diagnosis and right curing may be very rapid. Fifty years ago soul loss was common among the Wind River Shoshoni, and there were a number of medicine-men who were able in the state of trance to recover a lost soul. But the Shoshoni medicine-men of today only rarely make the diagnosis soul loss, and they never resort to the shamanistic ecstasy to cure a man who has lost his soul.[18]

It may be added that the notion of illness through soul loss constitutive for the theme of the Orpheus tradition also underlies the "sea-coast form." Among the Nootka, for example, soul loss was considered to be caused for the most part by the sea-beings.[19] Dramatic accounts have been given of the way in which "the Nootka shaman, in the full strength of his supernatural power, 'actually went down under the sea,' returning dripping wet and sometimes streaming blood at nose and temples, carrying the stolen soul in a little bunch of eagle down in his hands."[20] One may with a certain justification assume that what at bottom the "sea-coast form" has been intended to describe is the restoration to life of a drowning person.

2. Several circumstances indicate that the victim in the Orpheus drama, "Eurydice," was a seriously ill person who was treated by a shaman on the basis of the soul-loss diagnosis.

The person restored by Orpheus is as a rule a just previously deceased woman. It is true that in certain legends—e.g. the Stalo legend— she has been dead for several years before her husband sets off to save her. But such prolongations of the time factor have obviously been intercalated in the narrative later in order to give the hero a respite to acquire the visionary power of which he stands in such need if he is to be able to accomplish his mission. In the overwhelming majority of tales the decease

[16] Swanton 1928 a, 710.
[17] Swanton 1928 b, 654, 665 sq.; Swanton 1946, 798.
[18] Hultkrantz Ms.
[19] Drucker 1951, 206.
[20] Drucker, op.cit., 210 sqq.

is described in direct connection with the recovery: we witness how the deceased leaves her home or her grave to journey to the other world, and Orpheus follows her immediately—indeed, as we have seen, his journey is in many cases simultaneous with hers.

The departure of the deceased for the other world takes place immediately or shortly after her death. One asks oneself, however, how she can be dead before her soul has reached the land of the dead—the usual thing, in cases of soul loss, is for the person not to cease living until after his free-soul has crossed the threshold to Hades.[21] It is therefore natural to assume that in the Orpheus tradition the deceased has not been dead at all in the proper sense of the term, but merely unconscious, perhaps in a state of suspended animation. It is undoubtedly not a matter of chance that she is seldom or never represented as cremated or as having succumbed to fire:[22] the restitution to life is possible only if the whole body is preserved intact. The hypothesis of suspended animation is further strengthened by the Carrier narrative, which informs us indirectly that the deceased is not wholly incorporated in the sphere of death.[23] The entire situation appears to refer to a state which is, certainly, characterized more by death than by life, but which does nevertheless leave room for the possibility of restoration to life, which a really dead person does not have.

If we add to this that immediately after the "decease" Orpheus starts acting, we get a vision of the opening procedure in a shamanistic séance, where the goal is to restore an unconscious person to life.

3. A number of further circumstances indicate that Orpheus' rôle was originally that of the shaman in the shamanistic séance. In a large number of Orpheus tales he is represented as a person gifted with supernatural power: he has the right prerequisites for getting into contact with the supernatural world, for he is gifted with vision (and it is hinted that he has acquired this power through fasting, smoking, vigils and other ascetic means); he is directly stated to be the possessor of supernatural power or, as among the Carrier, a medicine-man; and he has, as emerges from several tales, guardian spirits at his disposition. It has been mentioned earlier that a person who in the living state journeys to the realm of the dead with the help of guardian spirits to restore a recently deceased

[21] Cf. above, pp. 234 sq.
[22] See above, pp. 62 sq. It is worth observing that according to the belief of the Chehalis Indians only those who have died of disease, and not those who have been burned to death, may return to life (Adamson 1934, 24 note 2).
[23] See above, p. 115. Cf. also the Isleta legend, above, p. 167.

person can only be a shaman.[24] The fear of him and of his supernatural power felt by the dead is a clear indication that he is not an ordinary mortal but a being of a higher order, a divinity or a medicine-man.[25]

The office of the shaman is above all connected with the restoration to health of a sick person. The therapeutic method corresponding to the diagnosis of soul loss consists in the restitution by the shaman—as a rule in deep trance—of the soul of the sufferer. If in this connection the escaped or ravished soul is wandering around in the world of the living or is still only on the way to the realm of the dead, the shaman is generally able without any great difficulty to catch it and bring it back.[26] But the moment the free-soul slips over the threshold to the world of the dead a new situation arises for the shaman: the patient is now no longer sick, he is "dead."[27] In a number of tribes this implies that he is irrevocably lost, either because it is not desired to bring back a "ghost,"[28] or because it is not in the shaman's power to enter the other world without risk to his own life.[29] Certain Orpheus legends seem to allude to this, above all the Sanpoil and Thompson legends.[30] Thus in the Thompson legend we are told that the young man who was looking for his mother had to leave his body behind at the frontier of the other world, i.e. die, in order to be able to visit her. According to the current religious belief among the Thompson Indians a shaman can sojourn in the realm of the dead "for only a very short time," and the soul of the sick person that arrives there must be caught "just upon its arrival."[31] It is also said that "whenever the soul reaches the spirit-land, the body immediately dies."[32] These data seem to testify that the shaman cannot without risk enter the realm of the dead, and that the capture of the soul actually takes place before the soul has crossed the boundaries of this realm. The Orpheus legend appears to be based upon this view: the mother has been in the other world for a long time, and the son cannot bring her home; he must, to be reunited with her, himself partake in the mystery of death.

However, as we know, the majority of Orpheus legends describe how a recently deceased person is restored to life, and to this corresponds the

[24] See above, pp. 84 sqq.
[25] See above, pp. 112 sq.
[26] Exceptions, see Hultkrantz, op.cit., 455.
[27] Hultkrantz, op.cit., 461.
[28] Among the Yana persons who had returned from death to life were considered to possess "bad power" (Sapir & Spier 1943, 282). Cf. also above, pp. 223 sq.
[29] Hultkrantz, op.cit., 456.
[30] See above, p. 49.
[31] Teit 1900, 364.
[32] Teit, op.cit., 360.

fact that in many places in North America the shamans have considered themselves able to bring back to life a "dead" person, i.e. an unconscious human, perhaps in a state of suspended animation. Shamanistic tales from different parts of North America confirm this.[33] Sometimes it is a special category of medicine-men who possess this power. Among the Chehalis "there are five classes of doctors. A doctor of the fifth class, that is, one who has five guardian spirits of the proper kind, can bring the dead back to life."[34] But "it is a very difficult job to get them back and very few succeed."[35] It is tempting to conceive a similar differentiation of the shamanistic capacity as underlying the contradiction between the Orpheus legend of the Hupa and their shamanistic ideology: according to the legend, Orpheus succeeds in entering the world of the dead and in bringing his wife home; but according to the religious belief obtaining a shaman can only journey to a definite place on the way to the realm of the dead, "red earth." "Thus far the spirit may go when a person is in a trance or a faint and return again."[36] Can the hero of the Orpheus legend have belonged to a shaman class with extraordinary accomplishments, or has the legend been automatically incorporated with the folklore of the tribe?

4. The sham burial of the Orpheus narrative constitutes, as a matter of fact, a reproduction of the outer effects of the shaman ecstasy in the shamanistic act, the cataleptic death-like rigidity in the state of trance.

We have earlier pointed out that one can understand the sham burial of the narrative as a means of transfering the Orpheus figure to an existence of another order, the supernatural world.[37] And this transference also finds expression in other ways: in some Orpheus tales we are told in so many words that Orpheus' soul leaves his body during a trance.[38] We have in the foregoing characterized the resurrection from the grave after successful restitution of the soul described in the narratives as an act of homeopathic magic intended to help the deceased back to life.[39] The whole of the "ritual complex" here referred to, the imitative burial and the resurrection of the two main personages from the grave, has its

[33] See e.g. Boas 1921 I, 718 sqq. (Kwakiutl), Parsons 1941, 38 sq. (Caddo), Hoffman 1891, 241 sq. (Ojibway). "I overpower death with my spirit," sings the Mide doctor among the Ojibway (Hoffman, op.cit., 268).
[34] Adamson 1934, 119 note 1.
[35] Adamson, op.cit., 29 note 3.
[36] Goddard 1903, 74.
[37] See above, p. 62.
[38] See above, pp. 68 sq.
[39] See above, p. 151.

exact counterparts in the train of events in the shamanistic trance in several quarters in North America. What appears to be the case is that in the course of time the original trance has been reinterpreted in the tradition and represented as an imitative burial. When the shamanistic basis of the tales has fallen into oblivion, a consistent "eschatological" interpretation has been applied.

Some examples of North American shaman séances from recent times should be able to confirm this explanation of the import of the sham burial. Especially close to the train of events in the Orpheus tradition is the following shamanistic rite among the Saulteaux, employed to resuscitate a newly "deceased" person. A Saulteaux Indian related that his father, a well-known medicine-man, was summoned by the family of a young girl who had fallen ill. "He found that it was too late to save her life. The day after he arrived where her father was encamped, she died." But the medicine-man did not give up. He "tied a piece of red yarn around the girl's wrist at once. Then she was dressed in her best clothes and laid out. 'After this,' said the narrator, 'my father lay down alongside of her. He lay in this position for a long time. He kept very still; he did not move at all. Then he began to move ever so little. The girl began to move a little also. My father moved a little bit more. So did the girl. Finally my father raised himself into a sitting posture and at the same time the girl raised herself up in the same way'." The medicine-man had, the bystanders were informed, journeyed after the deceased, i.e. deeply unconscious girl.[40] Only a very powerful medicine-man could attempt anything of this kind, and the father of the narrator was such an one. By lying down beside the girl he expressed symbolically that he was journeying to the realm of the dead at the same time as she —i.e. his soul was undertaking this journey. With the help of the red yarn he had readily identified her among the dead, and he had then come back to life with her soul, and "both returned to their 'senses' together."[41]

This account of a genuine shamanistic séance, which seems to repeat in detail the content of quite a number of Orpheus tales, is by no means isolated. Here are a further couple of séances of the same type, taken from other culture areas in North America. Lowie adduces the following from the Paviotso: "When a person 'died,' i.e., was very sick, the shaman would lie beside him and also 'die' for several hours in order to bring him

[40] To judge from the available evidence, one must presuppose a genuine shamanistic ecstasy.
[41] Hallowell, op.cit., 33.

back. On the return trip, they heard talking about mountains ... Sometimes the doctor's spirit coming back unsuccessful was heard crying. During the doctoring the shaman did not move but lay stiff as a board till his return."[42] Gifford's concentrated field-notes on the curing of soul loss among the Cocopa (on the lower Colorado river) run as follows: "Only in obstinate cases which lasted over night did doctor lie down beside patient and send own soul to land of dead. Afterwards doctor related adventures, how abducted soul locked in house in land of dead ... If any man wished to see land of dead, he and ghost doctor lay down together, and souls of both went there."[43]

The same imitative magical principle as that upon which the sham burial in the Orpheus tradition is based is found in these notes on shamanization in cases of soul loss. There can be no doubt but that the sham burial of the Orpheus tradition originally represented the shaman in the state of trance during an act of shamanization.

5. Orpheus' experiences and actions on the journey to the land of the dead and on the return trip have their precise counterparts in the experiences of the shaman on his search for a lost soul.

Like Orpheus, the shaman pursues the fleeing soul to the land of the dead. As in the Orpheus narratives, the soul gravitates to this goal.[44] And just as Orpheus can, at least for short moments or partly, descry the vanishing figure of the beloved,[45] so, too, the shaman can see, with visionary clairvoyance, the human on his way to the other world.[46] The land through which the shaman journeys is just as dream-like, fantastic and unreal as that which Orpheus has to traverse, this is confirmed by the accounts given by shamans, either after their journey or, in certain cases, simultaneously with this.[47] The rôle played by the guardian spirits during the shaman's journey has already been illustrated in the foregoing.[48] Also in this respect the points of agreement between the Orpheus tradition and the shamanistic séance are striking.

[42] Lowie 1924, 294.
[43] Gifford 1933, 311.
[44] Cf. also Hultkrantz, op.cit., 379.
[45] In one of the Haida versions of the "sea-coast form" a special shaman is summoned who is able with his clairvoyant gift to find out where the vanished woman has gone (Barbeau 1950 I, 284).
[46] See e.g. Kroeber 1929, 265 (Nisenan).
[47] During the shamanization among the Quinault the guardian spirit that had taken possession of the shaman and that spoke through his mouth described the places and dangers that were passed on the way. "While in the trance the shaman was only half conscious of things about him" (Olson 1936, 160).
[48] See above, pp. 85 sq.

Of particular interest is the fact that the magic songs sung by Orpheus on the journey to overcome the difficult obstacles[49] also have their counterpart in the shamanistic ritual. It is in general a common feature of shamanism that the shaman sings, or (if he is in a deep trance) his assistants sing, the songs the guardian spirit has given him: these invoke the spirit and ensure its collaboration in the cure, or they function as a magic spell, which binds and averts all resistance.[50] Presumably, these songs are prototypes of the ritual recitative intended as incantation which is employed by the Navajo medicine-man to free his soul from the powers of death in the underworld.[51] But in all probability they also formed the model for the ritual songs sent by the living after the deceased when he is on his way to the realm of the dead. Thus from the Northwest Coast we hear that "Singing after a death was an advantage to the traveling soul for it illuminated the trail, and according to the Haida, permitted the soul to enter its new abode with its head up."[52] And from the Dakota Riggs reports that "the last act of the conjurer is to sing a song to conduct the spirit over the wanagi taćanku, *the spirit's road*, as the milky way is called."[53]

The magic song also gives us a point of reference to the Greek Orpheus tale. Guthrie observes that "Orpheus is first and foremost the musician, with magic in his notes ... Closely allied with music in the Greek mind was magic, and for some the name of Orpheus was associated with charms, spells and incantations."[54] According to Macchioro, the Greek Orpheus used music to provoke ecstasy.[55] But the interpretation of the musical activity of the North American Orpheus advanced here accords better with the Greek text.

If we now return to the North American Orpheus tradition, we note further a couple of incidents on the journey which obviously reflect shamanistic experiences: the brief and risky sojourn in the realm of the dead, and the pursuit by ghosts on the journey home.[56] Both motifs are represented in the following account of shamanization in connection with soul loss among the Thompson Indians: "Shamans can stay for only a very short time in that country [= the land of the souls]. The shaman

[49] See above, pp. 80 sq.
[50] Cf. Bouteiller 1950, 128 sq.; Densmore 1953, 439 sqq., 1954, 109 sqq.
[51] Matthews 1888, 149 sqq. Cf. Reichard 1944, 13, 25.
[52] Goddard 1945, 133.
[53] Riggs 1893, 211 sq.
[54] Guthrie 1952, 39.
[55] Macchioro 1930, 133 sqq.
[56] In olden times the Tsimshian Indians knew that "dead men were very dangerous to shamans" (Boas 1916, 327; cf. op.cit., 476).

generally makes himself invisible when he goes to the spirit-land. He captures the soul he wants just upon its arrival, and runs away with it, carrying it in his hands. The other souls chase him; but he stamps his foot, on which he wears a rattle made of deer's hoofs. As soon as the souls hear the noise, they retreat, and he hurries on. When they overtake him once more, he stamps his foot again. Another shaman may be bolder, and ask the souls to let him have the soul he seeks. If they refuse, he takes it. Then they attack him. He clubs them, and takes the soul away by force."[57] Undoubtedly, this description constitutes a good parallel to the pursuit episode in many Orpheus tales.

There are not many intimations as to how long Orpheus' expedition to the beyond lasts, and the statements to this effect which do exist are often quite fantastic, presumably through the influence of the well-known folkloristic motif that one day in the other world is one year here. Certain statements do, however, allow more reasonable proportions to the duration; thus the Ojibway legend tells us that the female Orpheus figure returned "after an absence of one night only."[58] Such data concerning the time-interval are not incompatible with the rather sparse information as to the duration of the shamanistic séances. The Paviotso shaman "may stay in the trance from half an hour to two hours," but he has in this case only betaken himself to the realm of the dead to get information there.[59] When, on the other hand, he goes into a trance to fetch the soul of a sick person from the spirit world he may remain in this state "for several hours." "At times it was necessary to keep up the treatment for three or four nights."[60]

6. The receptacle motif in the Orpheus tradition corresponds to the use of the so-called soul-catcher or soul-tube in shamanism, an instrument in which the shaman keeps the soul after its capture. We have earlier hinted that also other factors may have influenced the receptacle motif in the Orpheus tradition, but that the model for the presumably more primary smaller receptacle should be sought in the soul-container of the shamanistic séance.[61]

Such tubes were in North America employed in the shamanizing acts among the Indians of the Northwest Coast and the Central Algonquin; I have not found any instances outside of these areas. The usage occurs

[57] Teit, op.cit., 364.
[58] Jenness 1935, 109.
[59] Park 1934, 105.
[60] Lowie, op.cit., 294.
[61] See above, p. 215.

chiefly on the Northwest Coast, where it was probably rather general.[62] Of the medicine-man among the Tlingit and Haida, Krickeberg reports that on his hunt for the soul of the sick person he manages "sie in einen hohlen, geschnitzten Knochen einzuschliessen und dann wieder in den Kopf des Patienten einzusetzen."[63] I do not know what sources Krickeberg has used here. That the Tlingit were familiar with the soul-tube in connection with shamanization is confirmed by later reports.[64] For the reference to the Haida Krickeberg is possibly indebted to Krause, who among the requisites of the shaman mentions "ein hohler, an beiden Enden offener Knochen, der auf der Aussenseite mit verschiedenen Zeichnungen versehen und bisweilen mit Perlmutter ausgelegt ist. In diesen Knochen kann er den Geist, 'Ka-tlun-dai,' wenn er eben den Körper verlässt, einschliessen, indem er die Enden mit etwas Cedernbast verstopft."[65] From the context one is rather inclined to conclude that the spirit referred to is the spirit of the disease. This cannot, however, be the case, since the name by which Krause refers to it is identical with a designation for the soul in Swanton's monograph on the Haida Indians.[66] That the soul is actually what is referred to emerges from an observation by Dawson, according to whom the Haida medicine-man, *ska-ga*, captured the souls of dying persons in hollow objects of bone, closed the ends with shred (sic) cedar-bark and restored the souls to their owners.[67]

Also the Tsimshian shaman caught fleeing souls in a bone tube.[68] In his work *Nordwest-amerikanische Indianerkunst* Adam reproduces two bone tubes,[69] which he explains as "Schamaneninstrumente der Haida und Tsimshian, aus Knochen, mit Perlmuttereinlagen. Beide Stücke stellen die fabelhafte Schlange Sisiutl dar, deren jedes Ende einen Kopf trägt und deren Berührung, ja nur Betrachtung, beim Menschen gewisse unheilvolle Wirkungen hervorruft.[70] Die Benutzung des Instruments durch den Schamanen (Medizinmann) geschieht bei der Krankenheilung

[62] Reminiscences of the custom occur as far up as the Alaska area, among the Eskimo (Jacobsen 1896, 199).
[63] Krickeberg 1922, 134.
[64] See Drucker 1955, 144, 145.
[65] Krause 1885, 308.
[66] Swanton 1905 b, 34. However, Swanton mentions that the Haida shaman "had a carved hollow bone through which he carried on his spiritual combats and blew away disease. The latter was also the treatment of Tlingit shamans" (Swanton, op.cit., 40).
[67] Dawson 1880, 121 sq., 123 B, 139 B.
[68] Drucker 1950, 227.
[69] Adam 1923, fig. 45. The objects are from Jacobsen's collection in the Berlin Museum (no. IV A, 798 and 812).
[70] Concerning *sisiutl*, see above, p. 80.

in der Weise, dass der Schamane die eine Öffnung des Instruments mit Werg verstopft, alsdann dem Kranken angeblich den Krankheitsdämon aus dem Körper saugt und den Dämon in das Instrument speit, worauf die andere Öffnung des letzteren gleichfalls geschlossen wird."[71] In all probability is was also possible to catch an escaped soul in this receptacle. Precisely similar receptacles from the Tsimshian and Tlingit are reproduced by Drucker and referred to by him as "soul-catchers."[72] A Haida specimen of the same type, reproduced in the ethnographic catalogue of the British Museum, is presented here as "soul-case."[73]

From the Haisla Lopatin describes a shamanistic séance in the course of which the shaman, in a light trance, gave a dramatic representation of the journey to the other world and the capture of the escaped soul. The shaman held the soul in his cupped hands and then transferred it to the patient's body. "Sometimes he did not restore the soul immediately, but placed the liberated soul in a small box which hung at his belt." A day or a couple of days later the soul was restored to its owner. Unfortunately, Lopatin's account of such boxes does not give us any clear idea of their appearance.[74]

The Rivers Inlet and Owikeno Kwakiutl believe that a mysterious being sometimes ranges along the coast at night and snaps up the souls of children. The shaman then assembles the children in his house, "takes a 'soul catcher,' made of cedar and funnel-shaped," and captures the lost souls when they have been enticed down through the smoke-hole.[75] Among both the Kwakiutl and the Nootka, for the rest, there occurred a practice according to which the shaman fetched a patient's soul in eagle's down.[76] Emmonds and Miles describe a soul-container of bone from one of the "southern tribes" of the Northwest Coast—probably the Kwakiutl or the Nootka. As among the more northerly coastal tribes, it is carved to represent the two-headed snake, *sisiutl*, and the open mouth at either end is intended to catch the fleeing soul of the sick person. The receptacle is carried around the neck.[77]

Finally, we meet with the soul-container in the Northwest Coast area also among the Coast Salish. Here, "the shaman went through a pantomime of searching all about the room with his arms extended and his

[71] Adam, op.cit., 43.
[72] Drucker 1955, 145.
[73] British Museum 1925, 265, fig. 250 c.
[74] Lopatin 1945, 73 sq.
[75] Olson 1954, 250.
[76] Drucker 1950, 227, 1951, 211.
[77] Emmonds & Miles 1939, 34, with adjoining plate.

eyes closed. According to some, his own soul actually left his body and went in search; others thought that he sent his possessing spirit all around the earth and the nether regions in quest of the vagrant or kidnapped soul of his patient. Finally, the soul was received in his cupped hands, on a piece of bark tow, or in a cup."[78]

Both among the tribes here mentioned and among other peoples in the vicinity (the Plateau tribes) the soul is also caught in the shaman's cupped hands—a procedure closely resembling the capture in a container.[79]

The use of receptacles in connection with shamanization is also found among the Central Algonquin. Concerning the Ottawa, J. B. Clicteur observes in the year 1828: "Ils disent qu'il y a des malades qui vivent, mais qui ont perdu l'ame. Le jongleur va la chercher, il la rapporte au malade dans un étui qu'il lui met dans la bouche."[80] The same type of soul-capture is practised among the Menomini by a special class of medicine-man, je'sako, who cure their patients during a so-called shaking-tent rite.[81] Concerning the activity of the medicine-man, we are told further: "Sometimes he coaxes the soul of a moribund patient, thought to be already well started on the journey to the Land of the Dead, to return and enter a small wooden cylinder where it is imprisoned and delivered to its relatives. These attach the cylinder to the patient's breast for four days, so that the soul may return to his body."[82] A similar tube, as we know, occurs in the Orpheus legend of these Indians.

Even if the reports concerning the use of soul-containers in North American shamanism are few and, in a couple of cases, not unequivocal, they seem to show that two such widely separated tribes as the Stalo (coastal Salish) and Menomini each possessed a background against which the notion of a soul-container could be combined with the Orpheus tradition quite independently. We do not, however, need to imagine that the association arose in several quarters. It may have persisted from a time when many of the now scattered east-western culture-elements in North America, chiefly represented by the Salish and Algonquin, formed a coherent block.[83] A significant fact is that Müller has found common features in the rites of death and renewal with a

---

[78] Barnett 1955, 215. See also Barnett 1939, 273.
[79] See Hultkrantz, op.cit., 263, 393.
[80] Clicteur in AAPF IV (1830—31), 479.
[81] Skinner 1921, 71. Concerning the shaking tent, see PM 27: 3—4 (1944).
[82] Skinner, op.cit., 72.
[83] In this connection one is reminded of e.g. the distribution of the practice of making an extra exit in the lodge for the carrying out of a dead person (see above, p. 74). In the field of the material culture it is especially instructive to observe the occurrence of the wooden armour.

shamanistic basis which occur in Northwest America and among the Central Algonquin.[84] Still more is revealed by the occurrence of the soul-loss complex, the fundamental shamanistic basis uniting the two culture zones: this complex has its main foci in North America precisely among the tribes of the Northwest Coast and the Central Algonquin.[85] One may even designate these as remanent "islands" in the great shamanistic distribution area which once—before the advance of the agrarian culture—extended without a break over the whole of North America and Siberia.[86]

The use of the soul-container is intimately connected with the soul-belief. First and foremost it is associated with soul-dualism, i.e. the notions of alternating body-soul and free-soul.[87] As a rule it is the free-soul of a sick person that the shaman catches in the container, but it may also be a matter of a body-soul (life-soul or ego-soul)—the notes from the shamanizations only rarely leave us in no doubt as to the nature of the soul. When a person is considered to have died (is in a state of suspended animation), the shaman's task may entail the recovery of both souls in a container—as is illustrated by the north-eastern Orpheus tales.[88] Since in its genuine form soul loss is not possible without the conception of dual souls (the free-soul leaves the body, the body-soul keeps the body alive),[89] soul-dualism may be said to constitute a prerequisite for the use of the soul-container. This agrees with the fact that in North America soul-dualism has its real anchorage in the north; it is, as is also the notion of soul loss, less common farther south.[90] The dualism thus occurs in its clearest form where shamanism is dominant.[91]

In one further respect the soul-belief shows a close connection with the use of the soul-container: wherever this latter has occurred, it has been possible to conceive the soul in a diminutive form. In an earlier work I have advanced a presumption that the soul received its outer, circumscribed form from, chiefly, shamanistic practice in connection with the curing of sick persons: the shaman seizes the escaped soul in his hand or in a little instrument, a soul-container.[92] Would it be too bold to assume that precisely the container has strongly contributed

[84] Müller 1955, 114 sqq., 121.
[85] See Clements 1932, 227, map 4.
[86] Cf. Eliade 1951, 301 sqq.
[87] See Hultkrantz, op.cit., 18 sqq.
[88] Cf. Hultkrantz, op.cit., 78, 87.
[89] Hultkrantz, op.cit., 284 sqq., 451 sq., 460 sq.
[90] Hultkrantz, op.cit., 110 sqq.
[91] The observation has been made by Paulson (Paulson Ms.).
[92] Hultkrantz, op.cit., 263 sq.

to the conception of diminutive souls? A couple of Orpheus tales seem to give an indication of how close the connection between the manikin soul and the container has been felt to be: while according to the Male-cite version the soul is enclosed in a nut, we are told in the closely related Micmac version that in order to be able to find room in "a little bag," the soul "became in an instant the size of a nut."[93] Particular attention should be paid to the circumstance that the notions of the soul in miniature form have been held chiefly among the tribes on the Plateau and in the coastal regions to the west of this, i.e. precisely in the area in which in shamanistic practice or oral tradition the soul-container has had its most coherent and concentrated distribution.[94] It is, finally, not un-natural to conceive that the miniature soul may have been formed on the model of the intrusive illness: as we shall soon find, the receptacle has sometimes also been used as an instrument for the extraction of the disease (the object causing the illness, the demon of the illness) from the patient, and in such cases the illness has naturally been conceived as a diminutive object or being.

In all probability the receptacle is not a primary or original element in North American shamanism—a circumstance that is indirectly illus-trated by the late appearance of the receptacle motif in the Orpheus tradition. As the foregoing collection of examples should have shown, the soul-container is chiefly associated with a type of shamanization that for want of a better term I should like to call "demonstrative shamanization": the shaman performs acts which afford evident con-firmation of the success of his commission; he shows the captured soul, or he dramatizes the transference of the soul to the patient. This type of shamanism is close to the so-called imitative séance, in which in dram-atic pantomime the shaman represents his journey to the beyond.[95] Ohl-marks is presumably right in supposing that this séance is historically secondary in relation to the genuine ecstatic séance with catalepsy.[96] The demonstrative séance occupies an intermediate position inasmuch as it is combined with the ecstatic or imitative séance as a strengthening ele-

[93] Cf. the circumstance that among the Kwakiutl the soul was fetched in eagle's down (see above, p. 252)—or looked like eagle's down! (Boas 1897, 561, 575 note 1).
[94] The conditions obtaining in Siberia throw less light on the subject, even if a rapid inventory shows that both the miniature soul and the soul-container (see below!) occur more frequently in eastern Siberia than farther westward. Cf., concerning the container, the data given below, and, concerning the diminutive soul, Eliade, op.cit., 201, 222 (Ugrians, Orochi), Harva 1938, 275 (Teleut, Yakut), Bogoras 1907, 332 sq. (Chukchee).
[95] See Ohlmarks 1939, 124 sqq.
[96] Ohlmarks, op.cit., 122 sq. Ohlmarks, however, is not quite consistent: see op.cit., 139.

ment. In principle it implies a weakening of the significance of the ecstatic act, and it is thus probably younger than the latter.

The soul-container of shamanism not only constituted an instrument for the capture of the souls of sick persons, as is apparent from a study of its distribution. We have already seen examples in North America of other functions which it served: by all the evidence the Indians of the Northwest Coast used the container as a suction tube through which the shaman was able to suck the illness out of the body.[97] This use of the receptacle has an entirely isolated occurrence, however, and among the Menomini, for instance, the receptacle and the suction tube are two distinct things.[98] It would appear that the suction tube was to begin with identical with the tobacco pipe.[99] Outside of North America the receptacle occurs with different functions, inter alia, as a soul-container.[100] It should in this connection be observed that a soul-container is not always the same as an instrument for the restoration of a patient's soul. From Africa, Celebes, Borneo, the Kei Islands and the Eskimo Frazer has collected instances of soul-boxes in which the soul is kept when it is exposed to danger; it is always the medicine-man who in such situations transfers the soul to the box.[101] The function of the Polynesian soul-containers was quite the contrary. Wizards on Hawaii were in the habit of catching the souls of living persons in calabashes and keeping them hidden until they had been ransomed by their owners.[102] On the Marquesas Islands spiteful magicians enclosed a man's soul between two coconut shells, which were then smashed with stones.[103] In its function of soul-catcher in cases of illness we find the receptacle, as we have seen, in North America, but also in easternmost Siberia—thus a rather coherent area.[104] The Siberian instances derive from the Buryat, the Gold and the Gilyak, among whom the soul-catcher has the form of a bottle,

[97] Cf. especially Drucker 1955, 144.
[98] Skinner 1921, 72.
[99] Birket-Smith 1929, 39.
[100] In a number of cases the soul (or the deceased) is enclosed in objects of another type. The Gold keep the spirit of the deceased in a black cushion until the great memorial feast for the dead (Lopatin 1922, 292 sqq.), the Tungus and Aymara shamans catch a fleeing soul in a doll (Shirokogorov 1935, 318; La Barre 1948, 222 sq.), and the Eskimo, Algonquin, Lamet and the population on Danger Island (Tuamotu) capture the soul or the deceased with snares and nets (Frazer 1927, 69 sq., 1934 II, 20, 35; Izikowitz 1941, 11, 24; British Museum 1925, 33, 171 sq.). Cf. also the Chinese practice of catching the spirit of the deceased in a movable pavilion (Körner 1938, 109 sq.).
[101] See Frazer 1949, 679 sq.
[102] Handy 1927, 236 sq. (quotes J. S. Emerson, *Some Hawaiian beliefs regarding spirits*, 1902, 11 sqq.).
[103] Handy, op.cit., 237 (quotes E. S. C. Handy, *The native culture in the Marquesas*, 1923, 274).
[104] I have not been able to find any instances from South America.

a leather bag or a kettle.[105] From the Gold, Zelenin reports also that after capturing the soul of the sick person the shaman concealed it in a hat. Zelenin opines that this procedure is a relic of an older usage, according to which disease-spirits were transferred by the shaman to cultic objects *(lekans)* or, more precisely, to their spirits, *ongons*.[106] It is, however, open to doubt whether the notion of soul loss developed in this way from the conception of intrusion.[107] Everything indicates that the association of the disease-spirit with the receptacle is a secondary phenomenon, and that from the outset the receptacle functioned as the shaman's soul-catcher. It has had this function both in north-eastern Asia and in North America.

The interpretation to be put upon the Polynesian data must then be that the receptacle originally had a positive function but was later used for black magic. Only the oral tradition—i.e. the Orpheus tradition—preserves the memory of its older significance. Eliade, too, has followed this line of interpretation. He observes that the original notion of illness as due to soul loss was in Polynesia superseded by various conceptions of intrusion, but observes at the same time that "l'idéologie chamanique est uniquement présente dans la mythologie" (without, however, introducing the receptacle motif in the Orpheus tradition into the discussion).[108] The occurrence of the receptacle motif in a couple of eastern Polynesian Orpheus legends thus need not be due to direct contact with the North American tradition: it is a specific form of shamanism that has set its stamp upon both of these traditional groups.

7. The process of soul-restitution proper, as this is described in the Orpheus tradition—the awakening to life, the normalization—also belongs to the experiences connected with shamanization, especially when the restitution applies to a person who has been in a deep coma. The resurrection from the grave spoken of in several Orpheus tales signifies, as has already been hinted, the awakening to consciousness on the part of the sick person (and the shaman).[109] Of particular interest are the observations in the Orpheus tradition concerning the location of the shamanistic act: the awakening to life takes place in several cases in a lodge, a closed lodge or a sweating house.[110] One is here reminded

[105] See Harva 1938, 543, Ohlmarks 1939, 136 sqq.
[106] Zélénine 1952, 41 sq.
[107] Hultkrantz, op.cit., 450 sq.
[108] Eliade 1951, 336.
[109] Cf. above, pp. 246 sq.
[110] See above, pp. 159 sq.

of the rôle played in shamanistic cures by the closed shaking tent and the sweating house.[111]

As in the Orpheus tradition, the restoration to life of the seriously ill person is for the Indians a difficult procedure, and it happens, naturally, that the patient dies despite the restitution of his lost soul by the shaman. The Orpheus tradition makes clear that the shaman cannot alone be blamed for such a sad issue. The person who has returned from "death" requires careful treatment, as his life-thread is so fragile; with half of his person he is lingering in the world of the dead. If anyone in his surroundings is not sufficiently careful—whether the shaman himself or some other person—the restored life may easily fly away. It has been pointed out earlier that it is the function of the numerous taboos in the Orpheus tradition, enjoined upon both Orpheus and other persons, to protect the deceased (i.e. the seriously ill individual) from injuries during the period of his (her) gradual incorporation in the world of the living.[112] Thus to these taboos correspond the precautionary measures which must be observed with a sick person as well during the actual shamanization (when the shaman must be at pains to treat the patient in the right way) as also after the return of consciousness (when relatives and friends must leave him in peace).

Not only the slow "normalization of the deceased" in the Orpheus tradition has its counterparts in actual life, also its theme of the failure to recover, the continued mental "existence in the beyond," has parallels in the world of reality. Especially certain narratives of persons in a state of suspended animation shed light in this connection. The Saulteaux Indian Mud-Turtle's Eye had been buried but dug up again after he had awakened to life and succeeded in making himself heard. "But he often acted strangely after this, as if he had not entirely detached himself from the spirit-world. Sometimes in the summer, when is was getting dark, Mud-Turtle's Eye would say: 'It's just coming daylight. There is going to be a game of lacrosse'. Then, instead of preparing for bed, he would dress himself and make ready to play the ball-game. As the night wore on and it got still darker he would make the motions of playing lacrosse, although he still remained in his wigwam. And he fell backwards all of a sudden and shouted, 'the ball struck my forehead'. He grabbed something and, sure enough, there in his hands was a rock,

---

[111] My own experience from the Arapaho supports the assumption that both lodges are still used in the curing of the sick.

[112] See above, p. 131.

shaped like a ball." The man was naturally playing lacrosse with the dead, who sleep during the day and dance and play during the night.[113] Hallowell, who adduces this narrative, considers that the man was suffering from "some mental disorder," and he refers to his informant's comment, "that Mud-Turtle's Eye did not seem to have all his senses, after he 'came back', but that half of his mind had remained in the spirit world."[114]

The viewpoints and instances adduced here should be sufficient to justify the assertion that in its American forms the Orpheus tradition reflects, at bottom, a shamanistic séance with a therapy based upon the diagnosis soul loss. Naturally it is the Orpheus legends of the hunting tribes that best reveal their shamanistic origin—best of all the Carrier tale in which Orpheus is actually represented as a medicine-man—, but also the Orpheus myths of the agrarian peoples have reminiscences of this background to the tradition. A couple of examples: The majority of versions of the Cherokee myth have "a conjurer or chief to direct proceedings," i.e. a medicine-man appears as advisor in connection with the fetching of the Sun's daughter.[115] In one of the Zuni versions it is the members of a medicine society who fix the taboos.[116]

Now it must not, however, be imagined that all the more striking and regularly recurring features in the narratives of Orpheus' mission derive from shamanization. This is not the case. A number of elements are shamanistic, but without having been taken from the shamanizing act as such. Thus one can probably not ascribe to the shaman séance Orpheus' bringing home of dances and other gifts. What is here most likely is that there has been a confusion due to some narrator between the act of shamanization (which sometimes included dancing, cf. below) and the shamans' initiation visions or the so-called fasting visions of ordinary persons. It is well known that the spirits in the visions of the North American Indians favour their suppliants with gifts, accomplishments and other privileges of various kinds. The medicine-men are not infrequently instructed to institute new dances or ceremonies, with the help of which the right therapy can be applied. The dance which according to the Orpheus tradition is brought to the tribe, and whose performance helps to restore the sick to health, quite obviously belongs

---

[113] Hallowell 1940, 32.
[114] Hallowell, op.cit., 32 note 3.
[115] Mooney 1900, 436.
[116] Benedict 1935 II, 158.

to such a context. That it has subsequently been connected with the ghost-dance doctrine is another matter (cf. below).

We have here spoken deliberately of the connection between the *American* Orpheus tradition and shamanization. It is my opinion, however, that in such widely separated quarters as North America and Europe the Orpheus tradition has had a common *structural* origin, viz, the shamanistic act in connection with the curing of soul loss. (This viewpoint renders the question of a direct cultural connection between e.g. the Greek myth and the North American tradition less important.) The points of resemblance between the two traditions are so striking that the explanatory hypothesis advanced here becomes meaningless unless it can also be applied in the Old World. It may of course be objected that there are as regards southern Europe no definite data concerning a shamanism of the kind here indicated. But in the first place we have only a very imperfect knowledge of the prehistoric religious picture in the area, and in the second place the narratives may have migrated far from their original territory.

How, then, is one to understand the origin and development of the Orpheus tradition on the assumption that in its plot and its general composition it reproduces the restitution of the soul by the shaman?

The origin of the Orpheus narrative is probably to seek in a memorable occurrence which once actually took place: a shaman's bold attempt to bring his deeply unconscious wife (or possibly some close relative) back to life. There is of course nothing remarkable about a shaman's curing of a close relative, a wife or a child of his own—we know of several cases of such cures in combination with soul-restitution from modern times.[117] But if the relation between the shaman and the person whose soul he brings back has some extra point, if it reveals an emotional span which captivates and delights and hereby enhances the dramatic character of the plot, then we have the necessary preconditions for a memorizing of the event. In the narrative form the romantic imagination can then elaborate on the pattern that is once given. It seems to me that the Manchu poem (Nishan saman) mentioned in the foregoing must have taken form and become so popular precisely on account of its romantic possibilities.[118] It marks, as it were, the transition between shamanization and the Orpheus narrative.[119]

[117] See e.g. Jenness 1935, 110 (Ojibway).
[118] See above, p. 192.
[119] Also Eliade realizes that the poem "démontre à quel point le thème 'descente d'Orphée' est proche des descentes chamaniques aux Enfers" (Eliade, op.cit., 219).

Now in North America we have several instances of the way in which shamanistic occurrences have merged into legend; we need here only remind the reader of the Tsimshian tales of the man who became "the great shaman,"[120] or the Alabama tale of the shaman who in a trance brought back from the realm of the dead the soul of a sick man that had been held back by the recently deceased friend of the latter.[121] If it has been so easy to construct stories on the ordinary shamanization theme, how much easier must it not be for a shamanistic séance with the general plot of the Orpheus drama to take literary form! It is undoubtedly no accident that so many of the Orpheus tales, as we have pointed out, deal with the relation between two lovers.[122] One is free to see in this the original background of the tradition or a later distortion of a similar original relationship.

Thus in my view the Orpheus tradition has from the outset been nothing other than the codification of a shamanization drama owing its fascination to special circumstances. Although it is so closely connected to the shamanistic act it has not constituted a sort of ritual text, but has formed a free narrative—a memorate which has merged into legend.[123] The narrative has retained its character of a real event since, as already hinted, it has had a considerable etiological function.

We have earlier given an account of the way in which the original occurrence, the shamanistic trance, has often been obscured in the tradition, embroidered, reinterpreted. In many tales the North American Orpheus has lost his connection with the shamanistic calling; the consciously developed trance has been replaced by the comatose state that may follow after deprivations and sufferings in connection with deep grief. But several versions of the narrative remind us that the memory of the "prototypical event" has not, despite all paraphrasing of the theme, altogether faded. It has been nourished and kept alive by the understanding for visionary ecstatic experiences general among North American Indians, an understanding which has its roots in the so-called "democratized shamanism" characteristic for North America (the guardian-spirit quest, the visions of puberty).[124]

It is possible indirectly to establish the link between the Orpheus tradition and the shamanistic act even in comparatively recent times by scrutinizing its function in connection with the ghost dance. As previ-

---

[120] Boas 1916, 322 sqq., 331 sqq.
[121] Swanton 1929, 143 sq.
[122] See above, p. 57.
[123] Cf. our discussion above, p. 16.
[124] The expression is Lowie's: Lowie 1934 a, 312.

ously pointed out, the institution of shamanism has given rise to many religious ideas, not least in the eschatological field.[125] It is well known that the originators of the ghost dance movement were two Paiute medicine-men, Tävibo and his son Wovoka.[126] Thus far, also the ghost dance has a shamanistic background. But the question is, whether the shamanistic element is not still stronger, whether the shamanistic act as such has not been prototypical. Unfortunately, the ideology of the ghost dance has not been made the subject for more exact analysis; up to the present, attention has been concentrated upon the dance as an acculturation phenomenon or a nativistic resistance movement with messianic elements deriving from Christianity. In so far as the original pagan features have been dealt with they have been given very summary and general treatment. Thus Fletcher finds that the notion of a restoration of the dead to life has been rendered possible by dreams: dream images "are considered to be reflections of actual persons and things . . . and, as the living can thus enter the presence of the dead and return unchanged to this life, so the restoration of the dead to the living is comparatively a simple thing."[127] But the case has scarcely been as simple as this! A more fruitful perspective is opened by a modern anthropologist, Cora Du Bois, in her tracing of the ghost dance notion of the return of the dead to the shaman's soul-restitution: "The communication of shamans with the dead was a concept frequently met in northern California. Soul restoration in cures was also known. If a soul could be restored to a body it had left, and the shaman could communicate with the dead, it was apparently not difficult for the Indians of many tribes to envisage a mass return of the dead as predicted by dreamers."[128] To the ghost dance belonged as an important element the conception of the return of the dead if one danced intensively the round-dance deriving from the Great Basin. Accounts of such collective dances are also given from shamanizing occasions; I adduce here an example from the Tillamook (after Boas): "A person had died. The body was kept in the house for five days, while the people were dancing a great shaman's dance, trying to bring him back. After the fifth night, the dead one arose and asked to be given something to eat."[129]

[125] See above, p. 240.
[126] Mooney 1896, 701 sqq., 764 sqq. The ghost dances of the years 1870 and 1890 are what is here referred to.
[127] Fletcher 1891, 58.
[128] Du Bois 1939, 137.
[129] Boas 1923, 11.

Data of this kind—and a good many more might be adduced—seem to testify to the close connection between the ghost dance and the shaman ecstasy in cases of the attempted cure of soul loss; here, too, one might speak of "democratized shamanism." Exactly the same connection with shamanization is revealed by the Orpheus tradition. We have earlier observed that in certain cases it functions as a kind of "institutional myth" for the ghost dance.[130] It appears probable that precisely the shamanistic background has constituted the necessary prerequisite for this. We may thus conclude that the Orpheus tradition was probably the document through which the shamanistic notions of importance for the ghost dance were preserved and handed down.

4. Elements of fertility mythology

The greatest change undergone by the Orpheus tradition has been that due to its incorporation in the schema of agrarian mythology. In this connection it has become more or less completely removed from its shamanistic origin, though not altogether to the point of unrecognizability. The historical development has been analysed in the foregoing.[1] Here we shall study the processes that have led to the transformation.[2]

To begin with it may be observed that in its spirit and content the Orpheus tradition is in complete contrast to the agrarian ideology. Its basic tone is individualistic, not collectivistic; it is founded on a shaman's ecstatic experiences, not upon the more sober therapeutic methods of a medicine society. The points of contrast are particularly in evidence in the Southwest culture, the most one-sidedly agrarian of the North American native cultures north of Mexico. As Benedict has put it, "no experiences are sought or tolerated among the Pueblos that are outside of ordinary sensory routine. The Pueblos will have nothing to do with disruptive individual experiences of this type. The love of moderation to which their civilization is committed has no place for them. Therefore they have no shamans."[3] Against this background it is scarcely surprising that within the frame of the advancing agrarian culture the Orpheus tradition should sometimes have changed character, sometimes

---

[130] See above, pp. 145 sq.
[1] See above, pp. 216 sqq.
[2] See also pp. 188 sqq.
[3] Benedict 1946, 68.

have been lost completely. We have no definite data concerning the last-mentioned eventuality, but since in the Southwest culture the Orpheus tales are relatively few in number, as well as being very much modified, it is at least plausible to conceive a certain loss of the tradition within the area.

If one now wishes to define more closely the position of the Orpheus tradition within the frame of the North American agrarian cultures, one may venture to assert that the Orpheus tradition has been in part absorbed by the fertility myth, and has in part influenced the latter. A region in which it has been to a great extent absorbed in the fertility mythology is the Southwest (the Pueblo culture).

Especially instructive is the Taos Orpheus myth, in which the deceased is represented as identical with the corn woman, who is lost to men but is regained and brought back to this world in a corn-cob—i.e. with the ripening corn. The deceased is called Yellow Corn woman or Yellow Corn girl, and her sister (in one of the versions) is Blue Corn girl. The names are eloquent enough, they refer to the goddess of growth, who among the Pueblo is conceived as distinct from the earth goddess.[4] The corn mother, corn woman or corn girl constitutes a personification of the corn, and her death and return symbolize the vegetative cycle. The events of the Orpheus narrative have thus been reinterpreted in accordance with the requirements of the prevailing agrarian ideology. Also other details in the Taos myth are equally plain in their implications. The corn woman comes to life when the rain spirits sing over her, or when it rains and thunders. She is transported, as mentioned above, in a corn-cob—the receptacle motif has thus been adapted to the agrarian mythology. The corn-cob is, for the rest, a natural form for the goddess to reveal herself in, for in this shape she sometimes appears in the fertility myths of the Southeast.[5] Finally, it may be mentioned that Yellow Corn woman brings back to the world of men as gifts of the rain spirits "different kinds of fruits, huckleberries, chokeberries, green corn." She throws the green corn outside her house, and at the same time she fetches water.

The fertility mythology has not to the same extent set its stamp upon the other Orpheus traditions in the Pueblo area, but it has not left them untouched. In this connection we must mention a Pueblo tradition constituting a remarkable hybrid between fertility myth and Orpheus tale, without its being possible to class it with either category: I am thinking

[4] See Parsons 1939 I, 208, table 2.
[5] Hatt 1951, 855. Cf. op.cit., 877: the corn-cob as a fetish in the Southwest.

of a tale from San Juan noted down by E. C. Parsons, which the chron-
icler has generously called "the Tewan Orpheus Tale."[6] The plot is
briefly as follows. Olivella Flower has lost his beloved wife, Yellow
Corn girl. Shortly after her death, he discovers, at dusk, the glow of a
fire to the south. He goes to it, finds a cabin there and peers in through the
window: inside stands Yellow Corn girl, combing her hair. She explains
that she is "a kind of wind," and that on this particular evening she is
preparing to "go home," i.e. set off on the journey to the realm of the
dead. Against her advice ("be a man and a woman!") he lies with her.
But the smell of decay that she emanates makes him recoil, he springs
up and flies from the spot, pursued by the deceased. He flies from
shrine to shrine, is finally shot up into the sky, where he becomes a star,
closely followed by his wife, who becomes another star.[7] In its present
form this tale contains elements from the Pueblo myth of the first death,
the Orpheus tradition, the tales of *vagina dentata* and the arrow-chain,
and the myth of the corn maiden; and if one is to characterize the tale
more precisely, it must be adjudged a star-myth with a hint of ghost
story.[8] It is possible, however, that it once had the form of an Orpheus
myth understood in the setting of the agrarian ideology.

At the same time as in the Southwest the agrarian myth has absorbed
the Orpheus tradition, its own pattern has in some measure been influenced by the latter. To elucidate this relationship we must refer to
Hatt's researches.

Hatt has found that the fertility myths in America have been of two
types, which he designates as "the immolation myth" and "the flight
myth." The first-mentioned myth (which is, for the rest, closely connected with the fertility sacrifices of human beings among the Aztecs
and the Pawnee, and thus probably constituted a ritual myth) describes
how the corn goddess is killed and her body dragged around, whereupon it gives rise to corn and other crops.[9] This myth is for us not so
interesting as the other, and according to Hatt younger, myth, which
tells of the flight and return of the fertility goddess: for some reason,
e.g. impertinence in the part of some male person, the corn goddess flies
from men, with the result that the corn no longer affords any nourish-
ment; but the husband of the goddess seeks her out and receives from

[6] Parsons, op.cit., 93.
[7] Parsons 1926, 22 sqq.
[8] See above, pp. 29 sq., and Gayton 1935, 271, 272.
[9] Hatt, op.cit., 854 sqq., 906; Witthoft 1949, 77 sqq. According to Baumann, this
myth gives expression to an idea which emanates from the high culture in the Old
World (Baumann 1955, 254, 285 sq., 291 sqq., 365 sq., 376).

her crops and rites, and she returns to this world.[10] Curiously enough, the flight myth is in the New World known only from North America —chiefly from the Southwest, Mexico and the Eastern Woodland area, from the Plains it is reported from the Comanche—whereas it is absent in South America, except for the northern edges of this continent.[11] This distribution may *in et per se* arouse the suspicion that the flight idea was developed in an earlier Orpheus tradition assimilated with the agrarian mythology. Probably, however, such a suspicion would be over-hasty, as the story of the flight and return of the goddess of growth coincides well with the rhythm of the vegetative cycle and is, moreover, also instanced in the Old World.[12] Instead, we venture to assert that in consequence of its resemblance to the Orpheus tradition the flight myth has been attracted by the latter, the "flight motif" being in this connection supplemented with the motif of the searching lover. The connection has already been indicated by Hatt, who speaks of "the Orpheus element or the searching for and finding of the Corn Mother after her flight."[13] The difference between the Orpheus myth and the flight myth is simply that the former—as in the above-adduced Taos case—expressly states that the lost woman is a ghost; the fertility concept at the same time plays, in spite of everything, a more obscure rôle.

This, however, is a very vague delimitation, and in certain cases one may be in two minds as to which of the two myths has supplemented the basic pattern. The great majority of the flight myths of which Hatt gives an account were undoubtedly at the outset genuine fertility myths, which were only secondarily influenced by the Orpheus tradition.[14] What is less certain is whether the Aztec song cited after Sahagun, which really seems to allude to a flight myth, is at bottom an Orpheus myth, as Hatt believes. In the song we are told how the "priest" Piltzintecutli weeps when he is searching for Xochiquetzal. "I shall go to the Land of Decay," he says. Hatt adduces, with approval, Seler's view to the effect that the song describes how the goddess of the flowers and of love dies and is sought out in the realm of the dead by her lover,[15] and continues: "In other words, this seems to be a version of the Orpheus tale—which is so widespread in North America."[16]

[10] Hatt, op.cit., 856 sq., and passim; cf. below, note 14.
[11] See above, pp. 218 sq.
[12] See chap. III: 2.
[13] Hatt, op.cit., 906; cf. op.cit., 872.
[14] See Hatt, op.cit., 857 (Seneca, Shawnee), 860 (Zuni, San Juan?), 865 (Comanche), 866 sq. (Cora, Huichol), 867 sq. (Tepecano).
[15] Seler 1904, 1032 sqq.
[16] Hatt, op.cit., 872; cf. op.cit., 906.

It is not here contested that the myth *may* possibly have been originally an Orpheus tale. But we must not forget the proper character of the personages. Piltzintecutli ("young prince") is identical with the god of sprouting vegetation, Macuilxochitl or Xochipilli, and also with the important corn god Cinteotl. He appears also to have been identified with the sun god Tonatiuh. His beloved or wife Xochiquetzal ("flower-feather") is the goddess of sprouting vegetation, the goddess of flowers and the goddess of love.[17] In another myth, this also adduced by Hatt, Piltzintecutli and Xochiquetzal are represented as the parents of Cinteotl.[18] As the person who plays the rôle of Orpheus so obviously functions as the fertility deity, it is difficult to imagine him as originally an Orpheus figure. A further consideration is that the song referred to appears to have a cultic background, as has been pointed out by Soustelle: "L'idée fondamentale semble bien être que la végétation disparaît, 'enlevée' pendant les mois d'hiver, pour ne revenir sur la terre qu'avec le printemps. Pendant la saison sèche, elle est endormie, et c'est pourquoi on entonne en l'honneur de la déesse un *tozozcuicatl*, 'chant de réveil' . . .'' The weeping priest is Xochipilli, "le compagnon et doublet masculin de la déesse," and the place to which he betakes himself the realm of the dead, i.e. the underworld, "où dort la végétation pendant la saison d'hiver. L'analogie avec le mythe gréco-latin de Proserpine est tout à fait frappante."[19]

If in its present form the Aztec myth were to be classified with the Orpheus tales is would be necessary, to be consistent, to include here also the majority of the more northerly fertility myths of the flight type. Consider, for instance, the Seneca myth of the corn goddess, the daughter of the earth goddess, who was held captive by "the Bad Minded" (= the evil twin) "in his darkness under the earth, where she languished, lamenting her lost fields; when a searching sun ray discovered her and guided her back to her lands."[20] The sun god, who seeks out the fertility goddess in the realm of the dead, occurs also in the Old World. And here, as in America, the myth telling of his deeds is probably a fertility myth with strong elements from the Orpheus tradition. In all probability the Aztec myth should be judged in the same way.

It is not difficult to constate the factors that have brought the Orpheus tradition and the fertility myths of the flight type together.[21]

---

[17] See e.g. the mythological lists in Soustelle 1940, 86 sqq., Vaillant 1941, 182 sqq.
[18] Hatt, op.cit., 869.
[19] Soustelle, op.cit., 40.
[20] Converse 1908, 64.
[21] Cf. above, p. 189.

In the first place we may observe that a similar pattern has existed for the plots in both cases, the flight of a dear and loved person to another world, and her return thence. We may note further that the combination between the two types of narrative must have been facilitated by certain preconditions common to both: 1. The fleeing corn deity is always a woman, and in the majority of Orpheus tales the deceased person is a woman. 2. The relation between Orpheus and his spouse constitutes a close parallel to the relation between the fertility goddess and her lover, or between the sky-father and the earth-mother in the archaic high cultures.[22] 3. The dead and the fertility-giving beings are often identical with each other in the agrarian cultures (cf. e.g. the Pueblo culture). The causes of this have been explained earlier.[23] The realm of the dead (in the underworld) is the place of abode of both the dead humans and the vegetation spirits that have withdrawn for the winter. 4. In the agrarian cultures the return of the dead is as an idea not altogether impossible; the life of human beings is understood on analogy with that of the plant world, and the earth burial implies the notion of rebirth.[24]

In the Eastern Woodland area the agrarian mythological disguise of the Orpheus drama has not left such deep traces.[25] But certain agrarian influences are demonstrable: among the Alabama the corn-cob is used as a missile,[26] among the Seneca, Yuchi and other tribes the woman is transported home in a pumpkin or a calabash,[27] and among the Micmac Orpheus brings agricultural products home with him.[28] To say that all these influences have derived from the corn mythology would perhaps be to say too much; but undoubtedly this is the case with the majority of them.

Of particular interest are the reports of Orpheus bringing agricultural products home with him. Curiously enough, this is mentioned in Le Clercq's Micmac legend, although the Micmac were outside the agri-

---

[22] Concerning the notion of the parents of the world, see Baumann, op.cit., 256 sqq., 262, 267, 377.
[23] See above, p. 101.
[24] Alexander 1916, 289.
[25] It should also be noted that in these traditions the realm of the dead is not conceived as subterranean—the subterranean realm of the dead belongs of course to the agrarian religion.
[26] See above, p. 128.
[27] See above, p. 156.
[28] See above, p. 147.

cultural zone.[29] In the stakes fixed by the ruler of the other world with the Micmac Orpheus, corn, tobacco and fruits figured as "the most precious and rarest things which the dead possessed in the Land of Souls." Orpheus and his companion won the stakes and therewith came into possession of these precious things. The ruler of the dead "commanded them to plant these in Gaspesia, assuring them that all the nation would receive therefrom an inconceivable advantage. This, say our Indians of to-day, is the manner in which the Indian corn and the tobacco have come into their country, according to the tradition of their ancestors."[30] Unless the motif is, as Dr. and Mrs. Wallis presume, of French origin (which appears rather improbable), it may very well have been taken from the fertility mythology: with the returning goddess of growth the crops, too, return.

One asks oneself whether a closely related motif in the Orpheus tradition may not, at least in a certain measure, be referred to the same agrarian mythological pattern: the food which magically increases.[31] We have shown earlier that this is an old folkloristic motif.[32] But it cannot be altogether without significance that both among the Shawnee and among the Yuchi it is combined with the female ruler of the other world, who is at the same time the goddess of fertility. The Yuchi goddess who received the four Orpheus men "planted a hill of corn, a hill of beans, and a hill of squash for each man ... Even then the plants began to sprout and grow up, and soon they fruited, and it was not long before they gathered the corn, beans and squashes, and were ready to eat."[33] The motif of the magic food appears to be well-adapted in the Orpheus traditions with elements from agrarian mythology.

To the influences from agrarian ideology one may in the Eastern Woodland area also refer the occurrence of female rulers of the dead.[34] In many Orpheus tales the latter have taken over the functions belonging earlier to male divinities.[35]

[29] Both Wallis and Müller find the statement of the tradition curious (Wallis & Wallis 1955, 19 sq.; Müller 1956, 16 note 4).
[30] Le Clercq 1910, 210 sq.
[31] See above, pp. 101 sq., 112. On the other hand, it would be too far-fetched to see influences from agrarian ideology in the account of the food served to Orpheus by the deceased in the Huron narrative (cf. also Beauchamp 1898, 201), or in the statement in the Yokuts legend to the effect that Orpheus brought home "some seeds made up into a little ball".—according to Gayton "a choice food, not seed for planting" (Gayton 1935, 268 note 1).
[32] See above, p. 175 note 59.
[33] Speck 1909, 145.
[34] See above, pp. 101 sq.
[35] Cf., for instance, the Shawnee legends (see above, p. 100).

In western North America the elements from the fertility mythology are few and slight—they are restricted to the Plateau region and the tracts around Puget Sound, and have been defined and explained in the foregoing.[36] We have mentioned, inter alia, the remarkable Chehalis narrative of Orpheus type which tells how the culture hero received from the realm of the dead both berries and fruits for men.[37] May it therefore be a reflex of these conceptions and trains of thought when the medicine-men in the neighbouring tribe, the Twana, "profess to bring berries from the other world, and if so, the bushes in this world will bear abundantly the next season"?[38] Or have we here to do simply with ordinary shamanistic magic?

One may also ask oneself whether the notion of the importance of the alternations of the seasons that is firmly connected with the agrarian ideology has left any traces in the North American Orpheus narratives. One sometimes imagines that one sees hints of this: the Comanche Orpheus regains his wife in the spring, but loses her in the autumn; the male Orpheus figures among the Alabama set off for the sky in the month of March (but it takes them a year to arrive!); the Pheasant of the Puyallup pays an annual visit to the realm of the dead. But these notes are too scattered and incidental for one to be able to attach any importance to them. A seasonal myth that is intimately connected with the vegetative cycle, on the other hand, is the interesting Orpheus tradition of the Cherokee.[39]

As appears from its name, "The Daughter of the Sun", this narrative constitutes a sun myth. It begins with a section which is reminiscent of other folktales of the sun in North America: In rage at human beings for not enjoying her as much as the Moon, the Sun burns the earth and thereby kills many people. The humans then turn to "the Little Men," i.e. the thunder beings[40]—or, according to several versions, to "a conjurer or chief"[41]—and these helpers dispatch a rattle-snake to bite the Sun. By mistake, however, it is the Sun's daughter that is struck with the fang of the snake and dies. In her grief the Sun shuts herself up in her daughter's house, and the world lies in darkness. The Little Men tell the people that if they want the Sun back they must fetch her daughter

[36] See above, pp. 217 sq.
[37] Cf. above, p. 147.
[38] Eells 1889, 678.
[39] Mooney 1900, 252 sqq.
[40] The so-called Thunder Boys, "beneficent wonder workers, of great power" (Mooney, op.cit., 438).
[41] Mooney, op.cit., 436.

from the realm of the dead, "the Darkening land in the west." They select seven men for this mission. Provided with a box, the seven set off to the other world, wandering westwards for seven days.[42] On their arrival in the land of the dead they capture the girl while she is taking part in the dance of the ghosts, and shut her up in the box. They now turn their faces homewards and travel in an easterly direction. The girl repeatedly begs them to let her out, or at least to leave the lid a little ajar. At first they do not heed her, but finally they lift the lid a little so that she shall not be stifled—whereupon she flies away as a bird. The Sun is now more inconsolable than before, but men are at last able to placate her with dancing and singing.

This tale, which is one of the chief myths of the Cherokee,[43] is clearly connected with the seasonal rhythm (and the twenty-four hour rhythm). At the same time it constitutes a particular form of the Orpheus tradition. It is not easy to decide whether it was originally a sun myth or an Orpheus narrative; in modern times it has constituted a hybrid between the two.

[42] We may here possibly have to do with astral speculation. See above, p. 59.
[43] Mooney, op.cit., loc.cit.

V. THE FUNCTION AND CULTURE-VALUE
OF THE ORPHEUS TRADITION

After having discussed the origin and development of the Orpheus tradition from historical, psychological and sociological viewpoints we shall conclude by dwelling somewhat upon its significance, firstly as a document concerning North American eschatology, secondly as a factor serving to authorize religious belief for the Indians themselves. It is thus here a matter of two distinct types of problem: the importance of the tradition as a source for comparative religious research (sub-chapter 1), and the importance of the tradition as a norm for Indian beliefs and customs (sub-chapters 2—3).

1. Value of the tradition as a document for comparative religious research

The problem of the significance of the Orpheus tradition for religious research is of such a character that the careful reader might perhaps have preferred to have seen it discussed in the introduction to this study. This is, moreover, to a certain extent what has been done.[1] But as it has been my intention to show, little by little, in how high a degree this tradition is traceable to religious conceptions and customs, it has seemed most natural to me to postpone the definitive exposition of the research value of the tradition until now.

What is here chiefly in question is the extent to which we may count on the reliability of the Orpheus tradition as source-material in a reconstruction of North American Indian eschatology. In other words, does the content of the Orpheus tradition correspond to the current conceptions of popular belief concerning the dead and their world? The researchers who have hitherto considered the problem have arrived at

---

[1] See the Introduction.

different views. Let us first listen to these, and then try to define our own attitude to the problem.

In support of her account of the eschatology of the Algonquin Conard adduces several Orpheus narratives. After reproducing Le Clercq's relation of the Micmac Orpheus legend she writes: "Dans cette histoire apparaissent la plupart des traits qui figurent dans les mythes relatifs à l'autre monde."[2] The implication seems to be that the Orpheus tradition is well suited as a basic document for the reconstruction of the native eschatology, that it may, as a matter of fact, be regarded as the best source for this. Gayton finds that "the descriptions of the afterworld in the tales are compatible with local beliefs concerning it,"[3] and she points out that the tradition has fulfilled an important function as *aition* to the problem of the realm of the dead and the fate of the dead.[4] Thompson opines that "the relation of this story to the religious concepts of the various tribes where it is told is especially interesting, since the story frequently gives us the clearest picture we have of the current conception of the abiding place and condition of the dead."[5]

A more negative attitude is adopted by Wyman, Hill and Osanai, as also by Ruth Benedict. These writers have in their field investigations compared the Orpheus tale with popular beliefs and have found that discrepancies exist. The three first-mentioned researchers have the following to say concerning the Navajo tradition: "... in our experience the Navajo version was volunteered only twice in full form and once as a fragment in response to questioning concerning the afterworld. The Navajo versions are well integrated with native eschatology, except for certain more characteristically 'Orpheus' items (e.g. pursuit motive, chief of afterworld, tabu and lack of fulfillment), but the lack of some of these latter (e.g. the chief, skeletons) in the generalized eschatology may mean that the myth has been more influenced by it than vice versa. This is difficult to prove, however, at least without more data."[6] It is obvious that an Orpheus narrative which contains eschatological elements without anchorage in living belief can scarcely be taken as the basis for an account of the eschatology. A still more radical discovery was made by Ruth Benedict. "Among the Serrano of Southern California," she writes, "I was repeatedly told that they knew nothing of the fate of the soul and had no concepts of an after-life.

[2] Conard 1900, 223 sq.
[3] Gayton 1935, 283.
[4] Gayton, op.cit., 285.
[5] Thompson 1946, 351.
[6] Wyman, Hill & Osanai 1942, 33.

But on the same afternoon they might tell the story of Orpheus with considerable detail of the habits and food and life of the people of the dead. I am convinced that there was no contradiction in their minds."[7] Here, then, the narrative seems to have been regarded as a fiction.

From what has here been adduced it emerges that those researchers who have stressed the agreement between the tradition and the conventional eschatological belief have done so without having subjected the religious value of the individual narratives to a closer investigation (it must here be admitted that it is only in passing that Gayton has had occasion to go into this question), while the researchers adopting the more negative attitude have studied the narrative in its functional milieu. Their pronouncements therefore carry great weight. Their criticism, which we must here consider and judge, resolves itself into two vital theses: that the tradition has sometimes had the character of the fairy-tale, and that through its homogeneity as a tradition it has run counter to the regionally differentiated religious conceptions.

In the following I shall try to show that Gayton's and Thompson's line does nevertheless present the Orpheus tradition in the correct perspective, that, in other words, the picture of the eschatological conceptions which it gives must be considered correct.

Our first task will be to consider the question as to whether the Orpheus tradition has by the Indians themselves been regarded as a fictive fairy-tale or a true story, i.e. a myth or a legend.[8] We have found that among the Serrano it has been noted down as a fairy-tale. But what is the position in all other cases?

Without some preliminary discussion it is unfortunately practically impossible to classify all the versions of the North American Orpheus tradition treated here as myths, legends and fairy-tales, since the majority of the versions have been published simply as "texts," without reference to the circumstances attending the narration, the reaction of the audience and so forth. And it is likewise rarely the case that the author or publisher of the texts in question states whether there exist different categories of narrative, and in which category, in this event, the individual tales are to be classified. Only researchers with a deeper interest in the psychology of tradition, such as Radin and Devereux, give any more detailed information in these questions, so essential for the student of comparative religion.

---

[7] Benedict 1923 a, 104.
[8] See the classification of the tradition-material in the Introduction.

To Radin we shall revert presently. Devereux, who, like Radin, has a psycho-analytic schooling, discusses in great detail the placing of the Orpheus narrative among the Mohave.[9] He concludes that it does not belong to the myths and the clan-traditions proper, but is to be classed with the group of "Coyote Tales."[10] This includes "a wide variety of narratives, ranging from semihistorical, novelistic legends to nursery tales, and to obscene anecdotes of the Trickster type."[11] The Mohave are themselves uncertain concerning the historical basis of these tales; the events they describe "may or may not have actually happened in the past," opined Devereux' informant. Devereux goes on: "The events of the remote past apparently tend to assume a distinctly mythical character, and are likely to become incorporated into the major myths and song cycles. Relatively recent events, on the other hand, seem to gravitate toward the less formalized Coyote tales."[12] Thus, if the classification used in the present work be adopted, the Mohave Orpheus tale is to be regarded rather as a legend.

It is seldom that one finds such excellent elucidations of the functional definition of the Orpheus tradition in the ethnographic folkloristic literature. As Thompson remarks, the publishers of Indian folktales "call them with seeming indifference tales, myths, legends, or traditions." Thompson finds this, however, understandable. He writes: "Some students of these primitive tales have indeed observed that the tribes themselves have a tendency to differentiate between ordinary tales and those about an ancient world preceding the present. But in this respect there is the greatest difference between individual tribes, and a strict classification of these tales into myths and non-myths is quite impossible."[13] It is true that there is a difficulty in this point—the above-adduced interpretation of the Mohave Coyote tales shows that these do not entirely fall under our category of "legends." But the difficulty must not be exaggerated. In the first place, in North America one can, as a matter of fact, observe that the natives have, quite generally, distinguished between myths and legends;[14] and in the second place, it is from the viewpoint of comparative religious research a desideratum that, independently of the Indians' own classification, the tales should be graded with reference to their alleged value as truth.

[9] Cf. above, pp. 23 sqq.
[10] Concerning the classification of the Mohave tales, see Kroeber 1925, 770 sqq., 1951, 108 sq.
[11] Devereux 1948, 233.
[12] Devereux, op.cit., 236 sq.
[13] Thompson 1955, 484.
[14] Wissler 1950, 208.

To ascertain to which category the Orpheus tradition belongs, and therewith its value as a religious source, we cannot immediately address ourselves to the individual narratives. We must try a detour, bring forward indirect proof. Our evaluation of the traditional material must be determined from the point of departure of what in general we may consider we know about the North American folktale material in its entirety. And what, then, do we know about this? In an unpublished study to which I have already made reference in the introduction to this work I have attempted to show, against the background of an extensive investigation, that the North American Indians have for the most part reckoned with only two categories of tradition, myths and legends. Fairy-tales have existed among some tribes, but their number has always been rather limited.

Let us take some random samples: the Coyukon distinguish between ridiculous stories (which are without importance), myths and tribal traditions, and stories with a less exact historical background.[15] The Tsimshian are acquainted with only two narrative categories, myths and "tales," which latter are identical with our legends—thus we find here only stories regarded as true. Boas points out that the same distinction is drawn among all Northwest Coast tribes.[16] It recurs also among the Californian Yuki.[17] Concerning the Owens Valley Paiute, Steward tells us that "their myths, properly speaking, were all folktales."[18] And every tale was considered to be true.[19] "In Zuni, tales fall into no clearly distinguishable categories," reports Benedict.[20] The Mandan and Hidatsa distinguish between "stories" and "sacred stories"; all are old, and when one listens to them one must smoke and "offer smoke to all those involved in the story."[21] The Winnebago draw a similar distinction (see below). We have earlier asserted that the Saulteaux regard all their tales as true.[22] The Cherokee set up several narrative categories, all of which seem to be listable as myths and legends.[23] The Huron, finally, classify their narrative material as myths, legends and fairytales.[24]

[15] Jetté 1908, 299.
[16] Boas 1916, 565. The trickster cycle, however, is considered to contain elements of dubious value as truth.
[17] Foster 1944, 200 sq.
[18] Steward 1936, 357.
[19] Steward, op.cit., 358.
[20] Benedict 1935 I, XXX.
[21] Beckwith 1938, XVI.
[22] See above, p. 14.
[23] Mooney 1900, 229.
[24] Barbeau 1915, 2.

This representative selection of Indian narrative classifications makes it clear that the great majority of North American tales have had the form of the myth or the legend, i.e. have been regarded as true. The fairy-tales have been relatively rare—the question is whether they do not for the most part constitute degeneration phenomena, i.e. belong to a later period that has seen the old traditions broken down or doubted, and that has also seen the import of European fairy-tales. Thompson finds it probable that "the distinction between *Märchen* and other types of folk narrative is largely confined to Western culture."[25] I share his view, and in this connection I should like to adduce Boas' comparison of European fairy-tales and primitive narratives: the former, in contradistinction to the latter, are integrated with a completely vanished culture.[26] They can for this reason not be taken seriously. To mention a single example: in Europe one can list among fairy-tales so-called pedagogical "ficts," regarded as true only by the children; among the Wind River Shoshoni I found such tales to be objects of genuine religious belief also among the adults.[27] By this I do not wish to be understood to mean that original native fairy-tales do not exist among the Indians of North America. Many humorous tales —and, as we have seen, sometimes tales belonging to the trickster cycle —should be classified as fairy-tales.[28]

We may now apply the insights we have gained to the evaluation of the Orpheus tradition. There is, actually, nothing in this tradition to motivate its inclusion in the category of fairy-tales. It deals with a subject belonging to the serious sector of existence. The trickster stories that in the Plateau area are combined with the Orpheus tradition may, certainly, sometimes have the character of the fairy-tale; but in combination with the motif of the visit to the dead they can scarcely retain this character (even if certain trickster elements do recur, such as the trickster's game with the bones of the dead). And a further consideration is that almost all of these Orpheus tales with the trickster motif constitute *aitia* to the divorce between the living and the dead. Only in rare cases, as among the Serrano, has the Orpheus narrative been a fairy-tale—at least in more recent times. We shall revert to this matter.

---

[25] Thompson, op.cit., 485.
[26] Boas 1927, 332. Cf. Jacobs & Stern 1947, 224, Herskovits 1949, 419.
[27] Hultkrantz 1957 b, 207 sq.
[28] Cf. above, pp. 14 sq. Much too crude is Müller's dismissal of the Sioux tales to the class of harmless tales for entertainment, "plattester Zeitvertreib ohne jeden Höhenflug" (Müller 1956, 151, 165, 304). The Sioux have several fairy-tales, but also a number of remarkable myths.

The Orpheus tradition has thus probably been regarded as a true story, its content has been believed in. "Belief" is here to be understood relatively. Not everyone has believed in it, at all events not strangers and agnostics. And there is in any case a possibility that in a few Indian communities it has belonged to—and been believed by—only a certain fraction of the population, a family group, a clan. Finally, it must be borne in mind that the religious individual lives in different "strata of belief," that different religious configurations may alternate with one another: what is believed in one connection does not coincide with what is believed in another.[29] Thus the myth and practical religion may imply different types of belief.[30] It has probably been possible for an individual to believe in the data concerning the realm of the dead in the Orpheus narrative, even if these have in some respect diverged from his private eschatological belief.

On the assumption that practically all Orpheus traditions have given expression to prevailing eschatological conceptions, i.e. have been regarded as authoritative and true, it is possible to determine more precisely their distribution between the two narrative categories relevant in this connection, the myth and the legend. The criteria to which we shall here have recourse are firstly the time for the action, secondly the character of the two main personages, and thirdly (even if in a lesser degree) the form of the tradition.[31]

In the form of the legend the Orpheus tradition occurs everywhere on the Northwest Coast right down to Puget Sound; its main personages are here, as Gayton expresses the matter, "people, either real or mythical."[32] Also in the "sea-coast form" we find the Orpheus tradition as legend. Several Plateau versions of the Orpheus tradition are of legend type (Carrier, Thompson, Sanpoil), but they are not characteristic for this region (cf. below). The great majority of Californian Orpheus tales, on the other hand, occur in legendary form. Gayton observes: "Invariably the story is told as an historic event, i.e., a tale, although myths are a favorite literary form with Yokuts, Western Mono, and Tübatulabal."[33] In the Southwest and in Mexico the narratives from Zuni and Nayarit may be accounted legends. The Great Basin and Plains versions are all legends, and in the whole of eastern North America all the tales except the Cherokee narrative belong to this category.

[29] Hultkrantz, op.cit., 211 sq.
[30] Cf. Arbman 1939.
[31] See above, p. 12.
[32] Gayton, op.cit., 278.
[33] Gayton, op.cit., 269.

According to this survey, the great majority of Orpheus tales should be regarded as descriptions of events that once took place on the human plane. But some of them have such an anchorage in the supernatural world that they verge on the limits of the myth. This appears to be the case with the Orpheus tale of the Winnebago. The Winnebago distinguish in the main in the same way as we have done between myths and legends, but in addition to these there is a mixed category that Radin refers to as "myth-tales."[34] Such a narrative may easily glide between the extreme categories; if it resembles a myth type it may on these grounds be classified as a myth. The Winnebago Orpheus tradition is such a "myth-tale." It is a legend in so far as it is "the semi-historical account that the founder of the Ghost Dance professed to give of the origin of that dance. It is definitely of the nature of a fasting experience." But it is a myth inasmuch as it includes "motifs and incidents from the mythological background ... These mixed roots of the story are reflected in the designation given to it by the Winnebago, a 'myth-tale'."[35]

It is, then, not surprising if in many quarters the Orpheus tradition has assumed the form of the myth. We seldom find it as a serious primeval myth in the strict sense, to be precise, only among the Nisenan, Modoc, Navajo, the Taos Indians and the Cherokee. Here the acting persons are exalted supernatural beings, and at least the one of the two main personages can be identified as a divinity. The Navajo myth is, as has already been pointed out, systematized with the rest of the mythology of the tribe. Of less sacred character are the myths connected with the culture hero or the trickster.[36] Although they often constitute origin-tales of the separation of the dead from the living, they are on the borderline of jocular entertainment. It is these myths of Coyote, Eagle and their peers that Gayton defines as "animal tales"; as she observes, they are characteristic of the southern Plateau, and they are also found among certain tribes in the southern part of Puget Sound that have had contact with the Shahaptin tribes in the interior.[37] Finally, they also have offshoots in northern California, among the Shasta. One may remark that the elevation of the Orpheus tradition to myth, i.e. sacred or at all events true narrative of divinities, has in the main

---

[34] Radin 1926, 18 sqq.
[35] Radin, op.cit., 22.
[36] Cf. the Introduction, note 10.
[37] Gayton, op.cit., 278. The tribes here referred to are the Sinkaietk (cf., however, below), the Kalispel, Klikitat, Yakima, Tenino, Nez Percé, Snuqualmi, Puyallup, Skopamish, Quinault, Chehalis, Wishram and Wasco.

taken place in regions where the mythology has had a dominant influence, as in the Plateau area, or where the fertility mythology has spread, as in the Southwest. The transition from legend to myth should not constitute any problem for us, as we have already been able to remark how easily one and the same tradition may pass between two such essentially different narrative categories as the myth and the fairy-tale.[38]

It thus seems probable that the Orpheus tradition in North America occurs most frequently as a legend, and that in practically all other cases it has constituted a myth. How, then, is one to judge the Serrano narrative; does it constitute an isolated case, or has it had counterparts elsewhere? As we have seen, the Orpheus tradition occurs among the Serrano as a fairy-tale; the Indians do not seem to believe that it can give us information concerning the realm of the dead. I think it probable that a similar situation has in more recent times overtaken the Orpheus tradition also in other quarters: it has lost its original value with the abandonment of the old eschatology. The old conceptions have lost their significance in the religious belief, but they have been formally retained intact in the already established narrative tradition. Such a state of affairs appears to obtain among the Sinkaietk. In their Orpheus myth the land of the dead is described as a country behind a river, but according to the current belief the land of the dead is reached without crossing a river and by journeying upwards—in this belief one can obviously trace influences from Christian teaching.[39] Christianity and modern agnosticism have destroyed the significance of the Orpheus tradition as a source for the eschatological belief.[40]

The Orpheus tradition as a fairy-tale is thus a product of modern times. It may be taken for granted that in so far as it does survive as tradition, it will do so to an increasingly lesser extent as myth or legend. This is not to say that its value for the student of comparative religion will evaporate completely. We have earlier pointed out that among primitive peoples the motifs of the fairy-tale commonly have an obvious value as realism, since they have been taken from the worlds of culture or religious belief.[41] It is, for example, scarcely likely that a fairy-tale concerning the realm of the dead in an Indian tribe should describe this realm otherwise than it was conceived in the old eschato-

[38] See above, pp. 14 sq.
[39] Cf. Spier 1938, 169, with op.cit., 235 sq.
[40] It is, however, conceivable (though I do not consider it likely) that as regards the Serrano the natives were disinclined to discuss their religious conceptions with outsiders. Drucker complains of the unwillingness of the Serrano to give information (Drucker 1937, 6).
[41] See above, pp. 14, 163 sq.

logical belief.[42] Where on account of pressure from Western civilization the Orpheus tradition has declined to the level of the fairy-tale it does nonetheless show, in its complex of elements, how in heathen times the world of the dead was conceived.

We constate: in the period before the days of the Christian mission the Orpheus tradition was probably everywhere regarded, even among the Serrano and Sinkaietk, as a true account of events which actually took place on the supernatural plane, or on the supernatural and natural planes. That this has been the case is confirmed not least by its important authorizing and etiological functions, to which we shall have occasion to revert later.

We now come to our second great problem: if both in respect of the course of events and the complex of elements the Orpheus tradition represents a fairly constant picture, how, then, can it be expected to reflect the various eschatological notions in widely separated culture areas? It is a well-known fact that the North American Indians' conceptions of the realm of the dead show rich variety; conceptions of the type "happy hunting grounds" alternate with ideas of paradise in the sky or beyond the ocean, and to the happy realms of the dead correspond the less happy, often subterranean, places. Even the interiors from the land of the dead vary in character, and different religious and social valuations have determined the rank and the activities of the dead. It seems impossible that a tradition which has everywhere had the same basic pattern should be able to serve as a source in an account of Indian beliefs concerning the realm of the dead.

There is, however, nothing to support the notion that the Orpheus tradition has not been understood as a true, realistic description of the world of the dead, wherever it has been narrated. Against the background of what has been said above this may appear strange, but it finds its natural explanation in the following circumstances.

In the first place, as has already been mentioned, religious belief does not constitute a close-welded, logically built-up whole.[43] It permits of inconsistencies and several "truths," valid for different groups or for one and the same individual in different situations. The following note by Drucker concerning the Nootka attitude to an eschatological tale closely related to the Orpheus tradition is typical: "There was a well-known variant of the widespread myth about a person who went to

[42] Concerning the Navajo, see below, p. 289.
[43] See above, p. 278.

the Land of the Dead, in an Underworld, but was sent back for fastidiously refusing food consisting of cooked fleas, nits, and the like. For
some reason however the journey to this Land of the Dead seems not
to have been accepted as explaining the fate of souls in general, but was
regarded as a unique adventure of one person."[44] Thus we find here
that the account given in the "myth" of the life after this did not have
a normative character. In the same way, an eschatology in the form of
the Orpheus tradition diverging from the general notion of the realm
of the dead may have had a "supplemental" religious value. As we shall
soon find, however, nothing has so far emerged which might confirm
that the Orpheus tradition has in principle represented a divergent
eschatology. The so-called "sea-coast form" has, it is true, a less common eschatology, but this holds for the drowned, and independently of
its epic frame it has been embraced along the whole of the Northwest
Coast.

In the second place, it can in some cases be definitely established that
the Orpheus tradition has formed the belief, i.e. changed earlier existing eschatological notions in accordance with its own eschatological
standards.[45] Thus the conceptions of the happy character of the underworld obtaining among the Karuk are in all probability traceable to
the influence of the Orpheus tradition: an originally gloomy underworld
eschatology has been coloured by the as a rule brighter atmosphere in
the realms of the dead in the Orpheus tradition.[46]

In the third place the Orpheus tradition has been spread chiefly among
tribes having an optimistic eschatology.[47] Here it has found its natural
point of contact, here it has been possible for its peculiar character to
be asserted and the assimilation with the native eschatology has been
able to proceed without friction. As has been pointed out earlier, the
Orpheus tradition has rarely been spread to tribes with a gloomy
eschatological perspective, such as the Athapascans.[48]   .

In the fourth place, it transpires on closer investigation that the
eschatology of the Orpheus tradition is, certainly, homogeneous in respect of its basic ideology, but at the same time it shows rich variety
as regards the details—the location of the land of the dead, its material
and social structure. These details show close agreement with the local
culture patterns, as we have earlier been able to establish.[49] This can

[44] Drucker 1951, 156 note 34.
[45] Cf. above, p. 208.
[46] See above, pp. 91 sq.
[47] See above, pp. 92 sq.
[48] See above, pp. 33, 223 sq.
[49] See above, pp. 35 sqq., 91, 106 sq.

only mean that wherever it has gone the Orpheus tradition has also absorbed local eschatological notions.[50] In other words, the Orpheus tradition has both stimulated and adapted itself to the prevailing religious pattern.

Let us further elucidate what has been said by trying to analyse the diffusion process of the Orpheus tradition. This may be characterized as implying in succession the three phases of transmission, adaptation and integration. The tradition hos been transmitted to tribes which have provided the conditions necessary for its acceptance—i.e. they have had a relatively bright view of the dead and the life beyond the grave.[51] For this would seem to be the basic feature in the eschatology of the Orpheus tradition; a number of other eschatological elements, which possibly occurred very early in the Orpheus tradition but which have also had their place in popular belief, have been listed in the foregoing.[52] It is clear that this eschatology, with its broad lines and relative paucity of detail, has been well-adapted to strike root in the most widely varying culture milieus. The process of adaptation must have run the same course as among the Bella Coola, where "stories of foreign origin, when told sufficiently often, tend to be considered indigenous and the facts recorded in them accepted and incorporated into Bella Coola belief."[53] We have already remarked how the eschatology of the Orpheus tradition has been able to transform the actual evaluation of the world of the dead. Its influence does not, however, seem to have extended further than this; it has then itself fitted in with the eschatological milieus of the different narrators and cultures. Its integration in these has been almost total.

One may arrive at this conclusion from two circumstances, the cultural integration and the eschatological points of agreement in certain cases open to control.

It has already been stressed in an earlier connection how completely integrated with local culture patterns the content of the Orpheus tradition has been, and it was there pointed out that this integration shows indirectly in what a high degree a narrative with a supernatural content reflects current popular belief.[54] The conclusion is obvious: the Orpheus tradition must have presented the other world precisely as this was

[50] See above, pp. 21, 38 sq.
[51] But that there are certain essential exceptions in this point has been seen in the foregoing.
[52] See chap. II: 3—4.
[53] McIlwraith 1948 I, 511.
[54] See above, p. 35.

283

conceived by its narrators and hearers. Now one may of course ask oneself whether such a generalization is permitted; have not, for example, the myth, the legend and the fairy-tale different levels of integration? And is not an older narrative better integrated than a younger and imported one? It is here not possible to take up these great problems for debate in their whole extent; I will content myself with a short discussion to which I will append my own conclusions.

No-one doubts that a myth is as a rule extremely firmly anchored in the culture within which it is recounted: it expresses the social, ethical and religious values prevailing in that culture.[55] Radin, it is true, declares that among the Winnebago the myth proper reflects the culture in a very slight degree, in contradistinction to the ordinary narrative, where the connection with the cultural background is very apparent.[56] This must not, however, be misunderstood: the myth moves on a supernatural, cosmic plane, it thus has less connection with this world; but this is not to say that its elements run counter to the culture structure.

Before we discuss the cultural integration of the legend it may be as well to try to ascertain the connection between the fairy-tale and the culture, as several researchers have from this point of view drawn a comparison between the myth and the fairy-tale. Boas, who makes a distinction between myths and tales,[57] by which he seems to be referring to what we have here called fairy-tales, declares that "a detailed study of mythologies shows clearly that ... they reflect in detail the cultures of which they form part."[58] The pronouncement seems to imply that the fairy-tale does not in the same way reflect the culture, it is more nourished by fantasy and imagination. At the international folklore conference in Bloomington, Indiana, in the summer of 1950, Dr. Bidney made the following statement: "If we accept Malinowski's contention that myths served in part to validate a culture, I think that would mean that insofar as we are concerned with genuine myths there is bound to be a one-to-one correlation between the types of myths which are found and the socio-cultural conditions which they are intended to validate. On the other hand, insofar as we are dealing with folk tales pure and simple, where the interest is primarily on the story, then I think it would be extremely unlikely that you would find any one-to-one correlation between social conditions and the folk tale."[59] To this

[55] See above, pp. 12 sq.
[56] Radin 1926, 18 sqq., 21.
[57] Though not so strictly as Bidney thinks: cf. Boas 1938, 609 with Bidney 1950, 20 sq.
[58] Boas, op.cit., 616.
[59] Thompson 1953 a, 301 sq.

Thompson objected: "I doubt whether the distinction between tale and myth can be properly drawn on the basis of the relationship or lack of relationship with the social background of the people who tell them."[60] Thompson's caution seems justified. Malinowski by no means rules out a culture integration for the fairy-tale, even if he finds it limited: "While in the mere fireside *tale* the sociological context is narrow, the *legend* enters much more deeply into the tribal life of the community, and the *myth* plays a most important function."[61] Both the myth and the fairy-tale generally have a strong anchorage in the culture in which they are handed down; the myth belongs naturally to it, while the fairy-tale is sometimes very superficially integrated — it is perhaps a migratory tale which has just been adopted, or it has its origin in a very alien culture.[62] It is typical that the fairy-tales among the Coyukon (Ten'a) "may serve to illustrate native customs and to give an insight in the Ten'a thought, but make no pretence to historical exactness."[63]

This grading of the cultural integration of the different oral narrative types places the legend between the myth and the fairy-tale, as Malinowski asserted. Its integration probably corresponds to that of the myth in many cases, but as a rule it holds that it does not come far after that of the myth; and in certain details the legend even seems able to excel the myth in depth of integration. Since the Orpheus tradition exists as myth or legend—and only in a degenerative form as a fairy-tale—, the problem of its level of integration may probably be regarded as solved. From the purely practical viewpoint, moreover, the particular category to which a narrative may belong does not seem to play any very considerable rôle as a criterion of its cultural integration. Ethnologists and folklorists have reconstructed entire cultures on a narrative material including myths, legends and fairy-tales.[64]

Of greater importance seems the second problem indicated above, the connection between the cultural integration of a narrative and its age and alien derivation. Now it is, as we have seen, probable that the Orpheus tradition in North America goes back to a very early date; and its local manifestations, too, appear to be very recent, as our study of the cultural integration in an earlier chapter was able to show.[65] (The

[60] Thompson, op.cit., 302.
[61] Malinowski 1954, 146; cf. op.cit., 101 sqq., 106.
[62] See above, p. 35. Cf. below.
[63] Jetté 1908, 299.
[64] Cf. e.g. Hultkrantz 1956, 24, Elbert 1956, 99, with the sources listed in these articles.
[65] See chap. I: 4.

Lipan Apache tradition is a striking exception, but it is nonetheless remarkably well adapted to the existing cultural and religious conditions.) If, on the other hand, an at all events relatively new narrative has been introduced from a very alien source, the problem becomes more apparent. This eventuality seems to exist in the Navajo Orpheus myth, which, as we have seen, is fitted into the origin-tradition of the tribe. Katherine Spencer has observed that the last-mentioned myth reflects only incompletely the Navajo culture, and she finds the probable explanation of this to be that the myth has been adopted from the originally alien Pueblo culture.[66] One is thus here confronted with the curious situation that a sacred, deeply believed text has not to any degree worth mentioning been integrated in its cultural milieu. On the other hand, there is nothing in this myth that runs counter to the milieu, as is the case with many of the fairy-tales adopted by the Indians from the Europeans.[67] The question is, whether in this connection the Navajo myth should not be compared with the Winnebago myths adduced in the foregoing, which do not, either, reflect the cultural environment in any considerable degree. However this may be, it is evident that the thesis to the effect that the religious value of a popular tradition is directly related to its cultural integration is not incorrect, provided that it is not applied negatively: defective cultural integration it not always *in et per se* a sign of a tottering religious foundation.

At the same time as the Orpheus tradition has been assimilated with the culture to which it has been introduced, its eschatology has obviously —and as a consequence of this—been modified to agree with the living belief in the culture in question. It is not altogether easy to prove this in detail, as the ethnographers and folklorists who have noted down the Orpheus tradition generally refer to this when the popular eschatological conceptions are touched upon. In several cases, however, eschatological material has been reported that has not been directly connected with the Orpheus tradition, although the latter has existed at the same time; generally this new material is supplied by another researcher than the one who has noted down the tradition. Let us consider some examples.

That the conceptions of the realm of the dead in the Orpheus tradition of the "sea-coast form" correspond closely to the popular notions of this realm for the drowned along the Northwest Coast has already been pointed out.[68] Morice's information on the eschatological con-

[66] Spencer 1947, 116 sq. Concerning the migrations of the myth, cf. above, p. 204, note 92.
[67] See, e.g., Radin 1915 a, 48, and 50 note 1.
[68] See above, pp. 47 sqq.

ceptions of the Carrier agree very well with the representation of the land of the dead in the Orpheus legend from the same tribe noted down by Jenness. Thus in both accounts there is mention of the road to the beyond ending on a high hill, from which the traveller has a wide view over the river dividing this world from the village of the dead with its black and red houses.[69] The traveller must cross the river in a black canoe that he summons from the other shore by yawning. The food in the land of the dead consists of frogs and snakes.[70] Olson has carefully reproduced the topography of the other world among the Quinault, and the description of the different villages with fishing nets etc. scattered along a river in that world gives precisely the milieu depicted in the Orpheus myth noted down by Farrand. Olson is even able to state exactly which village it was that Bluejay visited.[71] Loeb's data from the Pomo seem to show that the journey to an island out in the sea described in the Orpheus legend is perfectly compatible with the current notions of the life beyond the grave.[72] Among the Tübatulabal Orpheus and his deceased wife follow a road leading over a mountain which is the abode of a crow that pecks out people's eyes. According to Dr. Wheeler-Voegelin, this is the same road that in "general belief" is taken by the dead. The agreement is not, however, complete: the Orpheus couple journey westwards, the dead, in the popular belief, travel to the east.[73] It is of course possible that Dr. Wheeler-Voegelin has here noted the wrong direction.

The Orpheus tales from the Zuni show good internal agreement and also conform well with other reports of the life among the dead—the latter often conceived as fertility beings, *kachinas*[74]—in the underworld. As in the Orpheus tales, the dead are believed to spend their lives dancing *kachina*-dances in the festively adorned dancing-house at the bottom of a wonderful lake; the uninitiated may not take part in the dancing but may observe it at a distance.[75] In the Comanche tradition the realm of the dead presents precisely the appearance it has in popular belief: a happy realm beyond the mountains in the west, "happy hunting grounds" of the classical type, where the same life is lived as among the living, though in a more perfect form.[76] As it is reported by Swanton,

[69] Cf. above, p. 40.
[70] Morice 1889, 159 sq.
[71] Olson 1936, 161 sqq.
[72] Loeb 1926, 292 sq.
[73] Voegelin 1938, 62.
[74] The dead and *kachinas* (in Zuni *koko*) are not, however, altogether identical concepts in Zuni: see Bunzel 1932, 510, 516 sq.; Parsons 1933, 71, 1939 I, 164, II, 951, 965.
[75] Stevenson 1898, 35, 1904, 20, 32 sq., 308; cf. also Parsons 1923, 140 sq.

the living popular belief among the Alabama is acquainted with all the perils and difficulties met with by the Orpheus of the Alabama on his way to the realm of the dead: the great expanse of water, the dangerous serpents, the great battle and so forth. Common to both the Orpheus narratives and the popular belief, furthermore, is the notion that the dead go to the land of the Creator somewhere up in the sky.[77]

The Orpheus tradition communicated by Jenness from the Ojibway on Parry Island agrees almost exactly with the eschatological notions obtaining among these Ojibway as noted down by him, and rather well with the descriptions of the journey to the land of the dead given much earlier by Kohl from different Ojibway groups: one recognizes the terrible dog, the shaking bridge consisting of a tree-trunk, and much else.[78] Jenness observes, nevertheless, that "the jumble of beliefs" among the Parry Island Ojibway does, certainly, more or less conform with what we find in the Orpheus tradition, but at the same time introduces "a few variant ideas."[79] But this is of course only what is to be expected. The Shawnee, for example, have information concerning "Our Grandmother's" dwelling from descriptions supplied by latter-day visionaries and from the Orpheus narrative "which differs from those who have made personal observations in emphasizing the spaciousness of the dwelling."[80] There is, then, a difference, but it is minimal.

Instances might be multiplied, but those adduced must suffice. They seem to support the assumption that the eschatology of the Orpheus tradition has been well integrated in the religious patterns of the geographically widely separated tribes and become one with their eschatology. It can not of course be denied that discrepancies do sometimes exist; but it is easy to explain them.[81] In a number of cases it has not been possible to correlate the eschatology of the Orpheus tradition with that of popular belief, since the latter has either been forgotten, as for example among the Shasta, or been changed in Christian time, as among the Sinkaietk and Iroquois.[82] In many tribes the Orpheus narrative has

[76] Wallace & Hoebel 1952, 186 sqq.
[77] Swanton 1928 b, 513 sq.
[78] Jenness 1935, 108 sq.; Kohl 1859 I, 288 sq., 292 sq.
[79] Jenness, op.cit., 109.
[80] Voegelin 1936, 5.
[81] Cf. also above, p. 246 (Hupa).
[82] The Orpheus legend of the Seneca Iroquois gives an eschatological picture from an older time than that represented by the popular belief in the 19th century (see Morgan 1954 I, 162 sqq., 168 sqq.). Hewitt's presentation of the eschatological conceptions is a résumé based upon the Orpheus legend noted down by himself (Hewitt 1895, 109). Its eschatology disappeared from the Seneca tribe when the Christian-influenced teaching of Handsome Lake spread about 1800, with descriptions of heaven and hell (see Beauchamp 1897, Parker 1913, Deardorff 1951).

been connected with one of several simultaneously existing eschatological patterns. Thus a closer analysis of the eschatology of the Pomo
tradition shows that this coincides with the religious conceptions obtaining among only two of sixteen Pomo groups, the Shanel and the
Mukanno.[83] The geographic splitting up of the Thompson Indians is
presumably the chief cause of the poor agreement of their Orpheus
legend with the eschatology communicated by Teit: in the legend the
land of the dead is reached exclusively over water, in the popular
belief the journey is overland; the only common feature seems to be
that the journey takes place in a fog that gradually lifts.[84] It should,
however, be observed that by some the legend is told to the effect
that a compromise between the two modes of travelling is arrived at:
the journey proceeds first overland and across a river, then over a lake.[85]
There need scarcely be any doubt but that the Thompson Indians, like,
for example, the Wind River Shoshoni investigated in the field by myself, simultaneously embraced several divergent views of the realm of
the dead and the road thither.

   Also the above-discussed Navajo version of the Orpheus tradition
should be judged in the light of these facts.[86] The numerous and widely
dispersed Navajo are distributed among several local groups, and can
therefore scarcely be expected to have an uniform eschatology.[87] Their
Orpheus tradition *may* possibly include eschatological elements having
only a restricted distribution. The authors of *Navajo Eschatology* have,
moreover, overshot the mark when they assert that the ruler of the realm
of the dead mentioned in the Orpheus myth is lacking in the living belief:
he is referred to in a tale of a dream-journey to the land of the dead
published in the same work.[88]

   All things considered, it seems to me justified to make the general
pronouncement that the Orpheus tradition possesses a source-value of
the first rank as a document of current popular belief among the Indians
of North America. In certain cases, it is true, Christian belief has dis-
turbed the absolute correlation between the religious eschatology and
that of the popular tradition, but such cases can easily be discovered
and isolated. As a rule, where both popular belief and the tradition
give information in the same field the respective statements, where they

[83] Gifford & Kroeber 1937, 158.
[84] Teit 1900, 342 sq.
[85] Teit 1898, 117 note 274.
[86] See above, p. 273.
[87] Cf. their beliefs concerning the soul, Hultkrantz 1953, 105 sq.
[88] Wyman, Hill & Osanai 1942, 35.

are not identical, are able to supplement each other. If the popular belief has not been noted down, one can generally reconstruct it from the tradition[89]—the strong cultural integration of the tradition may be taken as a proof of agreement between it and the popular belief.

And finally, we have the assertions of the Indians themselves to the effect that they know the life after this through the Orpheus tradition.

2. The tradition as a sanction of the eschatology

The Orpheus tradition is, as has been pointed out earlier, not merely a tale for entertainment, a fairy-tale. It is myth or legend, and therewith considered as a true story of events which have really taken place. In more recent times the Indians have probably been conscious of its shamanistic origin only in exceptional cases, but they have retained the memory that the tradition was once connected with a real experience, an event in the past.. The narratives of the journey to the realm of the dead and of the stay there have had a markedly realistic character. They have presumably not afforded many new insights into the physiognomy of the other world, but to already existing eschatological notions they have lent weight and authority. The Orpheus tradition has constituted a source of belief, a document, that has confirmed the belief in a life after death. As a myth is has given an account of the way in which the divine Orpheus hero of primeval times fixed the order at present obtaining, according to which after their decease people go to his kingdom;[1] as a legend it has given a voice to people from the past to tell of the way in which life is lived beyond the grave.

There are several instances of the way in which the belief in the land of the dead is by the Indians themselves referred to the Orpheus tradition (what is less common is for the belief in ghosts and in reincarnation to be motivated with the same tradition).[2] As these instances are very essential for our assessment of the Orpheus tradition as a religious document, they will all be adduced here. As we shall find, there

---

[89] From the Cowichan Hill-Tout reports that "it is almost impossible to learn anything by direct questioning concerning the beliefs of the Indians on the subject of the Hereafter, but happily we may gather some idea of these beliefs indirectly from their myths." As one of these "myths" Hill-Tout cites the Orpheus tradition (Hill-Tout 1904 b, 321).

[1] Cf. especially above, pp. 104 sq.

[2] One may observe that the Orpheus tradition actualizes directly the belief in a realm of the dead, indirectly the belief in the ghost bound to the grave, while it does not at all actualize the belief in the wandering ghost, reincarnation or transmigration.

is no evidence that the "sea-coast form" has had an authorizing function for the eschatology. This is probably at least in part connected with the fact that their hereafter for drowned persons is in the first place the domain of the supernatural animals, and not of deceased human beings.[3] Another reason for this circumstance will be mentioned in a later context.[4]

The Tlingit legend of the "inland form" has quite obviously an informative character, as appears clearly from its detailed mention of e.g. the canoe on the lake of the dead.[5] In one of the Chehalis myths we find information concerning the respective fates of those who are burned to death and those who die of illness.[6] One of the Skopamish myths, telling of Owl's journey to the realm of the dead, relates a good deal about the conditions obtaining there, concluding with the words: "Owl found out all these things."[7] Among the Modoc, according to Curtin, the Orpheus myth has had an important etiological function. "When old men are asked what their ideas are regarding life hereafter they tell of Kumush's visit to the great house in the underground world; of what he saw there, and of the terrible effort he made to bring spirits to the upper world, and create Indians."[8]

The Yokuts relate that through their Orpheus hero they became acquainted with the life in the land of the dead.[9] In one Yokuts version we are told that the hero was taken out of the realm of the dead by his deceased wife after he had seen everything there. "She bade him tell his people all the wonders and then return to her on the third day. He ran back and called his tribe together and related all he had seen. He finished telling it and died."[10] Gayton remarks that "most Yokuts informants said that the tale showed what the land of the dead was like, and more than one informant voluntarily told the story in response to inquiries concerning their belief in a future life."[11] Also Dr. Wheeler-Voegelin's informant among the Tübatulabal explained the nature of the life in the hereafter by adducing the Orpheus legend.[12]

[3] See above, pp. 46 sq.
[4] See below, p. 297.
[5] Swanton 1909, 249.
[6] Adamson 1934, 24.
[7] Ballard 1929, 131.
[8] Curtin 1912, 382 sq.
[9] Kroeber 1907 c, 218; Gayton 1948 II, 237 note 176.
[10] Hudson 1902, 105.
[11] Gayton 1935, 269. Gayton also constates that the conceptions of the life after this introduced in the Yokuts ghost dance had been formulated in the Orpheus tradition (Gayton 1930 a, 77).
[12] Gayton 1935, 269 note 1; cf. Voegelin 1938, 47.

Wyman, Hill and Osanai find it curious that they only heard the Navajo Orpheus myth narrated three times in response to their questions concerning the life after this.[13] These writers evidently think it was not related frequently enough. Here we will content ourselves with the observation that the reference to the Orpheus tradition was at all events made, and we shall presently revert to the question of how often it has been adduced.

According to Dorsey, the Wichita consider that their knowledge and that of their ancestors concerning the other world and man's fate after death dates from the event eternalized in the Orpheus legend, which took place not so long after the Great Flood.[14] After reproducing the Carrier Orpheus tradition Jenness writes: "It was from this medicine-man, and from the salmon boy,[15] that the Indians learned where people go when they die. They alone of all living beings have visited the land of the dead."[16] The Parry Island Ojibway "learned all about the after-life" from "Sky-woman loin cloth," who followed her deceased husband to the realm of the dead and freed him from its grip.[17] Brébeuf observes that among the Huron the conception of a life after this "is kept up among them by means of certain stories which the fathers tell their children," inter alia, the Orpheus tradition.[18] Concerning the Micmac Orpheus legend Le Clercq says: "This it is, and this only, which makes our Indians believe in the immortality of souls."[19] In another place in his work, however, Le Clercq mentions a man who in an unconscious state visited the land of the dead and was given permission by the powers ruling there to return to life, "in order to give the Gaspesians [=Micmac] news of the Land of Souls, which had been up to that time unknown to them..."[20] Presumably both traditions contributed to the belief in a world beyond the grave.

The instances adduced confirm Dr. Gayton's thesis that the Orpheus tradition answers the question of the fate of the dead, and likewise the desire of the sceptic to know how this knowledge has been arrived at.[21] As an older researcher, John W. Chapman, found among the Ingalik, a narrative of the other life constitutes the firm foundation for belief,

[13] Wyman, Hill & Osanai 1942, 33.
[14] Dorsey 1904 a, 21. Cf. also the Pawnee (Dorsey 1906, 411 note 1).
[15] See above, p. 232.
[16] Jenness 1934, 145.
[17] Jenness 1935, 109.
[18] JR X, 147. Cf. above, pp. 25 sq.
[19] Le Clercq 1910, 213.
[20] Le Clercq, op.cit., 208.
[21] Gayton 1935, 285.

customs and speculation referring to this other life.[22] Both on account of the clear information it gives[23] and because of its in the majority of cases alleged high age, the Orpheus tradition forms a natural authoritative foundation for the eschatological hopes of the Indians.

It must not, however, be forgotten that the Indians have also other sources for their belief in another world. Like the Orpheus tradition, many of these have the character of ancient tales: we find myths concerning the culture hero's visit to the realm of the dead, we find legends of the sojourning there of heroes from olden times.[24] And we have, furthermore, the numerous memorates of recent experiences, journeys in ecstasy, dream and coma to the world of the dead by persons now living or deceased within living memory.[25] In support of his eschatological notions the believer adduces now his own experiences, now those of others, now again the established tradition. The Northern Shoshoni, for example, assert that Coyote "told them that the dead go to another world,"[26] but they nonetheless take their information concerning this world from the experiences of latter-day visionaries.[27] The Fox were instructed in the mysteries of the land of the dead by the culture hero,[28] but this notwithstanding, they are acquainted with this land chiefly through the visits paid to it in twilight states by contemporary Fox.[29] The Sia Indians tell of an occasion in olden times when the dead in corpore visited the living; "it was then that the Sia first learned all about their future home."[30] But subsequently, visionaries who have made their way to the realm of the dead and then returned have told of its secrets.[31] And so forth.

Despite its commonly authorizing function, the Orpheus tradition has not, any more than these tales, been the sole source of the conceptions of the land of the dead and the sole ground for the belief in this. It is characteristic that in the Orpheus tradition from the Ottawa related by Schoolcraft it is said of the hero that "he had heard the old people say that there was a path that led to the land of souls."[32] In other words, the knowledge did not arise with the Orpheus legend, it

[22] Chapman 1912, 66 sq.
[23] See Thompson 1946, 351.
[24] See above, pp. 231 sq.
[25] See above, pp. 232 sqq.
[26] Lowie 1909 a, 239.
[27] Lowie, op.cit., 226.
[28] Michelson 1925, 405.
[29] Michelson, op.cit., 399 sq.; Jones 1907 a, 207 sqq.
[30] Stevenson 1894, 143.
[31] Stevenson, op.cit., 144.
[32] Schoolcraft 1851 I, 321.

existed before this. The Orpheus tradition has been adduced as a source for the eschatology *as well as* other documents, and it would seem that in importance and value it is frequently overshadowed by the narratives of the other world based upon the subjective experiences of latter-day ecstatics and dreamers. Thus this is the case among the Navajo, whose eschatology, despite the existence of an Orpheus tradition, has "recent dreams as the main source."[33] It is also worth pointing out that immediately after reproducing the Orpheus legend of the Ojibway Jenness writes the following: "To substantiate this doctrine of the afterlife the Indians narrate the experiences of their forefathers, and even the experiences that come to themselves in dreams."[34] It seems logical that the Orpheus tradition of the Lipan Apache, which is of course strictly speaking a memorate of recent date absorbed by the North American Orpheus narrative, is presented as a document of the first rank concerning the conditions obtaining beyond the grave. "You are afraid to die," says the main personage to his fellow tribesmen on his return. "But I know it is a better place. So you people need not tell me about the lower world."[35] The Cherokee, on the other hand, do not adduce their Orpheus myth—as an astral myth is has an all too slight element of human personal experience, and it does not, moreover, give much information concerning the life beyond the grave. Instead, they derive their eschatological knowledge from a man who in a fever dream following a snake bite sojourned in the realm of the dead, "came back seven days after and described it all."[36]

The vision complex dominates the majority of North American Indian religions. It is therefore natural that to the personal visionary experiences should be ascribed a value that frequently exceeds that of the fixed tradition. Miss Conard, in her study of Algonquin eschatology, was surprised that the Indians, when seeking authority for their religious conceptions, did not attach greater importance to myths and traditions than to extraordinary experiences by contemporary fellow-tribesmen.[37] The significance of the visionaries in such connections has also been stressed by Hallowell, who met with the same situation among the Saulteaux. "When I made inquiries about life after death," he writes, "it was the alleged experiences of these individuals that were first mentioned."[38] Where there is no authorizing eschatological tradition the

[33] Wyman, Hill & Osanai 1942, 33.
[34] Jenness 1935, 110.
[35] Opler 1940, 101. Cf. Opler 1945, 130 sqq.
[36] Mooney 1900, 437.
[37] Conard 1900, 227.
[38] Hallowell 1940, 30.

visionary experiences acquire an immense importance; if they do not include visits to the realm of the dead there are scarcely any of the prerequisites for a belief in such a land.[39] As a rule, however, the eschatological belief grew out of the living tradition—myths or legends in combination with the ecstatic experiences of contemporaries—and was deepened and confirmed by subjective experiences occurring *in conformity with* the tradition handed down. For natural reasons the experiences frequently came to modify the belief. "Versions of the spirit world differ somewhat," remarks Harris of the White Knife Shoshoni, "since a number of individuals whose *muguwa* [=soul] had traveled there and returned contributed constant variations to the concept."[40]

It is thus not so surprising if it is sometimes possible to observe distinct differences between the tradition and the experience, although as a rule the latter has been based upon the conceptual material of the tradition. We have been able to note some such discrepancies in the foregoing.[41] Let us take a further example, the Northern Shoshoni in Idaho. These have several traditions concerning the land of the dead, inter alia in the form of an Orpheus legend and a myth regarding Coyote's instruction on this realm.[42] This notwithstanding, Lowie reports of the Shoshoni Indian Enga-gwacu Jim, who had undertaken several journeys to the world of the dead, that he "has questioned Shoshone medicine-men concerning a hereafter; but mistrusts both their statements and those of the missionaries, because they fail to tally with his personal experiences."[43] One thus finds that if a person's own experiences of the land of the dead diverge from the current norm, he trusts only his own experiences.[44] It is, however, rather unlikely that such an acute state of tension between the tradition and personal experience should have persisted for any length of time. In those cases in which there have been divergences these have, to all appearances, soon been overcome; the balance has been restored through the interaction between the experience and the tradition: they have approached each other, transformed each other. The Orpheus tradition has as a rule expressed the current eschatological belief (the great exception, of course, is constituted by the "sea-coast form"); and it has, I venture to

[39] Cf., e.g., the Washo (Lowie 1939, 322 sq.), the Walapai (Kroeber 1935, 149).
[40] Harris 1940, 66.
[41] See above, p. 288 (Ojibway, Shawnee).
[42] Concerning the last-mentioned myth, cf. above, p. 293.
[43] Lowie 1909 a, 226.
[44] Cf. also Steward 1943, 287. We must of course not overlook the possibility that special local conditions *may* have played a certain rôle: the Shoshoni are very individualistic, and a further consideration is that the break between heathendom and Christianity has created a certain insecurity in many as to the value of the older tradition.

295

assert, been constantly adapted to the changes in this belief motivated by more recent "revelations."

Finally, it is worth pointing out that the Orpheus tradition has generally had an advantage over other eschatological accounts—above all recent memorates—inasmuch as its telling has never been the subject of a taboo. We have, it is true, found earlier that in certain cases a taboo restricted in point of time has existed for the hero.[45] This taboo has not, however, been characteristic for the Orpheus tradition in general; instead, its hero has in many cases been charged by the powers ruling in the other world to tell the living what he has seen. And later generations have been free to recount the tale. One may compare this with the memorates: the recounting of the narrator's own experiences of the supernatural world is very often considered to entail his death. The Orpheus tale has not been burdened with such taboos, because it has passed from memorate to tradition and as such been intended, inter alia, to sanction the eschatological conceptions.

3. Etiological function of the tradition

At the same time as the Orpheus tradition has authorized the religious belief in a life after death it has in many places come to serve as an origin myth or origin legend for certain conditions in the natural environment and the cultural milieu of the tribes possessing it. On this subject Gayton writes: "The story of a Visit to the Afterworld answers the question: what is the fate of the dead, as well as the skeptic's request to know how man came by this knowledge. The Orpheus story, by far the more popular form, answers both these human queries, and at the same time satisfies two others. It supplies a motivation for the remarkable, the incredible journey, and explains why, since the dead live elsewhere, there can be no intercourse between the two worlds."[1] As we shall see, a number of other "explanations" are supplied by the Orpheus tradition. It has, in other words, functioned as an etiological narrative. To a certain extent one can also refer its function as sanction for the eschatology to this context. But it is in this case perhaps not quite legitimate to use the designation "etiological narrative": as a source

[45] See above, p. 137 note 88, and p. 291.
[1] Gayton 1935, 285.

for the eschatology the tradition fulfils a task that is congruent with its basic tendency, whereas the etiological elements are generally both secondary and incidental additions.[2]

Thus to begin with, the Orpheus tradition probably had no etiological function in the strict sense of the term to fulfil. Its etiological features have been later imposed upon it or automatically added when the tradition has been contaminated with some other tradition. In the following will be given a survey of the different explanatory elements in the Orpheus tradition. These are of extremely various character, some of them being rather inessential and irrelevant for the tradition as such, while others are more meaningfully connected with its main theme, and socially or culturally significant. As we shall find, no *aitia* are connected with the "sea-coast form." This has obviously not played the same important rôle in the mythology and the popular belief as the ordinary Orpheus tradition.

We shall here touch only lightly upon the above-mentioned rather meaningless explanatory motifs arbitrarily attached to the Orpheus tradition.

The Twana legend, which tells how the medicine-man Rat helped the Orpheus hero and the latter's deceased comrade to return to the world of the living, concludes with the information that "ever since then the rats come in the night to claim the reward for the rescue of the dead man."[3] The Snuqualmi myth about Pheasant's journey to the realm of the dead ends with the following words: "If Old Man Pheasant had brought all the children back, we should now have many pheasants with us."[4] This pronouncement may be regarded as a variation of the more common theme of the origin of death (see below). The Upper Puyallup myth describes how "the transformer," i.e. the culture hero, fails in his attempt to restore two children but succeeds in restoring one child to life. "For the future people it shall not be well to have two children at one time," he declares. "There shall be one child each time."[5] There are signs indicating that in older times the Puyallup, like so many other primitive peoples, not least in North America, put their twins to death.[6] A Skopamish myth which tells of Owl's descent to the realm of the dead gives the explanation of the nocturnal activities of owls:

[2] See Waterman 1914.
[3] Curtis 1913 IX, 164.
[4] Ballard 1929, 129.
[5] Ballard, op.cit., 131.
[6] Ballard, op.cit., 131 note 133. Cf., however, Smith 1940, 180 sqq.

297

"The owl is below at night when it is daylight in the graves."[7] Among the Wishram the fate of the dead in the Orpheus myth is intimately connected with the regulation of the seasons, as we shall soon see. The Orpheus legend of the Telumni Yokuts tells us that after his return home the hero was bitten by a rattlesnake and died. According to Dr. Gayton's informant, the story was told to children, so that they should not run far away from home and get bitten by rattlesnakes.[8]

All the cases recounted here have a westerly distribution, and if we except the Yokuts narrative—where the explanation does not belong to the actual narrative as such, but is added afterwards as an independent commentary—all the tales belong to the southernmost part of the Northwest Coast culture. It may thus on good grounds be assumed that we have here to do with a local myth-pattern, a local tendency to insert explanations of various phenomena in the myths.[9] But also east of the Rocky Mountains the same "loose" etiology does, in one case, occur: the Cherokee myth, according to which the daughter of the Sun flies out of the box in the shape of a redbird, becomes at the same time the origin tradition for these birds.[10]

Of a different character to the *aitia* so far mentioned are the cases in which the Orpheus tradition occurs as origin tale for the introduction of maize and other agrarian products. We have earlier touched upon this motif, pointing out that it has probably been taken from the fertility mythology closely akin to the Orpheus tradition.[11] Still closer to the main theme of the tradition come the *aitia* explaining the origin or inevitability of death, the right attitude to death, and the origin of certain rituals connected with the conceptions of death and of the dead. We shall here consider these more closely.

The Orpheus traditions which tell of the failure of the project not infrequently become tales recounting and explaining the origin of death, or the divorce between the living and the dead. The psychological prerequisites for this process have been indicated earlier; it was pointed out that the negative issue of the expedition might easily be generalized, the tale becomes, and not least thanks to its character of primeval and unique event, a tale of the dead in general.[12] One must not, how-

---

[7] Ballard, op.cit., 131.
[8] Gayton, op.cit., 269.
[9] Observe that Waterman, who has treated the etiological element in North America, took field experiences from precisely this area as his point of departure.
[10] Mooney 1900, 254.
[11] See above, pp. 146 sq., 268 sq.
[12] Cf. above, pp. 20, 119 sq., 122 sq.

ever, get the idea that this development took place automatically. The narratives of the origin of death and of the motifs connected herewith occur as an independent chain of tradition in North America, they had originally nothing to do with the Orpheus tradition.[13] The Orpheus tradition has been contaminated with these tales; its in many cases negative issue paved the way for the connection.[14] Before we set about analysing this more closely, however, we shall consider the forms taken by the idea within the Orpheus tradition.

The motif of the origin of death—or, more adequately expressed, the origin of the divorce between the living and the dead—occurs within the frame of the Orpheus tradition chiefly in north-western and south-eastern North America. The north-westerly instances come from the Plateau and the southernmost Northwest Coast, an area whose acquaintance we have already made several times as the milieu for a type of mythology of predominantly trickster character with strongly expansive tendencies. The Orpheus myths containing the motif here in question derive from the Sinkaietk, Kalispel, Yakima, Klikitat, Tenino, Nez Percé, Chehalis, Wishram and Wasco; the Shasta in California may be accounted a southern offshoot. One distinguishes the following groups stemming from this motif: 1. The inevitability of death is established. 2. The dead cannot return. 3. We cannot visit the dead. In all groups it is assumed that death has already taken place; it is thus in no case a matter of any myth proper concerning the origin of death; but it should be observed that even in the independent tales based on this motif the first death is often a fact before the supernatural powers decide upon death as the common lot of mankind.

The inevitability of death is constated in the Kalispel myth. It mentions Coyote's victorious game with the dead children in the realm of the dead and observes that the issue had fatal consequences. "The game in the lodge was to decide the question of life and death; had the children won, life would have conquered, and there would now be no death."[15] The Yakima myth concerning Coyote's and Eagle's journey to the beyond relates how Coyote quite deliberately desired the death of human beings. Eagle wanted to let them rise to new life, but Coyote "deemed it best after this that the dead should remain in the land of the dead."[16]

The majority of myths represent the catastrophic issue of the ex-

---

[13] Cf. Boas 1917 b, Dangel 1928.
[14] Cf. above, p. 143.
[15] Curtis 1911 VII, 97.
[16] Lyman 1904, 249.

pedition as the cause of the dead being unable to return.[17] When in the Sinkaietk tale Coyote has transgressed the taboo on coitus and thus lost his wife, the ruler of the dead declares: "If you did what I told you and didn't sleep with the woman until you got back, then when the Indians came, whenever anyone died, they could have come after him. But now you spoiled it."[18] The already cited Kalispel myth shows men's fate being decided when out of curiosity Coyote opens the bag he is carrying, so that all the dead in it disappear. "Did I not tell you not to look into the bag?" he hears his daughter cry. "If you had waited until you got home, you would have found your grandchildren [= mankind], but now you have lost them forever, and I am lost too!"[19] In the Orpheus myths among the Wishram, Wasco and Yakima Coyote destroys the chances for the dead to return in the same way, and his companion, Eagle, makes a remarkable pronouncement, which in a Wishram variant runs as follows: "If we had brought these dead all the way back, people would not die forever, but only for a season, like these plants, whose leaves we have brought. Hereafter trees and grasses will die only in the winter, but in the spring they will be green again. So it would have been with the people." As in the Orpheus legend of the Paviotso (see below), furthermore, the location of the land of the dead is moved, in order to render more difficult the communications between the living and the dead.[20]

In some cases it is Coyote or his peer, Bluejay, who in desparation at the failure to restore their own dead fling a curse on all mourners. "Babies shall die and go to the World of the Dead, and no one shall go to get them," declares the Chehalis Bluejay.[21] The Nez Percé myth puts a similar pronouncement in the mouths of the dead ("Henceforth when people die, they will be dead forever"), after which it goes on: "Then Coyote cried, and said, 'I shall not be the only one to mourn a child. All people shall do the same as I. When a person dies, they shall never see him again'."[22] In a Yakima variant Coyote rejects Eagle's proposal to make another attempt to restore the dead to life with the following words: "No, I am tired. Let the dead stay in the land of the dead forever and forever."[23]

[17] Thus among the Sinkaietk, Kalispel, Yakima, Klikitat, Tenino, Nez Percé, Wishram, Wasco; a diverging variant among the Snuqualmi, see above, p. 297. The Klikitat have the same motif also in the tale of "Skeleton-Baby" (see above, p. 173).

[18] Spier 1938, 236.

[19] Curtis, op.cit., loc.cit.

[20] Curtis 1911 VIII, 129.

[21] Adamson 1934, 29.

[22] Boas 1917 a, 179.

[23] Clark 1953, 195.

Finally, we have the group of myths which stress that on account of Orpheus' failure we are no longer able to visit the dead. We find this explanation among the Chehalis and the Shasta. The Shasta myth, which describes Coyote's unsuccessful attempt to bring home his son from the realm of the dead, concludes with the following words: "After that time, no one could follow after the dead to their country. It was as it is now."[24] The Humptulip myth (Chehalis) has the addition that also the dead are unable to visit us.[25]

This survey shows clearly that the motif of "death's origin" has been characteristic for the Orpheus traditions of the Plateau and coastal tribes. Nowhere else in North America does it so frequently occur in combination with the Orpheus theme as here. A part of the cause is doubtless to seek in the tendency found here to provide the tales with etiological commentaries (see above), but it is mainly to be sought in the circumstance that in this area the Orpheus tradition has the character of a primeval myth associated with the person of the culture hero-trickster; and every act performed by the latter forms a precedent, including the mistakes he commits as trickster—and as included in these mistakes we must probably account the definitive separation of the dead from the living. This motif has not crept into the Orpheus myth quite mechanically; one can observe how the latter has in a couple of points been altered. Thus it is typical that the myth often speaks of a number of dead persons that the hero tries to restore to life.[26] Sometimes these are presented as the close relatives of the culture hero. Thus the Kalispel speak of Coyote's grandchildren, by whom is obviously meant people in general. In complete conformity with this motif, the container in which the dead are fetched is represented as very roomy.[27]

Just to the south-east of the Plateau region we find the combination Orpheus tradition and tale of the divorce between the living and the dead among the Paviotso. The land of the dead, we are told, lay originally in a great valley, but after Orpheus' failure it was moved by "the Father" and his wife to a place over the water between the clouds, whence the dead can not return.[28] In southern and south-western North America we find the same origin-motif in the Orpheus legends in Zuni and Nayarit. The hero in the Zuni narrative loses his beloved when

[24] Dixon 1910, 19.
[25] Adamson, op.cit., 303. Cf. op.cit., 24 (Upper Chehalis).
[26] See above, p. 142. Among the Klamath and Modoc the bringing back of the dead to life is part of the endeavour by the culture hero or god to repopulate the world, an enterprise that he can carry out successfully.
[27] See above, p. 154.
[28] Gayton, op.cit., 278 (quotes W. Z. Park, Paviotso Field Notes).

he is on the way home with her through the infringement of a taboo; for this reason people cannot arise from the dead, and this is a good thing, as otherwise the world would be overpopulated.[29] In the Nayarit legend we are told that since the failure of Orpheus' project no soul in the land of the dead has been reunited with the living.[30]

The Southeast has possibly constituted another centre for Orpheus traditions with this secondary motif. We may cite tales of this type from the Alabama, Cherokee and Pawnee—the latter, like other Caddoan tribes, probably had an at least partly cultural origin in the southern civilization that lingered for a long time among the peoples of the Southeast. The Pawnee legend describing a father's desperate attempt to recover his deceased son concludes with the following words: "So he was forgotten; for had he not caught his son and held him so long, then the spirits and the people were to have lived once more together, and death was to have been unknown."[31] In one of the Alabama versions it is stated that on account of the failure of the Orpheus men the dead cannot return to the earth.[32] Similar information is given in the Cherokee myth reproduced by Mooney, earlier analysed in detail.[33] Here we are told that "if the men [= those fetching the daughter of the Sun] had kept the box closed, as the Little Men told them to do, they would have brought her home safely, and we could bring back our other friends also from the Ghost country, but now when they die we can never bring them back."[34] In one variant, on the other hand, it is pointed out that it was the intention of the creators—who are "a number of beings"—that people should live for ever. "But the Sun, when he passed over, told them that there was not land enough and that people had better die."[35] However, the Sun's own daughter was the first to die.

As we have seen, the traditions of this type outside the Plateau area are, with one exception—the Cherokee—, not myths, but legends. It is difficult to show the existence of any historical connection between the Plateau myths and the other tales. Rather is it the case that the independent traditions concerning the origin of death in the different regions have served as prototypes. Sometimes, too, one can see how the tales of the origin of death have been entirely incorporated with the Orpheus tradition. Boas has shown that the whole of western North America

[29] Cushing 1931, 32.
[30] Bancroft 1875 III, 530.
[31] Dorsey 1904 b, 78.
[32] Swanton 1929, 143.
[33] See chap. IV: 4.
[34] Mooney 1900, 254.
[35] Mooney, op.cit., 436. In this variant the Sun is a male being.

is dominated by one myth based on the motif of the origin of death, and this myth describes how two supernatural beings decide man's fate. The myth exists in two forms, a western and an eastern one. In the more westerly form the two exalted beings come to an agreement after a discussion, where the party with the negative attitude triumphs through his obstinacy; in the more easterly form the decision is arrived at through divination.[36] Now the foregoing collection of instances shows that both these forms of the myth have been absorbed by the Orpheus tradition, though not precisely according to the geographic distribution indicated above. Thus the first-mentioned form of the myth, the decision by agreement, occurs in the Orpheus tales of the Yakima and Cherokee, while the other form of the myth, the decision through divination, is found in the Orpheus narrative of the Kalispel. The motif according to which the decease referred to constitutes the first in the world, which plays such a great rôle in the myths concerning the origin of death, occurs separately in the Orpheus tales of the Nisenan, Navajo and Yuchi.[37] It should, finally, be pointed out that the combination of the Orpheus tale with the tale of the origin of death is, as far as I have been able to ascertain, peculiar to North America.[38] It is, of course, psychologically natural; behind both narratives lies what Boas has drawn attention to concerning the myth of the origin of death, "the desire to see the dead alive again."[39]

The Karuk Orpheus legend shows a variation of the motif of the origin of death: the two girls who have followed their lovers to the realm of the dead are charged by the dead on their return to take with them "salmon backbone meat" to their home country, and then, as soon as anyone dies, to smear him round the mouth with it. "Then nobody will die any more." For some time thereafter there are no deaths. But soon the supernatural specific comes to an end, and herewith the deaths begin again.[40] Here it is immortality considered as medicine that is taken back to the living. We have earlier adduced another legend, in which immortality is the longed-for heavenly treasure that the representative of human life tries to gain: the legend of the Ojibway Indian

---

[36] Boas 1917 b, 490.
[37] In the introduction to the Yuchi legend noted down by Speck the four heroes resolve to kill their wives. They do so, and thereby introduce death to the earth (Speck 1909, 144).
[38] Abrahamsson's list of myths concerning the origin of death in Africa shows no connection between these myths and any tradition based on the Orpheus motif (Abrahamsson 1951).
[39] Boas 1915, 348.
[40] Harrington 1932, 34.

Ogauns.[41] The same motif also appears in another north-eastern legend, viz., in a tale from the Montagnais communicated by Le Jeune; this is reminiscent now of the Orpheus motif, now of the myth of Pandora: "Our Savage related to Father Brebœuf that his people believe that a certain Savage had received from Messou the gift of immortality in a little package, with a strict injunction not to open it; while he kept it closed he was immortal, but his wife, being curious and incredulous, wished to see what was inside this present; and having opened it, it all flew away, and since then the Savages have been subject to death."[42] Thwaites compares this legend with the Micmac Orpheus tale.[43] One can, however, scarcely characterize it as a corrupted Orpheus tradition, even if it has the container motif in common with many tales based on the Orpheus motif.

On the other hand, the resemblance between the gift of immortality and the beloved deceased in the Orpheus tradition is obvious. In those Orpheus traditions which also include the motif of the origin of death "Eurydice" becomes a symbol for immortality, which with her return to the dead is forever lost for mankind.

At the same time as in this way the Orpheus tradition frequently stresses that death is inevitable because Orpheus failed to bring home the deceased from the realm of the dead, it seeks to regulate our behaviour in the face of this fact of reality. The Orpheus legend of the Lipan Apache gives us a salutary reminder not to fear death. "Now I'm not afraid to die," says the man who has just visited the land of the dead. "I've seen the place. I know it's a good place."[44] This was the happy message of the Orpheus tradition to many tribes.

The grief over the departure of a loved person may be heavy, but it is dangerous to abandon oneself to it, opine the Zuni Indians. One of their Orpheus tales ends with an account of the way in which Orpheus pines away with weeping at the supernatural lake in which his wife has vanished. "And that is why, when a husband or wife dies, we tell the one who is left not to weep or he will die soon."[45] The two heroines in the Karuk Orpheus legend, on the other hand, are said to have been the originators of a popular saying with almost the contrary import: "They are the ones that said it: 'I do not care how bad one feels over his dead one; he will never die for that. When he gets sick, then

[41] See above, pp. 31, 142.
[42] JR VI, 159.
[43] JR VI, 328 note 17.
[44] Opler 1940, 101.
[45] Benedict 1935 II, 134.

he will die.' It is talk of long ago: 'One will not die, I do not care how bad he feels for his dead one, he will think that he is going to die but he will not die'."[46]

In the course of time the Orpheus tradition has in addition acquired a third important etiological function: it has become a "cultic" narrative, origin myth or origin legend for present-day ritual. It tells us how the ritual "dances"—read: ceremonies—originated through which people can recover from illness, and it sanctions their use. The Orpheus tradition is, certainly, not the only eschatological narrative that fulfils this function. The reader may here be reminded that in the Ojibway medicine society *midewiwin* the initiation to the *mide*-dignity follows a pattern going back to the culture hero Minabozho's visit to the land of the dead, "land of the sleeping sun." According to the tradition Minabozho penetrated to this country "to destroy the 'Ghost Gambler' and to liberate the many victims who had fallen into his power." The initiate to the medicine society is identified with the culture hero, his actions in the sacred lodge, *midewigan,* reflect Minabozho's in the realm of the dead.[47]

No eschatological tradition in North America has, however, meant more than the Orpheus tradition as a cultic origin tradition. It nowhere occurs, it is true, as a ritual text, as a continuous commentary to a cultic act. But it figures as the ultimate cause of such an act. The connection is, as has been mentioned, not original, but has been added afterwards. Either the Orpheus narrative has been intercalated in an earlier origin tale, or else it has been made the object of a new interpretation.

The first of these alternatives is the case with the Navajo Orpheus myth, which constitutes a part of the origin myth of the curing ceremony Upward-Reaching Way. Its ritual "attacks the ghosts of deceased natives and was and is the first chantway with this exclusive purpose."[48] The ceremony includes, inter alia, a phase in which the patient and the singer recite a prayer of liberation, "talking (to return) upward or out of a lower place." Its aim is to "talk the ghost down into ghostland and then to lead the patient upward restored from its spell."[49] The Navajo Orpheus myth describes how the deceased "woman speaker's" husband seeks his wife in the land of the dead but is then obliged to fly thence.

---

[46] Harrington, op.cit., loc.cit. Cf. op.cit., 31 note 66, 33 note 77.
[47] Hoffman 1891, 280.
[48] Haile 1942, 415 sq.
[49] Haile, op.cit., 417. Cf. Wyman & Bailey 1943, 42.

Upward-Reaching Way connects up with this tale. The liberation of "woman speaker's" husband from the realm of the dead "typifies what mortals should do when inhabitants of ghostland 'bother' them," declares Haile. And he adds that "the 'upward-return-prayer' as provided in Upward-reaching-way alone will remedy that condition."[50]

In one of the Zuni legends we are told how after the return from the dead Orpheus' wife slept in the daytime and was awake at night. He then gave her to the medicine society Ciwanakwe. "They held their ceremony and danced all night." The woman was then instructed to refrain from eating meat for four days and not to sleep with her husband for four nights. She followed the instructions and became normal again. "That is why, when people are sick, they join a medicine society."[51]

As Gayton has observed, the Orpheus tale on the Plains has been influenced by a literary pattern that is rather common there: "without suffering any major alteration the story is made to account for the origin of a ceremony or sacred object by simply having the hero receive these as gifts in the afterworld."[52] The sacred objects are mentioned in the Orpheus tales among the Pawnee and the Blackfoot. In one Pawnee legend the dead hand over to the Orpheus hero a sacred bundle with the appropriate ceremony.[53] The Blackfoot Orpheus legend is said to illustrate "how the people came to possess the Worm Pipe." This sacred pipe, which was the ghosts' gift to Orpheus and his wife, was brought home by them and given to the Piegan band bearing the name "the Worm People."[54] The Pawnee and Blackfoot tales thus represent the dead as appearing in a very atypical rôle: they show such benevolence to Orpheus that they even hand over their dearest possessions to him. It is obvious that this representation of the attitude of the dead is not original, but a by-product of the etiological motive.

We have, finally, the numerous testimonies, both from the Plains and elsewhere, to the effect that the Orpheus tradition has functioned as origin tale for a religious ceremony or rite, a "dance." These dances and their import have been described in the foregoing.[55] It appeared that some of them are identical with the so-called ghost dance, which at the end of the last century swept over California, Great Basin, the Plateau and the Plains as a reaction against the supremacy of the whites and the decay of indigenous cultures. Behind the ghost-dance

[50] Haile, op.cit., 420.
[51] Benedict 1935 II, 158.
[52] Gayton 1935, 284.
[53] Dorsey 1904 b, 76, 77.
[54] Grinnell 1912, 131.
[55] See above, pp. 124, 145 sqq., 261 sqq.

movement one can, however, discern an older stratum, a dance connected with shamanistic experiences and rites and intended to restore the seriously ill to life. This dance is found preserved among the Sarcee and Winnebago, and is among them intimately connected with the Orpheus tale, which is its origin tradition. It is not hard to see in what way the narrative and the rite have been connected with each other: in remote times there must have been a contamination between the Orpheus tradition and tales (memorates?) concerning the initiation visions of shamans.[56] In the vision in which the shaman is called to his vocation he has received a rite, a dance, intended to be performed in connection with the curing of the sick. The Orpheus narrative, which goes back to shamanistic experiences, has come to be accepted as the narrative of this shaman's experiences, and has as such become the origin tale of the rite. In later times, when the rite for the curing of the sick has merged into a rite for the return of the dead, the Orpheus tradition has in some quarters automatically become the "institution myth" of the ghost dance.

[56] See above, p. 259.

SUMMARY AND CONCLUSIONS

It has been the author's intention in the present work to investigate the North American Orpheus tradition from comparative religious viewpoints; the literary analysis has already been given by A. H. Gayton. Attention has been directed above all to the original import of the Orpheus tradition and to its general significance as a document for comparative religious research. To attain full clarity in these respects I have at the same time presented the whole of the ethnographic-folkloristic material from North America containing the Orpheus motif, weeded out irrelevant tales and analysed the remaining, relevant material (listed in the appendix, see below).

In the first chapter the Orpheus tradition in North America is scrutinized from general points of departure. The narrative of the man or woman who sets out for the realm of the dead to bring back a recently deceased loved one, only, as a rule, to fail in this—for so the content of the tradition may be defined—occurs in large parts of North America, though the distribution is concentrated mainly to the western parts of the country.[1] In its plot and motif-cycle the tale is relatively constant, at the same time as it is well integrated with the different culture-milieus in which it occurs and in consequence of which it shows special local forms (oikotypes). The most remarkable of these is without doubt the so-called "sea-coast form," which is of widespread occurrence in the Northwest Coast culture. It is strictly speaking a formally independent tale associated with the notion of the abode of the drowned among the marine beings; but in point of structure and content of ideas it coincides with the commoner Orpheus tradition which is here distinguished from it by the term "inland form."

To come to closer grips with the problem the author proceeds in the second chapter to a collocation and analysis of the more important or from the comparative religious viewpoint more remarkable motifs. Among the phenomenologically interesting features connecting the Orpheus tale with other eschatological descriptions from North America belong the obstacle motifs on the journey to the land of the dead and the guardian and the chief of the dead, the latter personage often a divinity (creator-god, mother-goddess, twin-god). The other world itself may be of varying character, but is generally a happy place—a characteristic feature for the Orpheus tradition. A number of details reflect the connection of the Orpheus tradition with dream and trance experiences: ritual vigil, visions of supernatural beings (guardian spirits) and the acquisition of supernatural power are here chiefly to be mentioned. A consistent feature is the great difference in essence between the living, personified by the Orpheus hero, and the dead, represented by "Eurydice" and the ghosts in the land of the dead. This distance leads to oppositions, manifested in, inter alia, the resistance to Orpheus' plans by the dead, and their pursuit of him on his journey home. Of interest is the rôle played by the dance as a corporate factor among the dead.

Certain circumstances attending the start of the journey and its termination throw an explanatory light over the situation reflected by the Orpheus tradition. In order to be able to follow the deceased, Orpheus sometimes submits to a "sham burial" with her, i.e. he lies down by her side; and the return to life is often conceived to take place as a resurrection from the grave—or in a closed lodge, e.g. a sweat-lodge. The scene appears to have a ritual character and may be designated as an example of homeopathic magic: when Orpheus lies down by the side of the deceased he is transported to her world; when he rises from the grave the deceased returns to life. Sometimes we are told that the deceased is brought home in a diminutive form in a container. In certain versions the receptacle contains the spiritual constituent parts of the deceased, the soul and the life. Another typical feature is that the revivification takes the form of a slow, progressive process of "normalization," corresponding to the convalescence and recovery of a seriously ill person. The process is jeopardized if certain of the taboos imposed by the powers of the other world are infringed. In other words, the many different taboo prescriptions of the Orpheus tradition are intended to protect the person restored to life, i.e. in reality the seriously ill person, from various dangers like a blow or a shock etc.

The next stage in the investigation comprises historical, psychological and sociological analysis. In the historical analysis in the third chapter it is at first established that the Orpheus tradition constitutes an independent narrative in a fixed mould that has not been decisively influenced by other tales in North America, though in form and content many of the latter come rather close to it. It is further constated that there is no decisive evidence in favour of the assumption that the North American Orpheus tradition is an offshoot of the coherent block of Eurasiatic Orpheus tales, even if it is not possible to rule out the possibility of a connection between the American and the Oceanic tales. In these circumstances the history of the Orpheus tradition in North America must be reconstructed against an American background alone, and on the assumption of a relative formal constancy throughout. There are many indications that the tradition originally arose in a shamanistic hunting milieu, and that it was distributed over North America before the agrarian culture spread from the south. When southern North America adopted an agrarian economy the Orpheus tales existing here were suppressed or transformed.

In the fourth chapter an attempt is made to establish the origin and development of the Orpheus tradition with the aid of historical, sociological and psychological criteria. If we proceed on the assumption that the milieu is that of the shamanistic hunting community and that the tale is based upon a person's actual experiences in psychic twilight states—various data indicate this, as shown above—and at the same time subject the tradition in its older and younger forms to a phenomenological analysis, we arrive at the following schema for its development:

1. The oldest Orpheus tale was probably the narrative of a shaman's ecstatic journey to the land of the dead to fetch the soul of a seriously ill person (possibly one in a state of suspended animation). The so-called "sham burial" or imitative burial mentioned in the Orpheus tradition represents the shamanistic rite in its final phase, the ecstasy, while the container motif also mentioned in the tradition corresponds to the so-called soul-catcher or soul-tube, an instrument (for the most part in the form of a hollow tube) into which the shaman stuffs the soul of the sick person after catching it. The container motif belongs to a younger form of genuine shamanism ("demonstrative shamanization") and, moreover, also to a later version of the Orpheus tradition.—Probably the main personages in the prototypical rite stood in a romantic or blood relationship with each other, which has facilitated the formation of the legend.

2. Through the so-called democratized shamanism widespread in North America (the guardian-spirit quest, puberty-visions) it has been possible to keep alive the understanding for the basic experiences of the

Orpheus tale, and the tale has herewith been preserved in a form reflecting the original experience.

3. The tale has, however, also been modified and reinterpreted to conform with new viewpoints. Thus in many quarters Orpheus' experiences have been rendered as adventures in a comatose state caused by deep grief, and in the agrarian cultures the tale has been understood in conformity with or has been contaminated by the fertility myths. To a certain extent the latter have also incorporated elements from the Orpheus tradition (flight motif).

The North American Orpheus tradition is of interest for comparative religious research not only because it goes back to a religio-magic situation, an ecstatic shamanization procedure, but also because it constitutes a valuable documentary contribution to our knowledge of Indian religious conceptions, in the first place Indian eschatology. While space has not permitted of an all-round presentation of this eschatology in the form in which it is given in the Orpheus tradition,[2] the fifth chapter is devoted to some more important viewpoints concerning the function of the tradition as a source for the eschatology and for certain rites connected with this, in the first place the ghost dance. It has emerged that the Orpheus tradition has by the Indians themselves been understood as a true account of the life after this—it is myth or legend, not fairy-tale—, and a closer investigation has shown that its eschatology coincides in the main with that of the popular belief (also indirect evidence may be adduced in this connection: the cultural integration is an important criterion of the adaptation of the tradition to the religious conceptual pattern). Its function is above all to sanction the eschatology, even if there are, in addition to it, both other traditions and recent memorates fulfilling the same function. At the same time the Orpheus tradition has an etiological function: it explains the origin of death and constitutes the origin tale for the well-known 19th century revivalist movement among the Indians of North America, the so-called ghost dance.

The connection with the ghost dance is not new. As I have tried to show, the ghost dance is probably traceable to an older rite with the same name, which was used in the curing of the sick. The story of the origin of this rite or "dance" was incorporated in the Orpheus tale when in remote times a contamination occurred between the Orpheus tradition and narratives of shamans' initiation visions. The cause of the contamination is to seek in the common shamanistic background. To this may be added the observation that in shamanism the curing of a sick

[2] See, however, chap. II: 3—4.

person often implies a "dance," and that the dance in the Elysian fields is a frequently recurring feature in the original Orpheus tale.

The Orpheus tradition may thus be said, according to the interpretation presented here, to have arisen on the basis of an extraordinary ecstatic experience, which, via memorates, has been transformed to tradition. It is, however, obvious that it is the epic frame that has its origin in dreams and visions, and it is only in exceptional cases that the individual motifs have this origin.[3] The Orpheus tradition can thus not have added many new elements to the eschatological notions over and above what was already known in the popular belief. Rather do its significance and peculiar character in this connection reside in the fact that it has modified already existing material and welded it into a whole which, thanks to the dramatic and romantic plot, has become an unusually graphic and vivid presentation of the afterworld.

[3] See above, pp. 75 sqq. Cf. also Swahn 1955, 412.

APPENDIX

Table of sources of the North American Orpheus tales

The Orpheus tales listed here have in chap. I: 3 been described as relevant or almost so; a number of dubious cases have been noted in the foot-notes. Other traditions, noted by Barbeau, Gayton or Thompson, which according to the foregoing investigation cannot be considered to possess the character of the genuine Orpheus narrative, have not been included. Orpheus traditions of the type "sea-coast form" (see chap. I: 4) are marked with an asterisk.

Alabama: Swanton 1929, 141—142, 142—143.

Assiniboin: Lowie 1909 b, 168—169.

Bella Bella: see Rivers Inlet.

Bella Coola: Boas 1895 b, 259*.

Blackfoot: Grinnell 1912, 127—131.

Carrier: Jenness 1934, 143—145.

Chehalis: Adamson 1934, 21—24, 24—27, 27—28, 29, 293—303, 349—350.

Cherokee: Mooney 1900, 252—254.

Comanche: Linton—see above, chap. I: 1.

Cowichan: see Nanaimo, Stalo.

(Fox: Jones 1907 a, 207—211.[1])

Gabrielino: Reid 1926, 40—44; Kroeber 1925, 625.

Haida: Deans 1899, 71—75*; Swanton 1905 a, 244—247*, 338—340*; Swanton 1905 b, 202—203*, 220*; Swanton 1908 a, 495—500*; Barbeau 1953, 290—295*, 295—296*.

Haisla, see Kitlobe.

Hupa: Goddard 1903, 74.

Huron: JR X, 149—153 (=Brébeuf 1636). Cf. Wyandot!

Kalapuya: Frachtenberg, Gatschet & Jacobs 1945, 199—203 (Yamhill), 226—236 (Mary's River).

Kalispel: Curtis 1911 VII, 95—97.

Karuk: Harrington 1932, 31—34; Kroeber 1946, 14—15, 15—17; de Angulo & Freeland 1931, 212—221; Olden 1923, 102—105.

---

[1] The tale entitled "Painter's dream" contains Orpheus elements and is of Orpheus type, but can in itself scarcely be classified as an Orpheus legend. The main personage, who is the grandfather of the informant, falls down from a tree, and his spirit wanders to the world of the dead, there meeting with a woman he had loved long ago. It is, however, never a matter of her restoration to life. Nonetheless, the possibility remains that, as Gayton presumes, the tale was shaped according to the pattern of an Orpheus tradition unknown to us, and for this reason it has been listed here.

Kitlobe (Haisla): McIlwraith 1948 I, 508—510.

Klamath: Spier, *Klamath Tales*, Ms. (see Gayton 1935, 279).

Klikitat: Jacobs 1929, 227—231; Jacobs 1934 I, 55, 190.

Koasati: Swanton 1929, 189—190.

Kwakiutl: Boas 1910 a, 445—447.

Lipan Apache: Opler 1940, 100—101.[2]

Malecite: Mechling 1914, 88—90.

Menomini: Bloomfield 1928, 125—129.

Micmac: Le Clercq 1910, 208—213.

Miwok: Hudson 1902, 106.

Modoc: Curtin 1912, 40—45.

Mohave: Devereux 1948, 249—252.[3]

Montagnais: see Micmac.

Nanaimo: Boas 1895 b, 55*.

Navajo: Haile 1942, 411—414; Hill, *Navajo Field Notes*, Ms. (see Gayton 1935, 271).

Nayarit: Bancroft 1875 III, 529—530.

Nez Percé: see Shahaptin.

Nisenan: Powers 1877, 339—340.

Nootka: Sapir & Swadesh 1939, 63—67*.

Ojibway: Jenness 1935, 109.

Ottawa: Schoolcraft 1851 I, 321—323.

Paviotso: Park, *Paviotso Field Notes*, Ms. (see Gayton 1935, 277—278).

Pawnee: Dorsey 1904 b, 71—73, 74 —78; Dorsey 1906, 411—413, 536 —537.

Pomo: Loeb 1926, 292—293; Barrett 1933, 379.

Puyallup: Ballard 1929, 129, 131.

Quinault: Farrand 1902, 100—102.

Rivers Inlet (Bella Bella): Barbeau 1950 I, 289*.

Sanpoil: Boas 1917 a, 112—113 (M. K. Gould).

Sarcee: Jenness 1938, 97—98.

Sechelt: Hill-Tout 1904 b, 52—54.

Seneca: Curtin & Hewitt 1918 II, 570 —573.

Serrano: Benedict 1926, 8—9.

Shahaptin (Nez Percé): Boas 1917 a, 178—179 (L. Farrand).

Shasta: Dixon 1910, 19, 21; Voegelin 1947, 52—53.

Shawnee: Gregg 1954, 387—388; Voegelin 1936, 5.[4]

Shoshoni: Steward 1943, 287.

Sinkaietk: Spier 1938, 235—236.

Skopamish: Ballard 1929, 129—130, 130, 131, 132—133.

Snuqualmi: Ballard 1929, 128—129.

Stalo: Hill-Tout 1904 a, 339—341.

Taos: Parsons 1940, 23—27, 27—28.

Tenino: Murdock, *Tenino Field Notes*, Ms. (see Gayton 1935, 278).

Thompson (River): Teit 1898, 84—85; Teit 1912 a, 379.

Tlingit: Swanton 1909, 249—250; op.cit., 26—27*, 215—217*.

Tolowa: Barnett 1937, 185.

Tsimshian: Boas 1912, 147—192*; Boas 1895 b, 299*; Krause 1885, 275 —278*; Barbeau 1950 I, 279—280*, 282—283*; Barbeau 1953, 269—273*, 280—284*.

---

[2] This tradition has with a certain hesitation been classed among the Orpheus tales. See the motivation in chap. IV: 1.

[3] Also this tradition can only with much hesitation be designated as an Orpheus tradition. See further chap. I: 2.

[4] Gregg's work was published for the first time in 1844 (Orpheus legend, 239—40). Voegelin 1936, like Gayton 1935, bases his assumptions upon unpublished field-notes by E. W. Voegelin.

Tübatulabal: Voegelin 1935, 203—205.

Tututni: Barnett 1937, 185.

Twana: Curtis 1913 IX, 163—164.

Wasco: Spier & Sapir 1930, 277—278.

Western Mono: Gifford 1923, 340—341.[5]

Wichita: Dorsey 1904 a, 300—305, 306—310.

Winnebago: Radin 1926, 33—37.

Wishram: Sapir 1909 b, 107—117; Curtis 1911 VIII, 126—129.

Wyandot: Spence 1914, 260—262.

Yakima: Lyman 1904, 248—249; G. B. Kuykendall in Evans 1889 II, 80; Clark 1953, 193—195.

Yokuts: Hudson 1902, 104—105, 105; Kroeber 1907 c, 216—218, 228; Gayton 1930 a, 77—78; Gayton 1935, 267—269.

Yuchi: Speck 1909, 108, 144—146; Wagner 1931, 82—89.

Yurok: Kroeber 1925, 47.

Zuni: Cushing 1931, 18—32; Parsons 1916, 250; Benedict 1935 II, 133—134, 157—158, 288—289, 299.

[5] See also under Yokuts.

ABBREVIATIONS

Aa	Aarne-Thompson's classification of folktales.
AA	American Anthropologist. Washington, New York, Lancaster, Menasha.
AA (O.S.)	American Anthropologist, Old Series.
AAPF	Annales de l'Association de la Propagation de la Foi. Paris.
AAR	Annual Archaeological Report. Toronto.
AH	Anthropological Handbooks, American Museum of Natural History. New York.
AMNHHS	American Museum of Natural History, Handbook Series. New York.
ANA	Anthropology in North America, by Franz Boas et al. New York 1915.
APAM	Anthropological Papers of the American Museum of Natural History. New York.
AR	Anthropological Records. Berkeley & Los Angeles.
ARBAE	Annual Reports of the Bureau of American Ethnology. Washington D.C.
ARSI	Annual Reports of the Board of Regents of the Smithsonian Institution. Washington D.C.
ARW	Archiv für Religionswissenschaft. Leipzig.
BAAS	Reports of the Meetings of the British Association for the Advancement of Science. London, etc.
BAMNH	Bulletins of the American Museum of Natural History. New York.
BBAE	Bulletins of the Bureau of American Ethnology. Washington D.C.
BCDM	Bulletins (and Annual Reports) of the Canada Department of Mines, National Museum of Canada. Ottawa.
BCIS	Bulletins of the Cranbrook Institute of Science. Bloomfield Hills, Mich.
BFMUP	Bulletins of the Free Museum of Science and Arts, University of Pennsylvania. Philadelphia.
BMB	Bernice P. Bishop Museum Bulletins. Honolulu, Hawaii.
BPMCM	Bulletins of the Public Museum of the City of Milwaukee. Milwaukee.
CED	Culture Element Distributions (Berkeley).
CIWP	Carnegie Institution of Washington, Publications. Washington D.C.
CMAI	Contributions from the Museum of the American Indian, Heye Foundation. New York.
CNAE	Contributions to North American Ethnology, U.S. Geographical and Geological Survey of the Rocky Mountain Region. Washington D.C.
CUAS	Catholic University of America, Anthropological Series. Washington D.C.
CUCA	Columbia University Contributions to Anthropology. New York.
EPS	Essays Presented to C. G. Seligman, ed. by E. E. Evans-Pritchard, R. W. Firth, B. Malinowski & I. Schapera. London 1934.
ERE	Encyclopaedia of Religion and Ethics. Edinburgh.
ES	Ethnologische Studien. Leipzig.

316

FFC	FF Communications. Helsingfors.
FL	Folklore. London.
GSA	General Series in Anthropology. Menasha.
HSAI	Handbook of South American Indians, ed. by J. H. Steward. I—VI. BBAE 143. Washington D.C. 1946—50.
HTR	Harvard Theological Review. Cambridge, Mass.
IAE	Internationales Archiv für Ethnographie. Leiden.
ICA	Proceedings of the International Congress of Americanists. Paris etc.
IJAL	International Journal of American Linguistics. New York & Bloomington.
IN	Indian Notes, Museum of the American Indian, Heye Foundation. New York.
INM	Indian Notes and Monographs, Museum of the American Indian, Heye Foundation. New York.
JAFL	Journal of American Folklore. Boston, New York, Richmond (Virg.).
JR	Jesuit Relations and Allied Documents. Travels and Explorations of the Jesuit Missionaries in New France 1610—1791, ed. by Reuben Gold Thwaites. Vols. I—LXXIII. Cleveland 1896—1901.
JRAI	Journal of the Royal Anthropological Institute of Great Britain and Ireland. London.
JSAP	Journal de la Société des Américanistes. Paris.
KDVSS	Det Kongelige Danske Videnskabernes Selskabs Skrifter. Copenhagen.
MAAA	Memoirs of the American Anthropological Association. Lancaster, Menasha.
MAES	Monographs of the American Ethnological Society. New York.
MAFLS	Memoirs of the American Folklore Society. Boston, New York.
MAGW	Mitteilungen der Anthropologischen Gesellschaft. Wien.
MAMNH	Memoirs of the American Museum of Natural History. New York.
MAR	Mythology of All Races, ed. by. J. A. MacCulloch. Boston.
MCDM	Memoirs of the Canada Department of Mines, Geological Survey. Ottawa.
MIJAL	Memoirs of the International Journal of American Linguistics. Baltimore.
NYSMB	New York State Museum Bulletins. Albany.
OAHQ	Ohio Archaeological and Historical Quarterly. Columbus.
OCMA	Occasional Contributions from the Museum of Anthropology of the University of Michigan. Ann Arbor.
PAES	Publications of the American Ethnological Society. New York.
PCI	Proceedings of the Canadian Institute. Toronto.
PCS	Publications of the Champlain Society. Toronto.
PM	Primitive Man. Washington D.C.
PPFA	Papers of the Robert S. Peabody Foundation for Archaeology. Andover, Mass.
RGG	Die Religion in Geschichte und Gegenwart. 2. and 3. eds. Tübingen.
RHR	Revue de l'Histoire des Religions. Paris.
RLC	Race, Language and Culture, by Franz Boas. New York 1940.
ROB	Religion och Bibel. Nathan Söderblom-sällskapets årsbok. Uppsala.
RUSNM	Reports of the United States National Museum. Washington D.C.
SCK	Smithsonian (Institution) Contributions to Knowledge. Washington D.C.
SEMMS	Statens Etnografiska Museum, Monograph Series. Stockholm.
SEU	Studia Ethnographica Upsaliensia. Uppsala.
SM	Scientific Monthly. New York.
SMC	Smithsonian (Institution) Miscellaneous Collections. Washington D.C.

317

SP	Sherman Pamphlets. Riverside, Calif.
SWJ	Southwestern Journal of Anthropology. Albuquerque.
TASJ	Transactions of the Asiatic Society of Japan. Yokohama & Tokyo.
UCP	University of California Publications in American Archaeology and Ethnology. Berkeley & Los Angeles.
UNMB	University of New Mexico Bulletins, Anthropological Series. Albuquerque.
UNMPA	University of New Mexico Publications in Anthropology. Albuquerque.
UOMSA	University of Oregon Monographs, Studies in Anthropology. Eugene, Oregon.
UPMAP	University of Pennsylvania Museum Anthropological Publications. Philadelphia.
UUÅ	Uppsala Universitets Årsskrift. Uppsala.
UWPA	University of Washington Publications in Anthropology. Seattle.
YUPA	Yale University Publications in Anthropology. New Haven.
ZE	Zeitschrift für Ethnologie. Berlin.

BIBLIOGRAPHY

Aarne, Antti
  1930. Die magische Flucht. FFC 92.
Aarne, A., & Thompson, S.
  1928. The Types of the Folk-tale in World Literature. A Classification and Bibliography. FFC 74.
Abrahamsson, Hans
  1951. The Origin of Death. Studies in African Mythology. SEU 3.
Ackerknecht, Erwin H.
  1949. Medical Practices. HSAI V.
Adam, Leonhard
  1923. Nordwest-amerikanische Indianerkunst. Orbis Pictus 17. Berlin.
Adamson, Thelma
  1934. Folk-tales of the Coast Salish. MAFLS 27.
Aginsky, Burt W.
  1943. Central Sierra. AR 8: 4 (CED XXIV).
Alexander, H. B.
  1916. North American Mythology. MAR 10.
  1953. The World's Rim: Great Mysteries of the North American Indians. Lincoln.
Andræ, Tor
  1926. Mystikens psykologi. Uppsala.
Anesaki, Masaharu
  1928. Japanese Mythology. MAR 8.
de Angulo, J., & Freeland, L. S.
  1931. Karok Texts. IJAL 6.
Arbman, Ernst
  1927—28. Tod und Unsterblichkeit im vedischen Glauben. ARW 25—26.
  1939. Mythic and Religious Thought. In: Dragma, Martino P. Nilsson ... dedicatum. Lund.
  1955. Shamanen, extatisk andebesvärjare och visionär. In: Primitiv Religion och Magi, ed. by Å. Hultkrantz, Stockholm 1955.
Ballard, Arthur C.
  1929. Mythology of Southern Puget Sound. UWPA 3: 2.
Bancroft, H. H.
  1875—76. The Native Races of the Pacific States of North America. I—V. London & New York.
Bar, Francis
  1946. Les Routes de l'autre monde. Mythes et Religions 17. Paris.
Barbeau, C. M.
  1915. Huron and Wyandot Mythology. MCDM 80.
  1950. Totem Poles. I—II. BCDM 119.
  1952. The Old-World Dragon in America. In: Tax 1952.
  1953. Haida Myths Illustrated in Argillite Carvings. BCDM 127.

319

Barnett, H. G.
1937. Oregon Coast. AR 1: 3 (CED VII).
1939. Gulf of Georgia Salish. AR 1: 5 (CED IX).
1955. The Coast Salish of British Columbia. UOMSA 4.

Barrett, S. A.
1933. Pomo Myths. BPMCM 15.

Bascom, W. R.
1953. Folklore and Anthropology. JAFL 66.
1954. Four Functions of Folklore. JAFL 67.

Baumann, Hermann
1955. Das doppelte Geschlecht. Ethnologische Studien zur Bisexualität in Ritus und Mythos. Berlin.

Bayard, S. P.
1953. The Materials of Folklore. JAFL 66.

Beaglehole, Ernest & Pearl
1935. Hopi of the Second Mesa. MAAA 44.

Beals, Ralph L.
1933. Ethnology of the Nisenan. UCP 31: 6.

Beauchamp, W. M.
1897. The New Religion of the Iroquois. JAFL 10.
1898. Indian Corn Stories and Customs. JAFL 11.

Becker, E. J.
1899. A Contribution to the Comparative Study of the Medieval Visions of Heaven and Hell. Baltimore.

Beckwith, Martha Warren
1930. Mythology of the Oglala Dakota. JAFL 43.
1938. Mandan-Hidatsa Myths and Ceremonies. MAFLS 32.

Bendann, E.
1930. Death Customs. London.

Benedict, Ruth Fulton
1922. The Vision in Plains Culture. AA 24: 1.
1923a. A Matter for the Field Worker in Folk-Lore. JAFL 36.
1923b. The Concept of the Guardian Spirit in North America. MAFLS 29.
1926. Serrano Tales. JAFL 39.
1928. Psychological Types in the Cultures of the Southwest. ICA 23.
1932. Configurations of Culture in North America. AA 34: 1.
1935. Zuni Mythology. I—II. CUCA 21.
1946. Patterns of Culture. London.

Bertholet, Alfred
1931. Tod und Totenreich, religionsgeschichtlich. RGG 5 (2. ed.).

Bezemer, T. J.
1904. Volksdichtung aus Indonesien. Sagen, Tierfabeln und Märchen. Der Haag.

Bidney, David
1950. The Concept of Myth and the Problem of Psychocultural Evolution. AA 52: 1.

Birket-Smith, Kaj
1929. Drinking Tube and Tobacco Pipe in North America. ES I: 1—2.

Birket-Smith, K., & de Laguna, F.
1938. The Eyak Indians of the Copper River Delta, Alaska. KDVSS.

Bloomfield, Louis
1928. Menomini Texts. PAES 12.

Blumensohn, Jules
1933. The Fast among North American Indians. AA 35: 4.

Boas, Franz
1888. The Central Eskimo. ARBAE 6.
1889a. Notes on the Snanaimuq. AA (O.S.) 2: 4.

1889b. Preliminary Notes on the Indians of British Columbia. BAAS 58.
1890. First General Report on the Indians of British Columbia. BAAS 59.
1891. Second General Report on the Indians of British Columbia. BAAS 60.
1895a. Fifth Report on the Indians of British Columbia. BAAS 65.
1895b. Indianische Sagen von der Nord-pacifischen Küste Amerikas. Berlin.
1896. Sixth Report on the Indians of British Columbia. BAAS 66.
1897. The Social Organization and the Secret Societies of the Kwakiutl Indians. RUSNM 1895.
1898. The Mythology of the Bella Coola Indians. MAMNH 2.
1909. Die Resultate der Jesup Expedition. ICA 16.
1910a. Kwakiutl Tales. CUCA 2.
1910b. Soul. BBAE 30: 2.
1912. Tsimshian Texts (New Series). PAES 3.
1915. Mythology and Folk-tales of the North American Indians. In: ANA.
1916. Tsimshian Mythology. ARBAE 31.
1917a. Folk-tales of Salishan and Sahaptin Tribes, collected by J. A. Teit, M. K. Gould, L. Farrand, H. J. Spinden, and ed. by F. Boas. MAFLS 11.
1917b. The Origin of Death. JAFL 30.
1918. Kutenai Tales. BBAE 59.
1921. Ethnology of the Kwakiutl. I—II. ARBAE 35.
1923. Notes on the Tillamook. UCP 20.
1927. Primitive Art. Instituttet for sammenlignende kulturforskning. Ser. B: 8. Oslo.
1932a. Bella Bella Tales. MAFLS 25.
1932b. Current Beliefs of the Kwakiutl Indians. JAFL 45.
1933. Relations between North-West America and North-East Asia. In: Jenness 1933.
1935a. Kwakiutl Culture as Reflected in Mythology. MAFLS 28.
1935b. Kwakiutl Tales, New Series. CUCA 26.
1938. Mythology and Folklore. In: F. Boas (ed.), General Anthropology. New York.
1940. Romance Folk-lore among American Indians. RLC.

Boas, F., & Hunt, G.
1902. Kwakiutl Texts. MAMNH 5: 1—2.

Bogoras, Waldemar
1902. The Folklore of Northeastern Asia, as compared with that of Northwestern America. AA 4: 4.
1907. The Chukchee: II. Religion. MAMNH 7.

Bourke, John G.
1889. Notes on the Cosmogony and Theogony of the Mojave Indians. JAFL 2.

Bousset, D. W.
1901. Die Himmelsreise der Seele. ARW 4.

Bouteiller, Marcelle
1950. Chamanisme et guérison magique. Paris.

British Museum
1925. Handbook to the Ethnographical Collections (of the British Museum). London.

Bunzel, Ruth L.
1932. Introduction to Zuñi Ceremonialism. ARBAE 47.

Buschan, Georg (ed.)
1922. Illustrierte Völkerkunde, 3. ed. I. Stuttgart.

Bushnell, David I. Jr.
1909. The Choctaw of Bayou Lacomb, St. Tammany Parish, Louisiana. BBAE 48.
1920. Native Cemeteries and Forms of Burial East of the Mississippi. BBAE 71.
1927. Burials of the Algonquian, Siouan, and Caddoan Tribes West of the Mississippi. BBAE 83.

Castrén, M. A.
1853.* Nordische Reisen und Forschungen. Vol. III. S:t Petersburg.

Chamberlain, B. H.
1883. "Ko-ji-ki," or "Records of Ancient Matters." TASJ, Suppl. to Vol. X. Yoko-hama.

1888. Aino Folk-tales. The Folk-lore Society Publications, Vol. 22. London.

Chang, K.
1956. A Brief Survey of the Archaeology of Formosa. SWJ 12: 4.

Chapman, J. W.
1912. The Happy Hunting-Ground of the Ten'a. JAFL 25.

Clark, Ella
1953. Indian Legends of the Pacific Northwest. Berkeley & Los Angeles.

Clark, K. M.
1896. Maori Tales and Legends. London.

Clements, Forrest E.
1932. Primitive Concepts of Disease. UCP 32.

Codrington, R. H.
1891. The Melanesians: Studies in their Anthropology and Folk-lore. Oxford.

Conard, E. Laetitia Moon
1900. Les Idées des indiens algonquins relatives à la vie d'outre-tombe. RHR 42.

Contenau, Georges
1941. Le Déluge babylonien. Paris.

Converse, Harriet Maxwell
1908. Myths and Legends of the New York State Iroquois. NYSMB 125.

Coolidge, D. & M. R.
1930. The Navajo Indians. Boston & New York.

Cooper, John M.
1936. Notes on the Ethnology of the Otchipwe of Lake of the Woods and Rainy Lake. CUAS 3.
1941. Temporal Sequence and the Marginal Cultures. CUAS 10.

Curtin, Jeremiah
1912. Myths of the Modocs. Boston.

Curtin, J., & Hewitt, J. N. B.
1918. Seneca Fiction, Legends, and Myths. I—II. ARBAE 32.

Curtis, Edward S.
1907—13. The North American Indian. I—IX. Cambridge, Mass.

Cushing, Frank Hamilton
1931. Zuñi Folk Tales. New York.

Dangel, Richard
1928. Mythen vom Ursprung des Todes bei den Indianern Nordamerikas. MAGW 58.
1929. Tirawa, der Höchste Gott der Pawnee. ARW 27.

Davis, Edward H.
1919. The Diegueño Ceremony of the Death Images. CMAI 5: 2.

Dawson, G. M.
1880. Report on the Haida Indians of the Queen Charlotte Islands. Geological Survey of Canada, Report of Progress for 1878—1879. Montreal.

Deans, James
1899. Tales from the Totems of the Hidery. Archives of the International Folk-lore Association, II. Chicago.

Deardorff, Merle H.
1951. The Religion of Handsome Lake: Its Origin and Development. BBAE 149.

Deloria, Ella
1932. Dakota Texts. PAES 14.

Denig, Edwin Thompson
1930. Indian Tribes of the Upper Missouri. ARBAE 46.

Densmore, Frances
1929. Chippewa Customs. BBAE 86.
1939. Nootka and Quileute Music. BBAE 124.

1953. The Use of Music in the Treatment of the Sick by American Indians. ARSI 1952.
1954. Importance of Rhythm in Songs for the Treatment of the Sick by American Indians. SM 79: 2.

De Smet, Father P. J.
1905. Life, Letters and Travels of Father Pierre-Jean De Smet, S. J., 1801—73. I—IV. Editors: H. M. Chittenden & A. T. Richardson. New York.

van Deursen, A.
1931. Der Heilbringer. Groningen.

Devereux, George
1948. Mohave Coyote Tales. JAFL 61.

Diels, H.
1922. Himmels- und Höllenfährten von Homer bis Dante. Neue Jahrbücher.

Dieterich, Albrecht
1913. Mutter Erde. 2. ed. Berlin.

Dittmer, Kunz
1954. Allgemeine Völkerkunde. Braunschweig.

Dixon, Roland B.
1905. The Mythology of the Shasta-Achomawi. AA 7: 4.
1907. The Shasta. BAMNH 17: 5.
1909. The Mythology of the Central and Eastern Algonkins. JAFL 22.
1910. Shasta Myths. JAFL 23.
1916. Oceanic Mythology. MAR 9.
1933. Contacts with America across the Southern Pacific. In: Jenness 1933.

Dorsey, George A.
1902. The Dwamish Indian Spirit Boat and Its Use. BFMUP 3.
1903. Indians of the Southwest. Santa Fé.
1904a. The Mythology of the Wichita. CIWP 21.
1904b. Traditions of the Skidi Pawnee. MAFLS 8.
1906. The Pawnee Mythology. CIWP 59.

Dorsey, James Owen
1889a. Indians of Siletz Reservation. AA (O.S.) 2: 1.
1889b. Teton Folk-lore. AA (O.S.) 2: 2.
1894. A Study of Siouan Cults. ARBAE 11.

Driver, Harold E.
1937. Southern Sierra Nevada. AR 1: 2 (CED VI).
1939. Northwest California. AR 1: 6 (CED X).

Drucker, Philip
1937. Southern California. AR 1: 1 (CED V).
1943. Archeological Survey on the Northern Northwest Coast. BBAE 133.
1950. Northwest Coast. AR 9: 3 (CED XXVI).
1951. The Northern and Central Nootkan Tribes. BBAE 144.
1955. Indians of the Northwest Coast. AH 10.

Du Bois, Cora
1939. The 1870 Ghost Dance. AR 3: 1.

Du Bois, C., & Demetracopoulou, D.
1931. Wintu Myths. UCP 28: 5.

Duff, Wilson
1952. The Upper Stalo Indians of the Fraser Valley, British Columbia. Anthropology in British Columbia, Mem. 1. Victoria.

Eastman, Mary
1849. Dahcotah; or, Life and Legends of the Sioux around Fort Snelling. New York.

Eberhard, Wolfram
1937a. Chinese Fairy Tales and Folk Tales. London.
1937b. Typen chinesischer Volksmärchen. FFC 120.

323

Edsman, C. M.
1949. Ignis Divinus. Lund.

Eells, Myron
1889. The Twana, Chemakum, and Klallam Indians. ARSI 1887: 1.

Ehnmark, Erland
1939. Anthropomorphism and Miracle. UUÅ 1939: 12.

Ehrenreich, Paul
1905. Die Mythen und Legenden der südamerikanischen Urvölker und ihre Beziehungen zu denen Nordamerikas und der alten Welt. ZE 37, Suppl.

Elbert, S. H.
1956. The Chief in Hawaiian Mythology, I. JAFL 69.

Eliade, Mircea
1951. Le Chamanisme et les techniques archaïques de l'extase. Paris.

Elmendorf, William W.
1952. Soul Loss Illness in Western North America. In: Tax 1952.

Emmonds, G. T., & Miles, G. P. L.
1939. Shamanistic Charms. Ethnologia Cranmorensis 1939: 4. Chislehurst.

Emmons, George T.
1914. Portraiture among the North Pacific Coast Tribes. AA 16: 1.

Erkes, Eduard
1925—26. Chinesisch-amerikanische Mythenparallelen. T'oung Pao, Vol. 24.

Essene, Frank
1942. Round Valley. AR 8: 1 (CED XXI).

Evans, Elwood
1889. History of the Pacific Northwest: Oregon and Washington. I—II. Portland.

Farrand, Livingston
1902. Traditions of the Quinault Indians. MAMNH 4: 3.

Fenton, William N.
1941. Iroquois Suicide: A Study in the Stability of a Culture Pattern. BBAE 128.

Fewkes, J. Walter
1901. An Interpretation of Katcina Worship. JAFL 14.

Firth, Raymond
1955. The Fate of the Soul. An Interpretation of Some Primitive Concepts. The Frazer Lecture. Cambridge.

Fisher, Margaret W.
1946. The Mythology of the Northern and Northeastern Algonkians in Reference to Algonkian Mythology as a Whole. In: Johnson 1946.

Flannery, Regina
1939. An Analysis of Coastal Algonquian Culture. CUAS 7.

Fletcher, Alice C.
1891. The Indian Messiah. JAFL 4.
1904. The Hako: A Pawnee Ceremony. ARBAE 22: 2.

Fletcher, A. C., & La Flesche, F.
1911. The Omaha Tribe. ARBAE 27.

Florenz, K.
1925. Die Japaner. In: Chantepie de la Saussaye, Lehrbuch der Religionsgeschichte, 4. ed., ed. by A. Bertholet & E. Lehmann, Vol. I. Tübingen.

Forde, C. Darryll
1931. Ethnography of the Yuma Indians. UCP 28: 4.

Foster, George M.
1944. A Summary of Yuki Culture. AR 5: 3.

Frachtenberg, L. J., Gatschet, A. S., & Jacobs, M.
1945. Kalapuya Texts. UWPA 11: 3.

Frazer, Sir James G.
1910. Totemism and Exogamy. I—IV. London.
1927. Taboo and the Perils of the Soul. The Golden Bough, Vol. II. London.
1933—36. The Fear of the Dead in Primitive Religion. I—III. London.
1949. The Golden Bough: Abridged Edition. London.
Friederici, Georg
1929. Zu den vorkolumbischen Verbindungen der Südsee-Völker mit Amerika. Anthropos 24.
Garfield, Viola E.
1939. Tsimshian Clan and Society. UWPA 7: 3.
Gayton, A. H.
1930a. The Ghost Dance of 1870 in South-Central California. UCP 28: 3.
1930b. Yokuts-Mono Chiefs and Shamans. UCP 24: 8.
1935. The Orpheus Myth in North America. JAFL 48.
1948. Yokuts and Western Mono Ethnography. I—II. AR 10: 1—2.
van Gennep, A.
1910. La Formation des légendes. Paris.
Gifford, E. W.
1923. Western Mono Myths. JAFL 36.
1926. Clear Lake Pomo Society. UCP 18: 2.
1933. The Cocopa. UCP 31: 5.
1936. Northeastern and Western Yavapai. UCP 34: 4.
Gifford, E. W., & Kroeber, A. L.
1937. Pomo. UCP 37: 4 (CED IV).
Gill, W. W.
1876. Myths and Songs from the South Pacific. London.
Gillin, John
1954. Ralph Linton 1893—1953. AA 56: 2.
Goddard, Pliny Earle
1903. Life and Culture of the Hupa. UCP 1: 1.
1931. Indians of the Southwest. AMNHHS 2.
1945. Indians of the Northwest Coast. AMNHHS 10.
Gregg, Josiah
1954. Commerce of the Prairies. Norman.
Grinnell, George Bird
1893. Pawnee Hero Stories and Folk-tales. London.
1909. The Story of the Indian. New York.
1912. Blackfoot Lodge Tales. The Story of a Prairie People. London.
Gruppe, O.
1897—1909. Orpheus. In: W. H. Roscher, Ausführliches Lexikon der griechischen und römischen Mythologie, Vol. III. Leipzig.
Gunther, Erna
1925. Klallam Folk Tales. UWPA 1: 4.
1928. A Further Analysis of the First Salmon Ceremony. UWPA 2: 5.
Guthrie, W. K. C.
1952. Orpheus and Greek Religion. A Study of the Orphic Movement. 2. ed. London.
Haeberlin, H. K.
1916. The Idea of Fertilization in the Culture of the Pueblo Indians. MAFLS 3: 1.
1918. SbEtEtda'q, A Shamanistic Performance of the Coast Salish. AA 20: 3.
Haeberlin, H. K., & Gunther, E.
1930. The Indians of Puget Sound. UWPA 4: 1.
Haile, Father Berard
1942. Navaho Upward-Reaching Way and Emergence Place. AA 44: 3.
Haekel, Josef
1956. Zum heutigen Forschungsstand der historischen Ethnologie. In: Die Wiener Schule der Völkerkunde, Festschrift, Wien.

Hale, Horatio
1890. "Above" and "Below." JAFL 3.

Hallowell, A. Irving
1940. The Spirits of the Dead in Saulteaux Life and Thought. JRAI 70: 1.
1946. Concordance of Ojibwa Narratives in the Works of Schoolcraft. JAFL 59.
1947. Myth, Culture and Personality. AA 49: 4.

Handbook of American Indians North of Mexico
1907—10. Ed. by Frederick Webb Hodge. I—II. BBAE 30: 1—2.

Handy, E. S. Craighill
1927. Polynesian Religion. BMB 34.

Harmon, D. W.
1903. A Journal of Voyages and Travels in the Interior of North America. New York.

Harrington, John Peabody
1932. Karuk Indian Myths. BBAE 107.
1934. A New Original Version of Boscana's Historical Account of the San Juan Capistrano Indians of Southern California. SMC 92: 4.
1942. Central California Coast. AR 7: 1 (CED XIX).

Harris, J. R.
1906. The Cult of the Heavenly Twins. Cambridge.

Harris, J. S.
1940. The White Knife Shoshoni of Nevada. In: Linton 1940.

Harrison, J. E.
1923. Prolegomena to the Study of Greek Religion. 3. ed. Cambridge.

Harrison, Rev. C.
1892. Religion and Family among the Haida, Queen Charlotte Islands. JRAI 21.

Hartland, E. S.
1914. Mythology and Folktales: Their Relation and Interpretation. Popular Studies in Mythology, Romance, & Folklore, No. 7. 2. ed. London.

Harva, Uno
1925. Vänster hand och motsols. Rig 1925: 1—2.
1927. Finno-Ugric, Siberian Mythology. MAR 4.
1938. Die religiösen Vorstellungen der altaischen Völker. FFC 125.

Hatt, Gudmund
1949. Asiatic Influences in American Folklore. KDVSS, Historisk-Filologiske Meddelelser, Vol. XXXI: 6.
1951. The Corn Mother in America and in Indonesia. Anthropos 46.

Heckewelder, J.
1821. Nachricht von der Geschichte, den Sitten und Gebräuchen der indianischen Völkerschaften, welche ehemals Pennsylvanien und die benachbarten Staaten bewohnten. Göttingen.

Heine-Geldern, Robert (von)
1951. Significant Parallels in the Symbolic Arts of Southern Asia and Middle America. (Together with G. F. Ekholm.) In: Tax 1951.
1954. Die asiatische Herkunft der südamerikanischen Metalltechnik. Paideuma V: 7—8.
1955. Das Problem vorkolumbischer Beziehungen zwischen Alter und Neuer Welt und seine Bedeutung für die allgemeine Kulturgeschichte. Anzeiger der Österreichischen Akademie der Wissenschaften, philosoph.-histor. Klasse, Vol. 91: 24. Wien.

Herskovits, Melville J.
1949. Man and His Works: The Science of Cultural Anthropology. New York.

Heurgon, J.
1932. Orphée et Eurydice avant Vergile. Mélanges d'archéologie et d'histoire de l'école française à Rome, Vol. XLIX.

Hewitt, J. N. B.
1895. The Iroquoian Concept of the Soul. JAFL 8.
1910. Teharonhiawagon. BBAE 30: 2.
Hill, W. W.
1944. The Navaho Indians and the Ghost Dance of 1890. AA 46: 4.
Hill-Tout, Charles
1899. Haida Stories and Beliefs. BAAS 68.
1904a. Ethnological Report on the StsEe'lis and Sk'aulits Tribes of the HalkomelEm
Division of the Salish of British Columbia. JRAI 34.
1904b. Report on the Ethnology of the Siciatl of British Columbia, A Coast Division
of the Salish Stock. JRAI 34.
1905. Report on the Ethnology of the StlatlumH of British Columbia. JRAI 35.
1907. British North America: The Far West, the Home of the Salish and Déné.
London.
Hoffman, W. J.
1890. Mythology of the Menomini Indians. AA (O.S.) 3: 3.
1891. The Mide'wiwin or "Grand Medicine Society" of the Ojibwa. ARBAE 7.
1896. The Menomini Indians. ARBAE 14: 1.
Holmes, W. H.
1919. Handbook of Aboriginal American Antiquities, I. BBAE 60: 1.
Holmberg (-Harva), see Harva
Holmström, Helge
1919. Studier över svanjungfrumotivet i Volundarkvida och annorstädes. Lund.
Holt, Catharine
1946. Shasta Ethnography. AR 3: 4.
Hooke, S. H.
1933. Myth and Ritual. Oxford.
1953. Babylonian and Assyrian Religion. London.
Hooper, Lucile
1920. The Cahuilla Indians. UCP 16: 6.
Hrdlicka, Ales
1907. Medicine and Medicine-men. BBAE 30: 1.
Hudson, J. W.
1902. An Indian Myth of the San Joaquin Basin. JAFL 15.
Hulbert, A. B., & Schwarze, W. N. (eds.)
1910. David Zeisberger's History of the Northern American Indians. OAHQ
19: 1—2.
Hultkrantz, Åke
1953. Conceptions of the Soul among North American Indians. A Study in Religious
Ethnology. SEMMS 1.
1954. The Indians and the Wonders of Yellowstone Park. A Study of the Inter-
relations of Religion, Nature and Culture. Ethnos 1954: 1—4.
1955. The Origin of Death Myth as found among the Wind River Shoshoni Indians.
Ethnos 1955: 2—3.
1956. Religious Tradition, Comparative Religion and Folklore. Ethnos 1956: 1—2.
1957a. Amerika. I. Ethnologisch. RGG 1 (3. ed.).
1957b. Configurations of Religious Belief among the Wind River Shoshoni. Ethnos
1956: 3—4.
Ms. Wind River Shoshoni Field Notes.
Hyman, S. E.
1955. The Ritual View of Myth and the Mythic. JAFL 68.
Izikowitz, Karl Gustav
1941. Fastening the Soul. Some Religious Traits among the Lamet (French Indo-
china). Göteborgs högskolas årsskrift 47: 14. Göteborg.
Jacobs, Melville
1929. Northwest Sahaptin Texts. UWPA 2: 6.
1934. Sahaptin Texts, I—II. CUCA 19.

Jacobs, M., & Stern, B. J.
  1947. Outline of Anthropology. New York.
Jacobsen, J. A.
  1896. Reisen in die Inselwelt des Banda-Meeres. Berlin.
James, E. O.
  1927. The Concept of the Soul in North America. FL 38.
Jenness, Diamond
  1932. The Indians of Canada. BCDM 65.
  1933. The American Aborigines. Their Origin and Antiquity. Papers, ed. by D.
    Jenness. Toronto.
  1934. Myths of the Carrier Indians of British Columbia. JAFL 47.
  1935. The Ojibwa Indians of Parry Island, Their Social and Religious Life.
    BCDM 78.
  1937. The Sekani Indians of British Columbia. BCDM 84.
  1938. The Sarcee Indians of Alberta. BCDM 90.
  1941. Prehistoric Culture Waves from Asia to America. ARSI 1940.
  1943. The Carrier Indians of the Bulkley River. BBAE 133.
Jetté, Rev. Julius
  1908. On Ten'a Folk-lore. JRAI 38.
Joffe, Natalie F.
  1940. The Fox of Iowa. In: Linton 1940.
Johnson, Frederick (ed.)
  1946. Man in Northeastern North America. PPFA 3.
Jones, L. F.
  1914. A Study of the Thlingets of Alaska. New York.
Jones, William
  1907a. Fox Texts. PAES 1.
  1907b. Mortuary Observances and the Adoption Rites of the Algonkin Foxes of
    Iowa. ICA 15: 1.
  1939. Ethnography of the Fox Indians (ed. by M. W. Fisher). BBAE 125.
Jones, W., & Michelson, T.
  1919. Ojibwa Texts. PAES 7: 2.
Karutz, R.
  1925. Die Völker Nord- und Mittelasiens. Stuttgart.
Keith, A. Berriedale
  1927. Indian Mythology. MAR 6.
Kennard, E. A.
  1937. Hopi Reactions to Death. AA 39: 3.
Keysser, Ch.
  1911. Aus dem Leben der Kaileute. In: R. Neuhaus, ed., Deutsch Neu-Guinea, Vol.
    III. Berlin.
Kinietz, W. Vernon
  1947. Chippewa Village. The Story of Katikitegon. BCIS 25.
Kluckhohn, Clyde
  1942. Myths and Rituals: A General Theory. HTR 35: 1.
Kluckhohn, C., & Leighton, D.
  1947. The Navaho. Cambridge, Mass.
Knight, Julia
  1913. Ojibwa Tales from Sault Ste. Marie. JAFL 26.
Koch-Grünberg, Theodor
  1920. Indianermärchen aus Südamerika. Jena.
Kohl, J. G.
  1859. Kitschi-Gami oder Erzählungen vom Obern See. I—II. Bremen.
Koppert, Vincent A.
  1930. Contributions to Clayoquot Ethnology. CUAS 1.

Körner, *Theo*
1938. Das Zurückrufen der Seele in Kuei-chou. Ethnos 1938: 4—5.
Krause, *Aurel*
1885. Die Tlinkit-Indianer. Jena.
Kretschmar, *Freda*
1938. Hundestammvater und Kerberos. II. Stuttgart.
Krickeberg, \W.
1922. Amerika. In: Buschan 1922.
1935. Beiträge zur Frage der alten kulturgeschichtlichen Beziehungen zwischen Nord- und Südamerika. ZE 66: 4—6.
Kroeber, *Alfred L.*
1907a. Gros Ventre Myths and Tales. APAM 1: 3.
1907b. The Religion of the Indians of California. UCP 4: 6.
1907c. Indian Myths of South Central California. UCP 4: 4.
1907d. The Yokuts Language of South Central California. UCP 2: 5.
1922. Elements of Culture in Native California. UCP 13: 8.
1925. Handbook of the Indians of California. BBAE 78.
1929. The Valley Nisenan. UCP 24: 4.
1935. Walapai Ethnography (ed. by A. L. Kroeber). MAAA 42.
1936. Karok Towns. UCP 35: 4.
1946. A Karok Orpheus Myth. JAFL 59.
1948. Anthropology. New York.
1951. A Mohave Historical Epic. AR 11: 2.
Kunike, *Hugo*
1926. Zur Astralmythologie der nordamerikanischen Indianer. IAE 27.
La Barre, *Weston*
1948. The Aymara Indians of the Lake Titicaca Plateau, Bolivia. MAAA 68.
Labitte, *Charles*
1842. La Divine Comédie avant Dante. Revue des Deux Mondes, Vol. 31. Paris.
Ladd, *John*
1957. The Structure of A Moral Code. Cambridge, Mass.
Lafitau, *J. F.*
1724. Moeurs des sauvages amériquains, comparées aux moeurs des premiers temps. I—II. Paris.
La Flesche, *Francis*
1889. Death and Funeral Customs among the Omahas. JAFL 2.
Layard, *John*
1934. The Journey of the Dead from the Small Islands of North-Eastern Malekula. In: EPS.
Leach, *Maria (ed.)*
1949—50. Standard Dictionary of Folklore, Mythology and Legend. I—II. New York.
Le Clercq, *Father Chrestien*
1910. New Relation of Gaspesia. With the Customs and Religion of the Gaspesian Indians. PCS 5.
van der Leeuw, *G.*
1956. Phänomenologie der Religion. 2. ed. Tübingen.
Lessa, *William A.*
1956. Oedipus-Type Tales in Oceania. JAFL 69.
Leuba, *James H.*
1912. A Psychological Study of Religion. Its Origin, Function, and Future. New York.
Lindgren, *E. J.*
1949. The Collection and Analysis of Folk-lore. In: Bartlett, Ginsberg, Lindgren & Thouless, The Study of Society: Methods and Problems. London.

Lindquist, G. E. E.
1926. Bland Nordamerikas indianer. Uppsala.

Linton, Ralph
1936. The Study of Man. An Introduction. New York & London.
1940. Acculturation in Seven American Indian Tribes, ed. by R. Linton. New York & London.
1943. Nativistic Movements. AA 45: 2.

Ljungberg, Helge
1946. Ambivalens. Ett religionsfenomenologiskt utkast. ROB 5.

Locher, G. W.
1932. The Serpent in Kwakiutl Religion. A Study in Primitive Culture. Leiden.

Loeb, E. M.
1926. Pomo. Folkways. UCP 19: 2.
1931. The Religious Organizations of North Central California and Tierra del Fuego. AA 33: 4.
1932. The Western Kuksu Cult. UCP 33: 1.

Lopatin, Ivan A.
1922. Goldy. Vladivostok.
1945. Social Life and Religion of the Indians in Kitimat, British Columbia. Los Angeles.

Loskiel, Georg Heinrich
1789. Geschichte der Mission der evangelischen Brüder . . . in Nordamerika. Barby.

Lowie, Robert H.
1908. The Test-Theme in North American Mythology. JAFL 21.
1909a. The Northern Shoshone. APAM 2: 2.
1909b. The Assiniboine. APAM 4: 1.
1917. Ojibwa. ERE 9.
1922. The Religion of the Crow Indians. APAM 25: 2.
1924. Notes on Shoshonean Ethnography. APAM 20: 3.
1925a. On the Historical Connection between certain Old World and New World Beliefs. ICA 21: 2.
1925b. Primitive Religion. London.
1934a. An Introduction to Cultural Anthropology. New York.
1934b. Religious Ideas and Practices of the Eurasiatic and North American Areas. In: EPS.
1935. The Crow Indians. New York.
1937. The History of Ethnological Theory. London.
1939. Ethnographic Notes on the Washo. UCP 36: 5.
1942. Studies in Plains Indian Folklore. UCP 40: 1.
1954. Indians of the Plains. AH 1.
1956. Notes on the Kiowa Indians. Tribus 4—5.

Lumholtz, Carl
1904. Bland Mexikos indianer. I—II. Stockholm.

Luomala, Katherine
1940. Oceanic, American Indian, and African Myths of Snaring the Sun. BMB 168.

Lyman, William D.
1904. Myths and Superstitions of the Oregon Indians. PAAS 16: 2.
1909. The Columbia River. New York.

Maass, E.
1895. Orpheus, Untersuchungen zur griechischen-römischen altchristlichen Jenseits-dichtung und Religion. München.

Macchioro, V.
1930. From Orpheus to Paul: A History of Orphism. Constable.

MacCulloch, J. A.
1911. Descent to Hades. ERE 4.

330

Malinowski, Bronislaw
1926. Myth in Primitive Psychology. London.
1954. Magic, Science and Religion and other Essays. Garden City.
Martin, P. S., Quimby, G. I., & Collier, D.
1948. Indians before Columbus. Chicago.
Mason, J. Alden
1912. The Ethnology of the Salinan Indians. UCP 10: 4.
Matthews, Washington
1888. The Prayer of A Navaho Shaman. AA (O.S.) 1.
1897. Navaho Legends. MAFLS 5.
McClintock, Walter
1923. Old Indian Trails. London, Bombay, Sidney.
McIlwraith, T. F.
1948. The Bella Coola Indians. I—II. Toronto.
McLaughlin, Marie L.
1916. Myths and Legends of the Sioux. Bismark, N.D.
McLean, John
1892. The Indians of Canada. Their Manners and Customs. London.
Mechling, W. H.
1914. Malecite Tales. MCDM 49.
Merriam, C. Hart
1955. Studies of California Indians. Berkeley & Los Angeles.
Métraux, Alfred
1949. Religion and Shamanism. HSAI V.
Michelson, Truman
1925. Notes on Fox Mortuary Customs and Beliefs. ARBAE 40.
Mooney, James
1891. The Sacred Formulas of the Cherokees. ARBAE 7.
1896. The Ghost-Dance Religion and the Sioux Outbreak of 1890. ARBAE 14: 2.
1900. Myths of the Cherokee. ARBAE 19: 1.
Morgan, L. H.
1954. League of the Ho-de-no sau-nee or Iroquois. I—II. New Haven.
Morgan, William
1936. Human-Wolves among the Navaho. YUPA 11.
Morice, A. G.
1889. The Western Dénés—Their Manners and Customs. PCI, Ser. 3, No. 7.
1906. The Canadian Dénés. AAR 1905.
1910. Carrier Indians. ERE 3.
1911. Dénés. ERE 4.
Mortier, F.
1930. L'Expansion chinoise. Le Pays de Fou-Sang est-il l'Amérique? Bulletin de la Société des Américanistes de Belgique, Déc. 1930. Bruxelles.
Müller, Werner
1955. Weltbild und Kult der Kwakiutl-Indianer. Wiesbaden.
1956. Die Religionen der Waldlandindianer Nordamerikas. Berlin.
Nevermann, Hans
1947. Götter der Südsee. Die Religion der Polynesier. Stuttgart.
Nieuwenhuis, A. W.
1924. The Differences between the Conception of Soul (Animus) and of Spirit (Spiritus) among the American Indians. ICA 21.
Nilsson, M. P:n
1935. Early Orphism and Kindred Religious Movements. HTR 28.
1941. Geschichte der griechischen Religion, Vol. I. München.
Nomland, G. A.
1935. Sinkyone Notes. UCP 36: 2.

Nordenskiöld, Erland
1912. Indianerleben. Leipzig.
1933. Origin of the Indian Civilizations in South America. In: Jenness 1933.
Nyberg, H. S.
1937. Irans forntida religioner. Uppsala.
O'Bryan, Aileen
1956. The Dîné: Origin Myths of the Navajo Indians. BBAE 163.
Ohlmarks, Åke
1939. Studien zum Problem des Schamanismus. Lund.
Olden, S. E.
1923. Karoc Indian Stories. San Francisco.
Olson, Ronald L.
1930. Chumash Prehistory. UCP 28: 1.
1936. The Quinault Indians. UWPA 6: 1.
1940. The Social Organization of the Haisla of British Columbia. AR 2: 5.
1954. Social Life of the Owikeno Kwakiutl. AR 14: 3.
1955. Notes on the Bella Bella Kwakiutl. AR 14: 5.
Opler, Morris Edward
1940. Myths and Legends of the Lipan Apache Indians. MAFLS 36.
1941. An Apache Life-Way. The Economic, Social, and Religious Institutions of the Chiricahua Indians. Chicago.
1945. The Lipan Apache Death Complex and Its Extensions. SWJ 1: 1.
Park, Willard Z.
1934. Paviotso Shamanism. AA 36: 1.
1938. Shamanism in Western North America. Northwestern University Studies in the Social Sciences, 2. Evanston & Chicago.
Parker, A. C.
1913. The Code of Handsome Lake, the Seneca Prophet. NYSMB 163.
Parsons, Elsie Clews
1916. A Few Zuñi Death Beliefs and Practices. AA 18: 2.
1923. The Origin Myth of Zuñi. JAFL 36.
1925. Micmac Folklore. JAFL 38.
1926. Tewa Tales. MAFLS 19.
1929. The Social Organization of the Tewa of New Mexico. MAAA 36.
1932. Isleta, New Mexico. ARBAE 47.
1933. Hopi and Zuñi Ceremonialism. MAAA 39.
1936. Taos Pueblo. GSA 2.
1939. Pueblo Indian Religion. I—II. Chicago.
1940. Taos Tales. MAFLS 34.
1941. Notes on the Caddo. MAAA 57.
Paulson, Ivar
1952. The "Seat of Honor" in Aboriginal Dwellings of the Circumpolar Zone, with Special Regard to the Indians of Northern North America. In: Tax 1952.
1956. Untersuchungen über die primitiven Seelenvorstellungen mit besonderer Rücksicht auf Nordeurasien. Ein vorläufiger Forschungsbericht. Ethnos 1956: 1—2. Ms. Die primitiven Seelenvorstellungen der nordeurasischen Völker.
Pettazzoni, Raffaele
1954. Essays on the History of Religions. Studies in the History of Religions, I. Leiden.
Popham, Robert E.
1954. Trepanation as a Rational Procedure in Primitive Surgery. University of Toronto Medical Journal, 31: 5.
Powers, Stephen
1877. Tribes of California. CNAE 3.
Pratt, James B.
1945. The Religious Consciousness. A Psychological Study. New York.

Quimby, George I.
1948. Culture Contact on the Northwest Coast, 1785—1795. AA 50: 2.
Radin, Paul
1909. Winnebago Tales. JAFL 22.
1914. Some Myths and Tales of the Ojibwa of Southeastern Ontario. BCDM 48.
1915a. Literary Aspects of North American Mythology. BCDM 16.
1915b. Religion of the North American Indians. In: ANA.
1923. The Winnebago Tribe. ARBAE 37.
1926. Literary Aspects of Winnebago Mythology. JAFL 39.
1933. The Method and Theory of Ethnology. New York.
1937. Primitive Religion: Its Nature and Origin. New York.
1944. The Story of the American Indian. New York.
1948. Winnebago Hero Cycles: A Study in Aboriginal Literature. MIJAL 1.
1951. Die religiöse Erfahrung der Naturvölker. Albae Vigiliae 11. Zürich.
1954. Monotheism Among Primitive Peoples. 2. ed. Basel.
Radin, P., Kerényi, K., & Jung, C. G.
1954. Der göttliche Schelm. Ein indianischer Mythen-Zyklus. Zürich.
Rand, Silas T.
1894. Legends of the Micmacs. New York.
Ränk, Gustav
1949—51. Das System der Raumeinteilung in den Behausungen der nordeurasischen Völker. Ein Beitrag zur nordeurasischen Ethnologie. Stockholm.
Ray, Verne F.
1942. Plateau. AR 8: 2 (CED XXII).
Reichard, Gladys A.
1921. Literary Types and Dissemination of Myths. JAFL 34.
1928. A Few Instances of Cultural Resistance in Southwest North America. ICA 22.
1944. Prayer: The Compulsive Word. MAES 7.
1947. An Analysis of Coeur d'Alene Indian Myths. MAFLS 41.
1950. Navaho Religion: A Study of Symbolism. I—II. New York.
Reid, Hugo
1926. The Indians of Los Angeles County. Los Angeles.
Riggs, S. R.
1893. Dakota Grammar, Texts, and Ethnography. CNAE 9.
Rink, H.
1875. Tales and Traditions of the Eskimo. London.
Rönnow, Kasten
1943. Zagreus och Dionysos. ROB 2.
Rooth, Anna Birgitta
1951. The Cinderella Cycle. Lund.
1957. The Creation Myths of the North American Indians. Anthropos 52.
Rose, H. J.
1945. A Handbook of Greek Mythology, Including Its Extension to Rome. 3. ed. London.
St. Clair, H. H., & Frachtenberg, L. J.
1909. Traditions of the Coos Indians of Oregon. JAFL 22.
Sapir, Edward
1909a. Takelma Texts. UPMAP 2: 1.
1909b. Wishram Texts. PAES 2.
Sapir, E., & Spier, L.
1943. Notes on the Culture of the Yana. AR 3: 3.
Sapir, E., & Swadesh, M.
1939. Nootka Texts. Philadelphia.
Scherman, Lucian
1892. Materialien zur Geschichte der indischen Visionslitteratur. Leipzig.

Schmidt, Wilhelm
1930. Handbuch der vergleichenden Religionsgeschichte. Ursprung und Werden der Religion. Münster in Westfalen.
1933. High Gods in North America. Oxford.

Schoolcraft, H. R.
1851—57. Historical and Statistical Information Respecting the History, Condition and Prospects of the Indian Tribes of the United States. I—VI. Philadelphia.

Seler, Eduard
1904. Gesammelte Abhandlungen zur amerikanischen Sprach- und Altertumskunde, Vol. II. Berlin.

Shirokogorov, S. M.
1935. Psychomental Complex of the Tungus. Shanghai & London.

Skinner, Alanson
1911. Notes on the Eastern Cree and Northern Saulteaux. APAM 9: 1.
1913. Social Life and Ceremonial Bundles of the Menomini Indians. APAM 13: 1.
1916. Plains Cree Tales. JAFL 29.
1920. Medicine Ceremony of the Menomini, Iowa, and Wahpeton, Dakota, etc. INM 4.
1921. Material Culture of the Menomini. INM.
1923. Observations on the Ethnology of the Sauk Indians. BPMCM 5: 1.

Smith, E. A.
1883. Myths of the Iroquois. ARBAE 2.

Smith, Marian W.
1940. The Puyallup-Nisqually. CUCA 32.
1956. The Cultural Development of the Northwest Coast. SWJ 12: 3.

Soustelle, Jacques
1940. La Pensée cosmologique des anciens mexicains. Paris.

Speck, F. G.
1909. Ethnology of the Yuchi Indians. UPMAP 1: 1.
1935. Naskapi. Norman.
1940. Penobscot Man. Philadelphia.

Spence, Lewis
1914. Myths and Legends of the North American Indians. Boston.

Spencer, Katherine
1947. Reflection of Social Life in the Navaho Origin Myth. UNMPA 3.

Spier, Leslie
1928. Havasupai Ethnography. APAM 29: 3.
1930. Klamath Ethnography. UCP 30.
1933. Yuman Tribes of the Gila River. Chicago.
1935. The Prophet Dance of the Northwest and Its Derivatives: the Source of the Ghost Dance. GSA 1.
1938. The Sinkaietk or Southern Okanagon of Washington, ed. by L. Spier. GSA 6.

Spier, L., & Sapir, E.
1930. Wishram Ethnography. UWPA 3: 3.

Spinden, Herbert Joseph
1908. The Nez Percé Indians. MAAA 2: 3.

Standard Dictionary of Folklore, see Leach, Maria.

Steller, G. W.
1926. Von Kamtschatka nach Amerika. Leipzig.

Stevenson, Matilda Coxe
1894. The Sia. ARBAE 11.
1898. Zuñi Ancestral Gods and Masks. AA (O.S.) 11: 2.
1904. The Zuñi Indians. Their Mythology, Esoteric Fraternities, and Ceremonies. ARBAE 23.

Steward, Julian H.
1933. Ethnography of the Owens Valley Paiute. UCP 33: 3.
1936. Myths of the Owens Valley Paiute. UCP 34: 5.
1938. Basin-Plateau Aboriginal Sociopolitical Groups. BBAE 120.
1943. Northern and Gosiute Shoshoni. AR 8: 3 (CED XXIII).
1949. South American Cultures: An Interpretative Summary. HSAI V.
Stewart, Kenneth M.
1946: Spirit Possession in Native America. SWJ 2: 3.
Stewart, Omer C.
1941. Northern Paiute. AR 4: 3 (CED XIV).
1942. Ute-Southern Paiute. AR 6: 4 (CED XVIII).
Ström, Folke
1956. Loki. Ein mythologisches Problem. Göteborgs Universitets Årsskrift LXII: 8.
    Göteborg.
Swahn, Jan-Öjvind
1955. The Tale of Cupid and Psyche. Lund.
Swan, James G.
1870. The Indians of Cape Flattery. SCK 220.
Swanton, John R.
1905a. Haida Texts and Myths. BBAE 29.
1905b. Contributions to the Ethnology of the Haida. MAMNH 8: 1.
1907. Mythology of the Indians of Louisiana and the Texas Coast. JAFL 20.
1908a. Haida Texts. MAMNH 14: 2.
1908b. Social Condition, Beliefs, and Linguistic Relationship of the Tlingit Indians.
    ARBAE 26.
1909. Tlingit Myths and Texts. BBAE 39.
1911. Indian Tribes of the Lower Mississippi and Adjacent Coast of the Gulf of
    Mexico. BBAE 43.
1921. Tlingit. ERE 12.
1928a. Aboriginal Culture of the Southeast. ARBAE 42.
1928b. Religious Beliefs and Medical Practices of the Creek Indians. ARBAE 42.
1928c. Social and Religious Beliefs and Usages of the Chickasaw Indians. ARBAE 44.
1929. Myths and Tales of the Southeastern Indians. BBAE 88.
1946. The Indians of the Southeastern United States. BBAE 137.
von Sydow, C. W.
1941. Våra folksagor. Stockholm.
1942. Rite. Folkkultur. Lund.
1948. Selected Papers on Folklore. Copenhagen.
Tax, Sol (ed.)
1951. The Civilizations of Ancient America. Chicago.
1952. Indian Tribes of Aboriginal America. Chicago.
Teit, James
1898. Traditions of the Thompson River Indians of British Columbia. MAFLS 6.
1900. The Thompson Indians of British Columbia. MAMNH 2.
1906. The Lillooet Indians. MAMNH 4: 5.
1909. The Shuswap. MAMNH 4: 7.
1912a. Mythology of the Thompson Indians. MAMNH 12: 2.
1912b. Traditions of the Lillooet Indians of British Columbia. JAFL 25.
1930. The Salishan Tribes of the Western Plateaus. ARBAE 45.
Thompson, Stith
1919. European Tales among the North American Indians. Colorado College Pub-
    lications, Language Series, 2.
1929. Tales of the North American Indians. Cambridge, Mass.
1932—36. Motif-Index of Folk-Literature, I—VI. FFC 106—109, 116, 117.
1946. The Folktale. New York.
1953a. Four Symposia on Folklore. Indiana University Publications, Folklore Series
    No. 8. Bloomington.

1953b. The Star Husband Tale. Studia septentrionalia 4. Oslo.
1955. Myths and Folktales. JAFL 68.

Thrum, T. G.
1907. Hawaiian Folk Tales. Chicago.

Trowbridge, C. C.
1938. Meearmeear Traditions. OCMA 7.
1939. Shawnee Traditions. OCMA 9

Tylor, Edward B.
1871. Primitive Culture: Researches into the Development of Mythology, Philosophy, Religion, Art, and Custom. I—II. London.

Underhill, Ruth M.
1945. Indians of the Pacific Northwest. SP 5.
1948. Ceremonial Patterns in the Greater Southwest. MAES 13.
1954. Intercultural Relations in the Greater Southwest. AA 56.

Vaillant, George C.
1941. Aztecs of Mexico. Origin, Rise and Fall of the Aztec Nation. Garden City.

Vignaud, H.
1922. Le Problème du peuplement initial de l'Amérique et de l'origine éthnique de sa population indigène. JSAP 14.

Voegelin, C. F.
1935. Tübatulabal Texts. UCP 34: 3.
1936. The Shawnee Female Deity. YUPA 10.

Voegelin, Erminie W.
1938. Tübatulabal Ethnography. AR 2: 1.
1942. Northeast California. AR 7: 2 (CED XX).
1947. Three Shasta Myths, including "Orpheus." JAFL 60.

Voegelin, C. F., & Voegelin, E. W.
1944. The Shawnee Female Deity in Historical Perspective. AA 46: 3.

de Vries, Jan
1925—28. Volksverhalen uit Oost-Indie. I—II. Zutphen.

Wagner, G.
1931. Yuchi Tales. PAES 13.

Walker, J. R.
1917. The Sun Dance and Other Ceremonies of the Oglala Division of the Teton Dakota. APAM 16: 2.

Wallace, E., & Hoebel, E. A.
1952. The Comanches: Lords of the South Plains. Norman.

Wallis, Wilson D.
1936. Folk Tales from Shumopovi, Second Mesa. JAFL 49.
1945. Inference of Relative Age of Culture Traits from Magnitude of Distribution. SWJ 1: 1.

Wallis, W. D., & Wallis, R. S.
1955. The Micmac Indians of Eastern Canada. St. Paul.

Wassén, Henry
1954. Viss parallellism mellan lapska och indianska födelseföreställningar. Västerbotten 1954.

Waterman, T. T.
1914. The Explanatory Element in North American Mythology. JAFL 27.
1930. The Paraphernalia of the Duwamish "Spirit-Canoe" Ceremony. IN 7: 2.

Weisinger, Herbert
1956. Some Remarks on the Ritualist Controversy. JAFL 69.

Weltfish, Gene
1937. Caddoan Texts: Pawnee, South Band Dialect. PAES 17.

336

White, John
1886—89. The Ancient History of the Maori, his Mythology and Traditions. I—IV. Wellington.

Wied, Prinz Maximilian zu
1839—41. Reise in das Innere Nord-America in den Jahren 1832 bis 1834. I—II. Coblenz.

Wike, Joyce
1952. The Role of the Dead in Northwest Coast Culture. In: Tax 1952.

Wilkes, Charles
1845. Narrative of the United States Exploring Expedition... I—V. Philadelphia.

Wilson, Rev. E. F.
1889. Report on the Sarcee Indians. BAAS 58.

Willey, Gordon R.
1955. The Prehistoric Civilizations of Nuclear America. AA 57: 3.

Wisse, Jacob
1933. Selbstmord und Todesfurcht bei den Naturvölkern. Zutphen.

Wissler, Clark
1906. The Blackfoot Indians. AAR 1905.
1907. Some Dakota Myths. JAFL 20.
1911. The Social Life of the Blackfoot Indians. APAM 7: 1.
1950. The American Indian. 3. ed. New York.

Witthoft, John
1949. Green Corn Ceremonialism in the Eastern Woodlands. OCMA 13.

Wyman, L. C., & Bailey, F. L.
1943. Navaho Upward-Reaching Way. UNMB 4: 2.

Wyman, L. C., Hill, W. W., & Osanai, I.
1942. Navajo Eschatology. UNMB 4: 1.

Yarrow, H. C.
1880. Introduction to the Study of Mortuary Customs among the North American Indians. Washington.

Zeisberger, see Hulbert & Schwarze

Zélénine, D.
1952. Le Culte des idoles en Sibérie. Paris.

Zimmern, Heinrich
1909. Der babylonische Gott Tamuz. Abhandl. der Kgl. Sächs. Gesellsch. der Wiss., philosoph.-historische Klasse, Vol. 27: 2. Leipzig.

SUBJECT INDEX

www.ingramcontent.com/pod-product-compliance
Lightning Source LLC
Chambersburg PA
CBHW020524270326

41927CB00006B/439